MW00612263

Blockchain Development for Finance Projects

Building next-generation financial applications using
Ethereum, Hyperledger Fabric, and Stellar

Ishan Roy

BIRMINGHAM - MUMBAI

Blockchain Development for Finance Projects

Copyright © 2020 Packt Publishing

All rights reserved. No part of this book may be reproduced, stored in a retrieval system, or transmitted in any form or by any means, without the prior written permission of the publisher, except in the case of brief quotations embedded in critical articles or reviews.

Every effort has been made in the preparation of this book to ensure the accuracy of the information presented. However, the information contained in this book is sold without warranty, either express or implied. Neither the author, nor Packt Publishing or its dealers and distributors, will be held liable for any damages caused or alleged to have been caused directly or indirectly by this book.

Packt Publishing has endeavored to provide trademark information about all of the companies and products mentioned in this book by the appropriate use of capitals. However, Packt Publishing cannot guarantee the accuracy of this information.

Commissioning Editor: Sunith Shetty
Acquisition Editor: Aniruddha Patil
Content Development Editor: Nazia Shaikh
Senior Editors: Jack Cummings and Sofi Rogers
Technical Editor: Utkarsha S. Kadam
Copy Editor: Safis Editing
Project Coordinator: Aishwarya Mohan
Proofreader: Safis Editing
Indexer: Tejal Daruwale Soni
Production Designer: Alishon Mendonsa

First published: January 2020

Production reference: 1310120

Published by Packt Publishing Ltd.
Livery Place
35 Livery Street
Birmingham
B3 2PB, UK.

ISBN 978-1-83882-909-4

www.packt.com

Packt.com

Subscribe to our online digital library for full access to over 7,000 books and videos, as well as industry leading tools to help you plan your personal development and advance your career. For more information, please visit our website.

Why subscribe?

- Spend less time learning and more time coding with practical eBooks and Videos from over 4,000 industry professionals

- Improve your learning with Skill Plans built especially for you

- Get a free eBook or video every month

- Fully searchable for easy access to vital information

- Copy and paste, print, and bookmark content

Did you know that Packt offers eBook versions of every book published, with PDF and ePub files available? You can upgrade to the eBook version at www.packt.com and as a print book customer, you are entitled to a discount on the eBook copy. Get in touch with us at customercare@packtpub.com for more details.

At www.packt.com, you can also read a collection of free technical articles, sign up for a range of free newsletters, and receive exclusive discounts and offers on Packt books and eBooks.

Table of Contents

Section 2: Blockchain Workflows Using Smart Contracts

Section 3: Securing Digital Documents and Files Using Blockchain

Section 4: Decentralized Trading Exchanges Using Blockchain

Preface

Blockchain technology will play a disruptive role in **banking, finance services, and insurance** (BFSI) in the coming years. Experts estimate annual savings of up to 20 billion dollars from this technology. This book will help you build fully fledged financial applications using blockchain, enabling you and your enterprise to build transparent and secure business processes.

This book will walk you through reimagining some of the most popular products and services of BFSI. The book starts with common blockchain concepts and the impact of blockchain technology in the BFSI sector. Next, we look at re-designing existing banking processes and building new financial applications using blockchain. This will be accomplished through eight detailed blockchain projects. You'll be guided through the entire process, from environment setup to building the frontend portals/dashboards along with the system integration and testing aspects for the applications. You will gain hands-on experience with Ethereum, Hyperledger Fabric, and Stellar. You will learn how to use ancillary platforms such as IPFS, the Truffle Suite, QpenZeppelin, and MetaMask to build applications as well.

By the end of the book, you will have an in-depth understanding of how to leverage distributed ledgers and smart contracts for financial use cases.

Who this book is for

This book is for blockchain/DApp developers and start-ups who are looking for a one-stop guide to building innovative and highly secure solutions in the FinTech domain using real-world use cases. It is also suitable for developers working in financial enterprises and banks and for solution architects looking to build brand-new process flows using blockchain technology. Working experience with Solidity and prior knowledge of finance/trade is required to get the most out of the book.

What this book covers

Chapter 1, *Blockchain in Financial Services*, introduces you to enterprise blockchain solutions for the BFSI sector. It briefly discusses the opportunities for implementing blockchain in the domain and the challenges that you might face when introducing the concept of blockchain in your organization. There is a discussion of the various most common implementation strategies, including coverage of the architecture models that are relevant for each strategy. Brief walk-throughs are given of Ethereum, Stellar, and Hyperledger Fabric and their relevant use cases for the domain.

Chapter 2, *Building a Blockchain Wallet for Fungible and Non-Fungible Assets*, looks at the blockchain wallet, which is the most integral part of any enterprise blockchain application. It can take many shapes and forms, such as a payment wallet, a digital identity card, a land title portfolio, or a stock portfolio. This chapter focuses on creating a blockchain wallet suited for multiple enterprise applications. You will learn how to create and deploy a smart contract wallet for fungible (ERC20), and non-fungible assets (ERC721). You will also learn how to implement the Web3js library as part of your blockchain application. The end goal is to create a fully functional peer-to-peer wallet using HTML, Node.js, and Solidity that is suitable for use cases beyond payment.

Chapter 3, *Designing a Payment Gateway for Online Merchants*, focuses on creating a merchant solution for online retailers. The solution will enable users to accept payments on a blockchain network akin to the leading fiat payment networks today. Special focus is given to push/pull payments, reconciliation, payment confirmation, and settlement on a blockchain platform. The technologies used are HTML, Node.js, and Solidity.

Chapter 4, *Corporate Remittances and Settlement*, focuses on the Hyperledger Fabric platform and its application in financial systems. You are given a walk-through on configuring the plug-and-play modules that make up the Hyperledger Fabric ecosystem. You will then be taught how to leverage them to create a permissioned blockchain network that can be used for B2B payments.

Chapter 5, *Enabling Cross-Border Remittances with Real-Time KYC/AML Verification*, focuses on creating a multi-currency cross-border remittance network using Stellar. Special focus is given to real-time document exchange, KYC/AML verification, Nostro account visibility, and integration with legacy banking systems.

Chapter 6, *Building a Letter of Credit Workflow Module Using Smart Contracts*, looks at smart contracts, which provide us with a foundation to build faster and efficient enterprise workflows. This is possible through automation and an immutable ledger accessible to all the stakeholders. This chapter looks at using Solidity smart contracts to build a more efficient letter of credit workflow. This knowledge can then be leveraged to design similar financial products, such as bank guarantees and smart contract-based insurance products

Chapter 7, *Building a Tamper-Proof Record-Keeping and Document Management System*, introduces you to the Hyperledger Fabric framework. You will be deploying your own chaincode and using it to build an immutable record management system. This system employs the power of the SHA256 algorithm and blockchain consensus to ensure that all records are tamperproof and can be reverted to their original state in the case of a cyber attack.

Chapter 8, *Building a Decentralized Trading Exchange on Blockchain*, explores decentralized exchanges, which aim to bring more transparency to the trading of assets and commodities. They eliminate the middleman and can thus ensure faster settlements. They also help control fraudulent practices such as price manipulation. This project looks at creating a price-time priority matching engine using Solidity smart contracts. This matching engine can then operate on a decentralized orderbook that can accept orders from all the participants on the network.

Chapter 9, *Developing a Currency Trading Exchange for Market Making*, looks at leveraging the market maker module of the Stellar platform to create a currency swap exchange. This currency swap exchange operates in real time and can be used either as an asset trading platform or to provide liquidity for cross-currency cross-border remittances.

Chapter 10, *Looking into the Future*, provides a short summary of the skills you will have acquired in your journey through the book. It also talks briefly about how we see blockchain technology evolving and the new concepts on the horizon that you might want to look at.

Chapter 11, *Appendix: Application Checklist*, This chapter provides step-by-step instructions for setting up an Ethereum, Stellar, and Hyperledger Fabric development and production environment. This is a pre-requisite for the aforementioned projects. This chapter also focuses on enterprise security and scalability essentials for implementing a blockchain application in a live production scenario. A basic checklist is provided with respect to design, development, testing, and deployment.

To get the most out of this book

The following is what you will need to get the most out of this book:

- Elementary to moderate knowledge of Ethereum and Solidity
- Elementary knowledge of Hyperledger Fabric and Stellar
- Moderate knowledge of JavaScript and Node.js
- Elementary knowledge of ReactJS

Download the example code files

You can download the example code files for this book from your account at www.packt.com. If you purchased this book elsewhere, you can visit www.packtpub.com/support and register to have the files emailed directly to you.

You can download the code files by following these steps:

1. Log in or register at www.packt.com.
2. Select the **Support** tab.
3. Click on **Code Downloads**.
4. Enter the name of the book in the **Search** box and follow the onscreen instructions.

Once the file is downloaded, please make sure that you unzip or extract the folder using the latest version of:

- WinRAR/7-Zip for Windows
- Zipeg/iZip/UnRarX for Mac
- 7-Zip/PeaZip for Linux

The code bundle for the book is also hosted on GitHub at https://github.com/PacktPublishing/Blockchain-Development-for-Finance-Projects. In case there's an update to the code, it will be updated on the existing GitHub repository.

We also have other code bundles from our rich catalog of books and videos available at https://github.com/PacktPublishing/. Check them out!

Download the color images

We also provide a PDF file that has color images of the screenshots/diagrams used in this book. You can download it here: `https://static.packt-cdn.com/downloads/9781838829094_ColorImages.pdf`.

Conventions used

There are a number of text conventions used throughout this book.

`CodeInText`: Indicates code words in text, database table names, folder names, filenames, file extensions, pathnames, dummy URLs, user input, and Twitter handles. Here is an example: "Now, let's create a simple wallet app in `react.js` to manage tokens."

A block of code is set as follows:

```
import "openzeppelin-
solidity/contracts/token/ERC20/ERC20Detailed.sol";
import "openzeppelin-
solidity/contracts/token/ERC20/ERC20Capped.sol";
import "openzeppelin-solidity/contracts/ownership/Ownable.sol";
```

When we wish to draw your attention to a particular part of a code block, the relevant lines or items are set in bold:

```
const HDWalletProvider = require('truffle-hdwallet-provider');
module.exports = {
networks: {
development: {
host: "127.0.0.1",
port: 8545,
network_id: "*",
}
prod: {
host: "<Live geth host IP>",
port: 8545,
network_id: "1",
}
},
compilers: {
solc: {
version: "0.5.2",
settings: {
optimizer" {
enabled: false,
runs: 1000,
```

```
},
}}}}}
```

Any command-line input or output is written as follows:

```
truffle console
```

Bold: Indicates a new term, an important word, or words that you see onscreen. For example, words in menus or dialog boxes appear in the text like this. Here is an example: "Click on the **GreenGables Bank** button to log in as a bank user."

 Warnings or important notes appear like this.

 Tips and tricks appear like this.

Get in touch

Feedback from our readers is always welcome.

General feedback: If you have questions about any aspect of this book, mention the book title in the subject of your message and email us at customercare@packtpub.com.

Errata: Although we have taken every care to ensure the accuracy of our content, mistakes do happen. If you have found a mistake in this book, we would be grateful if you would report this to us. Please visit www.packtpub.com/support/errata, selecting your book, clicking on the Errata Submission Form link, and entering the details.

Piracy: If you come across any illegal copies of our works in any form on the Internet, we would be grateful if you would provide us with the location address or website name. Please contact us at copyright@packt.com with a link to the material.

If you are interested in becoming an author: If there is a topic that you have expertise in and you are interested in either writing or contributing to a book, please visit authors.packtpub.com.

Reviews

Please leave a review. Once you have read and used this book, why not leave a review on the site that you purchased it from? Potential readers can then see and use your unbiased opinion to make purchase decisions, we at Packt can understand what you think about our products, and our authors can see your feedback on their book. Thank you!

For more information about Packt, please visit packt.com.

1
Section 1: Blockchain Payments and Remittances

Blockchain was first used for transferring and establishing the provenance of assets between individuals and organizations without depending on a middleman. This makes payments and remittances the oldest and most mature application of blockchain technology. Today, the technology has evolved to support a number of enterprise use cases revolving around payments and remittances, including retail payments, cross-border remittances, and corporate remittances. Several banks and financial enterprises around the world have recognized the disruptive nature of this technology in payments and are actively experimenting with workflows and applications that will form a core component of their IT infrastructure in the near future.

In the next five chapters, we will look at four such applications. We'll start by introducing blockchain in financial services and will then proceed toward building a wallet for transferring and storing assets. Next, we'll build a blockchain-enabled payment gateway for an e-commerce website. Lastly, we'll look at how we can leverage blockchain to cut out the inefficiencies and delays in corporate remittances and retail cross-border remittances.

This section comprises the following chapters:

- Chapter 1, *Blockchain in Financial Services*
- Chapter 2, *Building a Blockchain Wallet for Fungible and Non-Fungible Assets*
- Chapter 3, *Designing a Payment Gateway for Online Merchants*
- Chapter 4, *Corporate Remittances and Settlement*
- Chapter 5, *Enabling Cross-Border Remittances with Real-Time KYC/AML Verification*

1
Blockchain in Financial Services

Blockchain technology is expected to revolutionize how our industries and enterprises operate. Experts estimate that it will business process flows and enable organizations to build products and services that are more secure, transparent, fraud-resistant, and cost-efficient. Banking and financial enterprises and start-ups have been the first to experiment with and adopt this disruptive technology. Reports and surveys suggest that, within the next decade, these organizations will go through rapid stages of innovation to establish blockchain as the Backbone for their day-to-day operations and the services they offer to their customers. In this book, we'll be looking at some prominent applications of this technology for the banking and finance industry through projects. Each project is implemented using a popular distributed ledger platform.

By the end of the book, you will have a better understanding of how to leverage blockchain technology to build applications for financial use cases. You will also have sufficient knowledge of building blockchain solutions using the Ethereum, Hyperledger Fabric, and Stellar distributed ledger platforms.

In this chapter, we'll be looking at the current state of financial systems and how blockchain can make a difference. We'll also try to understand how to approach implementing such a solution and some of the popular blockchain platforms we can consider for developing a financial application. The topics covered are as follows:

- Present-day banking and finance systems
- Understanding the blockchain technology
- Blockchain for financial services
- How to approach implementing a blockchain solution
- The popular distributed ledger platforms for financial applications

Present-day banking and finance systems

The global banking and financial system plays a huge role in the life of the modern human being. It moves more than a trillion dollars around the world in a day, and more than a billion people are directly or indirectly served by it every day. It is the backbone of global trade finance and it enables enterprises, from start-ups to conglomerates, to run their businesses smoothly in any part of the world. The technology that makes this ecosystem tick has evolved in leaps and bounds in the last two decades, especially with the advent of the internet.

However, owing to compliance restrictions, reliance on legacy systems, and a conservative outlook on technology, most banking IT systems today are yet to adapt to advancements in technology and are unable to keep up with the nefarious means employed by malicious individuals. As a results close to half of banking customers have been expose to frauds and cyber crimes while dealing with payment gateways, stock exchanges, money transfer agencies, and so on.

Add to this the fact that the system has added layer after layer of middlemen and intermediaries owing to the limitations of conventional IT systems. This, in turn, has resulted in high fees and delays for the customers, not to mention a massive amount of paperwork arising from complex workflows. It also exposes the customer to the possibility of financial fraud and corruption. Lastly, the system in many cases is highly exclusive and denies basic access to financial products and services to a number of people around the world.

Generally, bankers have resisted sweeping changes to the current way the underlying technology works as they do not want to upset the apple cart and want to ensure that businesses that rely on them are able to continue working smoothly without any change in their user experience. However, the inefficiencies and faults in the system mean that such changes are the need of the hour. Disruptive innovation that can make the customer's experience even better is required to ensure that the system keeps chugging along and customers are able to operate their businesses without being slowed down or stopped by the technology on which their businesses are built. Enter blockchain.

Blockchain technology has numerous features and advantages that enable us to re think and re-engineer how modern financial services operate and serve the end customer. It enables us to design modern workflows minimizing middlemen, maximizing security, enabling transparency, and promoting high levels of interoperability between different players of the financial ecosystem.

Understanding blockchain technology

Blockchain technology was invented to be the backbone for Bitcoin, the popular cryptocurrency. It is a distributed ledger spread across a permissioned or permissionless network. The participants of this network are referred to as nodes. Each node contains a copy of the ledger. To update the ledger, the participants in the network will propose a transaction or a set of transactions that should be added next to the ledger. Once the participants in the network come to an agreement on the next set of transactions, they will add the transactions to their local copy of the ledger. This way, the sanctity and uniformity of the ledger across the nodes are maintained.

Data is added in "blocks" of transactions. Each block contains the hash value of the header of the previous block. (A hash function generates a unique output of fixed length for an input data of any length.) This ensures that the sequential order of the blocks is maintained in the ledger. Each block header has a set of parameters, including a Merkle root hash of the transactions in the block. If any transaction data is tampered, it results in the Merkle root of the block being altered. This causes a mismatch in the hash of the header of the block and the hash of the header of the block stored in the following block, effectively 'breaking the chain'. This will result in the local copy of the ledger being broken and the node being thrown out of sync with the other copies of the distributed ledger disabling it from adding any further transactions to the ledger.

Transactions submitted to the network are signed using a private key or a secret key that is held by the network participant and the public key is included in the transaction as part of the transaction. This means that the other participants on the network can validate the identity of the transaction submitter.

The multiple copies of the ledger and the hash-chain ensure that any data written to the ledger is immutable. If there is a mismatch between the local copy of the ledger held by a node and the copy of the ledger held by the other network participants (nodes), the node is disengaged from the network and cannot broadcast new transactions. This ensures that the sanctity of the ledger is maintained. To further maintain the uniformity of the ledger, blockchain allows network participants only to append new data to the ledger and does not allow participants to remove or modify existing data in the ledger. As such, any transaction data written to the blockchain is preserved and cannot be modified.

Since the ledger is universal, there needs to exist a mechanism to ensure that transactions are added in the same order across all copies of the ledger. This is typically achieved through a consensus mechanism. A consensus mechanism is basically a set of steps that ensures that transactions are written in the same order across the nodes. Additionally, it ensures that the transactions in all the copies of the ledger are the same.

Consensus can be achieved through various means. Traditional public permissionless blockchains, such as those running cryptocurrencies such as Bitcoin or Ethereum 1.0, rely on the solving of a cryptographic puzzle to pick the network participant who gets to write the next set of transactions to the ledger. This network participant is called a **miner**. After successfully solving the cryptographic puzzle, the miner will create a "block" of what they believe the next transactions in the ledger should be. They then add this block with the transactions and their solution to the puzzle to their local copy of the ledger and broadcast this block to all the other nodes in the network. The other nodes will validate the authenticity of this block before updating it to their local ledger. The difficulty of the cryptographic puzzle is set such that only one network participant can solve the puzzle in a fixed window of time. After the puzzle is solved, a new cryptographic puzzle is generated and the next miner needs to solve this puzzle.

Permissioned blockchains follow a slightly different approach. Permissioned blockchains are blockchains where we know all the network participants and the participants cannot connect to the network without prior permission of the participants. Since the identity of all the network participants is known, these blockchains follow a slightly more relaxed approach to consensus. They might use a simple queuing mechanism to order the transactions. Some may also follow a round-robin approach. A round-robin approach is one where each network participant is allowed to submit and write its own block to the ledger. This continues until every participant has had a chance to submit a block, and then the process is repeated.

In recent times, the term **Distributed Ledger Technology** (DLT) has been interchangeably used with the term blockchain. All Blockchains are DLTs but not all DLTs are Blockchains. In common parlance, the term DLT is generally used to refer to a platform that does not use 'blocks' or 'chains'. Instead they add data in singular transactions. These platforms are being actively used to build financial applications. Most of these platforms use a variation of the **Practical Byzantine Fault Tolerance** (PBFT) mechanism to achieve a transactional-level consensus between the various copies of the ledger. As they are PBFT-based, several of them suffer from the same limitations as PBFT. They are able to solve this problem using intelligent network design or by making modifications to the traditional PBFT algorithm. A good example is the Stellar platform, which follows the **Federated Byzantine Agreement** (FBA) consensus model and restricts the Validation Nodes on its public network. DLT platforms are preferred over blockchains in certain use cases because they often permit higher transactions per second. This makes them suitable for payment networks, trading exchanges, and so on.

Lastly, let's look at the concept of smart contracts. Smart contracts are computer protocols that enable the execution of condition-based business flows. The authenticity of conditions and the execution of the terms of the contract can be satisfactorily verified by all the parties who are affected by the execution of the contract without trusting a third party.

This is possible by writing and deploying such business flows to a distributed ledger and by leveraging blockchain technology. Let's say Alice wants to sell a car and Bob wants to buy it. But Alice wants to ensure that Bob gets possession of the car only when she gets paid. In such a case, Alice and Bob can write a smart contract. Bob can transfer the funds he needs to pay Alice to the smart contract's account. Alice can transfer a secret password that will unlock a digital copy of the documents of the car to the smart contract. The smart contract will ensure that Bob gets access to the password and Alice gets her payment without them depending on a third-party middleman. If the deal does not go through, the contract can also return the assets to the original owners.

This is better than traditional means because a human intermediary can be influenced by Alice or Bob. They might also have to pay some fees to the intermediary. Additionally, there might be a delay in executing the deal owing to a backlog of requests or an inefficient intermediator. If the third-party turns out to be fraudulent, they could even run away with the money and possession of the car! Since in a distributed system the smart contract code is deployed on a blockchain network, it cannot be altered by Alice or Bob or a malicious individual due to the immutable nature of the blockchain. This ensures that the deal will always go through with a limited risk of fraud.

Blockchains for financial services

There are many advantages offered by blockchain technology that make it suitable for application in financial services. The technology can help us overcome numerous shortcomings and inefficiencies of present day Banking and Financial systems. The following are some of these areas:

- **Reconciliation**: Reconciliation is an expensive and time-consuming affair across almost all financial products and services. The delayed visibility of transactions or information across organizations leads to delayed settlement for the end customer. Cross-border and domestic payments, trade settlement, trade finance, and letter-of-credit settlement are examples of some workflows that are more time-consuming and expensive due to the effort spent on reconciling data between organizations. Blockchains can help eliminate or reduce reconciliation costs and time. Transactions and information can be posted to a shared ledger. All parties that are participants of the shared ledger get instant visibility of the transaction or information. Since the ledger is immutable, data once added cannot be removed. Additionally, the immutability of the ledger also provides us with an audit trail for all asset transfers and transactions that have been successfully executed.

- **Information sharing**: Currently, banks carry out the KYC(Know Your Customer) process for all new customers. This is a laborious and time-consuming affair for the customer. Additionally, if the customer has accounts across different banks, their KYC information could be different at each bank. Add to this the fact that many banks and financial institutions today use extremely inefficient and insecure workflows for sharing KYC and AML(Anti-Money Laundering) data between them. Given this, it becomes imperative to design a system that can securely share customer KYC and AML data between transacting parties. This concept can be extended to sharing other confidential information as well. It can also enable us to create a unique KYC identity for the customer that can be updated annually or quarterly.

- **Automated workflows**: Owing to the distributed nature of blockchain networks, it is easier to script workflows that span organizations. Traditionally, such workflows would involve human operators at each organization analyzing and validating data and information before initiating the next steps. Smart contracts can allow us to automate or semi-automate such workflows. This reduces dependency on manual intervention. Additionally, we could use an "oracle" for off-chain information or inputs required to automate a blockchain workflow. An oracle is a third-party service that provides external data/off-chain data to the blockchain.

- **Secure document sharing**: Blockchain can enable secure document sharing between organizations. A hash signature of the document can be stored on the shared ledger. This signature will allow us to verify the integrity of the document after successfully receiving the document and in the future. Additionally, we can tag these hash signatures to transactions so they can be referred for audit purposes in the future. A good application of this concept could be storing hash signatures of the Purchase Order and Invoice for Corporate Remittances and tagging them to the settlement transaction.

- **Decentralized systems**: Blockchains can be used to build decentralized trading exchanges or marketplaces. This can help bring down the intermediary cost, bring in more transparent workflows, and reduce reliance on a central authority. It also reduces the settlement time for the end customers.

- **Inclusive finance**: Owing to public-private key encryption and a distributed ledger at its heart, it is extremely easy, cost-efficient, and secure to maintain customer accounts and transactions using blockchains. This can help us to design, build, and extend cost-effective financial services to the unbanked, refugees, and the less privileged at a fraction of the expense.

The following is a list of potential banking and finance use cases where blockchain can have a sizeable impact:

- Cross-border remittance
- Domestic payments
- Back office reconciliation
- Inter- and intra-organizational information sharing
- Trade finance
- KYC/AML
- Secure IPOs(Initial Public Offer)
- Asset tracking

How to approach implementing a blockchain solution

The following is a list of discussion points and activities that IT practitioners should consider and carry out before implementing blockchain technology within their organization:

- Identify business requirements that require provenance, audit ability, or distributed workflows.
- Recognize whether potential use cases can be executed with centralized databases or digital signatures without relying on a blockchain. (One example of a use case that requires blockchain could be an inter-organizational use case where no central organization or regulator exists to take ownership of the database.)
- Envisage the end benefits of implementing blockchain technology.
- Identify legacy workflows and modules that will need to be replaced or augmented.
- Analyze whether the end benefits from replacing the legacy workflow outweigh the costs.
- Identify new workflows and modules that will need to be built for use cases.
- Analyze whether the end benefits from implementing the solution outweigh the total cost of executing and implementing the project.
- Identify stakeholders and participants of the blockchain system.
- Agree on a governance framework for operating the network and build in accountability from the participants.

- Agree on an implementation strategy and identify integration with legacy systems, if any.
- Choose a blockchain platform based on your requirements.
- Identify essential enterprise tools that need to be built to successfully operate the blockchain solution. These include modules such as an identity service, security and access control policies, network directory, and so on.

Organizations should only proceed once they have successfully considered all the preceding points and have the answers to all of them.

Implementation strategies

There are different implementation strategies that organizations can look at to implement a blockchain network. These are as follows:

- All stakeholders own and maintain a node on the blockchain network. This node can be on-premises or on a cloud platform.
- A cloud-hosted blockchain network is operated by a trusted service provider. Organizations can view data and information and submit transactions based on access control. This is known as **Blockchain as a Service (BaaS)**.
- Accessing a public permissionless blockchain to record data so that it cannot be tampered with. A good example is storing the hash signature of a document to the public Bitcoin or Ethereum network. The transaction ID and the document is then shared with other stakeholders who need to validate the authenticity of the document in the future.

Organizations can choose to put either complete data and information on the blockchain or can just the hash of the data, document, or information on the blockchain.

The first case is applicable when the stakeholders need to share data in real-time between different stakeholders and ensure that the information shared is immutable and cannot be modified once it has been published to the shared ledger.

The second case is applicable when the stakeholders only need a blockchain to establish the provenance of documents, data, files, or any other assets. The actual data or asset is not shared through a blockchain. In such a case, we only publish a unique attribute of the asset to the blockchain. For documents, files, and information, this can be a hash of the file or document content. For assets such as gold, it could be the carat value.

Popular distributed ledger platforms for financial applications

The blockchain industry today is inundated with distributed ledger frameworks and platforms that can be used to implement solutions. For this book, I've selected three popular platforms that are being used by developers and architects to implement financial solutions. These platforms are as follows:

- Ethereum
- Hyperledger Fabric
- Stellar

These platforms have been used extensively for implementing blockchain projects globally. As with any framework, there are trade-offs when you settle on one for designing your solution. Let's look at these platforms.

Ethereum

Ethereum is probably the second most popular blockchain platform in the world. It was conceptualized by Vitalik Buterin. The technology stack is open source and is maintained by the Ethereum Foundation. Its native asset is ether. Users can also issue their own assets on the network. These assets are popularly known as tokens.

Ethereum was the first blockchain platform to implement smart contracts. Smart contracts are written using the Solidity language. Contracts are compiled and deployed to the blockchain in bytecode format. This bytecode is then broadcast to all the nodes in the network. Each node implements the **Ethereum Virtual Machine** (**EVM**), which is a runtime environment for Ethereum smart contracts. The popularity of Solidity has led other blockchain platforms to include it as an optional framework for writing and deploying smart contracts.

Ethereum implements a world state that keeps track of all user accounts and smart contract accounts. It uses the EthHash Proof-of-Work consensus mechanism to maintain ledger integrity. Owing to its popularity, its open source nature, the flexibility of the Solidity language, and how old the platform is, Ethereum has developed a huge online community that constantly contributes to the project and the ecosystem. This has helped the platform mature and add new features over time. One of the best examples is probably the **Ethereum Request for Comment** (**ERC**) initiative, which proposes standards for contract development. Two of the most popular ERC standards are ERC20 and ERC721, which propose standards for creating fungible and non-fungible tokens respectively.

There is also an entire ecosystem of applications, tools, and utilities that can be used with the Ethereum platform. These are called DApps, short for Distributed Apps. One of the most popular DApps is Metamask. Metamask is an Ethereum wallet that can be used to submit and receive transactions to and from an Ethereum blockchain network. We'll be using it extensively in our projects.

Hyperledger Fabric

Hyperledger Fabric is a project incubated by the Linux Foundation under the Hyperledger umbrella of projects. Hyperledger is used to refer to a collection of open source enterprise blockchain projects, tools, and utilities. The Hyperledger initiative's main purpose is to enable the collaborative development of enterprise blockchain. It has seen major contributions from IBM, Intel, SAP Ariba, and other global enterprises.

Fabric is one of the oldest and most mature projects under Hyperledger. It is intended to be a platform for developing blockchain solutions with a modular architecture. It allows different platform features such as consensus mechanisms, certificate authorities, and identity services to be available as plug-and-play features. To achieve this, it implements containerization, making it suitable for modern enterprise IT systems. Unlike other blockchain platforms, it does not implement native assets, accounts, or an unspent transaction model, making it suitable for a plethora of applications.

Hyperledger Fabric implements chaincodes, which are similar to smart contracts. One of the most important features it implements is a concept called channels, which are essentially private ledgers with a fixed number of participant nodes. Only authorized nodes and organizations can access a channel. Nodes can be members of multiple channels, and chaincodes, policies, and certificate authorities can be used across multiple channels.

Hyperledger Fabric takes a unique approach to consensus. It runs a stand-alone orderer peer. The orderer peer gathers transactions and transmits new blocks of transactions to the network peers. The orderer leverages an ordering mechanism based on Kafka or Raft to order transactions and create blocks.

To submit transactions, peers first send a proposed transaction to a select few peers in the network, known as endorsement peers. These peers are determined during channel creation. If the transaction does not violate the endorsement peer's internal state, it "endorses" the transaction and sends it back to the node that sent the proposal. The initiating node then gathers these responses and broadcasts these with the endorsements to the orderer. It also sends a read and write set that has the initial and final values of the state after the transaction has been executed.

The orderer will collect these transactions and generate a new block. Fabric allows users to modify block size and block generation time. The newly created blocks are then sent back to the peer nodes by the orderer. The peer nodes will first add the block to their private copy of the ledger. Next, they will check the transactions inside the block to ensure that the read and write set is in line with the value in their local state database. After this check, they will update their local state database with the new values resulting from the transaction.

Stellar

The Stellar platform is a decentralized protocol that was primarily designed for enabling fast, low-cost, cross-border payments. It is an open source project developed and maintained by the Stellar Foundation. The platform was conceived by Jed McCaleb, who is also the co-founder of Ripple.

Stellar implements transaction-level consensus using FBA, the modified version of PBFT, mentioned earlier. Its native asset is called the lumen (XLM). Owing to its focus on payments, the Stellar platform provides additional modules that work in conjunction with the core software to enable users to build customer-friendly apps that meet compliance and regulatory norms for payments.

Stellar's most interesting feature is probably that it implements a decentralized orderbook as part of its core technology stack. This feature allows you to carry out cross-asset transactions. This way, a customer can initiate a transaction in USD and terminate it in GBP. Since Stellar allows you to issue your own assets, the possible use cases where this feature can be used are endless. You can also use the orderbook to build a trading exchange by submitting buy and sell offers using the Stellar SDK. You can virtually build an entire application around this feature. Many decentralized exchanges have actually done this.

Globally, Stellar has been used by IBM to build the World Wire network to enable cross-border payments. It has also been used by a number of remittance providers across the world who have found the technology stack suitable for building payment applications.

Summary

I hope this chapter gave you insight into how blockchains will impact the financial services sector, how enterprises are adopting this technology, and what to consider when trying to implement a blockchain solution. It should also have helped you understand how to implement blockchain projects within an enterprise.

We started the chapter by looking at the present-day banking and finance industry and by understanding blockchain technology. Next, we went through the areas where we believe blockchain can make a difference in this industry. We also looked at how organizations need to approach implementing blockchain technology and what the different implementation models they can consider are. Lastly, we looked at some of the popular blockchain platforms of the day. We'll be using these to implement the projects that will follow in the coming chapters.

In the following chapters, we'll be developing blockchain projects suited for various financial applications. Each of these projects looks at leveraging blockchain technology to deliver a financial solution that is more secure, efficient, and transparent than the traditional alternative. In the next chapter, we'll be looking at leveraging a blockchain platform to design a wallet that can store fungible as well as non-fungible tokens.

Building a Blockchain Wallet for Fungible and Non-Fungible Assets

2

The blockchain wallet forms the most integral part of any enterprise blockchain application. It is the customer interface of the blockchain application. It can take many shapes and forms, depending on the use case being implemented. It could be a payment wallet, a digital identity card, a land title portfolio, or an assets portfolio.

This chapter focuses on creating blockchain wallets suited for financial applications. Our wallet will be managing assets that are issued on the blockchain. These assets will be issued using pre-defined smart contract standards. For this, we will look at the ERC20 and ERC721 smart contract standards. We will learn to write, migrate, and deploy our own smart contract codes using Truffle. We will also learn to create a token wallet frontend using ReactJS, and finally, we will run the app. We will also look at how to connect the wallet to the main Ethereum network.

The following topics will be covered in this chapter:

- Technical requirements
- Understanding ERC20 and ERC721 smart contract standards
- Writing the smart contract code
- Migrating the smart contract code using Truffle
- Creating the token wallet frontend using ReactJS

- Running our app
- Connecting to the main Ethereum network

Technical requirements

The code files of this chapter are available at the following link:

https://github.com/PacktPublishing/Blockchain-Development-for-Finance-Projects/tree/master/Chapter%202/Chapter%202

We'll be using the following to develop our project:

- Ganache Private Blockchain Server—https://trufflesuite.com/ganache/
- Trufflesuite—https://github.com/trufflesuite/truffle
- MetaMask plugin for Chrome/Firefox/Safari—https://metamask.io/

For installing Ganache on Ubuntu, you might need to change some settings. Click on the drop-down menu next to the Ganache directory name on the title bar. Select **Preferences**. Navigate to the **Behavior** tab. Under **Executable Text Files**, set the option to **Ask what to do**. Navigate back to the file downloaded from the Ganache download link. Right-click on the file and click on PROPERTIES. Select the **Permissions** tab. Select the option **Allow executing files as program**. Now, double-click on the file. The Ganache blockchain should start smoothly. It's probably best to do a global installation of Truffle to avoid any conflicts. For example, create a directory workspace called **truffle** and install Truffle using sudo npm install truffle -g.

I'm using Ubuntu 18.04.2 LTS for running the preceding applications and deploying my blockchain. This project assumes that you are working on a Unix operating system. Additionally, this project assumes you have **Node.js** and **npm** installed. I'm using **Node version 13.0.1** and **npm version 6.12.0**.

Lastly, we'll be using the **OpenZeppelin** library of smart contracts to write our contracts. To use this library, create a project folder in your Truffle workspace. Let's call it tokenwallet. Create a package.json file in the project folder and update it with the following values:

```
{
  "dependencies": {
    "babel-register": "^6.23.0",
    "babel-polyfill": "^6.26.0",
```

```
    "babel-preset-es2015": "^6.18.0"
  },
  "devDependencies": {
    "openzeppelin-solidity": "^2.2.0"
  }
}
```

Run `npm install` to install the OpenZeppelin library and Babel for your Truffle workspace.

Understanding ERC20 and ERC721 smart contract standards

To understand ERC20 and ERC721 contract standards, first, let's look at the concept of fungibility. Fungibility is used to describe the property of an asset where individual units do not hold a special value and can be replaced with another unit of the asset. A good example of this a 10 dollar bill. If you have a 10 dollar bill and I have a 10 dollar bill, they both hold the same value, which is 10 dollars. The bill would not have a higher or lower value depending on who is the owner of the bill. The bills can replace each other very easily. Hence, a 10 dollar bill is a fungible asset. All currency is essentially fungible in nature.

Now, take the case of a different kind of asset. If both of us owned a 400-square foot apartment and yours was in New York City and mine in New Delhi, the monetary value of both the apartments would be different because of the average price of a property per square foot being much higher in New York. In this case, the apartment is an example of a non-fungible asset—essentially, an asset that cannot be replaced by a random asset from the same group. The asset has some additional properties attached to it that make it "special."

In the world of finance, we use both fungible and non-fungible assets and goods extensively. Currency, loyalty tokens, food coupons, gift cards, commodities, and so on are fungible in nature, wherein one can replace the other. Real estate, people, pre-owned automobiles, artworks, and so on are non-fungible in nature, where each unit has some distinguishing features that make it irreplaceable.

The Ethereum community has devised numerous smart contract standards suited for different use cases. These are meant to be starting points for developers and introduce uniformity among developers coding for the public Ethereum blockchain. For fungible tokens, the most popular contract standard is ERC20. ERC20 tokens have been implemented in multiple use cases such as payment tokens, loyalty coins, gift cards, and so on but their most popular implementation by far is as **Initial Crypto Offering (ICO)** tokens. ERC20 contracts are easy to understand, build, and deploy and, owing to this, it is often this first contract standard that developers work with.

ERC 721 is the token standard used to build smart contracts that issue **Non-Fungible Tokens (NFTs)**. Popular implementations include government documents, land titles, digital identities, and real estate. In its native implementation, it does not define a protocol for capturing metadata of the token. However, OpenZeppelin provides us with a sample URI framework for implementing NFTs as part of its ERC721 contract templates.

Writing the smart contract code

For our project, we'll be creating one fungible and one non-fungible token. Our fungible token will be a payment token called MoolahCoin. Our non-fungible token will be an apartment ownership token called Condos. We'll also be creating a wallet that can hold both fungible and non-fungible tokens.

We will be using Truffle Suite and the Ganache blockchain for building and deploying our smart contracts. For writing our smart contract, we'll be using the OpenZeppelin Solidity library version 2.2. OpenZeppelin is a nifty resource that provides smart contract templates for developing DApps. It is a suite of tested and community-approved smart contracts that can be used as building blocks for production-grade blockchain applications.

The OpenZeppelin framework consists of reusable contract code for Ethereum and other **Ethereum Virtual Machine (EVM)**-based blockchains (for example, Quorum). It significantly cuts down the development time for building secure and safe blockchain applications and the time for writing smart contracts. It also helps to promote standardization.

Creating the ERC20 Token contract

We will start by creating a `.sol` file in your contracts directory. Let's name this file `MoolahCoin.sol`:

1. We'll begin writing our contract by first declaring the Solidity compiler version with the help of the following command:

   ```
   pragma solidity ^0.5.2;
   ```

2. Next, we will import the dependent sample contract templates from the `openzeppelin` library, as shown in the following code block:

   ```
   import "openzeppelin-
   solidity/contracts/token/ERC20/ERC20Detailed.sol";
   import "openzeppelin-
   solidity/contracts/token/ERC20/ERC20Capped.sol";
   import "openzeppelin-solidity/contracts/ownership/Ownable.sol";
   ```

   The imported contracts implement the following functionalities:

   - `ERC20Detailed` and `ERC20Capped` are sample contracts that allow us to encapsulate the inner workings of the ERC20 token. They are also used to initialize the parameters used to describe the ERC20 token during contract deployment.
   - `ERC20Detailed` allows us to define the token name, symbol, and the number of decimals the token is divisible up to.
   - `ERC20Capped` allows us to define the total supply, the total number of tokens that will be issued in the contract's lifetime. It also implements a `mint` method. The `mint` method permits us to issue new tokens and transfer them to any Ethereum address on the network.
   - `Ownable` is a sample contract that allows us to implement access controls on the smart contract.

3. The contract name is the same as our token name. The contract inherits the `ERC20Detailed`, `ERC20Capped`, and `Ownable` smart contracts from the `openzeppelin` library:

   ```
   contract MoolahCoin is ERC20Detailed, ERC20Capped, Ownable {
   ```

4. Next, as shown in the following code block, we will create a constructor for our token contract. During contract deployment, it initializes the descriptive parameters of our payment token:

```
constructor()
ERC20Detailed("Moolah Coin", "MC", 4)
ERC20Capped(10000000000)
payable public {}
}
```

Our constructor inherits the constructor methods for the contracts `ERC20Detailed` and `ERC20Capped` from the Open Zeppelin library. The following code demonstrates the `ERC20Detailed` constructor:

```
//ERC20Detailed Constructor
constructor (string memory name, string memory symbol, uint8
decimals) public {
_name = name;
_symbol = symbol;
_decimals = decimals;
}
```

The `ERC20Detailed` constructor sets the name of the token as **Moolah Coin**, the token symbol as MC, and the number of decimals the token is divisible up to (7 decimal places after zero).

The following code demonstrates the `ERC20Capped` constructor:

```
//ERC20Capped constructor
constructor (uint256 cap) public {
  require(cap > 0, "ERC20Capped: cap is 0");
  _cap = cap;
  }
```

The `ERC20Capped` constructor initializes the total supply of Moolah Coin (10,000,000,000 MC tokens in the token's lifetime) when the contract is deployed.

Putting it all together, `MoolahCoin.sol` will look something like this:

```
pragma solidity ^0.5.2;

import "openzeppelin-
solidity/contracts/token/ERC20/ERC20Detailed.sol";
import "openzeppelin-
solidity/contracts/token/ERC20/ERC20Capped.sol";
import "openzeppelin-solidity/contracts/ownership/Ownable.sol";
```

```
contract MoolahCoin is ERC20Detailed, ERC20Capped, Ownable {

constructor()
ERC20Detailed("Moolah Coin", "MC", 4)
ERC20Capped(10000000000)
payable public {}


}
```

5. We will compile our contract using Truffle. Copy and paste the contract file (MoolahCoin.sol) to the directory /contracts in your truffle workspace. Before bringing the Truffle console online, check whether your Ganache blockchain is running and the Solidity compiler version is set to 0.5.2 in the Truffle configuration file.

   To change the Solidity compiler version, open the truffle-config.js file. Under module.exports, add the compiler version and settings as shown in the following code block. Make sure the tags are uncommented and enabled. Also, make sure the development network tags are uncommented and enabled and the port tag is set to 8545. Refer to the following code block:

   ```
   module.exports = {
   networks: {
   development: {
   host: "127.0.0.1",
   port: 8545,
   network_id: "*",
   }},
   compilers: {
   solc: {
   version: "0.5.2",
   settings: {
   optimizer: {
   enabled: false,
   runs: 1000,
   },
   }}}}
   ```

6. Now, let's run the Truffle console with the help of the following command:

   ```
   truffle console
   ```

7. Next, in the command line, we will enter compile to compile the contract as shown in the following code:

   ```
   truffle(development)>> compile
   ```

You can check out the original ERC20 smart contract standard approved by the Ethereum Improvement Program here (`https://theethereum.wiki/w/index.php/ERC20_Token_Standard`). OpenZeppelin implements an encapsulated and safer version of the same contract. It's always recommended that you read the inherited template contracts in the `openzeppelin` contracts directory. You can locate the contract by following the folder path given in the import statement.

Creating the ERC721 Token contract

We will start by creating a `.sol` file in our contracts directory and will name this file `Condos.sol`:

1. We will begin writing our contract by first declaring the Solidity compiler version as shown here:

   ```
   pragma solidity ^0.5.2;
   ```

2. Next, as shown in the following code, we will import the dependent sample contract templates from the `openzeppelin` library:

   ```
   import "openzeppelin-
   solidity/contracts/token/ERC721/ERC721Metadata.sol";
   ```

`ERC721Metadata.sol` is an extremely useful resource for creating non-fungible tokens. It implements the hashmap TokenURI for storing token metadata. This helps as the native ERC721 standard does not implement a standard for capturing token metadata. It can be used to quickly create an ERC721 token with metadata as shown in the following:

```
contract Condos is ERC721Metadata {
```

You can choose to avoid using the internal hashmap implemented by `ERC721Metadata.sol` while creating an NFT. Simply import and inherit the `openzeppelin` contract, `ERC721.sol`, and define the metadata structure using a struct as per your requirement.

3. Our contract inherits the `ERC721Metadata` contract from `ERC721Metadata.sol`. Now, we define the `Id` parameter. The `Id` parameter holds the ID value of the last/latest token issued by our contract. The `MDTrack` hashmap maps each token ID to the Ethereum address that holds that token:

```
uint32 public Id;
mapping(address => uint32) public MDTrack;
```

In the preceding code, `Id` is a public variable used to hold the token ID and `MDTrack` is a public hashmap that maps addresses to token IDs, which are of the integer type.

4. Next, as shown in the following, let's create the constructor method that executes on contract deployment:

```
constructor()
ERC721Metadata("Condos Token", "CONDO")
payable public {
Id = 0;
}
```

Following is the constructor for the `ERC721Metadata` contract from its `.sol` file:

```
//ERC721Metadata Constructor Method

constructor (string memory name, string memory symbol) public {
  _name = name;
  _symbol = symbol;
  _registerInterface(_INTERFACE_ID_ERC721_METADATA);
  }
```

From the preceding code, we can make the following observations:

- The constructor initialized the name (`Condos Token`) and symbol (`CONDO`) for our token.
- It also registers a new ERC165 interface type for our non-fungible token. We also assign an initial value of `0` to our ID parameter.

5. Next, we will define a method for creating NFTs and a method for transferring NFTs, as shown in the following code:

```
//createNFT method
function createNFT(address receiver, string calldata metadata)
external returns (uint32)
{
Id++;
```

```
_mint(receiver,Id);
_setTokenURI(Id,metadata);
MDTrack[receiver] = Id;
return Id;
}
```

From the preceding code, we can make the following observations:

- The method mints new non-fungible tokens to the receiver's address. It also allows the owner to set initial metadata using the input parameters.
- The metadata is set using the setter for `TokenURI` from `ERC721Metadata.sol`. Every time a new token is issued, the `MDTrack` hashmap is updated to map the holding address to the token ID. Next, let's write a method for transferring the NFTs:

```
//transferNFT method
function transferNFT(address sender,address receiver, uint32
transId, string calldata metadata) external
{
_transferFrom(sender, receiver, transId);
_setTokenURI(transId,metadata);
delete MDTrack[sender];
MDTrack[receiver] = Id;
}
}
```

From the preceding code, we make the following observations:

- The method transfers non-fungible tokens between the sender and the receiver address. It also allows the owner to update the metadata of the token using the input parameters.
- The metadata is updated using the setter for `TokenURI` from `ERC721Metadata.sol`.
- For every transfer, the `MDTrack` hashmap is updated to map the receiver's address to the token ID and the sender's address is removed from the hashmap using `delete`.

Putting it all together, this is what `Condos.sol` looks like:

```
pragma solidity ^0.5.2;

import "openzeppelin-
solidity/contracts/token/ERC721/ERC721Metadata.sol";

contract Condos is ERC721Metadata {
```

```
uint32 public Id;
mapping(address => uint32) public MDTrack;
constructor()
ERC721Metadata("Condos Token", "CONDO")
payable public {
Id = 0;
}

function createNFT(address receiver, string calldata metadata)
external returns (uint32)
{
Id++;
_mint(receiver,Id);
_setTokenURI(Id,metadata);
MDTrack[receiver] = Id;
return Id;
}

function transferNFT(address sender,address receiver, uint32
transId, string calldata metadata) external
{
_transferFrom(sender, receiver, transId);
_setTokenURI(transId,metadata);
delete MDTrack[sender];
MDTrack[receiver] = Id;
}


}
```

6. Next, let's compile our contract now. Copy and paste the contract file
   `Condos.sol` to the directory `/contracts` in your truffle workspace. Now, we
   will run the Truffle console with the help of the following command:

   ```
   truffle console
   ```

7. Finally, in the command line, enter `compile` to compile the contract, as shown
   here:

   ```
   truffle(development)> compile
   ```

In this section, we created one fungible and one non-fungible token for our project. Now,
let's move ahead toward migrating and deploying the smart contract code in the next
section.

Migrating the smart contract code using Truffle

To work with our contracts, we first need to migrate these contracts to our test blockchain. Migrations carry out the following tasks:

- They deploy the compiled contract code to the blockchain.
- They establish interlinking between dependent contracts.
- They initialize the initial values through the constructor.
- Lastly, and most importantly, they manage the different versions of the contracts deployed. In the traditional model, every time a contract is deployed, a new Ethereum address is generated that then needs to be updated to the code of the blockchain application. Truffle allows us to abstract this concept and invoke the contract directly through a contract object instead of the address.

To deploy the smart contracts, first bring your Ganache blockchain online. Make sure your Ganache test server is running on `localhost:8545`. To do so, select the **New Workspace** option from the Ganache launch screen. Click on the **SERVER** tab on the **Workspace** screen. Set the port number to `8545`:

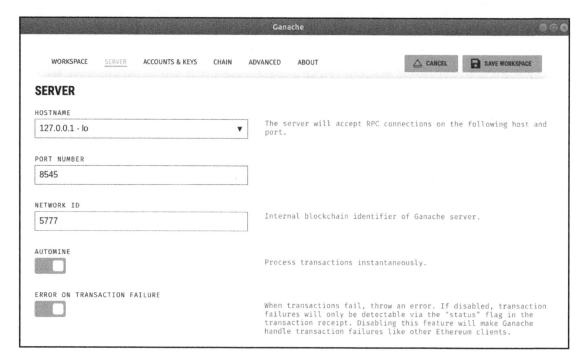

Click on **Save Workspace** in the upper-right corner. A blockchain network will be started as follows:

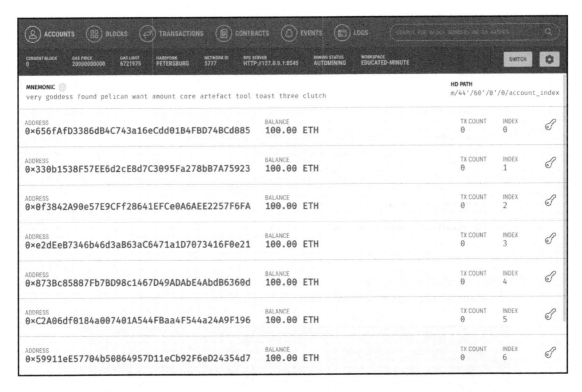

Now let's migrate the contracts we wrote earlier to our Ganache blockchain network:

1. We start with creating migrations for the two token contracts using the Truffle command line, as shown here:

```
truffle console
truffle(development)> create migration condos_migration
truffle(development)> create migration moolahcoin_migration
```

Two migration files will be created with the following nomenclature:

- *{timestamp}_moolahcoin_migration.js
- *{timestamp}_condos_migration.js

2. Replace the content of the `*{timestamp}_moolahcoin_migration.js` file with the following code:

```
let MoolahCoin = artifacts.require("MoolahCoin.sol");
module.exports = function(deployer) {
deployer.deploy(MoolahCoin);
};
```

3. Replace the content of the `*{timestamp}_condos_migration.js` file with the following code:

```
let Condos = artifacts.require("Condos.sol");
module.exports = function(deployer) {
deployer.deploy(Condos);
};
```

4. In the Truffle console, enter `migrate` to migrate the contracts to the blockchain, as shown in the following code:

```
truffle(development)> migrate
```

5. Now, check the Ganache UI. It will show that some blocks have been mined and the transactions have been created:

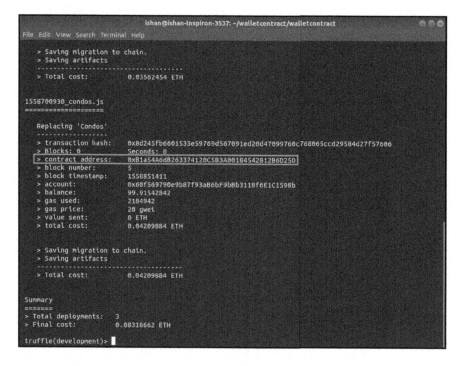

Note down the contract addresses from the console. We'll need this later. Now, let's create a token wallet frontend using ReactJS in the next section.

Creating the token wallet frontend using ReactJS

Now, let's create a simple wallet app in `react.js` to manage tokens. The wallet will have the following functionalities:

- It will allow the user to send ERC20 and ERC721 tokens.
- It can mint new tokens if the address owner is the contract owner for the token. Minting issues new ERC20 or ERC721 tokens and credits them to any Ethereum account on the network.
- It will approve an Ethereum account to spend the tokens on the user's behalf. Certain use cases and workflows might require the user account to approve or authorize an external party to debit their account and transfer tokens. The approve functionality allows us to achieve the same.

I am assuming that you will have a basic understanding of the React framework for this project. I'll be focusing on the sections where our app interacts with the token contracts. You can download the source code for the entire app from our GitHub repository at this link: `https://github.com/PacktPublishing/Blockchain-Development-for-Finance-Projects/tree/master/Chapter%202/Chapter%202/tokenwallet`.

We need to set up a MetaMask account before we can create our wallet frontend. To do so, follow these steps:

1. Start by installing MetaMask into your browser. It's available as a plugin for Chrome and Firefox. Create or import your wallet using the seed words.
2. Open the MetaMask wallet by clicking on the icon on the right-hand side. On the top right hand side of your Chrome or Firefox browser for test account. From the drop-down menu for the **network** tab in MetaMask, select the network as `Localhost 8545`.
3. Open the Ganache blockchain interface. Copy the secret key for an account. To do so, click the **key** icon next to the first Ethereum test account available in Ganache. Copy the secret key from the popup that appears.

4. Navigate back to your MetaMask wallet. Import the Ethereum account into MetaMask as an account. To do so, click on the account icon on the top right-hand side in your MetaMask wallet. Click on **Import Account**. Select and paste the private key and click on **Import**. Your Ganache address should now be available as an account on MetaMask.

We are now good to start working on the wallet.

Setting up the React app

Let's start building our React app:

1. We'll first create a new React app called token wallet using `npx`, as shown in the following:

   ```
   npx create-react-app tokenwallet
   ```

2. Next, we will update `package.json` with the following values:

   ```
   {
    "name": "tokenwallet",
    "version": "1.0.0",
    "dependencies": {
    "bulma-start": "0.0.2",
    "react": "^16.4.2",
    "react-dom": "^16.4.2",
    "react-scripts": "1.1.4",
     "web3": "^1.2.0"
    },
    "scripts": {
    "start": "react-scripts start",
    "build": "react-scripts build",
    "test": "react-scripts test --env=jsdom",
    "eject": "react-scripts eject"
    }
   }
   ```

3. Run the following command to install the dependencies:

   ```
   npm install
   ```

4. Next within the `src` folder, create a **Components** folder for the app components. Also, create a `Token` folder within `src`. We'll be using this to map the tokens supported by our wallet.

5. Finally, create a folder called **Contracts** in the `src` directory. From your build repository in the Truffle workplace, copy the `json` file for our tokens and the inherited contracts to this folder. You can also set `symlink` instead, to point to the build repository of your Truffle Suite.

Adding token interfaces to our app

We need to map the contract ABI and provide a suitable contract interface that our app can use for invoking the token smart contracts and calling the contract methods. Let's see how we can accomplish this:

1. Within the token folder, we will create two components for mapping ERC20 and ERC721 tokens. Let's call these `all20.js` and `all721.js`, as shown in the following code:

```
//all20.js

import MoolahCoin from './MoolahCoin';
const Tokens20 = [
 MoolahCoin
];
export default Tokens20;

//all721.js

import Condos from './Condos';
const Tokens721 = [
 Condos
];
export default Tokens721;
```

Currently, these files map our MoolahCoin token (ERC20) and Condos token (ERC721). As you add more tokens to the wallet, you need to add them to these files.

2. Next, we'll create two component files for our tokens. We'll label these `MoolahCoin.js` and `Condos.js`. Map the following parameters to each token js:

- **Address**—Address of the contract
- **Decimal**—Number of decimals after zero
- **Name**—Name of the token
- **Symbol**—Symbol of the token

- **Icon**—Pictorial icon to be shown on the wallet
- **ABI**—Contract ABI

This is how `Condos.js` looks:

```
export default {
address: "0xB1a54A6dB263374120C5B3A00184542812B6D25D",
decimal: 0,
name: "Condos",
symbol: "CONDO",
icon: "Condos.jpg",
abi: [
{
"constant": true,
"inputs": [
{
"name": "interfaceId",
........
........
........
"payable": false,
"stateMutability": "nonpayable",
 "type": "function"
    }
  ]
}
```

Every time you add a new token, you need to add a similar component and update all the relevant code files. Let's create the rest of our app components.

App components

Following are the main components of our app:

- `TokenBlock20.js`: This component renders the list of ERC20 tokens along with the option to send, approve, and mint tokens. It renders the token image, symbol, and wallet balance.
- `TokenBlock721.js`: This component renders the list of ERC721 tokens along with the option to send, approve, and mint tokens. It renders the token image and symbol as well as token ID and metadata. Since this is an ERC721 token, the last two are of special importance here.
- `ApproveHeader.js`: This component renders the wallet header for the Approve screen. It loads when the user clicks the **approve** button.

- `ApproveToken.js`: This component renders the wallet screen for the Approve screen. It loads when the user clicks the **approve** button. For ERC20 tokens, it asks for the address to approve and the balance to approve for that address. For ERC721, it asks for the address to approve and the token ID to approve.
- `MintHeader.js`: This component renders the wallet header for the Mint screen. It loads when the user clicks the **mint** button.
- `MintToken.js`: This component renders the wallet screen for the Mint screen. It loads when the user clicks the **mint** button. For ERC20 tokens, it asks for the address it needs to send the new tokens to and the number of tokens to mint. For ERC721, it asks for the address to which the new NFT will be tagged and the metadata for the new token.
- `TransferHeader.js`: This component renders the wallet header for the Transfer screen. It loads when the user clicks the **send** button.
- `TransferToken.js`: This component renders the wallet screen for the Transfer screen. It loads when the user clicks the **send** button. For ERC20 tokens, it asks for the address to send to and the number of tokens to send. For ERC721, it asks for the address to send to, the ID of the token to be sent, and the new metadata for the transfer.
- `InstallMetamask.js`: This component notifies the user to install MetaMask when it cannot detect injected `web3`.

> You can view and download the source code for all of the components at the GitHub link of this chapter.

Container.js

The `Container` component holds several other components, toggles components display as per state changes, and passes down their props to the components after it receives them from `app.js`:

1. We start by importing React and all of the dependent components.

> You can look at the `Container` component code file at the following GitHub repository for reference: `https://github.com/PacktPublishing/Blockchain-Development-for-Finance-Projects/blob/master/Chapter%202/Chapter%202/tokenwallet/src/Components/Container.js`.

2. The container checks the current state selected by the user. Accordingly, the user is navigated to the correct screen components. The state is checked using the `transferDetail20`, `transferDetail721`, `mintDetail20`, `mintDetail721`, `approveDetail20`, and `approveDetail721` state variables. The container then redirects the props it receives from `app.js` to the relevant component and renders it.

3. If the state variable is not set for an operation (approve, mint, or transfer), the container then renders the default token block.

4. The container also renders a separate panel for ERC721 tokens.

Next, let's look at our `App.js` file.

App.js

`App.js` has the following functions:

- Use the injected `web3` objected to connect to the Ganache blockchain and set the network in the navigation bar.
- Asynchronously access MetaMask for account authorization.
- Define the `Transfer`, `Approve`, and `Mint` methods for interacting with the token contracts.
- Set the state and pass the relevant props to the container component before each operation (`Approve`, `Mint`, and `Transfer`) is carried out.

Let's look at the code:

1. We will start writing `App.js` by first importing React, Web3, and the app components, as shown here:

```
import React, { Component } from 'react';
import Web3 from 'web3'
import Tokens20 from './Tokens/all20';
import Tokens721 from './Tokens/all721';
import Nav from './Components/Nav';
import Description from './Components/Description';
import Container from './Components/Container';
import InstallMetamask from './Components/InstallMetamask';
```

2. Next, we will define the constructor and set the initial values for the state variables. Check the `constructor` method in the `App.js` code available at the following link for reference: `https://github.com/PacktPublishing/ Blockchain-Development-for-Finance-Projects/blob/master/Chapter%202/ Chapter%202/tokenwallet/src/App.js`.

In the `constructor` method, we do the following:

- We import the token interfaces we created earlier and set the app name.
- We define the state variables for each operation being carried out, namely, `approveDetail20`, `approveDetail721`, `mintDetail20`, `mintDetail721`, `transferDetail20`, and `transferDetail721`.
- We also set the default and initial values for the form fields. We use `bind` to enable the child components to change the state.
- The `account` parameter stores the account of the Ethereum wallet being used for submitting transactions to the blockchain.

3. Next, we will define the `ComponentDidMount()` section to indicate the tasks to carry out after `App` is rendered, as shown in the following:

```
componentDidMount(){

  var account;

  if (window.Ethereum) {
  const Ethereum = window.Ethereum;
  window.web3 = new Web3(Ethereum);
  this.web3 = new Web3(Ethereum);

  Ethereum.enable().then((accounts) => {
  account = accounts[0];
  this.web3.eth.defaultAccount = account ;
```

Post November 2018, MetaMask does not inject the Ethereum provider with user accounts by default. Also, while the legacy `window.web3` option is still available (after disabling privacy mode in settings), it is not recommended to use it as it will be phased out in the long run. The Ethereum provider is now available at `window.Ethereum` in the new version. To access the user accounts, the DApp must asynchronously call the `Ethereum.enable()` method. This method requests access from the MetaMask app and the user must explicitly grant access to the DApp for using his or her MetaMask wallet. After granting permission, the method returns an array of the user's account with the active/current account at the 0th location.

Hence, for our app, we first check whether the `window.Ethereum` object is available. To provide compatibility with legacy code, we map the `window.Ethereum` object to `window.web3`. We also map the current app's Ethereum provider to `window.Ethereum`. Next, we asynchronously call MetaMask to ask for permission to the injected Ethereum provider with the user's accounts.

4. As shown in the following, we will set the local `account` parameter to the first account in the array of accounts returned by the `Ethereum.enable` method. We also set the default account for `window.web3`:

```
let app = this;

this.setState({
 account
 });

this.setNetwork();
this.setGasPrice();
```

From the preceding code, we can make the following observations:

- We initialized the `this` object for our app. We also set the account state variable to the default account.
- We also called the `setNetwork` (to set the Navbar to our local Ganache blockchain) and `setGasPrice` methods (to get the default gas price from the network) once we have access to the injected `web3`.

5. Next, we will use the `Tokens20` parameter to loop through all of the tokens listed in `all20.js`. For each ERC20 token, we set the contract parameter using its ABI and address. We call the `balanceOf` method to get the balance for each token for our primary account. We will fetch all of the other parameters from the token's component file. Finally, each token's details are pushed into the `token20` state array. Let's have a look at the following code:

```
Tokens20.forEach((token) => {
 let erc20Token = new
this.web3.eth.Contract(token.abi,token.address);

erc20Token.methods.balanceOf(account).call().then(function(response
){

 if(response) {
 let decimal = token.decimal;
```

```
let precision = '1e' + decimal;
let balance = response / precision;
let name = token.name;
let symbol = token.symbol;
let icon = token.icon;
let abi = token.abi;
let address = token.address;

balance = balance >= 0 ? balance : 0;

let tokens20 = app.state.tokens20;

if(balance > 0) tokens20.push({
decimal,
balance,
name,
symbol,
icon,
abi,
address,
});

app.setState({
tokens20
})
}
});
});
```

6. We will similarly loop through all of the ERC721 tokens available in `all721.js`.
   The only difference being that, for ERC721, we fetch `tokenId` and the mapped
   metadata for each token. We do this by accessing the `getter` method for
   `MDTrack` (the public hashmap for tracking token ID for an address) and
   the `tokenURI` method available in the base ERC721 contract:

```
Tokens721.forEach((token721) => {
 let erc721Token = new
this.web3.eth.Contract(token721.abi,token721.address);

 erc721Token.methods.MDTrack(account).call().then(function
(response) {
 if(response) {
 let name = token721.name;
 let symbol = token721.symbol;
 let icon = token721.icon;
 let abi = token721.abi;
 let address = token721.address;
```

```
let tokenid = response;

tokenid = tokenid >= 0 ? tokenid : 0;
if(tokenid!==0)
{
erc721Token.methods.tokenURI(tokenid).call().then(function
(response) {
if(response) {
let metadata = response;
let tokens721 = app.state.tokens721;

tokens721.push({

name,
symbol,
tokenid,
icon,
abi,
address,
metadata,
});

app.setState({
tokens721
})
}
});
}
}
})
})
```

7. Next, we define the individual methods for each operation. The `Transfer` method is used to transfer token between Ethereum addresses. You can find the code for the `Transfer` method at the `App.js` code at the link here: https://github.com/PacktPublishing/Blockchain-Development-for-Finance-Projects/blob/master/Chapter%202/Chapter%202/tokenwallet/src/App.js.

From the code, we can make the following observations:

- The `Transfer` method starts by setting the `inProgress` state variable to `true` so child components can recognize that the current state is a transfer in progress.
- After establishing `defaultAccount`, we initialize our contract object depending on whether the token is `ERC20` or `ERC721`. We do this by checking whether the `transferDetail721` state variable is storing any metadata.
- Next, we assign the values of the state variables to our local variables and then call our token contract for the transfer.
- For our ERC20 tokens, this is the `transferFrom` method. For ERC721, this is the `transferNFT` method.
- On successful response, we reset the app using the `resetApp` method, which resets the state variables and sets `inProgress` to `false`.

8. Now, we will write the mint method. The `mint` method is similar to the `Transfer` method. It is invoked when the user clicks the mint button on the mint token screen:

   You can find the code for the `mint` method in the `App.js` file code at the following link: `https://github.com/PacktPublishing/Blockchain-Development-for-Finance-Projects/blob/master/Chapter%202/Chapter%202/tokenwallet/src/App.js`.

- The code checks whether the user is minting an ERC20 or an ERC721 token and searches the respective state variable for the token's details.
- If the token is an ERC20 token, it calls the mint method defined in the base ERC20 contract.
- For non-fungible tokens, it calls the `createNFT` method defined in our Condos contract for creating non-fungible tokens and allocating token metadata.
- It also toggles the `inProgress` state parameter on and off when minting is in process.

9. Next, we will write the `Approve` method:

   Please check the `App.js` file at the following link for the code for the `Approve` method: https://github.com/PacktPublishing/Blockchain-Development-for-Finance-Projects/blob/master/Chapter%202/Chapter%202/tokenwallet/src/App.js.

   - The `approve` method checks whether the user is approving an ERC20 token or an ERC721 token.
   - This it does by checking the `approveDetail20` state variable. Accordingly, it calls the `approve` function from the ERC20 base class or the approve function from the ERC721 base class.
   - In the case of the ERC20 contract, it needs to send the account to approve and balance. In the case of ERC721, it needs to send `tokenid` and the account to approve.

10. Lastly, we will build the `render` function:

    You can find the `render` method at this link for the `App.js` file: https://github.com/PacktPublishing/Blockchain-Development-for-Finance-Projects/blob/master/Chapter%202/Chapter%202/tokenwallet/src/App.js.

    - If the app can detect a `web3` instance, the app renders and sends the state parameters to the `Container` component, which then redistributes it between the child components.
    - If the app is unable to detect a `web3` instance, it shows a notification to the user asking him or her to install MetaMask. It does this by rendering the `InstallMetamask.js` component. The entire `app.js` source code can be found at the GitHub repository: https://github.com/PacktPublishing/Blockchain-Development-for-Finance-Projects/tree/master/Chapter%202/Chapter%202/tokenwallet.

Running our app

Let's bring our wallet online and run the application to see how it works. Make sure your Ganache blockchain is running and the contracts are deployed. Let's run our React development server:

1. Run the following command in the project directory:

   ```
   npm start
   ```

   By default, the app should run on port 3000.

2. To access the app, enter localhost:3000 in your browser. The app should open up in the browser, as shown in the following screenshot:

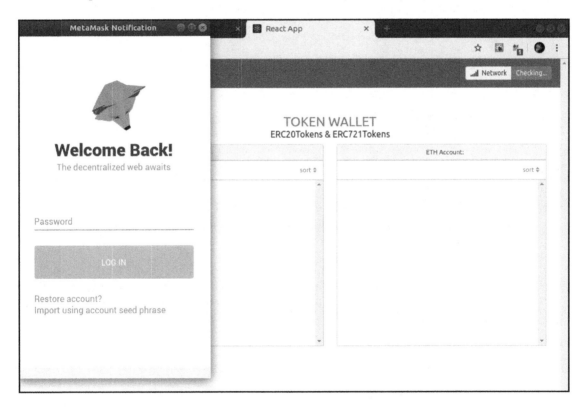

3. You need to sign in with your MetaMask credentials so the app can access your primary account. After signing in, you should get another popup, as shown in the following screenshot. You need to permit the app access to MetaMask:

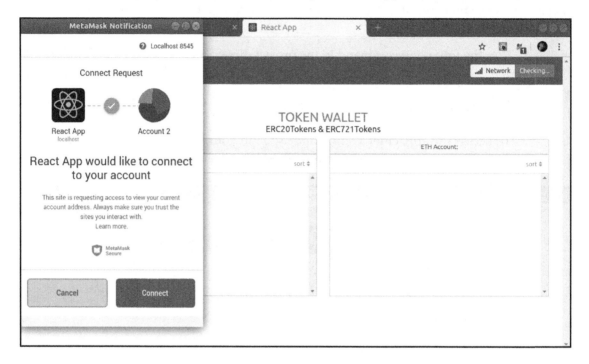

On granting access, MetaMask returns an array of accounts to the app including your primary account in the 0th location. Hence, the app should now be rendered with your primary Ethereum account visible.

4. Next, we will add the Condos and MoolahCoin tokens to your MetaMask wallet. To do so, select the hamburger menu icon in the top left-hand corner in MetaMask. From the sliding panel that appears, click on **Add Token**, as shown in the following screenshot:

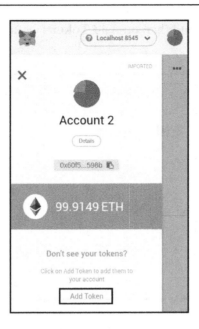

5. As shown in the following screenshot, select the **Custom Token** tab. Paste the contract address in the screen that appears. MetaMask should automatically recognize the details of your token contract on pasting the address:

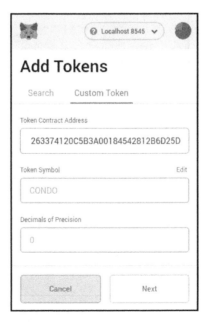

6. Then, click on **Next** and then on **Add Tokens**, as shown in the following screenshot:

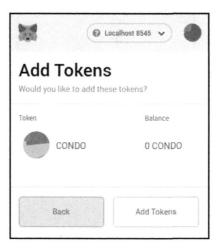

7. The following screenshot displays the details of **Account 2**. Now, we will repeat the process for both the MoolahCoin and Condos tokens:

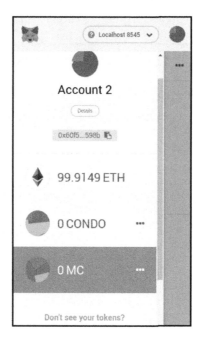

8. We need to mint an initial amount of tokens to ourselves before we start using the app. To do so, navigate back to the Truffle console and run the following code:

```
//Mint 10 MoolahCoins
MoolahCoin.deployed().then(function(instance) { return
instance.mint("<Your primary eth address>",100000);
}).then(function(responseb) {console.log("response",
responseb.toString(10));});

//Mint 1 Condo Token with metadata 'New Delhi'
Condos.deployed().then(function(instance) { return
instance.createNFT("<Your primary eth address>","New Delhi");
}).then(function(responseb) {console.log("response",
responseb.toString(10));});
```

Our token wallet app will now look like the following screenshot:

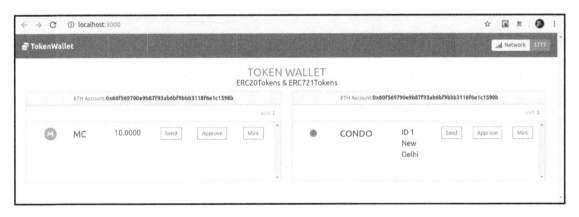

You will now see the MoolahCoin and Condo tokens in your wallet dashboard.

9. Let's try to send some tokens now. Click on the **Send** button for MC. The send MC screen will open as shown in the following screenshot:

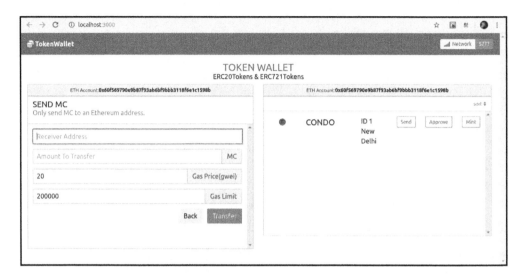

10. Copy an address from the list of auto-generated addresses from Ganache, as shown in the following screenshot:

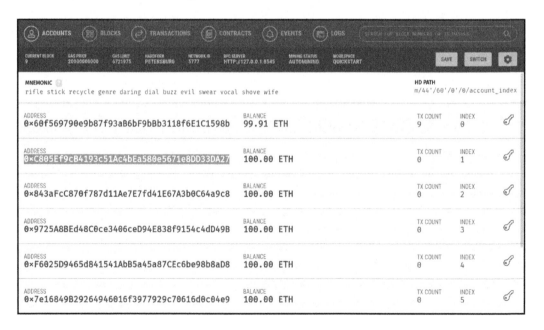

11. Copy the receiver's address field, enter an amount to transfer, and click on **Send**.

    MetaMask will pop up with a notification and ask the user's permission to transfer tokens:

12. Click on **Confirm** and the transaction will go through. MetaMask will give you a pop-up notification to let you know the transaction has gone through successfully. The balance change is reflected in the app interface:

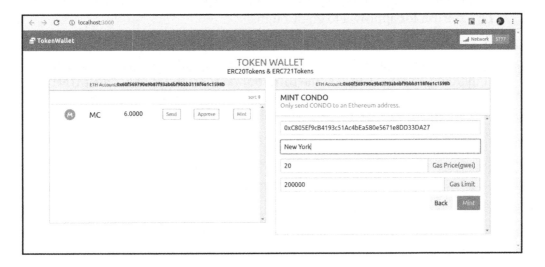

13. Let's try to approve now. Click on the **Approve** button for MoolahCoin. Enter an address to approve and the token balance permitted to move. Click on **Confirm** after entering the details, as shown in the following screenshot:

MetaMask asks for the user's permission. It also shows a notification indicating that the user is approving another address to spend tokens on their behalf. Click on **Confirm** for approval to go through.

14. Lastly, let's try out the Mint operation for the Condos token. As shown in the following screenshot, Mint allows you to create and assign new tokens to an Ethereum address. Click on the **Mint** button for Condos to get the **MINT** token screen. Enter an address to mint the new tokens to. Minting for Condos also allows you to allocate an initial metadata value to the token:

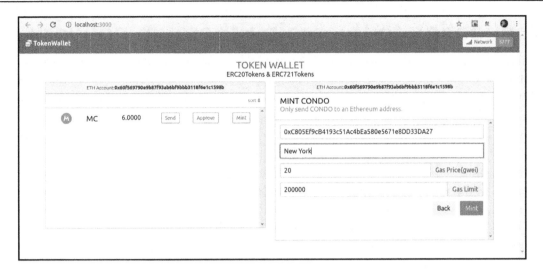

15. Click on **Mint** after entering the address and metadata as shown in the following screenshot. MetaMask pops up with a notification asking for the user's permission:

16. Click on **Confirm** to generate a new NFT mapped to the receiving address with the metadata mentioned on the screen.

Connecting to the main Ethereum network

In this section, we'll see how our wallet can be connected to the main Ethereum network and used for storing, transferring, and managing fungible and non-fungible assets on the Ethereum network:

1. To deploy the wallet and contracts in production, you need to have a `geth` instance running on the main Ethereum network. Geth is a popular Ethereum client used to run an Ethereum node and connect to the main network. Update the `truffle-config.js` file to point to the production `geth` instance as shown in the following. The network ID is set to `1` for the main network:

```
const HDWalletProvider = require('truffle-hdwallet-provider');
module.exports = {
networks: {
development: {
host: "127.0.0.1",
port: 8545,
network_id: "*",
}
prod: {
host: "<Live geth host IP>",
port: 8545,
network_id: "1",
}
},
compilers: {
solc: {
version: "0.5.2",
settings: {
optimizer" {
enabled: false,
runs: 1000,
},
}}}}}
```

2. Run the following command to launch an instance of the Truffle console pointed to your production `geth` instance:

```
truffle prod
```

3. Make sure your coinbase is set and your account is unlocked before executing `migrate`. Since you are deploying on the main Ethereum network, there will be associated gas that you need to pay to the network. Make sure your account has sufficient ethers to pay for gas. Run the following command to unlock your account:

```
personal.unlockAccount(eth.accounts[0],'passphrase',1000)
```

4. Run `migrate` on the console to deploy your contracts to the production `geth`:

```
migrate
```

5. Let's come to the app now. Point the MetaMask instance to the main Ethereum network by selecting it from the drop-down list as shown in the following screenshot:

Your wallet app should now be connected to the main Ethereum network. This is indicated on the network status tab, as shown in the following screenshot:

You can now start using your wallet app on the main Ethereum network.

Summary

So, we come to the end of our second chapter. If this is your first time building a blockchain application, this chapter should have helped you to identify the different components of a blockchain application. If you are new to creating and issuing tokens on blockchains, this should have helped you to grasp the concept and give you some ideas on how you can implement them as part of your projects.

We started this chapter by looking at the concept of fungible and non-fungible tokens and the business cases you can implement using these tokens. We also looked at the smart contract standards for these tokens and how they can be implemented using Solidity and OpenZeppelin. We created a mintable fungible token called MoolahCoin and a non-fungible token called Condos using these resources. Finally, we built a wallet app to manage the tokens we issued on the blockchain using ReactJS. The wallet allowed us to send tokens, approve requests from secondary addresses, and mint new tokens. Lastly, we looked at running our application and connecting our application to the main Ethereum network.

The main takeaway from this chapter is understanding the concept of tokens and how you can implement them as part of your business use cases. I also hope you were able to understand how to leverage `openzeppelin` to quickly write smart contracts. I hope you now have a clear understanding of creating a React app that can interact with your local Ganache blockchain or the main Ethereum network by leveraging MetaMask.

In the next chapter, we will learn to create a merchant solution for online retailers. The solution would enable users to accept payments on a blockchain network akin to the leading fiat payment networks of the day.

Designing a Payment Gateway for Online Merchants

3

A payment gateway is an integral tool in the kitty of any web developer designing an e-commerce solution. Payment gateways allow retailers to set up and scale businesses online. This chapter will guide you in building a payment gateway system and a payment ecosystem. The solution would enable users to accept payments on a blockchain network akin to the leading fiat payment networks of the day. This specific solution is built on the Ethereum platform and allows the merchant to accept ether as payment. It can easily be leveraged to accept an ERC20 token as payment as well for enterprise applications not implementing cryptocurrencies.

This chapter will cover the following topics:

- Defining our blockchain payment ecosystem
- Generating dynamic merchant addresses using HD wallets
- Creating an e-commerce website and payment gateway
- Creating an API for generating dynamic payment addresses
- Building the merchant HD wallet
- Running the payment ecosystem

Technical requirements

The code files of this chapter are available on the following link :

```
https://github.com/PacktPublishing/Blockchain-Development-for-Finance-Projects/
tree/master/Chapter%203
```

We'll be using the following to develop our project:

- Ganache Private Blockchain Server: `https://trufflesuite.com/ganache/`
- MetaMask plugin for Chrome/Firefox/Safari: `https://metamask.io/`

For installing Ganache on Ubuntu, you might need to change some settings. Click on the drop-down menu next to the Ganache directory name. Select **Preferences**. Navigate to the **Behavior** tab. Under **Executable Text Files**, set the option to **Ask what to do**. Navigate back to the file downloaded from the Ganache download link. Right-click on the file and click on **Properties**. Select the **Permissions** tab. Select the **Allow executing files as program** option. Now, double-click on the file. The Ganache blockchain should start smoothly.

Make sure your Ganache test server is running on `localhost:8545`. To do so, select the **New Workspace** option from the Ganache launch screen. Click on the **SERVER** tab on the workspace screen. Set the port number to **8545**:

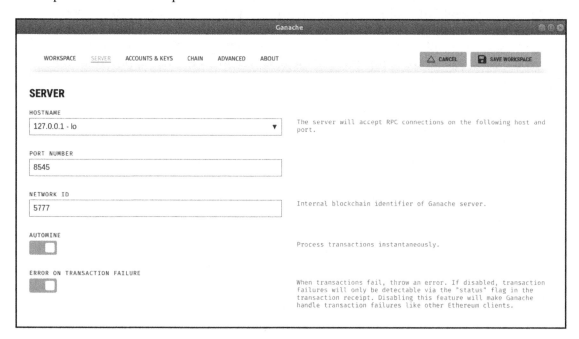

Click on **Save Workspace** on the upper-right corner. A blockchain network will be started, as follows:

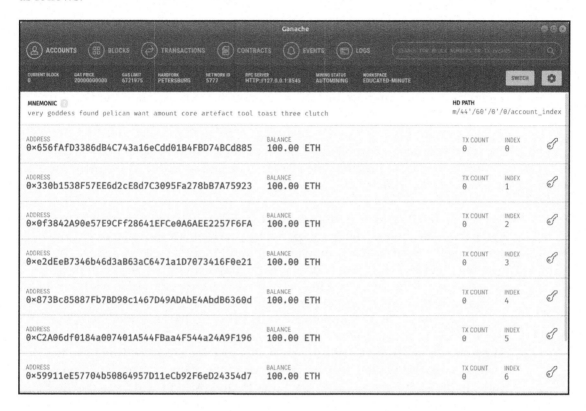

I'm using Ubuntu 18.04.2 LTS for running the preceding applications and deploying my blockchain. This project assumes that you are working on a Unix operating system. Additionally, this project assumes you have Node.js and npm installed. I'm using **Node.js version 13.0.1** and **npm version 6.12.0**.

Defining our blockchain payment ecosystem

Payment flows on a blockchain network have numerous characteristics similar to conventional fiat payments. However, owing to the unique architecture of blockchain systems, several features make them distinct from conventional payment networks. Additionally, owing to their decentralized nature, blockchains permit you to design payment systems that eliminate middlemen and directly credit the merchant's blockchain wallet.

For our project, we'll be building a payment ecosystem that illustrates the preceding benefits. The payment ecosystem will consist of three major components:

- A *faux* e-commerce web page with an ether payment gateway, which allows payment from MetaMask or other Ethereum wallets
- A merchant HD wallet generator, which dynamically generates a new address for each payment request
- A merchant wallet interface that tracks payments from customers and confirms payments on the blockchain network

Let's first look at the **e-commerce** web page. Our e-commerce web page will have a list of products that the customer can procure. The price will be listed in USD. A payment process will typically follow this workflow:

1. On clicking the **Buy Now** button, the customer is redirected to a landing page where they can choose whether to pay using the MetaMask wallet or any other ether wallet. The customer is shown the amount that they need to pay to the merchant in ether. This page is similar to the payment option selection page in fiat payments. Instead of choosing between credit cards, PayPal, bank transfer, or prepaid wallets, here, the customer can choose which Ethereum wallet they will use for payments. Our e-commerce website provides the customer the option to use either a MetaMask wallet or any other Ethereum wallet. Examples of other Ethereum wallets could be third-party wallet providers such as Coinbase and Kraken, hardware wallets such as Trezor, or true wallets such as the Ethereum wallet in the Mist browser, Jaxx, **My Ether Wallet** (**MEW**), and TrustWallet. You could also use paper wallets or transfer directly from the command line of an Ethereum client such as go-ethereum (**geth**).

2. If the customer selects **MetaMask Wallet**, the application will use the browser-injected web3 object for making the payment transaction. To do so, the application will first generate a dynamic Ethereum address from the merchant's wallet for receiving payments. This address will change for every payment request to the merchant's wallet. Next, the app will fetch the user's account from the injected web3 object and submit a transfer request from the user's account to the dynamically generated merchant address. At this point, MetaMask will notify the user of an outgoing payment and ask them whether they want to permit the transaction. If the user permits the transaction, the transaction amount is debited in ethers from this account and the amount is credited to the merchant's address.

The advantage of this workflow is that the user has to go through a very simple process to make a payment. Their experience is not very different from a conventional fiat wallet payment. Given the checks and balances implemented by MetaMask including notifying the user and seeking permission for each request, it also makes for a very secure workflow.

3. Optionally, if the customer selects **Other wallets**, the gateway will generate a dynamic address for accepting payments from the merchant's wallet and then track this address for 15 minutes for any incoming transactions. The Ethereum address to which the customer has to send the payment is displayed on the screen. They are also shown the 15-minute timer for the payment. The customer is expected to copy the merchant's address and then send a payment from their wallet to the address within the 15-minute window. Every 10 seconds, the gateway application checks the balance of the dynamic address. The timer will stop and payment will be confirmed only when the ether balance of the merchant address is equal to or greater than the payment expected by the merchant. The customer can also send the payment in multiple transactions, provided these transactions are within the 15-minute window and the total ether sent is greater than or equal to the payment amount. When the application confirms that the full payment has been received, it shows a confirmation message to the customer on the screen. Alternatively, if the full payment is not received in the 15-minute window, it shows a **Payment failed** message to the user. As you might realize, this a very cumbersome process for making payments, something that users new to crypto or blockchain might not be comfortable with. At the same time, the customer could make a mistake while copying the address or send the incorrect amount. Many applications try to avoid these complications by using a QR code that the customer can scan to populate the merchant's address. But it's not a secure process and the customer and the merchant could end up losing funds.

We'll also be designing a **merchant wallet** and a **merchant wallet interface**. A merchant wallet is significantly different from a traditional customer wallet on Ethereum. Privacy is of utmost importance for merchants. If the merchant uses a single Ethereum account for accepting payment every time, it will be easy for an external party to track their business transaction volumes and other relevant details from the peer-to-peer ledger. Hence, we need to generate dynamic addresses for each transaction. This will ensure the anonymity of transactions yet a transparent system for payments.

We also need to verify that each payment received by the merchant's wallet is confirmed. Blockchain transactions have the risk of being removed from the peer-to-peer ledger if they end up on a competing chain à la a fork. There is also no middleman in this scenario to cover the merchant's risk. Hence, it is important to create a foolproof system that will notify the merchant once the payment is secure and cannot be reversed or removed. The merchant will ship the product only after receiving the notification.

The industry standard is to wait for 6 blocks after your bitcoin transaction and 40 blocks after your Ethereum transaction before confirming the transaction and carrying out any dependent steps. Hence, we need to build a workflow that'll notify the merchant when the payment comes in and when it is 40 blocks old in the Ethereum blockchain. This process is referred to as **block confirmation**. Block confirmation will form an integral part of our merchant wallet interface.

Hence, we'll be building the following:

- An e-commerce payment gateway that generates a landing page for payments: this landing page will show a dynamically generated merchant account for receiving payments.
- An API service that the e-commerce payment gateway can call: this API will dynamically generate an address key linked to a merchant wallet and share that new address with the payment gateway.
- A merchant wallet interface that tracks all dynamically generated addresses linked to a common root node and seed kept safe by the merchant: the wallet interface tracks all of the payments to these dynamic addresses and notifies the merchant once the transaction is **confirmed** by the network (40 blocks old).

Generating dynamic merchant addresses using HD wallets

To generate dynamic addresses, we'll be creating a **Hierarchical Deterministic (HD)** wallet system for the merchant. HD wallets create a hierarchical tree of public and private keys from a single master node. This allows the user to generate and control a suite of public and private keys from the same seed phrase. The HD wallet owner can easily port their suite of keys to another hardware by porting the seed phrase used to derive the public-private key tree.

All addresses are generated from a master seed. Each time a new key pair is generated, the seed is extended at the end by a counter value. This means that, theoretically, you can generate 2^{512} key pairs from the same seed phrase. To back up their wallet, the user needs to back up just the master seed phrase. They can also move their key pairs easily between hardware by importing this key pair to a different infrastructure. This makes them extremely portable. This also means that the user needs to back up the seed phrase and keep it safe anytime they generate a new HD wallet as they might end up losing their funds otherwise.

As the name suggests, HD wallets use a hierarchical structure for deriving Ethereum addresses. To generate the addresses, we first create 12- or 24-word BIP39 mnemonic phrase or seed phrase. The BIP39 standard defines an implementation standard for generating deterministic wallets from a seed phrase. It has a predetermined 2,048-word list, which it uses to create a seed phrase with 12 or 24 words aligned in a selected order. The order of the words in the seed phrase is important. Random seed phrases can be used but they are not recommended due to the possibility of checksum errors.

From the seed phrase, we derive the binary seed, which is actually used to generate the key pairs. For a 128-bit seed, we use 12 words and for a 256-bit seed, we use 24 words in the seed phrase. The 256-bit implementation is considered more secure.

From this seed, we derive a master node and the corresponding master public and private key pair. We derive the child address nodes from this master node and subsequently the child public-private key pair and Ethereum address. The BIP32 standard defines the functions that are used to derive the child key pairs from this master public and private key. It also defines a hierarchical wallet structure and a nomenclature that would be used to refer to the child key pairs generated out of this mechanism.

The following nomenclature is a symbolic representation used to refer to a BIP32 HD wallet key pair:

$$\texttt{m/i}_\texttt{H}\texttt{/0/k}$$

Here, *m* indicates the master node, *i* indicates the account number derived from the master node, 0 indicates that the address is generated for the external keychain (used for generating public address), and *k* indicates the kth key pair generated. Additionally, you can set the third parameter to 1 instead of 0 for an internal keychain for addresses for other operations such as change addresses (addresses that store transaction change amounts) and generating addresses.

You can find the network diagram representing a BIP32 hierarchical public-private key structure in the following diagram:

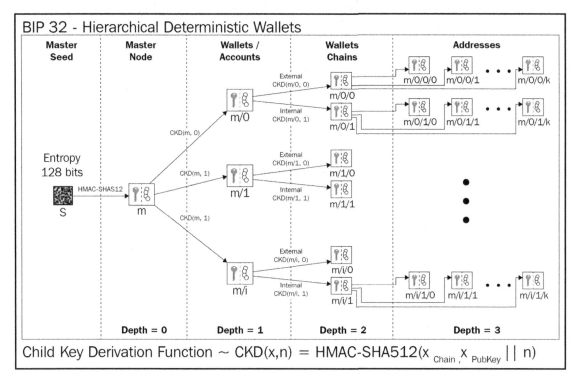

Figure 1: BIP32 HD wallets

The BIP44 standard builds on top of BIP32 and defines a derivation path with the following 5-level hierarchy:

```
m / purpose' / coin_type' / account' / change / address_index
```

This enables the HD wallet system to handle multiple accounts and asset types (such as Bitcoin and Ethereum).

In this representation, we have the following:

- m: This indicates the master node.
- purpose: This is a constant set to 44 to indicate that the derivation path is of BIP44 type.
- coin type: This is constant for each cryptocurrency. For Bitcoin, this is 0 and for Ethereum, this is 60. Additional coin types can be registered with the community.

- `account`: This is the account type; users can use multiple types of accounts. They can be split into various categories such as donations, savings, and expenses.
- `change`: This is set to 0 for public addresses and 1 for internal addresses such as those holding transaction change.
- `index`: This is used as a child index in BIP32 key derivation. It starts at 0 and increases sequentially whenever a new address is generated.

A typical derivation path may look as follows:

```
m/44'/0'/0'/0/0
```

For our purpose, we'll be using a BIP39 mnemonic and BIP44 derivation path to build our HD wallet. We'll be varying the address index starting from 0 to generate a key structure each linked to the same root node. The coin type will be set to `60` for Ethereum. All of the dynamically generated addresses can then be easily monitored and managed. Each address will be valid only for one payment request. The mnemonic generated for the merchant wallet will be constant throughout and the merchant needs to preserve it to be able to view their total balance and access their funds.

Let's move on to building our ecosystem, starting with the payment gateway.

Creating an e-commerce website and payment gateway

Let's start by creating a React app that'll act as our e-commerce portal and payment gateway:

1. Create a new React app called `gateway` with the help of the following command:

   ```
   npx create-react-app gateway
   ```

2. Open `package.json` within the app, and add the following dependencies:

   ```
   {
     "name": "gateway",
     "version": "1.0.0",
     "private": false,
     "dependencies": {
     "bulma-start": "0.0.2",
     "react": "^16.8.6",
     "react-dom": "^16.8.6",
     "react-scripts": "3.0.1",
   ```

```
"typescript": "^3.4.0",
"web3": "^1.2.0"
},
"scripts": {
"start": "react-scripts start",
"build": "react-scripts build",
"test": "react-scripts test",
"eject": "react-scripts eject"
}
}
```

3. Run the `npm install` command to install the dependencies.

We'll be building an e-commerce page for selling shoes online called **Sindbad Commerce**. On running the app, the user lands on a default page where they can choose to buy from a selection of five products. On clicking on the **Buy Now** button, they are redirected to a payments page where they can pay using the MetaMask wallet or any other wallet.

Next, we'll be focusing on the components of the gateway. Our app will contain the following components:

- `Container.js`: The `Container` component holds several other components, toggles components, display as per state changes, and passes down their props to the components after it receives them from `app.js`.
- `Nav.js`: This renders a navigation bar for the e-commerce page.
- `Description.js`: This renders a single-line description for the page.
- `Shoerack.js`: The `Shoerack.js` app component lists all of the shoes. It renders the e-commerce page for viewing and buying the shoes. On clicking the **Buy Now** button, the customer is redirected to the payment page.
- `Payment.js`: `Payment.js` renders a payment page. It dynamically fetches a new Ethereum address for payment using an API from the merchant wallet. It also sets the number of ether to be transferred for a successful payment. The user can pay using the MetaMask wallet or any other wallet.
- `PVerification.js`: This component is rendered when the user selects **Other Wallets**. It renders a tracking page that gives the user a 15-minute window to transfer to the merchant's address.
- `Timer.js`: The `Timer` component renders a 15 minutes timer and checks whether the complete amount has been transferred to the merchant's wallet at an interval of 10 seconds.

Additionally, we'll define an array constant called `Shoes.js`, which will dynamically list details about all of the items on sale.

We'll be looking at the important components in this section. Some understanding of how to build React apps is assumed for the next few steps. If you want to focus on just the blockchain part, you can download the entire app at the GitHub repository location, at `https://github.com/PacktPublishing/Blockchain-Development-for-Finance-Projects/tree/master/Chapter%203/gateway` and directly move on to the next steps.

Shoes.js

The `Shoes.js` object will have metadata about the products our website is selling. Let's start creating this interface:

1. Under the `src` directory, create a folder called `Items`, and within the `Items` folder, create a `.js` file called `all.js`. List out all of the shoes you want to display on the site within this file. This is how my `all.js` file looks:

    ```
    import Shoes1 from './Shoes1';
    import Shoes2 from './Shoes2';
    import Shoes3 from './Shoes3';
    import Shoes4 from './Shoes4';
    import Shoes5 from './Shoes5';

    const Shoes = [
     Shoes1,
     Shoes2,
     Shoes3,
     Shoes4,
     Shoes5,
    ];

    export default Shoes;
    ```

    The `Shoes` constant contains the details of all of the items listed and can be used to access their information.

2. Now, define the parameters of each individual shoe component. This is how my `Shoes1.js` file looks:

    ```
    export default {
     price: 200,
     name: "Badidas",
     logo: "Badidas.png",
    ```

```
image: "Shoe1.jpg"
}
```

Do this for all of the shoe components from `Shoes2` through to `Shoes5`.

Container.js

The `Container.js` file serves two main purposes:

- It renders components based on the current state of the app.
- It accepts the props from `app.js` and transfers them to the lower-level components.

Let's see how we will build the `Container.js` component:

1. Start by importing the three components for the app, `Shoerack`, `Payment`, and `PVerification`, as follows:

   ```
   import React, { Component } from 'react';
   import Shoerack from './Shoerack'
   import Payment from './Payment'
   import PVerification from './PVerification'
   ```

2. The render statement renders the `Shoerack`, `Payment`, and `PVerification` components based on the current state variables, as follows:

   ```
   this.props.paymentf ?
   <div>
   <PVerification mAddress={this.props.mAddress}
   PaymentDetail={this.props.PaymentDetail}
   amount={this.props.amount}
   diff={this.props.diff}
   closePayment={this.props.closePayment}
   minutes={this.props.minutes}
   seconds={this.props.seconds}
   />
   </div>:
   ```

3. When the `paymentf` flag is set, it indicates the customer is using a wallet other than MetaMask to make the payment. Setting this flag to `true`, it renders the `PVerification` page. The container component forwards the **Payment Details** parameter, the payment amount, and the minutes and seconds parameters for the timer.

4. If `paymentf` is set to `false`, the `container` component next checks whether the `PaymentDetail` props has `name` as a local property, as shown here:

```
this.props.PaymentDetail.hasOwnProperty('name') ?
<div>
<Payment PaymentDetail={this.props.PaymentDetail}
Conv={this.props.Conv}
mAddress={this.props.mAddress}
closePayment={this.props.closePayment}
MMaskTransfer={this.props.MMaskTransfer}
PaymentWait={this.props.PaymentWait}
startTimer={this.props.startTimer}
minutes={this.props.minutes}
seconds={this.props.seconds}
/>
</div>:
```

5. If the `name` property exists and `paymentf` is false, the `Container` component renders the `Payment` component. It also forwards the following state variables as props:

- The `Conv` state variable: Live conversion rate from USD into Ether
- The `mAddress` variable: Dynamically generated merchant wallet address
- `MMaskTransfer`: The method for initiating a transfer from the MetaMask wallet
- `PaymentWait`: The method for accepting a transfer when a customer pays using a wallet other than MetaMask
- `startTimer`: The method to start a timer interval
- `minutes` and `seconds`: Dynamic parameters for the timer

6. If none of the state variables are set, the container then renders the `Shoerack` component, which displays all of the shoes:

```
<div>
<Shoerack shoes={this.props.shoes}
newPayment={this.props.newPayment}
/>
</div>
```

That ends `Container.js`. Now, let's bring it all together by declaring the methods that will define and modify our state in the `App.js` file.

Writing the App.js file and declaring the methods

Let's create our main `App.js` file. The `App.js` file will define all the methods invoked by the components and set the initial state of the App:

1. We start writing our `App.js` file by importing the dependencies and the `app` components, as shown here:

```
import React, { Component } from 'react';
import Web3 from 'web3'
import Nav from './Components/Nav'
import Description from './Components/Description'
import Container from './Components/Container'
import Shoes from './Items/all'
```

2. Within the constructor, we initialize the global parameters of the requisite state variables. We also bind the methods that will be accessed by the child components for changing the state, as shown here:

```
class App extends Component {
 constructor(){
 super();
 this.appName = 'Sindbad Commerce';
 this.shoes = Shoes;
 this.newPayment = this.newPayment.bind(this);
 this.closePayment = this.closePayment.bind(this);
 this.PaymentWait = this.PaymentWait.bind(this);
 this.tick = this.tick.bind(this);
 this.bCheck = this.bCheck.bind(this);
 this.startTimer = this.startTimer.bind(this);

 this.state = {
 shoes: [],
 PaymentDetail: {},
 Conv: 250,
 defaultGasPrice: null,
 defaultGasLimit: 200000,
 paymentf: false,
 mAddress: '0x',
 amount: 0,
 diff: 0,
 seconds: '00', // responsible for the seconds
 minutes: '15', // responsible for the minutes
 tflag: true
 };
```

Let's start writing the methods. We'll be looking at the following methods in detail:

- newPayment()
- PaymentWait()
- MMaskTransfer()
- startTimer()
- tick()
- bCheck()
- Using the componentDidMount() function
- Using render() to invoke components

newPayment()

The newPayment() method is called every time a user clicks the **Buy Now** button next to an item. As the name suggests, it initiates a new payment:

1. We start by defining the method. The method takes index as a parameter, which basically refers to the shoe model, as shown here:

```
newPayment = (index) => {
var mAddress;
let app = this;
```

2. Next, we define two asynchronous calls:

- The first asynchronous call is to our local API, getMAddress, which dynamically generates a new Merchant address for receiving payments for each payment request. We'll talk more on this API later. This newly generated address is then updated to the state along with the details of the item for which the payment is being processed, as shown here:

```
(async function main(){
 await fetch('http://localhost:5000/api/getMAddress')
 .then(response => response.json())
 .then(data => {
 mAddress = data.MAddress;

 app.setState({
 PaymentDetail: app.state.shoes[index],
 mAddress
 })
 });
```

- The next asynchronous call is to fetch the live conversion details rate from USD to ETH (ether):

```
var Conv;
await
fetch('https://min-api.cryptocompare.com/data/price?fsym=ETH&ts
yms=USD')
.then(response => response.json())
.then(data => {
Conv=data.USD;

app.setState({
Conv
})
});
})();
};
```

CryptoCompare (`min-api.cryptocompare.com/data`) is a free service that returns the live conversion rate from USD to ETH. We store this conversion rate in the state variable, `Conv`. Since the e-commerce website displays all prices in USD, the `Payment` app component first converts the price of the product into ether and then notifies the customer of the number of ether they need to send to the merchant's wallet address.

PaymentWait()

This method is called to set the state variable every time the customer selects **Other Wallet** for payment, as shown here. It indicates the container component that a payment page needs to be rendered with a 15-minute window for accepting payments to the merchant's address. This is done through the `PVerification` component:

```
PaymentWait = (mAddress,amount) => {

this.setState({
paymentf: true,
amount,
mAddress
})

};
```

It sets the `paymentf` flag to `true`, indicating that a payment is being made by a wallet other than MetaMask and sets the state variable for the amount to be paid in ETH and the merchant address (`mAddress`) to which the transfer has to be made.

MMaskTransfer()

This method is called for initiating transfers through the MetaMask wallet of the customer directly to the merchant address, as shown here:

```
MMaskTransfer = (MRAddress,amount) => {

let app = this;
if (window.ethereum) {
const ethereum = window.ethereum;
this.web3 = new Web3(ethereum);
```

The following list shows exactly what this method does:

1. The method takes the merchant address and amount to be paid as input parameters.
2. On being called, it first checks whether the `window.ethereum` object is present, essentially checking whether the browser has injected `web3` through MetaMask.
3. If an injected `web3` is present, it maps the app's `web3` object to the injected `web3`.
4. Next, it makes an asynchronous call to request permission to access the array of accounts available on the user's MetaMask wallet. This is done through `Ethereum.enable`, as shown here:

```
Ethereum.enable().then((accounts) => {
let account = accounts[0];
this.web3.eth.defaultAccount = account ;
this.setGasPrice();
let tAmount = amount * 1000000000000000000;
```

On successful approval, it populates the primary account into the account parameter and sets it as the default account for the `web3` object, as shown next. It also converts the amount to be transferred into gwei.

Next, we set the `transObj` (transfer object) parameter and set the receiving address as the merchant's wallet address, the value as the amount to be sent, the default gas limit, and the default gas price. Then, we initiate a send transaction request using our `web3` object:

```
let transObj = {to: MRAddress, gas: this.state.defaultGasLimit,gasPrice:
this.state.defaultGasPrice, value: tAmount}
 this.web3.eth.sendTransaction(transObj,function (error, result){
if(!error){
console.log(result);
app.resetApp();
} else{
console.log(error);
```

```
    }
  });
});
}
}
```

startTimer()

The `startTimer()` method is used to set a timer for 15 minutes in the payment window as shown here. The customer has 15 minutes to make the payment from their wallet to the merchant's wallet address before the request expires:

```
startTimer = () =>{
if(this.state.tflag == true)
{
this.intervalHandle = setInterval(this.tick,1000);
this.intervalBalance = setInterval(this.bCheck,10000);

 let time = this.state.minutes;
 this.secondsRemaining = time * 60;
 this.setState({
 tflag: false
 });
}
}
```

Let's understand the various components of the `startTimer` method:

- `tflag` is set to `false` if the app has an ongoing 15-minute window. This prevents React from creating multiple timer intervals when a state variable is updated.
- If `tflag` is set to `true`, meaning no interval exists, the method sets up two intervals. The first interval calls the method tick at an interval of 15 minutes.
- The `tick()` method is the brains behind our timer. The second interval calls the `bCheck()` method at an interval of 10 seconds.
- The `bCheck()` method checks the balance of the merchant's wallet address within the 15-minute window.
- If the address receives an amount equal to or greater than the amount owed by the customer, it stops the timer and notifies the customer of the successful payment.

This method also initializes the `secondsRemaining` parameter to 600 seconds or 15 minutes. This will be used by the `tick()` method.

tick()

The `tick()` method, as shown in the following, sets a timer that runs for 15 minutes:

```
tick(){
var min = Math.floor(this.secondsRemaining / 60);
var sec = this.secondsRemaining - (min * 60);
this.setState({
 minutes: min,
 seconds: sec
})

if (sec < 10) {
 this.setState({
 seconds: "0" + this.state.seconds,
 })
}

if (min < 10) {
this.setState({
 minutes: "0" + this.state.minutes,
 })
}

if (min === 0 & sec === 0) {
clearInterval(this.intervalHandle);
clearInterval(this.intervalBalance);
}
this.secondsRemaining--;
}
```

Every interval, the `tick()` method sets the minutes and seconds state variable. It also fixes the formatting as per the `00:00` format when the seconds or minutes are single digits. When both minutes and seconds are equal to zero, it clears the timer interval and the balance check interval. This happens when the payment request expires. At the end of each interval, it decreases the `secondsRemaining` parameter by 1.

bCheck() – running a persistent balance check

The `bCheck()` method runs a balance check on the merchant's address 10-second intervals:

1. We start by setting the `web3` object, which we'll use to interact with the Ethereum blockchain as shown here. Since we do not have access to MetaMask's injected `web3` in this scenario, we would need to configure our `web3` provider to a local or third-party Ethereum node. I have a Ganache blockchain running at `localhost` on the `8545` port, which is why my provider is set to `http://localhost:8545`. You should update the provider to any node you have access to:

```
bCheck(){
let app = this;
let amount = this.state.amount;
let intervalHandle = this.intervalHandle;
let intervalBalance = this.intervalBalance;
this.web3 = new Web3(new
Web3.providers.HttpProvider("http://localhost:8545"));
```

2. Now that the `web3` object is set, we will check the balance of the merchant's address with the help of the following code:

```
this.web3.eth.getBalance(this.state.mAddress,function (error,
result){
if(!error){
let diff = result / 1000000000000000000;
if(diff >= amount )
{
clearInterval(intervalHandle);
clearInterval(intervalBalance);

}

app.setState ({
diff
})
}

else
{
console.log(error);
}

});
}
```

Let's understand the various components of this code block:

- The `web3.getBalance()` method checks the balance of `mAddress`, the merchant address, every 10 seconds. This balance is mapped to the `diff` variable.
- If the `diff` variable is greater than or equal to `amount`, `bCheck()` immediately clears the timer and balance check intervals and stops the timer.
- The `diXff` variable is also updated to the state. It is used by the `PVerification` component in the payment window to display to the customer how much of the payment has been received by the merchant's wallet address.

Using the componentDidMount() method to map the Shoes array

Within the `componentDidMount` method, we map the `Shoes` constant to our state variables, as shown here. We fetch the individual shoe details from the `Shoes.js` file that we declared earlier:

```
Shoes.forEach((shoe) => {
  let logo = shoe.logo;
  let price = shoe.price;
  let image = shoe.image;
  let name = shoe.name;
```

Each individual shoe is mapped in the `shoes` array and pushed to the state as shown in the following. From here, we will retrieve it within the `Shoerack` component:

```
shoes.push({
  logo,
  price,
  name,
  image,
});

app.setState({
  shoes

})
});
```

After each push, we set the app state to show a new product on the e-commerce website. Let's take a look at our `App.js` render method next.

render()

The render() method for App.js renders the Nav, Description, and Container components. It also passes all of the state and methods to the Container component for use by the child components:

```
render() {
return (
 <div>
 <Nav appName={this.appName} />
 <div> </div>
 <Description />
 <Container
 shoes={this.state.shoes}
 newPayment={this.newPayment}
 closePayment={this.closePayment}
 PaymentDetail={this.state.PaymentDetail}
 mAddress={this.state.mAddress}
 amount={this.state.amount}
 diff={this.state.diff}
 paymentf={this.state.paymentf}
 Conv={this.state.Conv}
 MMaskTransfer={this.MMaskTransfer}
 PaymentWait={this.PaymentWait}
 startTimer={this.startTimer}
 tick={this.tick}
 defaultGasPrice={this.state.defaultGasPrice}
 defaultGasLimit={this.state.defaultGasLimit}
 minutes={this.state.minutes}
 seconds={this.state.seconds}/>
 </div>
 )
 }
```

When the Container component is rendered, it will accept all props and forward them to the child components as and when they are rendered.

Running the gateway app

Let's run our gateway app to see how it works:

1. Navigate to the gateway app directory using the Terminal window.
2. Enter npm start to start the app. You should see the app as follows:

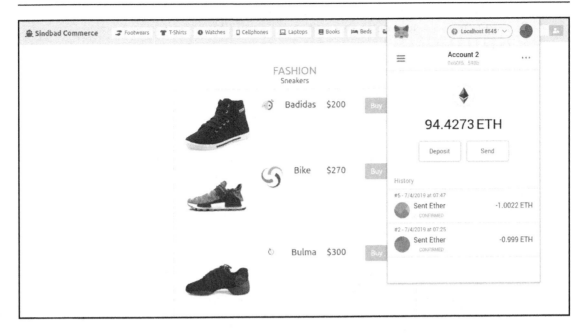

Let's now set up the other components of our payment ecosystem so we can run the app in its entirety.

Creating an API for generating dynamic payment addresses

For creating dynamic wallet addresses on the fly for each payment request, we will be setting up an HD wallet for the merchant who is accepting payment for their products from the e-commerce gateway.

HD wallets allow us to create a set of hierarchical wallet addresses derived from the same mnemonic. If the merchant can safely preserve one mnemonic phrase, they can manage all of the addresses using the same string of words.

For providing dynamically generated, hierarchically linked addresses to our payment gateway, we'll be setting up a Node.js app with a get API service. The payment gateway can use this service to fetch a new address from the merchant's HD wallet:

1. Create a new `Node.js` project directory as shown in the following. Let's call this `hdwallet`.
2. Run the `mkdir hdwallet` command.

3. Run `npm init` to create your `package.json` file.

4. Start by updating `package.json` to the following values:

```
{
  "name": "hdwallet",
  "version": "1.0.0",
  "description": "hdwallet",
  "main": "app.js",
  "scripts": {
  "test": "echo \"Error: no test specified\" && exit 1"
  },
  "author": "",
  "license": "ISC",
  "dependencies": {
  "bip39": "^3.0.2",
  "body-parser": "^1.19.0",
  "ethereumjs-tx": "^2.0.0",
  "ethereumjs-util": "^6.1.0",
  "express": "^4.17.1",
  "hdkey": "^1.1.1"
  }
```

5. Run `npm install` to install the dependencies.

6. Let's start writing out `app.js`. Start by declaring all of the dependencies for our app, as shown here:

```
const bip39 = require('bip39')
const hdkey = require('hdkey')
const ethUtil = require('ethereumjs-util')
const ethTx = require('ethereumjs-tx')
const express = require("express");
```

In the preceding code, `bip39`, `hdkey`, `Ethereumjs-util`, and `Ethereumjs-tx` will be used for generating a new mnemonic and the subsequent hierarchical addresses. We'll talk more about these later.

We'll be using the `express` framework to create our API.

7. Next, as shown in the following, we will declare our `middleware` layer. The `middleware` layer here allows **CORS** or **Cross-Origin Resource Sharing**. This is required so our gateway app can request a new merchant address from our API:

```
app.use(function (req, res, next) {

// Website to connect to. * indicates 'all'
res.setHeader('Access-Control-Allow-Origin', '*');
```

```
// Methods to allow access
 res.setHeader('Access-Control-Allow-Methods', 'GET, POST, OPTIONS,
PUT, PATCH, DELETE');

// Request headers to allow access
 res.setHeader('Access-Control-Allow-Headers', 'X-Requested-
With,content-type');

// Send cookies
 res.setHeader('Access-Control-Allow-Credentials', true);

// Move on to the next layer
 next();
});
```

8. Now, we will define our server settings. I am running mine on port 5000, as shown here. You can configure it as per your requirements:

```
var server = app.listen(process.env.PORT || 5000, function () {
var port = server.address().port;
console.log("App now running on port", port);
});
```

9. We will declare the pathid parameter. This parameter will keep a track of the last address index used to derive a hierarchical address and increment after generating a new address:

```
var pathid = 0;
```

10. We will now start writing our API service, as shown here. The API will be a get service available at http://localhost:5000/api/getMAddress:

```
app.get("/api/getMAddress", function(req,res){

const mnemonic = bip39.generateMnemonic(); //generates string
console.log(mnemonic);

var sendResponseObject={};
var address;
```

Let's understand this code block and how it generates the mnemonic:

- The `bip39` module is used to generate a random mnemonic string. This string can be used to recover a wallet or import the wallet to a third-party wallet service provider such as MetaMask.
- A mnemonic in the `bip39` format looks somewhat like **feature concert truth service energy egg able bind comfort candy harvest similar**.
- We also define our `response` object and `address` parameter.

11. Next, we derive our seed and root address node from the mnemonic, as shown here. To do so, we make an asynchronous call to the `bip39` method, `mnemonictoSeed`:

```
(async function main() {
  try {
  const seed = await bip39.mnemonicToSeed(mnemonic)
  console.log("Seed:",seed);
```

12. We derive the root node and the master public and private key for the root node, as shown here:

```
const root = hdkey.fromMasterSeed(seed)
const masterPrivateKey = root.privateKey.toString('hex');
console.log("Master private Key:",masterPrivateKey);
const masterPubKey = root.publicKey.toString('hex');
console.log("Master Public Key: ",masterPubKey);
```

13. Next, we set the path for deriving the hierarchical addresses as shown in the following. Notice the `pathid` parameter at the end. As we increment the `pathid` parameter, the address index in the path changes. Hence, we have a new hierarchical address:

```
var path = "m/44'/60'/0'/0/"+pathid;
console.log("root: ", root);
const addrNode = root.derive(path)
console.log("path: ", path);
```

14. We will use the `privateToPublic` method to service the public key for the derived address node, as shown in the following. We also derive the hierarchical address in hex format with checksum using the `publicToAddress` and `toCheckSumAddress` methods under `ethUtil`:

```
const pubKey = ethUtil.privateToPublic(addrNode._privateKey)
console.log("Pubkey as hex:",pubKey.toString('hex'));
```

```
const addr = ethUtil.publicToAddress(pubKey).toString('hex');
console.log("pubkey to Addr:",addr);

address = ethUtil.toChecksumAddress(addr);
console.log("Address with Check sum:",address)
```

We now have our derived address in the address variable. We'll now return this in the request.

15. We will add the MAddress key, which will hold the newly generated address and add this key and its value to the response body as shown in the following. We also increment the pathid parameter at the end of the asynchronous call so we get a new path and a new address next time.

    The app checks whether pathid is less than 100 before incrementing because the app is designed so that it loops between 100 hierarchical addresses. This is done so that the app only generates 100 new hierarchical addresses and then reuses the existing addresses. Our merchant wallet will track these 100 addresses for payments. If pathid is equal to or greater than 100, it resets it to zero instead of incrementing it again:

```
sendResponseObject['MAddress']= address;
let jsonString= JSON.stringify(sendResponseObject)
res.send(jsonString);

if (pathid < 100)
{
 pathid++;
}
else
{
pathid = 0;
}
}catch(error) {
 console.log(error);
 };
})();
```

    Now, we have our merchant wallet address generator ready.

16. Start the application using node App.js. The app will print the mnemonic in the console on its first run. This mnemonic is generated only once and all addresses generated will be mapped to it. So, we need to copy and keep the mnemonic safe for future purposes.

In the next section, we will build the merchant wallet interface.

Building the merchant HD wallet

The merchant wallet interface is a simple React app that tracks all of the addresses generated from the merchant's wallet mnemonic and checks whether any payment has been made to them from a customer. It also does block confirmation, that is, for each transaction, it checks whether 40 blocks have been transacted since the transaction was recorded in the blockchain.

The wallet interface app consists of the following components:

- `Container.js`: The `Container` component shown here holds the other components, toggles components display as per state changes, and passes down their props to the components after it receives them from `app.js`. It checks whether an account has been set in the state for retrieving transactions. If the account has been set, it renders the `WalletTrans.js` component; otherwise, it renders the `WalletMain.js` component:

```
render(){

return (
<section className="container">
<div className="columns">
<div className="is-half is-offset-one-quarter column">
<div className="panel">
{
this.props.acc?

<div>
<WalletTrans transactions={this.props.transactions}
acc = {this.props.acc}
/>
</div>:

<div>
<WalletMain accounts={this.props.accounts}
getAccountTransactions={this.props.getAccountTransactions}/>
</div>

}
</div>
</div>
</div>
</section>
```

- `WalletMain.js`: `Walletmain.js` maps the array of account addresses in the merchant wallet and displays the current balance. It fetches the account addresses and their balance from the accounts state parameters. On clicking the view transactions button, the user is redirected to the `WalletTrans.js` child component, which displays the transactions for the account.
- `WalletTrans.js`: `WalletTrans.js` maps the transaction's array and displays all transactions to the account since the genesis block (the first block in our blockchain). The following properties are mapped for each transaction:
  - Transaction index
  - Transaction hash
  - From account address
  - To account address
  - Block confirmations (the number of blocks since the transaction was added to the blockchain)
  - Transaction confirmed/unconfirmed
- `Mnemonic.js`: This component exports the mnemonic of the merchant HD wallet generated in the previous step.

Let's take a look at our `App.js` file that has all of the methods.

App.js

Start by importing the dependent modules and components, as shown here:

```
import React, { Component } from 'react';
import Web3 from 'web3';
import Container from './Components/Container';
import Mnemonic from './Components/Menmonic.js';
import ethTx from 'ethereumjs-tx';
const bip39 = require('bip39');
const hdkey = require('hdkey');
const ethUtil = require('ethereumjs-util')
```

We will be importing the HD wallet mnemonic from `Mnemonic.js` and deriving the individual addresses. The `web3` object enables us to interact with the Ethereum blockchain.

Constructor()

Within the constructor, we set the app name and define the following state parameters:

- mnemonic: The mnemonic used to generate the root node address of the HD wallet
- accounts: A list of merchant's HD wallet addresses
- acc: The merchant account address for which the app is displaying transactions in the WalletTrans component
- transactions: All transactions to date for the merchant address mapped to acc

We also bind the getAccountTransactions method so the child components can change the state, as shown here:

```
class App extends Component {
 constructor(){
 super();
 this.appName = 'Merchant Wallet';
 this.getAccountTransactions = this.getAccountTransactions.bind(this);
 this.state = {
 acc: null,
 accounts: [],
 transactions: [],
 mnemonic: Mnemonic
 };
 }
```

Let's have a look at the methods that load after the main component mounts next.

componentDidMount()

Within the componentDidMount() method shown here, we will create and populate our accounts array. This will be used further by the WalletMain component to display all of the derived address from the merchant's HD wallet:

1. We start by declaring the app variable to store the state of the app. We also store the accounts state array in the local account parameter. Lastly, we declare a variable called pathid:

```
componentDidMount(){
  let app = this;
  let accounts = this.state.accounts;
  let pathid = 100;
```

The `pathid` variable indicates the number of address indices we'll be deriving, essentially, the number of hierarchical addresses we'll be generating in the merchant's HD wallet. Hence, in the `m/44'/60'/0'/0/<address index>` expression, `pathid` indicates the range of values the address index can take starting from 0. For our case, we are assuming the merchant wallet only generates 100 addresses.

2. Next, we will set up a `web3` provider, which our application will interact with to get transaction data, as shown here:

```
this.web3 = new Web3(new
Web3.providers.HttpProvider("http://localhost:8545"));
```

In my case, I have a Ganache blockchain running at `localhost:8545` and hence my provider is pointed to the same. You can configure the provider as per the location of your Ethereum blockchain.

3. Next, we will derive our list of hierarchical address from the mnemonic, as shown here:

```
(async function main() {

  const seed = await bip39.mnemonicToSeed(app.state.mnemonic)
  const root = hdkey.fromMasterSeed(seed);
```

As per the preceding code, we will generate the wallet seed from the mnemonic using the `mnemonicToSeed` member of the `bip39` module. We also derive the root node from the seed using `hdkey`.

4. Next, as shown here, we will introduce a loop to generate the addresses from the mnemonic and check the current balance of each address. We loop our counter until it is within our range (`pathid`):

```
var i = 0;
  for (i = 0 ; i <=pathid; i++)
  {
```

5. For each loop, we generate the hierarchical checksum address for each counter value, as shown here:

```
var path = "m/44'/60'/0'/0/"+i;
const addrNode = root.derive(path);

const pubKey = ethUtil.privateToPublic(addrNode._privateKey)
const addr = ethUtil.publicToAddress(pubKey).toString('hex');
const address = ethUtil.toChecksumAddress(addr);
```

6. For each hierarchical address, we then check the current balance using the `web3.getBalance()` method, as shown here. After fetching the balance, we convert it from gwei into ether by dividing by 1,000,000,000,000,000,000:

```
app.web3.eth.getBalance(address,function (error, result){
if(!error)
{
let balance = result / 1000000000000000000;
```

7. For each account address, we push the checksum address and the balance to the `accounts` array, as shown here:

```
if (balance >0)
{
accounts.push({
address,
balance,
});
}
```

8. After each push, we set the app state, as shown here:

```
app.setState({
accounts
})
```

Hence, our state now has all of the derived addresses with their current balance. If any of these accounts received a payment from the customer, its balance will be populated and displayed in the `WalletMain` screen.

render()

The `render()` component shown here simply transfers the state and methods to the `Container` component, where it will be distributed to the various child components:

```
render() {

return (
<div>
<Container
acc={this.state.acc}
accounts={this.state.accounts}
transactions={this.state.transactions}
getAccountTransactions={this.getAccountTransactions}/>
</div>
)
}
```

Let's look at the method used to fetch the account transactions.

getAccountTransactions()

The `getAccountTransactions()` method shown here accepts a derived address as an argument and fetches all transactions to that account, from the genesis block to the current block. Hence, it fetches all payment transactions by customers to an address in the wallet. It then updates this transaction data to the state.

This array is then mapped by the `WalletTrans` component, which displays all of the transactions for a selected wallet address:

1. Let's look at this method:

   ```
   getAccountTransactions = (accAddress) => {
    const startBlockNumber = 0;
    let app = this;
    let transactions = this.state.transactions;
   ```

   The code block can be understood as follows:

   - `getAccountTransactions` accepts the `accAddress` argument, which is the merchant wallet address for which it needs to fetch transactions from the blockchain.
   - We also define the constants and local variables and capture the current app state.

- The `startBlockNumber` constant is set to 0 to indicate that we'll be searching from the initial block in the blockchain, otherwise known as the genesis block.

2. With an asynchronous call, we fetch the latest block using the `web3` method, `getBlockNumber`, as shown here. This will be our `endBlockNumber`, that is, the last block we search up to for transaction data:

```
(async function main () {
  const endBlockNumber = await app.web3.eth.getBlockNumber()

  console.log("Searching for transactions to/from account \"" +
  accAddress + "\" within blocks "  + startBlockNumber + " and " +
  endBlockNumber);
```

3. Now, we write a loop as shown here. Our counter loops from the `startBlockNumber` (0) to `endBlockNumber` (the current block):

```
for (var i = endBlockNumber; i > 0 ; i--) {
  var block = await app.web3.eth.getBlock(i, true);
```

For each loop, we fetch the block with block number equal to our current counter value. To do so, we use the `web3` method, `eth.getBlock`.

4. For each non-null block (blocks with transactions), we will check whether any of the transactions are to the merchant's address (the `accAddress` argument parameter), as shown here:

```
if (block != null && block.transactions != null) {
  block.transactions.forEach( function(e) {
  if (accAddress == "*" || accAddress == e.to) {
```

5. If a transaction is to the merchant's account, we fetch the details and update the current state. To do so, we will first capture the transaction properties in our local variables. The value of the transaction is divided by 1,000,000,000,000,000,000 to convert it from gwei into ether:

```
let hash = e.hash;
let blockNumber = e.blockNumber;
let transactionIndex = e.transactionIndex;
let from = e.from;
let value = e.value/1000000000000000000;
```

6. We also check how many blocks have been added to the blockchain after our transaction, as shown in the following. The confirmation parameter captures the difference between the latest block and the block number of the transaction. `cflag` captures whether this difference is greater than or less than 40. If the difference is greater than 40, the block is confirmed and the value of `cflag` is set to `true`; otherwise, `cflag` is set to `false` to indicate that the transaction is still awaiting 40 block confirmations:

```
var confirmations;
 var cflag;
if( i >= e.blockNumber)
  {
 confirmations = endBlockNumber - e.blockNumber
  }

 if(confirmations > 40)
  {
 cflag= "Confirmed";
  }
 else
  {
 cflag = "Unconfirmed";
  }
```

7. After setting our local parameters, we push a new element to the `transactions` array, as shown here:

```
transactions.push({
 transactionIndex,
 hash,
 blockNumber,
 from,
 value,
 confirmations,
 cflag
});
```

8. After each one, we use `setState` to set the new transactions state, as shown here:

```
app.setState({
 transactions
 })
```

With that, we come to an end for our `App.js` file and all of the related components. Let's now put all of the components together and see how the entire payment ecosystem operates.

You can find the source code of this chapter on the GitHub repository of this book.

Running the payment ecosystem

Let's run our entire payment ecosystem:

1. We'll start by initializing a local Ganache instance, as shown here. This will serve as the test blockchain for the payment ecosystem:

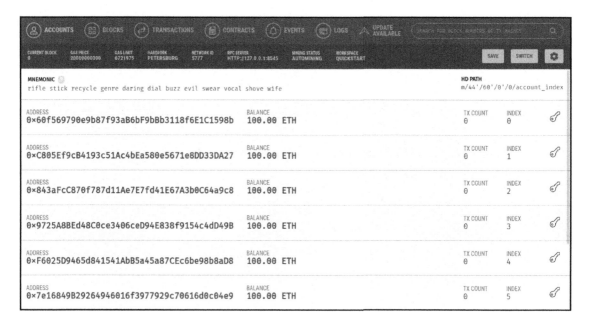

2. Now, let's bring our components online. First, start the e-commerce portal and payment gateway app, navigate to the app directory, and enter `npm start`, as shown here:

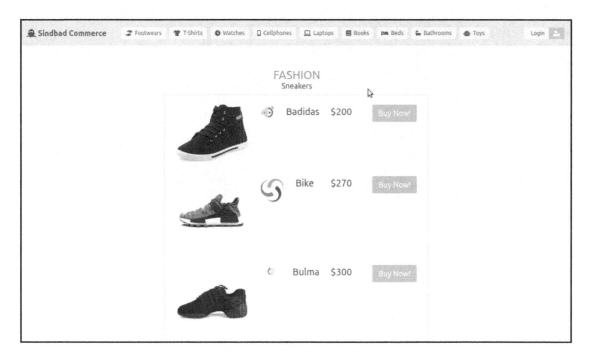

By default, my React app runs on port 3000:

3. Now, open the browser and open the app home page on localhost:3000, as shown here:

You should be able to see the app running and the landing page.

4. Next, we run our Node.js server that extends the `MAddress` API service for address generation. Navigate to the app directory and run `node MAddress`.

   You'll notice in the following screenshot that the app generates a mnemonic on the first run. Keep this handy. We'll need it for our merchant wallet:

   In my `MAddress` run, the mnemonic generated is right at the bottom of the console window in the screenshot. It's **share confirm story grocery check soon cool priority doctor cruise subway provide.** On calling the `MAddress` API, a new hierarchical address will be generated that is derived from this mnemonic. The mnemonic generated by BIP39 will be different for you but the steps to be followed are the same.

5. We now need to map our mnemonic to the merchant wallet. The merchant wallet will use the mnemonic to identify the merchant-owned addresses. To map the mnemonic, locate your `mnemonic.js` file. In my merchant wallet app directory, `mnemonic.js` is available under the `src/Items` directory. Update `mnemonic.js` with the mnemonic as follows:

```
1  const Mnemonic = "share confirm story grocery check soon cool priority doctor cruise subway provide"
2  export default Mnemonic;
```

Before we can bring our wallet online, we also need to change the port it runs on. React apps, by default, run on port 3000 but we already have our gateway app running on that port.

6. So, we need to change the port on which our merchant wallet app runs. To change the port, open the package.json file for the merchant wallet app and update the port for the start script, as follows:

```
"start" : "PORT=8000 react-scripts start"
```

You can find the preceding line of code in the following screenshot of the package.json file:

```json
14      "ethereumjs-util": "^6.1.0",
15      "hdkey": "^1.1.1"
16    },
17    "scripts": {
18      "start": "PORT=8000 react-scripts start",
19      "build": "react-scripts build",
20      "test": "react-scripts test",
21      "eject": "react-scripts eject"
22    },
23    "eslintConfig": {
24      "extends": "react-app"
25    },
26    "browserslist": {
27      "production": [
28        ">0.2%",
29        "not dead",
30        "not op_mini all"
31      ],
32      "development": [
33        "last 1 chrome version",
34        "last 1 firefox version",
35        "last 1 safari version"
36      ]
37    }
```

7. Now, let's bring our merchant wallet online. Navigate to the app directory and run `npm start`, as shown here:

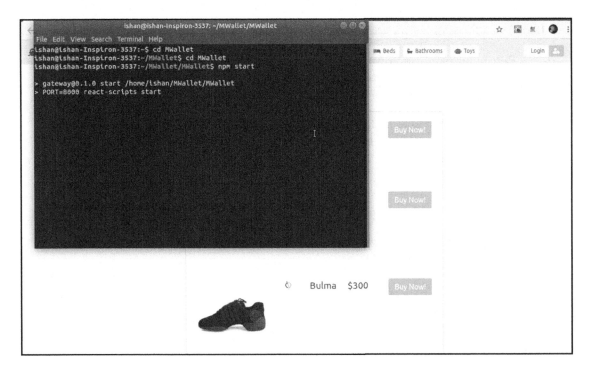

8. After the app is online, navigate to your browser and enter `localhost:8000`. You should be able to see the app as shown here:

Since we haven't carried out any transactions, the wallet is currently empty. As we carry out payments, you'll slowly see the wallet getting populated.

9. There's one last thing before we try out a payment. Connect your MetaMask wallet to your local Ganache blockchain (localhost 8545) and import an account from Ganache. To import an account, open the Ganache UI. Click the key icon next to any account. The secret key is revealed in a popup shown in the following screenshot. Select and copy the secret key:

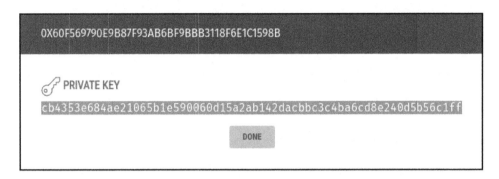

10. Go to MetaMask and select **Import Wallet** from the settings menu as shown in the following. From the screen that appears, select the private key option. Paste the key:

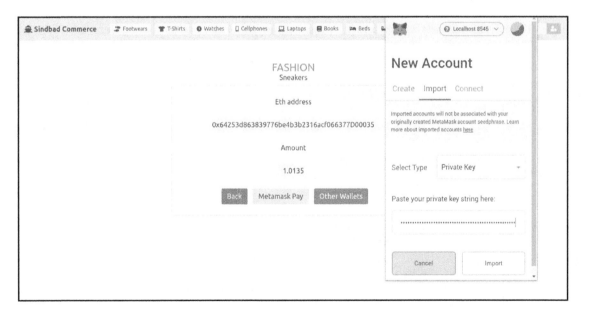

11. After pasting the secret key, click on **Import**. You should now be able to see this account in MetaMask, as shown in the following. By default, it has 100 ether at the start:

OK. We are now good to try a payment.

12. Navigate back to the landing page of the gateway app, as shown here:

13. Let's try to buy a Bulma shoe! Click on the **Buy Now** button. You'll notice the app directs you to a payment page like the one here:

The **Eth** address here is fetched from the MAddress API. In fact, if you open the Terminal window for the MAddress app, you should be able to see this address:

Did you notice the highlighted address? Compare it with the one on the payment page. You'll see that they match.

The amount on the payment page is the amount to be paid in ether. This amount is calculated after fetching the USD to ETH conversion ratio in real time from the `cryptocompare.com` API and using it to convert the price of the shoes from USD into ETH.

You'll also notice a timer for 15 minutes on the screen. The timer indicates that the conversion rate from USD to ETH used is valid for 15 minutes. Since the price of ether is highly volatile and can change during the payment, we need to fix a window for which our conversion rate will be constant. If the price of ether increases or decreases during this 15-minute window, the risk is borne by the merchant or the customer but since it will be low, it is bearable. After 15 minutes, the payment will expire.

Let's go back to our payment page, shown here:

You'll notice there are two payment options. **MetaMask** and **Other Wallets**. If the user has a MetaMask wallet with funds, the app uses MetaMask's injected `web3` to make the payment. Alternatively, if the user has another wallet or does not want to give access to MetaMask's injected `web3` to the app, they click on the **Other Wallets** option. For the **Other Wallet** option, the app then connects to a local `web3` provider and checks whether a payment has been made by the customer.

14. Let's first try a MetaMask payment. Click on the **MetaMask Pay** button. A popup, as shown here, will open. You might have to log in to MetaMask if you are logged out:

15. After login, as shown in the following, MetaMask will pop another window asking whether you trust the app and want to permit access to your accounts on MetaMask:

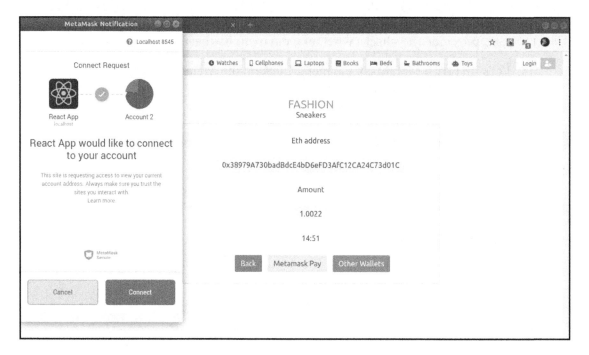

16. As shown in the previous screenshot, click on **Connect** to continue. When you click on **Connect**, the app gets access to the inject web3 provider and the string of accounts on MetaMask.

Now, you'll see a popup asking you whether you want to permit the send transaction to the merchant's account:

17. Click on **Confirm** to send the transaction from MetaMask to the merchant's wallet. The transaction should now go through and you'll get a confirmation notification, as here:

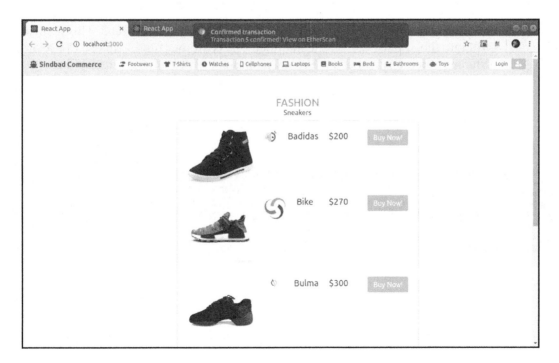

If you navigate to MetaMask, you should also be able to view the transaction there:

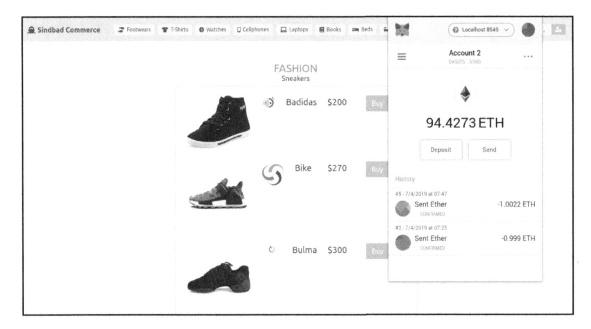

18. Next, let's try a payment without using MetaMask's injected web3. This feature is built into the app for use on the mainnet. The customer might choose to use a different Ethereum wallet such as a Coinbase or Jaxx Wallet. Here, we'll use the `truffle console` command for **Other Wallets**. To do so, first bring the Truffle console online. Go to your Truffle environment and run `truffle console`, as shown here:

```
                        ishan@ishan-Inspiron-3537: ~/walletcontract/walletcontract
File  Edit  View  Search  Terminal  Help
ishan@ishan-Inspiron-3537:~$ cd walletcontract
ishan@ishan-Inspiron-3537:~/walletcontract$ cd walletcontract
ishan@ishan-Inspiron-3537:~/walletcontract/walletcontract$ ls
 build              Condos.sol    ERC20.sol    LandTitle.sol    Migrations.sol    test
'Condos (copy).sol'  contracts    Item.sol     migrations       SmartWallet.sol   truffle-config.js
ishan@ishan-Inspiron-3537:~/walletcontract/walletcontract$ truffle console
```

19. Now, in the command line, set your `web3` default account to the first account in your Ganache HD wallet using the following command:

```
web3.eth.defaultAccount =
'0x60f569790e9b87f93aB6bF9bBb3118f6E1C1598b'
```

Once the preceding command is executed, this is what your Ganache HD wallet will look like:

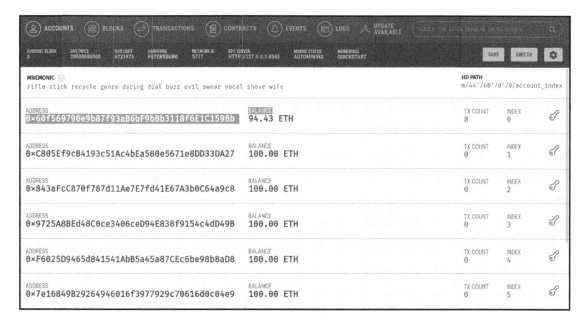

This is how your command looks in the command line:

```
ishan@ishan-Inspiron-3537: ~/walletcontract/walletcontract
File Edit View Search Terminal Help
ishan@ishan-Inspiron-3537:~$ cd walletcontract
ishan@ishan-Inspiron-3537:~/walletcontract$ cd walletcontract
ishan@ishan-Inspiron-3537:~/walletcontract/walletcontract$ ls
build          Condos.sol    ERC20.sol   LandTitle.sol  Migrations.sol   test
'Condos (copy).sol'  contracts  Item.sol  migrations     SmartWallet.sol  truffle-config.js
ishan@ishan-Inspiron-3537:~/walletcontract/walletcontract$ truffle console
truffle(development)> web3.eth.defaultAccount = '0x60f569790e9b87f93aB6bF9bBb3118f6E1C1598b'
'0x60f569790e9b87f93aB6bF9bBb3118f6E1C1598b'
truffle(development)> []
```

20. Now, let's try the second type of payment. Go back to the main page and click on a shoe, as shown here:

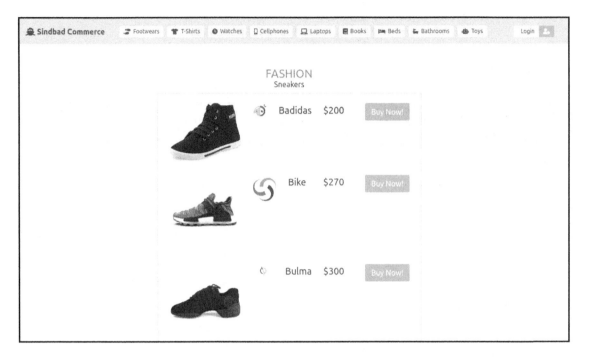

You will again be redirected to the payment page like before:

21. Click on the **Other Wallets** option this time, as shown here. The app will redirect you to a page that looks like this:

This page essentially tracks the generated MAddress to see whether any payment request is made in the 15-minute window. When the balance for the MAddress gets equal to or higher than the amount owed by the customer, it notifies the customer of the successful payment and stops the timer. It allows for part payment as well as long as the transactions happen in the 15-minute window.

22. Now, let's send some ether to the address and see how it works. Go back to your Truffle console and send 0.4 ether to the address and see how the app works. Run the following command in the console:

```
await web3.eth.sendTransaction({from: web3.eth.defaultAccount, to:
'0x315074C434eca2B79878f4a1A2323d12eE413fdb', value:
web3.utils.toWei('0.4', "ether")})
```

This command sends 0.4 ether to MAddress 0x315074C434eca2B79878f4a1A2323d12eE413fdb. You might remember we set defaultAccount earlier. It uses web3.utils.toWei to convert our value from ether into wei as web3 uses wei as the unit for sending transactions.

The blockchain should return you the transaction hash and other transaction details after execution. this is demonstrated in the following screenshot:

```
File Edit View Search Terminal Help
ishan@ishan-Inspiron-3537:~$ cd walletcontract
ishan@ishan-Inspiron-3537:~/walletcontract$ cd walletcontract
ishan@ishan-Inspiron-3537:~/walletcontract/walletcontract$ ls
 build              Condos.sol    ERC20.sol    LandTitle.sol    Migrations.sol    test
'Condos (copy).sol'  contracts    Item.sol     migrations       SmartWallet.sol   truffle-config.js
ishan@ishan-Inspiron-3537:~/walletcontract/walletcontract$ truffle console
truffle(development)> web3.eth.defaultAccount = '0x60f569790e9b87f93aB6bF9bBb3118f6E1C1598b'
'0x60f569790e9b87f93aB6bF9bBb3118f6E1C1598b'
truffle(development)> await web3.eth.sendTransaction({from: web3.eth.defaultAccount, to: '0x315074C434eca2B79878f4a1A2323d12eE413fdb', value:
web3.utils.toWei('0.4', "ether")})
{ transactionHash:
  '0xa3Bf7a4b932259978a0a4a95dc3400a2c55174bfb9e1d0e5bf557a4d4cfa1042',
  transactionIndex: 0,
  blockHash:
  '0x650f88bae303513d00dc0e9e9b924daf42a03cb43041596a6fd4bce15a54adbe',
  blockNumber: 7,
  from: '0x60f569790e9b87f93ab6bf9bbb3118f6e1c1598b',
  to: '0x315074c434eca2b79878f4a1a2323d12ee413fdb',
  gasUsed: 21000,
  cumulativeGasUsed: 21000,
  contractAddress: null,
  logs: [],
  status: true,
  logsBloom:
  '0x000000000000000000000000000000000000000000000000000000000000000000000000000000000000000000000000000000000000000000000000000000000000000000000000000000000000000000000000000000000000000000000000000000000000000000000000000000000000000000000000000000000000000000000000',
  v: '0x1b',
  r:
  '0xe75267cba2ba8ffd9524d6fc82333a2a03f3968af4380f0b2020368ce582aa1b',
  s:
  '0x5f42674ac8984d1e61ff05c38bf88c0cd56a6ceea3271091b3d5cddac27332aa' }
truffle(development)> []
```

Let's go back and check the payment page again:

You'll notice it tells you that it has received 0.4 ether. There might be a slight delay after you send the payment as the timer checks the balance every 10 seconds.

23. Now, let's send the rest of the amount, as shown here:

```
await web3.eth.sendTransaction({from: web3.eth.defaultAccount, to:
'0x315074C434eca2B79878f4a1A2323d12eE413fdb', value:
web3.utils.toWei('0.2683', "ether")})
```

On submission, you should be able to see the transaction submitted and the network's response on the Terminal window, as follows:

The payment page as shown here will reflect the following status once it can detect the balance in `MAddress`:

24. Now, let's go to the merchant's wallet interface to see whether the two transactions are recorded in their wallet. As shown here, navigate to the merchant's wallet interface. You might need to refresh the app to see the transactions:

25. In the following screenshot, you'll notice both the transactions we carried out are listed. Click on **View Transactions** for any one transaction:

You'll get a screen like the one shown previously. It shows the following details:

- Transaction **Index**
- **Hash**
- **Block No.** in which the transaction is recorded
- The account from which the transaction was sent
- Ether value of the transaction
- The number of blocks in the blockchain after the transaction came through
- Confirmed/unconfirmed

The last two points are especially significant. Generally, in the Ethereum mainnet, most people wait for 40 blocks to be added after the block in which your transaction was fired to confirm a transaction. This is to protect the merchant from losing out on their payment due to any forks in the network. If there is a fork, the transaction might be removed. Ideally, a merchant should wait for transaction confirmation before shipping the goods.

In Bitcoin, confirmation is after 6 blocks. In most Ethereum applications and in ours, it is set to 40 blocks though this number can vary. The app will automatically change the status to confirmed once the transaction has 40 blocks added. Once the status changes to confirmed, the merchant can ship their goods.

In the Ganache blockchain scope, confirmations don't have much value and don't work because Ganache doesn't generate blocks at regular intervals like the Ethereum mainnet or test net. However, if you connect this app to Ropsten or a bigger test net, you can see this feature in action.

With that, we come to the end of our payment ecosystem project.

Summary

So, we finally finished building our payment gateway and ecosystem. I really hope this project gives you insight into how blockchain apps work on the Ethereum mainnet with each other leveraging the shared ledger, especially in a financial scenario.

This ecosystem can easily be used in an enterprise environment as well. Replace ether with any ERC20-based asset token you need to work with, such as fiat currency, land, or commodities. You might also consider running this on Ropsten or a larger Ethereum test network after you build it on Ganache and compare it with how exchanges such as Coinbase or Binance or payment gateway services such as Bitpay or Coingate work.

We started this chapter by looking at what a payment ecosystem in a blockchain looks like and its components. We discussed HD wallets and block confirmations in blockchain payments. Then, we leveraged our knowledge to build an e-commerce portal with a payment gateway, a merchant HD wallet service with an API to generate dynamic addresses, and a merchant wallet interface for tracking transactions to this wallet. Then, we ran our entire ecosystem end-to-end using both MetaMask and the Truffle console command line as our wallets for making a payment and tracked it on the merchant's wallet

The main takeaway from this chapter is understanding how an ecosystem like this is built and how the components interact with each other, leveraging the blockchain. It also gives you insight into how payment systems are changing. With this particular system, the merchant directly receives payment to a wallet owned and maintained by themself minus a middleman. Hence, the merchant can avoid paying payment or operation fees to a third party.

In the next chapters, we'll see how we can use Hyperledger Fabric to build complex payment and remittance workflows for corporates and enterprises.

4
Corporate Remittances and Settlement

This chapter looks at leveraging blockchain to enable domestic and international remittances for corporate payments. Corporate payments require the exchange of documents and information about the transacting parties for compliance purposes. They are also prone to more cases of fraud and illegal activities when compared to retail remittances (payments between individuals or from a business to an individual). As such, blockchain technology is perfect for enabling such payments. It can enable banks and financial organizations to exchange compliance and **Anti-Money Laundering (AML)** information about the remittance request and the transacting parties in real time. It maintains an immutable and auditable log of all transactions that have been carried out in the payment network, along with a digital forensic record of compliance information shared with the transaction. Lastly, and probably most importantly, owing to distributed ledger technology, the time and costs associated with reconciliation in traditional payment systems are eliminated. Transactions posted to the distributed ledger are replicated in real time, across all the nodes that are part of the payment network.

In this chapter, we'll be building a four peers, two-participant organizations remittance network, using Hyperledger Fabric. Each participant will be a bank in our remittance channel. Each bank will have a corporate customer, who will be sending and receiving payments on this network. Lastly, we'll set up an **InterPlanetary File System (IPFS)** network between the two banks, for sharing documents and other artifacts that need to be shared with the remittance request as part of compliance requirements.

The following topics will be covered in this chapter:

- Technical requirements
- Understanding the blockchain corporate remittance application and network layout
- Setting up the Hyperledger Fabric bankchain network
- Creating blockchain identities for the banks

- Building the corporate remittance contract
- Setting up the IPFS network
- Setting up the bank databases
- Building the bank backend servers
- Building the transaction listeners for the banks
- Creating the corporate remittance app frontend in React
- Running the corporate remittance app

Technical requirements

You can access the code files for this chapter at the following GitHub link: `https://github.com/PacktPublishing/Blockchain-Development-for-Finance-Projects/tree/master/Chapter%204`.

For this project, we'll be working with the Hyperledgic Fabric 1.4 binaries, and Docker images provided in the Hyperledger Fabric GitHub repository.

You can find the step-by-step installation process at this link: `https://hyperledger-fabric.readthedocs.io/en/release-1.4/prereqs.html`.

Hyperledger Fabric assumes that you have the following dependencies installed:

- The latest version of the cURL tool
- The latest version of Docker and Docker Compose
- Go version 1.12.x
- Node.js version 10.15.3 and higher
- npm version 5.6.0 and above
- Python 2.7

After downloading and installing the dependencies, we need to download and install the binaries, samples, and Docker images for Hyperledger Fabric. To do this, we'll be using cURL to download the images from the Fabric repository, as follows:

```
curl -sSL http://bit.ly/2ysbOFE | bash -s 1.4.0
```

This will take up to 15 minutes to complete, depending on your net connectivity.

Additionally, we'll need to install IPFS and set up a private IPFS network. We'll look at this in the section on setting up the IPFS network.

Understanding the blockchain corporate remittance application and network layout

In this chapter, we'll be building a blockchain network using Hyperledger Fabric that we'll be using to carry out corporate remittances. We'll call this network Bankchain. The bankchain network will contain a private ledger called `bkchannel`. This channel will consist of two participants, Bank A and Bank B. Both Bank A and Bank B will have two nodes on the channel, labeled `peer0` and `peer1`. Hence, in total, the channel has four nodes. All transaction requests will be posted to these nodes. Additionally, the banks will monitor these nodes for any incoming transactions.

Apart from the Hyperledger Fabric network, both banks will also each host an IPFS node. IPFS is a distributed file-sharing system. It consists of a distributed network and nodes. Documents published by any IPFS node can be retrieved from any other node connected to the network. In our project, we'll be running a private IPFS network with two nodes. Each bank will own a node on the network. IPFS allows the banks to securely share compliance and AML documents for the remittance transactions.

The following screenshot shows a high-level architecture diagram of our project:

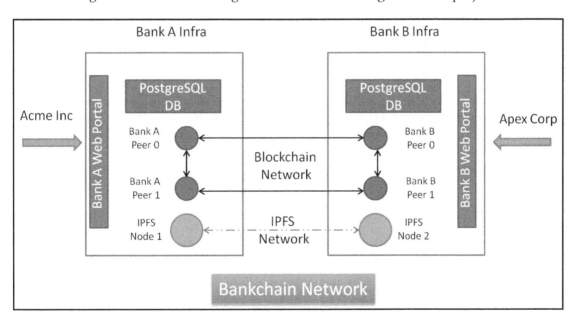

The postgresql database will consist of a customer table that stores customer details, and a transaction table that stores transaction details.

The bank portal has the following three components:

- A React frontend
- A Node.js backend server
- A Node.js transaction listener

The **React frontend** accepts remittance requests from the customers. In our project, Acme Inc is a customer with Bank A, and Apex Corp is a customer with Bank B. The React frontend also displays the details and documents of all the incoming and outgoing remittance transactions for the customer.

The **Node.js backend** is essentially a bridge between the frontend, the postgresql database, the blockchain network, and the IPFS network. It retrieves the customer information from the database for populating the frontend, accepts payment requests from the frontend, posts transactions to the Hyperledger Fabric network, and publishes the compliance and AML documents to the IPFS network. It also updates the customer's balance, after a transaction goes through successfully.

Lastly, we have a **Node.js transaction listener.** The transaction listener listens for all transactions posted to the channel. It does so by listening to an event that is broadcasted by our remittance smart contract whenever a new transaction is added. If the transaction pertains to the node participant, it fetches the details of the transaction from the blockchain. Thus, if the transaction listener for Node B detects a transaction where the receiving bank is Bank B, it will fetch the details of the transaction from the blockchain, for further processing.

After fetching the details of the incoming transaction, the transaction listener updates the balance of the customer receiving the transaction, adds the transaction to the transactions table in our postgresql database, and fetches the AML and compliance documents relevant to the transaction from the IPFS network to the local storage. The transaction, its relevant details, and attached compliance documents can now be viewed from the frontend by the customer.

We'll be carrying out the following steps in our project:

1. Setting up the Hyperledger Fabric network Bankchain with the `bkchannel` private channel and the node participants Bank A and Bank B.
2. Writing a corporate remittance chaincode (smart contract) that will allow us to submit remittance transactions and retrieve transaction details from the blockchain.

3. Setting up a postgresql database for each bank. The database will have a customer database that has the customer details and a transaction database that has details of all the transactions initiated and received by the bank.

4. Setting up a private IPFS network with two nodes between Bank A and Bank B, to privately and securely share remittance documents between Bank A and Bank B.

5. Setting up a node backend server that interacts with the blockchain network, the IPFS network, the postgresql database, and the React frontend. It fetches customer details to populate the frontend, fetches transaction details from the database, submits payment requests to the blockchain network, publishes compliance documents to IPFS, and updates the customer's balance after the transaction goes through successfully.

6. Setting up a Node.js transaction listener that will listen for incoming transactions to a customer of the bank, fetch transaction details and update these to the transactions database, update the customer's balance, and fetch the compliance documents pertaining to an incoming remittance request from the IPFS network.

7. Creating a React frontend that allows customers to submit remittance requests and view transactions on their accounts.

Let's start creating our project. We'll start by setting up the Hyperledger Fabric Bankchain network in the next section.

Setting up the Hyperledger Fabric Bankchain network

For this project, we'll be working with the Hyperledger Fabric binaries and Docker images provided in the Hyperledger Fabric GitHub repository that we downloaded earlier.

Next, let's set up the environment for our project. Download the Bankchain directory from the GitHub repository, at this link: `https://github.com/PacktPublishing/Blockchain-Development-for-Finance-Projects/tree/master/Chapter%204/bankchain`.

Save the directory to the `fabric-samples` repository that you would have downloaded while installing Hyperledger Fabric. In the next sections, we'll walk through the different artifacts in the repository that we have to create or modify, to build our network.

Creating the crypto-config file

Refer to the `crypto-config.yaml` file in the repository. The `crypto-config.yaml` file defines the components and participants of our network and passes them to the `cryptogen` utility to generate the network artifacts, including the identity certificates and private keys for each network participant.

Open the `crypto-config.yaml` file. Inside the file, the following two organization-type tags are defined:

- `OrdererOrgs`
- `PeerOrgs`

`OrdererOrgs` defines organizations that maintain and manage the orderer nodes for our blockchain network. The orderer is a node in the Hyperledger Fabric ecosystem that orders transactions and generates the blocks for our channel. The `crypto-config.yaml` file defines the attributes of such an organization, under the `OrdererOrgs` tag.

In our network, we'll bring the `orderer.example.com` node online, to order our transactions. The `Orderer` organization will have ownership of this node.

PeerOrgs defines organizations that own and manage peer nodes on the blockchain network. In our case, these are the `bankA` and `bankB` organizations. The peer node can read and write transactions to the blockchain ledger and execute chaincodes (smart contracts). The `crypto-config.yaml` file defines the attributes of such an organization, under the `PeerOrgs` tag.

In our network, we'll be setting up two peer organizations, `banka.example.com` and `bankb.example.com`. Each organization will have two peers, indicated by the tag `Count`. The nomenclature followed for the nodes will be `peer0.banka.example.com`, `peer1.banka.example.com`, `peer0.bankb.example.com`, and `peer1.bankb.example.com`. Lastly, we set the `Users` tag, to indicate that there will be one user (apart from the admin user) who will access the blockchain through these nodes.

As you can see, the `crypto-config` file defines a base network structure. Now, let's move on to the `configtx` file that will be used to generate the channel artifacts, including the genesis block (first block in the blockchain).

Creating the configtx file

Refer to the `configtx.yaml` file in the repository. The `configtx` file defines the elements that will be used by the network to create the channel artifacts, including the genesis block (first block). The `configtx` file is the input to the `configtxgen` utility, which uses the file to generate the artifacts.

Open the `configtx.yaml` file. You'll notice it is divided into five sections, as follows:

- **Organizations** define the organizations that are defined as part of the network. It is used to define the **Membership Service Provider** (**MSP**) that implements access controls on our blockchain ledger. Each organization has the following attributes:
    - Name of the organization.
    - Identity of the organization.
    - Policies that define which identities can read and write, and the admin identity.
    - The local directory (`MSPDir`), where the inputs for creating the MSP are available.
    - The anchor peers for the organization (that is, the node that broadcasts the block to all other peers of the organization).
- **Orderer** is used to defining the ordering mechanism, the block parameters, and the block-creation parameters for our network. Additionally, you can use it to configure a broker network if you are using a Kafka ordering mechanism.
- **Capabilities** define the versions of Hyperledger Fabric binaries that are supported by our channel. They allow you to configure individual compatible versions for channels, orderers, and applications that will interact with, or be a part of, our network.
- **Applications** define the values that must be encoded into a config transaction or genesis block for application parameters.
- **Channels** define the values that must be encoded into a config transaction or genesis block for channel parameters.
- The **Profile** section is used to define a set of network profiles that can be used to launch a network. We will be using the `TwoOrgsOrdererGenesis` network profile to launch our network. This profile creates a two-organization, solo-ordering service network.

That wraps up the `configtx` file. Next, let's look at the docker-compose files that define the containers that will host each component of the network.

Creating the docker-compose files

In addition to the artifacts defined earlier, we'll also need to define the `docker-compose` files that will be used to bring the network online. Each section of the docker-compose files defines a network component. When we invoke the `docker-compose` statement, it will launch a set of containers. Each container will house a network component.

For our network, we have three docker-compose files. These are as follows:

- `docker-compose-bankchain.yaml`: Defines the parameters used to bring the orderer and the peer containers online. The containers are `orderer.example.com`, `peer0.banka.example.com`, `peer1.banka.example.com`, `peer0.bankb.example.com`, and `peer1.bankb.example.com`. Additionally, it also creates the `cli` container, which hosts command-line tools, used to interact with the `peer0.banka.example.com` container.
- `docker-compose-ca.yaml`: Defines the parameters used to bring the **certificate authorities (CA)** online. We'll be running two CAs, `ca0` and `ca1`, one for each organization, Bank A and Bank B. The containers are named `ca_peerbanka` and `ca_peerbankb`.
- `docker-compose-couch.yaml`: Defines the parameters used to bring the CouchDB database online. The couch database stores the transaction data and the state database for a peer node. We'll be running four databases, one for each peer—`couchdb0`, `couchdb1`, `couchdb2`, and `couchdb3`.

You can check out these files in the repository, to see how they have been configured for running the network.

Launching the network

We need to carry out the following steps in the following order, to bring the network online:

1. Generate certificates for all channel participants, using the `cryptogen` utility.
2. Generate the network artifacts (including the genesis block), using the `configtxgen` utility.

3. Run the `docker-compose` statement with all the relevant `yaml` files as input, to launch the containers housing the network components.

4. Run the scripts to build the channel, using the fabric tools available in the `cli` container, and carry out end-to-end tests, to ensure the network and peers are up and running.

The repository contains a script that can be used to execute these actions back-to-back. Run the `startBankchain.sh` script in the repository, to build the Bankchain network and bring it online, as follows:

```
./startBankchain.sh
```

The script should bring all the containers online. You should get a confirmation message, like the one in the following screenshot:

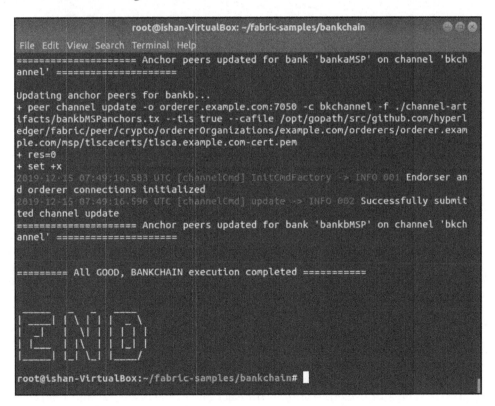

Run the `docker ps` command to view the launched containers. There should be 11 containers running, as shown in the following screenshot:

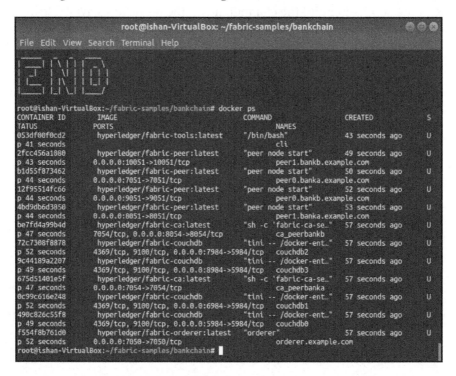

That takes care of our blockchain network. Now, let's move on to creating identities on the network for the `banka` and `bankb` organizations.

Creating blockchain identities for the banks

Before we can use our blockchain network for submitting and querying transactions, we need to create an admin user and a bank user for both banks.

The admin user will be authorized to create users, remove users, add user groups, and so on.

The bank user will be authorized to submit transactions to the network, and read transactions that have been submitted previously.

We'll be building two utilities—one for creating the admin user, and one for creating the bank user.

Creating the admin user

The `enrollAdmin-BankA.js` and `enrollAdmin-BankB.js` utilities will be used to create a new admin identity for Bank A and Bank B, respectively.

Creating a utility to enroll the admin user

We will need to create a `Node.js` utility that can be run to register a new admin user for Bank A and a new admin user `BankB`. This admin user will then be used to register the other users. Let's look at the steps to create this utility:

1. Create a new file, `enrollAdmin-BankA.js`, in the `fabric-samples/bankchain` directory.

2. Open the file in a code editor, and start writing the code. We start by importing all the required dependencies, as follows:

```
/*
 * SPDX-License-Identifier: Apache-2.0
 */

'use strict';

const FabricCAServices = require('fabric-ca-client');
const { FileSystemWallet, X509WalletMixin } = require('fabric-
network');
const fs = require('fs');
const path = require('path');
```

- The `fabric-ca-client` **software development kit (SDK)** is used to configure identities and user groups in CAs for Bank A and Bank B.
- We parse the `connection-banka.json` file for the network connection profile for `banka`.
- The file is generated as an artifact when we bring the Bankchain network online.
- The connection profile values are stored in the `ccp` object after parsing, as shown in the following code block:

```
const ccpPath = path.resolve(__dirname, 'connection-banka.json');
const ccpJSON = fs.readFileSync(ccpPath, 'utf8');
const ccp = JSON.parse(ccpJSON);
```

3. Next, we create a new `ca` object that points to the CA for Bank A, as follows:

```
main();
async function main() {
 try {
 const caInfo = ccp.certificateAuthorities['ca.banka.example.com'];
 const caTLSCACerts = caInfo.tlsCACerts.pem;
 const ca = new FabricCAServices(caInfo.url, { trustedRoots:
caTLSCACerts, verify: false }, caInfo.caName);
```

Next, we configure the `walletPath` object. The `walletPath` object points to the location of the wallet, where the keys for the admin and the user will be stored. If there is no existing wallet at the location, a new wallet is created.

The name of the wallet for Bank A is `wallet-BankA`, as shown in the following code block:

```
const walletPath = path.join(process.cwd(), 'wallet-BankA');
const wallet = new FileSystemWallet(walletPath);
console.log(`Wallet path: ${walletPath}`);
```

An `if` statement checks if the admin user is already registered and the identity exists in the wallet, as follows:

```
const adminExists = await wallet.exists('admin');
 if (adminExists) {
 console.log('An identity for the admin user "admin" already exists in the
wallet');
 return;
 }
```

Next, we call `ca.enroll`, to register the `admin` user with the password `adminpw`.

A new key pair is generated for the identity and added to the MSP for Bank A (`bankaMSP`).

Lastly, we import the certificate file and private key for the admin user, and store it in our wallet, by running the following code:

```
const enrollment = await ca.enroll({ enrollmentID: 'admin',
enrollmentSecret: 'adminpw' });
 const identity = X509WalletMixin.createIdentity('bankaMSP',
enrollment.certificate, enrollment.key.toBytes());
 await wallet.import('admin', identity);
 console.log('Successfully enrolled admin user "admin" and imported it into
the wallet');
```

A `catch` block catches any errors during execution, as follows:

```
catch (error) {
 console.error(`Failed to enroll admin user "admin": ${error}`);
 process.exit(1);
 }
}
```

That brings us to the end of the utility.

Changes for Bank B

For Bank B, create a new file, called `enrollAdmin-BankB.js`.

Replicate the preceding code. Only change the following parameters to the corresponding value for Bank B:

1. Change the connection profile file to `connection-bankb.json`, like this:

    ```
    const ccpPath = path.resolve(__dirname, 'connection-bankb.json');
    ```

2. Update the wallet path by running the following line of code (we'll be using a different wallet for the identities of Bank B):

    ```
    const walletPath = path.join(process.cwd(), 'wallet-BankB');
    ```

3. Update the MSP to the MSP and CA for Bank B, as follows:

    ```
    const caInfo = ccp.certificateAuthorities['ca.bankb.example.com'];
    ```

4. Update the CA for Bank B, as follows:

    ```
    const identity = X509WalletMixin.createIdentity('bankbMSP',
    enrollment.certificate, enrollment.key.toBytes());
    ```

Let's run our utilities.

Running the utility

Navigate to the Bankchain repository. Run the following command to enroll an admin user for Bank A:

```
node enrollAdmin-BankA.js
```

You should get a message on the console, informing you that a new admin has been registered and imported to the wallet. Repeat the same for Bank B, as follows:

```
node enrollAdmin-BankB.js
```

- The admin identities for the `banka` and `bankb` organizations should be added to the wallet for Bank A and Bank B.
- You can actually verify this. Navigate to the `wallet-BankA` and `wallet-BankB` directories. You'll be able to see a folder labeled `admin`. Inside, you'll find the private key file and certificate for the admin user.

Let's create the bank users next.

Creating the bank users

Next, we'll register a user for both Bank A and Bank B. To do so, we'll be building the `registerUser-BankA.js` and `registerUser-BankB.js` utilities for each bank.

Creating a utility to register users

We will create a new `registerUser-BankA.js` file in the `fabric-sample/bankchain` directory, as follows:

1. Open the file in a code editor, and let's start writing the code. We start by importing all the required dependencies, like this:

```
/*
 * SPDX-License-Identifier: Apache-2.0
 */

'use strict';

const { FileSystemWallet, Gateway, X509WalletMixin } =
require('fabric-network');
const path = require('path');
```

2. Next, we set the `ccpPath` object to the location of the network connection profile for Bank A, like this:

```
const ccpPath = path.resolve(__dirname, 'connection-banka.json');
```

3. We set the `walletPath` object to the wallet we created in the previous section, like this:

```
main();
async function main() {
  try {

    const walletPath = path.join(process.cwd(), 'wallet-BankA');
    const wallet = new FileSystemWallet(walletPath);
    console.log(`Wallet path: ${walletPath}`);
```

4. Next, we check to see if the user is already enrolled in the wallet, by running the following code:

```
const userExists = await wallet.exists('user1');
if (userExists) {
console.log('An identity for the user "user1" already exists in
the wallet');
return;
}
```

5. Next, we check if the admin identity exists in the wallet, by running the following code:

```
const adminExists = await wallet.exists('admin');
if (!adminExists) {
console.log('An identity for the admin user "admin" does not exist
in the wallet');
console.log('Run the enrollAdmin-BankA.js application before
retrying');
return;
}
```

6. We create a new gateway to connect to the peer node. We connect using the admin user we created earlier, like this:

```
const gateway = new Gateway();
await gateway.connect(ccpPath, { wallet, identity: 'admin',
discovery: { enabled: true, asLocalhost: true } });
```

7. We also create the `ca` client object for interacting with the CA for the Bank A organization, as follows:

```
const ca = gateway.getClient().getCertificateAuthority();
const adminIdentity = gateway.getCurrentIdentity();
```

8. Next, we register a new affiliation with the CA. An affiliation is like an intermediate certificate. Typically, it is a department or group, or sub-organization within the organization. In our case, we use `department1`.

9. We create a new affiliation, `department1`, for our `banka` organization, and register it with the CA. We use the admin identity to submit the request, like this:

```
let affiliationService = ca.newAffiliationService();
let affiliation = 'banka.department1'

await affiliationService.create({
name: affiliation,
force: true}, adminIdentity);
```

10. Next, we register a new user, `user1`, for the `department1` affiliation in the `banka` organization.

The `user1` user is registered with the CA, and their certificate and private key are imported to the wallet. A success message is printed on the console, as shown in the following code block:

```
const secret = await ca.register({ affiliation: 'banka.department1',
enrollmentID: 'user1', role: 'client' }, adminIdentity);
 const enrollment = await ca.enroll({ enrollmentID: 'user1',
enrollmentSecret: secret });
 const userIdentity = X509WalletMixin.createIdentity('bankaMSP',
enrollment.certificate, enrollment.key.toBytes());
 await wallet.import('user1', userIdentity);
 console.log('Successfully registered and enrolled user "user1" and
imported it into the wallet');
```

A `catch` block catches any errors during execution, like this:

```
catch (error) {
 console.error(`Failed to register user "user1": ${error}`);
 process.exit(1);
 }
```

Changes for the Bank B utility

Replicate the code for `registerUser-BankA.js` to `registerUser-BankB.js`. Save the code file in the Bankchain repository.

Make the following changes to the code so that it works for the Bank B organization:

1. Change the `ccpPath` object to the connection profile for Bank B, like this:

```
const ccpPath = path.resolve(__dirname, 'connection-bankb.json');
```

2. Change the `walletPath` object to the wallet for Bank B, like this:

```
const walletPath = path.join(process.cwd(), 'wallet-BankB');
```

3. Change the affiliation to `bankb.department1` at both places, like this:

```
let affiliation = 'bankb.department1'

const secret = await ca.register({ affiliation:
'banka.department1', enrollmentID: 'user1', role: 'client' },
adminIdentity);
```

4. Change the MSP to `bankbMSP`, like this:

```
const userIdentity = X509WalletMixin.createIdentity('bankbMSP',
enrollment.certificate, enrollment.key.toBytes());
```

After you've made the changes, save the files. Let's register both of the users.

Running the utilities

Let's register the users that will submit and read transactions to the blockchain for Bank A and Bank B

1. Navigate to the Bankchain repository. Run the following command to register a user for Bank A:

```
node registerUser-BankA.js
```

2. You should get a message on the console informing you that a new user, `user 1`, has been added to the wallet. Repeat the same for Bank B, as follows:

```
node registerUser-BankB.js
```

- The user1 identities for the banka and bankb organizations should be added to the wallet for Bank A and Bank B.
- You can actually verify this. Navigate to the wallet-BankA and wallet-BankB directory. You'll be able to see a folder labeled user1. Inside, you'll find the private key file and certificate for the admin user.

- Now, our network is ready to use. We can submit transactions to the network, and query transactions that have been added to the blockchain ledger. Next, let's write and deploy our corporate remittance smart contract.

Building the corporate remittance contract

To successfully carry out remittances on our blockchain network, we need to write and deploy a smart contract. The smart contract will define the transaction object, including the transaction parameters that will be captured in the channel ledger. The smart contract will allow authorized users to write transactions to the ledger and read transactions that have been written to the ledger.

We'll be creating a chaincode (smart contract) called corprem.js. It will have the following methods:

- createTx: This will submit a new corporate remittance transaction.
- queryTx: This will allow authorized users to fetch transactions already written to the blockchain.

OK. Let's start writing our contract.

Writing the corporate remittance contract

Let's write our corprem contract, with the help of the following steps:

1. Create a new file called CorpRem.js. We start writing the contract, by declaring the dependent fabric-contract-api library, which is used to define our contract object, like this:

```
/*
 * SPDX-License-Identifier: Apache-2.0
 */
'use strict';
```

```
const { Contract } = require('fabric-contract-api');
class corprem extends Contract {
```

2. Next, we will add the `createTx` method. The `createTx` method will create a new transaction in the ledger, as follows:

```
async createTx(ctx, txid,
  Sname,
  Saccount,
  Sbank,
  Saddr,
  Rname,
  Raccount,
  Rbank,
  Raddress,
  curr,
  amt,
  InvHash,
  BOEHash,
  DocHash ) {

  console.info('============== START : Create Transaction
  ===========');
```

The method takes the following parameters as input:

- `ctx`: The transaction context.
- `txid`: The transaction ID generated by the bank's internal system.
- `Sname`: The transaction sender's name.
- `Saccount`: The transaction sender's bank account number.
- `Sbank`: The transaction sender's bank.
- `Saddr`: The transaction sender's registered office address.
- `Rname`: The transaction receiver's name.
- `Raccount`: The transaction receiver's bank account number.
- `Rbank`: The transaction receiver's bank.
- `Raddr`: The transaction receiver's registered office address.
- `curr`: The currency of the transaction amount.
- `amount`: The transaction amount.
- `InvHash`: The hash of the invoice document, relevant to the corporate remittance being sent.

- BOEHash: The hash of the **Bill of Entry/Bill of Lading (BOE/BOL)** document, relevant to the corporate remittance being sent.
- DocHash: The hash of any other documents, relevant to the corporate remittance being sent.

A statement is printed to the console, to indicate the start of the method.

We create the transaction object, using the input parameters. We'll write this object to the ledger, like this:

```
const transaction = {
txid,
Sname,
Saccount,
Sbank,
Saddr,
Rname,
Raccount,
Rbank,
Raddress,
curr,
amt,
InvHash,
BOEHash,
DocHash,
DocType: 'transaction'
};
```

We use putState, to write the transaction object to the ledger. The transaction object will be referred by the transaction ID (txid) in the ledger, as follows:

```
await ctx.stub.putState(txid,
Buffer.from(JSON.stringify(transaction)));
```

Lastly, we fire a txCreated event, to indicate to all transaction listeners that a new transaction has been added, as follows:

```
ctx.stub.setEvent('txCreated',
Buffer.from(JSON.stringify(transaction)));
console.info('============= END : Create Transaction ===========');
}
```

We also print a message on the console, to indicate the end of the createTx method.

3. Next, we will write a `queryTx` method, to retrieve transactions written to the blockchain ledger, like this:

```
async queryTx (ctx, txid) {
```

The `queryTx` method takes the transaction ID (`txid`) as an input parameter.

```
const transaction = await ctx.stub.getState(txid); // get the
transaction from chaincode state
 if (!transaction || transaction.length === 0) {
 throw new Error(`Transaction does not exist`);
 }
 console.log(transaction.toString());
 return transaction.toString();
 }

module.exports = corprem;
```

It uses `getState()` to fetch the transaction details, using `txid` (the transaction ID). If the fetched transaction object is not empty, indicating the transaction exists, the transaction object is converted into a string object from the buffer and returned back to the requestor.

Lastly, we export the `corprem` contract as a module. That wraps up our chaincode contract. Now, let's deploy it to the blockchain.

Deploying the corprem smart contract

We need to set up a new `chaincode` directory for our contract. In your Hyperledger Fabric `fabric-samples` directory, navigate to the `chaincode` directory. By default, it will be at the following location:

```
/fabric-samples/chaincode/
```

Let's look at how to setup the contract project environment:

1. In the `chaincode` folder, create a new folder, with the name `corprem`.
2. In the `corprem` folder, create an `index.js` file, with the following values:

```
/*
 * SPDX-License-Identifier: Apache-2.0
 */

'use strict';

const corprem = require('./lib/corprem');
```

```
module.exports.corprem = corprem;
module.exports.contracts = [ corprem ];
```

This will declare the `corprem` object, which will be used by our peer chaincode to install and instantiate tools for deploying our chaincode within the blockchain.

3. Next, create a `lib` folder in the `corprem` directory. By default, your `lib` folder's `filepath` should be this:

   ```
   /fabric-samples/chaincode/corprem/lib
   ```

4. Copy and paste the `corprem.js` file with the `corprem` smart contract code that we wrote in the previous section. We need to install this smart contract to all four peers, `peer0.banka.example.com`, `peer1.banka.example.com`, `peer0.bankb.example.com`, and `peer1.bankb.example.com` of our Hyperledger Fabric network. To do so, we'll be using the `peer chaincode install` command.

   The utility `peer chaincode` is a tool available in the `cli` (command-line interface) Docker container, which is available by default as a Docker image in the Hyperledger Fabric repository. It allows us to interact with and carry out operations on chaincodes (a chaincode is the Hyperledger Fabric equivalent of a smart contract).

   Let's look at the `peer chaincode install` statement that we will be using to deploy our chaincode for the `peer0.banka.example.com` peer, as follows:

   ```
   docker exec
   -e CORE_PEER_LOCALMSPID=bankaMSP
   -e CORE_PEER_ADDRESS=peer0.banka.example.com:7051
   -e
   CORE_PEER_MSPCONFIGPATH=/opt/gopath/src/github.com/hyperledger/fabr
   ic/peer/crypto/peerOrganizations/banka.example.com/users/Admin@bank
   a.example.com/msp
   -e
   CORE_PEER_TLS_ROOTCERT_FILE=/opt/gopath/src/github.com/hyperledger/
   fabric/peer/crypto/peerOrganizations/banka.example.com/peers/peer0.
   banka.example.com/tls/ca.crt
   cli peer chaincode install -n corprem -v 1.0
   -p /opt/gopath/src/github.com/chaincode/corprem -l node
   ```

Let's go through the different parts of the command, one by one, as follows:

- The `docker exec` command is used to execute a command within the Docker container.
- The `-e` tag is used to set environment variables inside the Docker container before executing a command.
- The `CORE_PEER_LOCALMSPID` environment variable indicates the membership service provider for the node. The membership service provider is used to define the Root Certificate Authorities and Intermediate Certificate Authorities which will be used to issue identities for a trusted domain/organization on the blockchain network. Here, we set it to `bankaMSP`, which is the MSP service for Bank A.
- The `CORE_PEER_ADDRESS` environment variable indicates the external client port for `peer0` (Node 1 in our Hyperledger Fabric network), to which requests need to be submitted. We set it here to `peer0.org1.example.com:7051`, which is our node's client port.
- The `CORE_PEER_MSPCONFIGPATH` environment variable indicates the configuration file path for the Membership Service Provider, for `peer0` within `peer0`'s Docker container.
- The `CORE_PEER_TLS_ROOTCERT_FILE` environment variable indicates the location of the root certificate (CA certificate), for the digital signature used by `peer0`.
- `cli` indicates the container name where we are executing the `peer chaincode` command. This, as we discussed earlier, is the command-line interface Docker container.
- Lastly, we use the `-n` tag to indicate the chaincode name, `-v` to indicate the version of the chaincode, `-p` to indicate the path where the smart contract code is available, and `-l` to indicate the scripting language of the smart contract, which is node in our case.

5. Run the command as a Linux user with Docker privileges on the Terminal line. On successful execution, it should print a message similar to the one in the following code block. The message is from the command-line container:

```
2019-10-29 05:56:55.357 UTC [chaincodeCmd] install -> INFO 003
Installed remotely response:<status:200 payload:"OK" >
```

6. Now, craft a `peer chaincode install` statement for all the other nodes in our network, as follows:

```
//chaincode install statement for peer1 banka

docker exec -e CORE_PEER_LOCALMSPID=bankaMSP -e
CORE_PEER_ADDRESS=peer1.banka.example.com:8051 -e
CORE_PEER_MSPCONFIGPATH=/opt/gopath/src/github.com/hyperledger/fabr
ic/peer/crypto/peerOrganizations/banka.example.com/users/Admin@bank
a.example.com/msp -e
CORE_PEER_TLS_ROOTCERT_FILE=/opt/gopath/src/github.com/hyperledger/
fabric/peer/crypto/peerOrganizations/banka.example.com/peers/peer0.
banka.example.com/tls/ca.crt cli peer chaincode install -n corprem
-v 1.0 -p /opt/gopath/src/github.com/chaincode/corprem -l node

//chaincode install statement for peer0 bankb

docker exec -e CORE_PEER_LOCALMSPID=bankbMSP -e
CORE_PEER_ADDRESS=peer0.bankb.example.com:9051 -e
CORE_PEER_MSPCONFIGPATH=/opt/gopath/src/github.com/hyperledger/fabr
ic/peer/crypto/peerOrganizations/bankb.example.com/users/Admin@bank
b.example.com/msp -e
CORE_PEER_TLS_ROOTCERT_FILE=/opt/gopath/src/github.com/hyperledger/
fabric/peer/crypto/peerOrganizations/bankb.example.com/peers/peer0.
bankb.example.com/tls/ca.crt cli peer chaincode install -n corprem
-v 1.0 -p /opt/gopath/src/github.com/chaincode/corprem -l node

//chaincode install statement for peer1 bankb

docker exec -e CORE_PEER_LOCALMSPID=bankbMSP -e
CORE_PEER_ADDRESS=peer1.bankb.example.com:10051 -e
CORE_PEER_MSPCONFIGPATH=/opt/gopath/src/github.com/hyperledger/fabr
ic/peer/crypto/peerOrganizations/bankb.example.com/users/Admin@bank
b.example.com/msp -e
CORE_PEER_TLS_ROOTCERT_FILE=/opt/gopath/src/github.com/hyperledger/
fabric/peer/crypto/peerOrganizations/bankb.example.com/peers/peer0.
bankb.example.com/tls/ca.crt cli peer chaincode install -n corprem
-v 1.0 -p /opt/gopath/src/github.com/chaincode/corprem -l node
```

7. Run them on the Terminal window. You should get a successful peer installation message, like the one in the following code snippet, after each `peer install` command:

```
INFO 003 Installed remotely response:<status:200 payload:"OK" >
```

8. Next, we need to instantiate the chaincode across the nodes. To instantiate the chaincode, we'll use the following command:

```
docker exec
-e CORE_PEER_LOCALMSPID=bankaMSP
-e
CORE_PEER_MSPCONFIGPATH=/opt/gopath/src/github.com/hyperledger/fabr
ic/peer/crypto/peerOrganizations/banka.example.com/users/Admin@bank
a.example.com/msp cli peer chaincode instantiate
-o orderer.example.com:7050
-C bkchannel
-n corprem
-l node
-v 1.0
-c '{"Args":[]}'
-P 'AND('\''bankaMSP.member'\'','\''bankbMSP.member'\'')'
--tls
--cafile
/opt/gopath/src/github.com/hyperledger/fabric/peer/crypto/ordererOr
ganizations/example.com/orderers/orderer.example.com/msp/tlscacerts
/tlsca.example.com-cert.pem --peerAddresses
peer0.banka.example.com:7051
--tlsRootCertFiles
/opt/gopath/src/github.com/hyperledger/fabric/peer/crypto/peerOrgan
izations/banka.example.com/peers/peer0.banka.example.com/tls/ca.crt
```

Let's look at the environment variables, which are denoted by the -e tag.

The CORE_PEER_LOCALMSPID environment variable indicates the membership service provider for the node. The membership service provider is used to define the Root Certificate Authorities and Intermediate Certificate Authorities which will be used to issue identities for a trusted domain/organization on the blockchain network. Here, we set it to bankaMSP, which is the MSP service for Bank A.

The CORE_PEER_MSPCONFIGPATH environment variable indicates the configuration file path for the Membership Service Provider for peer0 within peer0's Docker container."

- The -C tag indicates the Hyperledger Fabric network channel to which this chaincode will be instantiated. In Hyperledger Fabric, channels are private blockchain ledgers, which can be read or written to only by the approved participants of the channel. We set it to the bkchannel channel we created earlier.
- The -n tag indicates the name of the chaincode being instantiated. Here, we set it to corprem.
- The -l tag indicates the scripting language, which in our case is node.

- The -v tag is the version number of the chaincode.
- The -c tag indicates the constructor arguments for the contract, if any.
- The -P tag indicates the member participants of the network.
- The --tls tag indicates that messages will be ssl-encrypted. The following tags, --cafile and --tlsRootCerFiles, indicate the certificate file for the orderer and peer0.banka.

Run the command in the Terminal window. If instantiation is successful, you will not get any message on the Terminal window.

That completes writing and deploying our corprem chaincode (smart contract). Let's move on to creating the IPFS network.

Setting up the IPFS network

In this section, we'll set up the IPFS network. The IPFS network will allow the banks to share important compliance and AML documents that are required to process corporate remittance transactions. Our IPFS network will consist of two nodes. Each node will be controlled by a bank.

The banks will publish the documents to the IPFS network. Only authorized participants will be able to retrieve the documents from the network, using the document's hash signature.

Downloading the binary and installing IPFS

We will be using IPFS for storing and sharing documents between the two banks. Let's look at the steps to setup the private IPFS network:

1. To install IPFS, you'll need to ensure that Go is installed in your system and the GOPATH object is set. You can check if Go is installed on your system, with the following command:

   ```
   go version
   ```

   If Go is installed, it'll let you know the current version. You can find steps to download and install it at this link: https://golang.org/doc/install.

Make sure the GOPATH variable is set. Otherwise, add the following lines to your .bashrc file in your home directory:

```
export GOROOT=/usr/local/go
export GOPATH=$HOME/gopath
export PATH=$PATH:$GOROOT/bin:$GOPATH/bin
```

2. Enter the source ~/.bashrc command in the Terminal, to add the preceding environment variables to your Linux profile.
3. Now, run the go version command. It should show you the current Go version.
4. Now, let's install IPFS. Run the following commands on the Terminal, to download the latest version of the IPFS binary, and move it to the Go executable path. At the time of writing, the latest version was 4.22.

My Go executable path is /usr/local/bin/, as shown in the following code block:

```
$wget
https://dist.ipfs.io/go-ipfs/v0.4.22/go-ipfs_v0.4.22_Linux-amd64.ta
r.gz
$tar xvfz go-ipfs_v0.4.22_Linux-amd64.tar.gz
$sudo mv go ipfs/ipfs /usr/local/bin/ipfs
```

Initializing the IPFS nodes

Next, we need to initialize the IPFS nodes for our system. Since we are setting up two nodes, we'll repeat the necessary steps twice, once for Node 1 and once for Node 2. Node 1 will be owned by Bank A, and Node 2 by Bank B.

1. First, initialize Node 1, using the following command on the Terminal. Make sure you are in the IPFS executable path, which in my case is /usr/local/bin/ipfs.

The IPFS_PATH parameter points to the location of the local node folder for the IPFS Node 1. By default, it is available at /home/<user name>/.ipfs.

2. Update this location to the IPFS_PATH parameter, by running the following command:

```
IPFS_PATH=~/.ipfs ./ipfs init
```

- A new peer ID will be generated. It will look something like this:
  `QmQVvZEmvjhYgsyEC7NvMn8EWf131EcgTXFFJQYGSz4Y83`.
- Keep it safe. We'll need it later for bootstrapping the nodes.

3. Next, repeat the same for Node 2 by executing the next few commands on the Terminal window.

   We first need to point the `IPFS_PATH` parameter to the location of the local node folder for the IPFS Node 2. I've set it to `/home/<user name>/.ipfs2` for Node 2.

4. Run the following command on the terminal to initialize IPFS Node 2:

   ```
   IPFS_PATH=~/.ipfs2 ./ipfs init
   ```

A new peer ID will be generated similar to before. Make sure you copy and store the peer ID for this node as well.

This will create two nodes and two-node configuration paths for IPFS in the same local machine.

Generating a key file for the network

Let's generate a secret key for the network. Only nodes with this secret key will be able to connect and share documents to our private IPFS network.

Run the following command to download the Swarm key generator utility:

```
go get -u github.com/Kubuxu/go-ipfs-swarm-key-gen/ipfs-swarm-key-gen
```

Run the following command to generate a new Swarm key for Node1:

```
ipfs-swarm-key-gen & > ~/.ipfs/swarm.key
```

Node2 will refer to this key for connecting to the private IPFS network. Copy the key file (`swarm.key`) to the folder for Node 2, `~/.ipfs2`. The key will be available under the path for the first node. This in my case is `/home/ishan/.ipfs/swarm.key`.

In my case, this is `/home/ishan/.ipfs2/`.

Configuring the nodes

Next, we'll configure the nodes to run them on one local machine. IPFS uses the following ports for communication and operation:

Gateway port: The default value is 8080.

Client port: The default value is 5001.

Swarm ipv4 and ipv6 ports. The default value is 4001.

To avoid conflict, we need to change the values of this port for Node 2. To do so, open the config file in your ~/.ipfs2 directory, and locate the Addresses: tag.

Change the values of these ports to those shown in the following code block to avoid a conflict with IPFS Node 1, which is running on the same machine:

```
"Addresses": {
    "API": "/ip4/127.0.0.1/tcp/5002",
    "Announce": [],
    "Gateway": "/ip4/127.0.0.1/tcp/8081",
    "NoAnnounce": [],
    "Swarm": [
      "/ip4/0.0.0.0/tcp/4002",
      "/ip6/::/tcp/4002"
    ]
  }
```

This should allow us to run both the nodes on the same local machine.

Bootstrapping the nodes

Next, we need to bootstrap the two nodes so that they can discover each other on the network.

1. Navigate to the ipfs executable folder. In my case, it is in /usr/local/bin/ipfs.
2. Run the following commands in the Terminal window for Node 1. Substitute the Peer ID we generated when initializing Node 1:

    ```
    $ IPFS_PATH=~/.ipfs ./ipfs bootstrap rm —all
    $ IPFS_PATH=~/.ipfs ./ipfs bootstrap add
    /ip4/192.168.10.1/tcp/4001/ipfs/<Peer ID for Node 1>
    ```

3. Repeat the same for Node 2, changing the IPFS directory and the client port. Also, substitute the Peer ID for Node 1 that we got when initializing the node, as follows:

```
$ IPFS_PATH=~/.ipfs2 ./ipfs bootstrap rm —all
$ IPFS_PATH=~/.ipfs2 ./ipfs bootstrap add
/ip4/192.168.10.1/tcp/4001/ipfs/<Peer ID for Node 1>
```

Now, we are ready to run our IPFS network.

Starting the nodes and testing the network

Now, let's start the network. To interact with IPFS, we need to bring the daemon for both the nodes online. Follow these steps:

1. Run the following command on a Terminal window to bring Node 1 online. Make sure you are in the directory with the IPFS executable, as shown in the following code block:

```
$ IPFS_PATH=~/.ipfs ./ipfs daemon
```

The daemon for `Node1` should now come online.

2. Open a new Terminal window and navigate back to the directory with the IPFS executable, Now bring the daemon for the second node online with the below command:

```
$ IPFS_PATH=~/.ipfs2 ./ipfs daemon
```

The daemon for `Node 2` should come online. Let's try publishing a file, and see if it is indeed shared between the nodes.

3. Create a sample file by entering the following code:

```
$ echo hello IPFS & > file.txt
```

4. Add it to IPFS `Node1` by entering the following code:

```
$ IPFS_PATH=~/.ipfs ./ipfs add file.txt
```

Note down the hash for the file generated by IPFS. It'll look something like this: `QmZULkCELmmk5XNfCgTnCyFgAVxBRBXyDHGGMVoLFLiXEN`.

5. Now, let's connect to Node 2 and try to read this file. Enter the following command to read the file from Node 2:

```
$ IPFS_PATH=~/.ipfs2 ./ipfs cat
QmZULkCELmmk5XNfCgTnCyFgAVxBRBXyDHGGMVoLFLiXEN
```

It should print the content of the file—that is, "hello IPFS"—on the Terminal.

With that, we have successfully set up our IPFS network. Next, let's set up the bank databases that will store customer data and transaction data.

Setting up the bank databases

We need to set up databases for both Bank A and Bank B, which will hold the customer data and transaction data. I'm using a postgresql database for the same. Feel free to use MySQL or any other database that you see fit for your purpose.

If you are not using postgresql , jump to the sub-section on creating the bank databases.

Installing postgresql

To install postgresql on Ubuntu, use `apt install`, as shown in the following code snippet:

```
$sudo apt install postgresql postgresql-contrib
```

For CentOS or **Red Hat Enterprise Linux (RHEL)**, use the following commands:

```
$sudo yum install postgresql-server postgresql-contrib
$sudo postgresql-setup initdb
$sudo systemctl start postgresql
```

Let's create the databases and relations for Bank A and Bank B.

Creating the bank databases

Next, we'll create two databases, banka and bankb, each corresponding to Bank A and Bank B. Additionally, we'll create two database users, banka and bankb, each corresponding to the banka and bankb databases. Each database will contain the customers table, which will hold customer data, and transactions table, which will hold transaction data.

Follow these steps:

Switch to the postgres user, like this:

```
$su - postgres
```

Create two new users for each database, like this:

```
$ createuser banka --pwprompt
```

Enter the password as banka, or anything else. We'll need this password later for connecting to the banka postgres database. Repeat the same for the bankb user, as follows:

```
$ createuser bankb --pwprompt
```

Enter the password as bankb, or anything else. We'll need this password later for connecting to bankb. Log in to the postgres command line, like this:

```
psql
```

Create a database each for Bank A and Bank B in the postgres command line. The owner will be banka and bankb respectively, as shown in the following code block:

```
postgres=# CREATE DATABASE banka OWNER banka;
postgres=# CREATE DATABASE bankb OWNER bankb;
```

Next, create two Unix users for each database. Log in to your root user and create a banka user and a bankb user. For Ubuntu, enter the following code:

```
$sudo adduser banka
$sudo adduser bankb
```

Change the passwords for each user. I've set it to **banka** and **bankb** for the banka and bankb users respectively, as follows:

```
$sudo passwd banka
$sudo passwd bankb
```

Let's create the relations we'll use.

Creating the database relations

Let's create the databases our application will use for storing and processing customer and transactions data.

Log in to the `banka` user with the password you created earlier, and connect to the postgres command line, like this:

```
$su - banka
$psql banka
```

Create a `customers` table for handling customer data. To do so, run the following query on the postgres command line:

```
CREATE TABLE customers(
 user_id serial PRIMARY KEY,
 name VARCHAR NOT NULL,
 address VARCHAR NOT NULL,
 account VARCHAR NOT NULL,
 balance INTEGER NOT NULL
);
```

The relation will store the `user_id` that is automatically generated, the customer's name, the customer's address, their account number, and their current balance.

Create a `transactions` table for handling customer data. To do so, run the following query on the postgres command line:

```
CREATE TABLE transactions(
 transactions_id VARCHAR PRIMARY KEY,
 sname VARCHAR NOT NULL,
 saddress VARCHAR NOT NULL,
 saccount VARCHAR NOT NULL,
 sbank VARCHAR NOT NULL,
 rname VARCHAR NOT NULL,
 raddress VARCHAR NOT NULL,
 raccount VARCHAR NOT NULL,
 rbank VARCHAR NOT NULL,
 currency VARCHAR(4) NOT NULL,
 amount INTEGER NOT NULL,
 invhash VARCHAR NOT NULL,
 boehash VARCHAR NOT NULL,
 dochash VARCHAR NOT NULL,
 transtype VARCHAR NOT NULL
);
```

Repeat the preceding steps for the bankb user. Log in to the Unix bankb user and connect to the postgres command line. Run the queries for creating the customers table and transactions table in the bankb database.

Inserting test customer data into the customers table

We need to insert some test customer data that we can run our application with. To do so follow the below steps -

Log in to the banka user account and connect to the postgres command line. Run the following query to insert test customer data into the customers relation in the postgres command line:

```
INSERT INTO customers (name, account, address, balance)
VALUES('Acme','ACMEAC8829','New Delhi',1000);
```

Next, log in to the bankb user account and connect to the postgres command line. Run the following query to insert test customer data into the customers relation in the postgres command line:

```
INSERT INTO customers (name, account, address, balance)
VALUES('Apex','APXAC09002','Dubai',1000);
```

Now, we have both bank databases set up with test data for the corporate customers Acme Inc and Apex Corp. Let's start building our backend server and transaction listeners for both of the banks.

Building the bank backend servers

The backend server is a bridge between the blockchain network, the IPFS network, the postgresql database, and the bank portal frontend. It takes a request from the frontend, processes it, and forwards it to the next component in the workflow.

The backend server extends a set of API endpoints, where the frontend can post requests. The API endpoints are listed as follows:

/customerinfo: Fetches the customer's info, including name, address, account, and balance from the banka or bankb database, and passes it to the bank portal frontend.

/payment: The bank portal frontend posts payment requests to this endpoint. It uploads the transaction documents, including invoices, BOL/BOE, and any other document to the bank server, posts the document to the IPFS network, and then fires the remittance transaction on the blockchain network. On a successful response from the blockchain network, it adds the transaction to the transactions table in the bank database and updates the customer's balance. It then returns the response **Transaction successfully submitted** to the bank frontend.

/gettrans: It fetches the customer's transaction details from the bank database and returns a transactions array to the bank portal frontend.

The backend server application contains the following methods:

iwrite: It takes the file path of the uploaded files as an input and adds the files to the IPFS network.

submitTrans: It takes the transaction ID, the transaction details, and the hash of the transaction documents as input parameters, and submits the transaction to the bankchain network.

updateBal: Updates the customer's balance in the database after the transaction has been successfully submitted to the network.

insertTrans: Inserts the transaction into the database after it has been successfully submitted to the blockchain and added to the channel ledger.

Let's start writing the code for the backend server. We'll write it for Bank A. Repeat the following steps for Bank B.

Creating the app environment

In your Node.js environment, run npm init to initialize the app.

Open the package.json file, and update the dependencies tag to the following:

```
{
..........
```

```
"dependencies": {
      "body-parser": "^1.19.0",
      "express": "^4.17.1",
      "multer": "^1.4.2",
      "fabric-ca-client": "~1.4.0",
      "fabric-network": "^1.4.4",
      "fs": "0.0.1-security",
      "ipfs-http-client": "^40.0.0",
      "pg": "^7.14.0",
   }
........
}
```

Run `npm install` to install the dependencies.

Create two files: `backend-BankA.js`, and `backend-BankB.js`.

Let's start writing the code for `backend-BankA.js`.

Writing the backend server code

Open the `backend-BankA.js` file in a code editor, and follow these next steps:

We start by importing the dependent node modules, as follows:

```
var express = require('express');
var app = express();
var multer = require('multer')
var bodyParser = require("body-parser");
const { FileSystemWallet, Gateway } = require('fabric-network');
const ipfsClient = require('ipfs-http-client')
const ipfs = ipfsClient('http://localhost:5001')
const pg = require('pg');
```

We are using the `express` framework for our app.

We are using `multer` to upload the transaction documents to the system.

`body-parser` allows us to parse the app request body.

The `fabric-network` module is used to connect to the blockchain network and submit transactions to our smart contract.

The IPFS client allows us to publish to and fetch files from the IPFS network. It is set to the client port of Bank A, which is `5001`.

The `pg` module is used to connect to the postgres database.

Next, we define the parameters for connecting to the `banka` postgres database.

The `conString` object is passed to the `pg` postgres client, to connect to the database. We add the postgres client port, the username, and password for the `banka` Unix user and the database to connect to the `conString` object, as follows:

```
const conString = "postgres://banka:banka@localhost:5432/banka";
const client = new pg.Client(conString);
client.connect();
```

`client.connect()` will connect the postgres client to our `banka` database.

Next, we define the `bodyParser` object to parse the `json` request body, as follows:

```
app.use(bodyParser.json());
app.use(bodyParser.urlencoded({ extended: true }));
```

The `CurrTxID` counter holds a numeric value that is used to generate the transaction ID, like this:

```
var CurrTxID = 1;
```

We set up a middleware to allow cross-origin requests. This will allow our frontend to post requests to our backend server's endpoints. The middleware passes the request to the next layer, after adding the required parameters to the headers, as follows:

```
app.use(function (req, res, next) {
res.setHeader('Access-Control-Allow-Origin', '*');
res.setHeader('Access-Control-Allow-Methods', 'GET, POST, OPTIONS,
PUT, PATCH, DELETE');
res.setHeader('Access-Control-Allow-Headers', 'X-Requested-
With,content-type');
res.setHeader('Access-Control-Allow-Credentials', true);
next();
});
```

Next, we set up the `server` object and bring the server online at the port `8000`, like this:

```
var server = app.listen(process.env.PORT || 8000, function () {
 var port = server.address().port;
 console.log("App now running on port", port);
 });
```

The `ccpPath` object stores the location of the connection profile used to connect and submit transactions to the blockchain channel, as a member of the Bank A organization. The connection profile is generated after the blockchain network is set up and online, It should be located in the Bankchain directory path, as shown in the following code snippet:

```
const ccpPath = '~/fabric-samples/bankchain/connection-banka.json';
```

Let's start writing the services.

Creating an endpoint to fetch customer data

The `/customerinfo` endpoint takes the `userID` as the request parameter and returns a response object, with the customer details matching the user ID, after fetching them from the bank database.

The service fetches the user ID from the request body. It then uses the `pg` client object to run a `SELECT` query on the `customers` table in the `banka` database, as follows:

```
var userId=request.body.userId;

client.query('SELECT name,address,account,balance from customers where
user_id = $1', [userId], (error, results)=> {
```

On the response from the `pg` client, we check for error responses. In the case of no errors, the customer's name, address, account, and current balance are added to the `json` response object and sent back to the requestor, like this:

```
if (error) {
 throw error
 }

if(results)
{
response.json({
name: results.rows[0].name,
address: results.rows[0].address,
account: results.rows[0].account,
balance: results.rows[0].balance
});

response.end();

}});
});
```

Next, let's look at the payment endpoint used to post transaction requests.

Creating an endpoint to post payment requests

The `/payment` endpoint will accept the payment requests from the bank portal frontend. It uses `multer` to accept the transaction object with the transaction details and upload the compliance and AML documents.

Before we write the code for the service, we define the `cpUpload` object that will be used to configure `multer`, to upload the documents.

The `cpUpload` object provides `multer` the configuration for the files to be uploaded. The files at the `invfile` (invoice file), `boefile` (BOE/BOL file), and `docfile` (other document) fields will be uploaded, as follows:

```
var cpUpload = upload.fields([{ name: 'invfile', maxCount: 1 }, {
name: 'boefile', maxCount: 1 }, { name: 'docfile', maxCount: 1 }])
```

The `upload` object is also configured with the location to which the files will be uploaded and with the naming format of the files, as follows:

```
var upload = multer({ storage: storage })

var storage = multer.diskStorage({
  destination: function (req, file, cb) {
  cb(null, '/home/ishan/CorpRemApp/CorpRemApp/public/uploads/')
  },
  filename: function (req, file, cb) {
  cb(null, 'BankA' + CurrTxID+'-'+file.fieldname+'.txt' )
  }
})
```

In my case, the files are uploaded to the `public/uploads` folder of the bank portal frontend React app. The naming convention for the uploaded file is `BankA <CurrTxID value> - <Fieldname(invfile/boefile/docfile)>.txt`.

Let's start writing our service, by running the following code:

```
app.post('/payment', cpUpload, function (request, response, next) {
```

When a request is posted to the `/payment` endpoint, the request body is first sent to `multer` for parsing.

The `multer` module will upload the files whose information is available under the `invfile`, `boefile`, and `docfile` request body fields, and stores them to the local storage at the location defined by us, with the nomenclature defined by us.

It then passes the details of the files and the other input parameters in the request body to the next layer, which is the business logic written in the `/payment` endpoint.

We store the location of the documents in the local storage to the `invpath`, `boepath`, and `docpath` variables, as follows:

```
var invpath = request.files.invfile[0].destination +
request.files.invfile[0].filename;
var boepath = request.files.boefile[0].destination +
request.files.boefile[0].filename;
var docpath = request.files.docfile[0].destination +
request.files.docfile[0].filename;
```

Next, we call the `iwrite()` method to publish the uploaded files to the IPFS network. The `iwrite()` method adds a file to the IPFS network between the bank and returns to us the hash value of the uploaded file. We add the hash value of the three files to the array object, `hasharray`, like this:

```
var hasharray = [];
iwrite(invpath).then(function(res,err){

if(res) {
hasharray[0] = res[0].hash ;
iwrite(boepath).then(function(res,err){

 if(res)
 {
hasharray[1] = res[0].hash ;
iwrite(docpath).then(function(res,err){

if(res)
 {
hasharray[2] = res[0].hash ;
```

Next, we generate the transaction ID for the outgoing transaction, like this:

```
var txID = 'BankA' + CurrTxID;
 console.log("Transaction ID",txID);
```

The transaction ID follows the format `BankA<CurrTxID>`. Thus, when the value of `CurrTxID` is 1, the transaction ID is `BankA1`. After every successful transaction submitted to the blockchain, the `CurrTxID` value is incremented by one, to get the next transaction ID.

Next, we call the `submitTrans()` method to submit the transaction to the blockchain network. The `txID` (transaction ID), `request.body` (request body with details of the transaction to be submitted), and `hasharray` (array object with the hash signatures of the three files) variables are sent as input parameters to the method, as follows:

```
submitTrans(txID, request.body, hasharray).then(function(err,res){
```

On the response from the `submitTrans()` method, we check for error responses. In the case of no responses, we call the `updateBal()` method to update the balance of the customer in the Bank A database.

We set the parameter object with the transaction amount and the sending customer's account number, and call `updateBal()`, as follows:

```
var paramsBal = {amount : request.body.amount,
  account : request.body.saccount};

updateBal(paramsBal,function(res){
console.log("Updated result",res);
```

On a successful response from the `updateBal()` method, we call the `insertTrans()` method to insert the transaction into the `transactions` table of the Bank A database.

We send the transaction ID (`txID`), the transaction details in the request body, and `hasharray` as input parameters to the `insertTrans` method, like this:

```
if(res)
 {

var paramsTx = {txID : txID,
det : request.body,
hasharray: hasharray};

insertTrans(paramsTx,function(res){
```

On a successful response from the `insertTrans()` method, we send the `response` object back to the `requestor` from the frontend with the success message, as shown in the following code block:

```
if(res)
{
response.json({
result: res,
});

CurrTxID++;
console.log(CurrTxID);
response.end();

}
```

We also increment the `CurrTxID` variable by 1 to get the next transaction ID. That wraps up our payment endpoint.

Creating a service to get transaction details

The endpoint `/gettrans` returns the incoming and outgoing transactions against an account when called from the bank portal frontend. It fetches the transactions from the `transactions` relation in the bank database, by running a `SELECT` query against it.

We start by fetching the customer's account from the request body, as follows:

```
app.post('/gettrans', function (request, response) {
const account = request.body.account;
```

Next, we fetch all the transactions from the `transactions` relation for the account in the request body, as follows:

```
client.query('SELECT * FROM transactions WHERE saccount = $1 OR
raccount = $1', [account], (error, results)=> {
```

On the response from the `pg` client, we check for an error response. In the case of no errors, we add the query result rows to the response object and send it back to the bank portal frontend, like this:

```
if (error) {
throw error
}

if(results)
```

```
{
console.log(results);
response.json({
tx: results.rows
});
response.end();
}
})
})
```

That brings us to the end of our /gettrans endpoint.

Let's look at the methods defined in our backend server next.

Writing a method to publish documents to the IPFS network

The iwrite() method accepts the location of a file in the local server storage as an input parameter. It then adds this file to the IPFS network and returns the hash of the document to the function invoker.

The method receives the path of the file in the filepath input parameter, as shown in the following code snippet:

```
async function iwrite (filepath) {
```

Next, it adds the file to IPFS by calling the ipfs client object. The client object submits the file to the IPFS client port 5001, as follows:

```
try
{
const results = await ipfs.addFromFs(filepath, { });
```

The IPFS client returns the hash of the file content. The iwrite() method returns this file hash to the invoker, like this:

```
return results;
}catch (error) {
  console.error(`Failed to write: ${error}`);
  }
}
```

A catch statement catches any errors while adding the file to the IPFS network.

That brings us to the end of the `iwrite()` method. Next, let's look at the method that submits the transaction to the blockchain network.

Writing a method to submit transactions to the blockchain network

The `submitTrans()` method accepts the transaction details from the `/payment` endpoint and adds a new remittance transaction to the blockchain ledger. Let's see how the method works:

1. The input parameters to the method are the transaction ID (`txID`), the `trans` object with the transaction details, and the `hasharray` object with the hash of the invoice document, the BOE/BOL document, and any other document shared for compliance purposes with the transaction request, as follows:

   ```
   async function submitTrans ( txID, trans, hasharray) {
   ```

2. We first check whether a valid user exists for Bank A for submitting transactions. We use the `user1` user we created for Bank A earlier. We set the `wallet` object to the location of the admin and user keys we created earlier. We check whether a private key and certificate exist for the `user1` user in the wallet, by running the following code:

   ```
   try {
    const wallet = new FileSystemWallet('~/fabric-
   samples/bankchain/wallet-BankA');
    const userExists = await wallet.exists('user1');
    if (!userExists) {
    console.log('An identity for the user "user1" does not exist in
   the wallet');
    console.log('Run the registerUser.js application before
   retrying');
    return;
    }
   ```

3. Next, we set the `Gateway` object and connect to the gateway with the `user1` user. The channel is set as `bkchannel`, our remittance channel in the Hyperledger Fabric network. The contract object is set to `corprem`, which is our corporate remittance chain code, as follows:

```
const gateway = new Gateway();
 await gateway.connect(ccpPath, { wallet, identity: 'user1',
discovery: { enabled: true, asLocalhost: true } });
 const network = await gateway.getNetwork('bkchannel');
 const contract = network.getContract('corprem');
```

4. We call the `submitTransaction` method in the contract object to submit a new transaction to the `corprem` chaincode, like this:

```
await
contract.submitTransaction('createTx',txID,trans.sname,trans.saccou
nt,trans.sbank,trans.saddress,trans.rname,trans.raccount,trans.rban
k,trans.raddress, trans.currency,
trans.amount,hasharray[0],hasharray[1],hasharray[2]);
```

The following are the input parameters to the transaction:

- `createTx`: Name of the method being invoked
- `txID`: Transaction ID
- `trans.sname`: Transaction sender's name
- `trans.saccount`: Transaction sender's account
- `trans.sbank`: Transaction sender's bank
- `trans.saddress`: Registered address of the transaction sender
- `trans.rname`: Transaction receiver's name
- `trans.raccount`: Transaction receiver's account
- `trans.rbank`: Transaction receiver's bank
- `trans.raddress`: Registered address of the transaction receiver
- `trans.currency`: Currency symbol of the transaction
- `trans.amount`: Transaction amount
- `hasharray[0]`: Hash of the invoice document
- `hasharray[1]`: Hash of the BOE/BOL
- `hasharray[2]`: Hash of other compliance documents

5. We print a message on the console after successful transaction submission and disconnect the gateway, like this:

```
console.log('Transaction has been submitted');
 await gateway.disconnect();
 return;
 }
catch (error) {
 console.error(`Failed to submit transaction: ${error}`);
 return 'Failed to submit transaction: ${error}';
 process.exit(1);
 }
};
```

A `catch` block catches any errors while submitting the transaction to the blockchain network. That brings us to the end of the `submitTrans()` method.

Writing a method to update the customer's balance

After the transaction is successfully submitted to the blockchain network, the customer's balance is updated in the `customers` table. The `updation` process is carried out by the `updateBal()` method.

The method accepts the transaction details through the `trans` object as an input parameter, as shown in the following code snippet:

```
var updateBal = function(trans,res) {
```

We fetch the customer balance from the `customers` table, like this:

```
client.query('SELECT balance from customers where account = $1',
[trans.account], (error, results)=> {
```

On the response from the `pg` client, we check for any error responses. In the case of no errors, we deduct the transaction amount from the customer's balance, and run an update query to update the balance, as follows:

```
if (error) {
 throw error
 }
 if(results)
 {
 var oldbal = results.rows[0].balance;
 var newbal = oldbal - trans.amount;
client.query('UPDATE customers set balance = $1 where account = $2',
[newbal, trans.account], (error, results) => {
```

We check for error responses from the pg client. If there are no errors, we return the control back to the function invoker, like this:

```
if (error) {
 throw error
 }
return res(newbal);
 })
 }
})
 }
```

That wraps up the updateBal() method. Next, let's look at the insertTrans() method.

Writing a method to add transactions to the database

The insertTrans() method will insert a new transaction to the transactions relation by using the pg client. It is invoked after the customer's balance is updated by the /payment endpoint.

The method runs an INSERT query to insert the transaction into the transactions database. Apart from the transaction details, an additional flag, transtype, is inserted with the data to indicate that the transaction is an Outgoing transaction, as shown in the following code block:

```
var insertTrans = function(trans,res) {

client.query('INSERT INTO transactions(transaction_id,sname,
saccount,sbank, saddress, rname, raccount, rbank, raddress, amount,
currency, invhash, boehash, dochash, transtype) values ($1, $2, $3, $4, $5,
$6, $7, $8, $9, $10, $11, $12, $13, $14, $15)',
[trans.txID,trans.det.sname,trans.det.saccount,trans.det.sbank,trans.det.sa
ddress,trans.det.rname,trans.det.raccount,trans.det.rbank,trans.det.raddres
s,
trans.det.amount,trans.det.currency,trans.hasharray[0],trans.hasharray[1],t
rans.hasharray[2], 'Outgoing'], (error, results) => {
```

We check the pg client for any error responses. In the case of no errors, we return control to the function invoked with the Transaction successfully submitted message. This message will then returned back to the bank portal frontend by the payment endpoint, as follows:

```
if (error)
 {
 throw error;
```

```
}

var msg = "Transaction successfully submitted";
console.log("Reached here",msg);
return res(msg);

})
}
```

That wraps up the `insertTrans()` method for our backend server.

Changes for backend server for Bank B

To create the backend server for Bank B, duplicate the backend server code for Bank A, and change the following details:

1. The `ipfs` object to the client port for Bank B, as follows:

    ```
    const ipfs = ipfsClient('http://localhost:5002')
    ```

2. postgres client values to the following code:

    ```
    const conString = "postgres://bankb:bankb@localhost:5432/bankb";
    ```

3. The server port to the following, to avoid conflict:

    ```
    var server = app.listen(process.env.PORT || 8001, function () {
    var port = server.address().port;
    console.log("App now running on port", port);
    });
    ```

4. The `ccpPath` object to the connection profile for `bankb`, as follows:

    ```
    const ccpPath = '~/fabric-samples/bankchain/connection-bankb.json';
    ```

5. The wallet path for `BankB`, as follows:

    ```
    const wallet = new FileSystemWallet('~/fabric-
    samples/bankchain/wallet-BankB');
    ```

6. Bring both the servers online by running the following commands on separate Terminals:

    ```
    $node backend-BankA.js
    $node backend-BankB.js
    ```

You should now have the backend servers online at the 8000 and 8001 ports, for Bank A and Bank B respectively.

Building the transaction listeners for the banks

We need to build a transaction listener, to detect incoming transactions to the bank's customers. We need one for Bank A and one for Bank B.

The transaction listener will carry out the following tasks:

- Monitor the blockchain for the txCreated event. The txCreated event is triggered by the corprem whenever a new transaction is created using the method createTx.
- In the case of an event being triggered, the listener checks the transaction payload to see if the receiving bank (trans.Rbank) is the bank hosting the transaction listener. Thus, the transaction listener for Bank A checks for transactions where the receiving bank is banka. Similarly, the transaction listener for Bank B checks if the receiving bank is bankb.
- If the transaction is intended for the bank, the transaction listener fetches the customer's current balance from the customers table. It fetches the transaction amount and the receiver's account from the transaction payload, and increments the receiving account's balance in the customers table with the transaction amount.
- Next, it inserts the incoming transaction details into the transactions table. The transtype flag is set to Incoming.
- Lastly, it calls the iread() method. The iread() method takes the hash of the compliance documents accompanying the transaction as an input parameter. It uses the hash value to fetch the documents from the IPFS node of the receiving bank and saves it to the local storage of the bank infrastructure.
- A catch block catches any errors while executing the preceding tasks.

The transaction listener has the following two methods:

- Transactionlisten(): The listener method checks for any incoming transactions and processes the tasks listed previously.
- iread(): This uses the IPFS client to fetch the compliance documents from the IPFS network and saves them to the local storage.

Let's start building the transaction listener. The following steps are for the transaction listener for Bank A. Repeat the steps for Bank B.

Creating the app environment

In your Node.js environment, run `npm init` to initialize the app.

Open the `package.json` file, and update the `dependencies` tag to the following:

```
{
..........
"dependencies": {
        "body-parser": "^1.19.0",
        "express": "^4.17.1",
        "fabric-ca-client": "~1.4.0",
        "fabric-network": "^1.4.4",
        "fs": "0.0.1-security",
        "ipfs-http-client": "^40.0.0",
        "pg": "^7.14.0",
    }
........
}
```

Run `npm install` to install the dependencies.

Create two files: `TransListener-BankA.js` and `TransListener-BankB.js`.

Let's start writing the code for `TransListener-BankA.js`.

Writing the transaction listener code

Open the `TransListener-BankA.js` file in a code editor, and proceed as follows:

We start by importing the dependencies for building our transaction listener, like this:

```
const { FileSystemWallet, Gateway } = require('fabric-network');
const ipfsClient = require('ipfs-http-client')
const ipfs = ipfsClient('http://localhost:5001')
const fs = require("fs");
const pg = require('pg');
```

The `fabric-network` module is used to connect to the blockchain network and listen to events triggered by our `corprem` smart contract.

The IPFS client allows us to publish to and fetch files from the IPFS network. It is set to the client port of Bank A, which is `5001`.

The `fs` module allows interaction with the local filesystem.

The `pg` module is used to connect to the postgres database.

Next, we define the parameters for connecting to the `banka` postgres database.

> The `conString` object is passed to the `pg` postgres client to connect to the database. We add the postgres client port, the username, and the password for the `banka Unix` user and the database, to connect to the `conString` object, as follows:
>
> ```
> const conString = "postgres://banka:banka@localhost:5432/banka";
> const client = new pg.Client(conString);
> client.connect();
> ```
>
> The `ccpPath` object stores the location of the connection profile for connecting and submitting transactions to the Bank A node. We'll use it to connect our transaction listener to the blockchain gateway. Lastly, we call the `Transactionlistener`, as follows:
>
> ```
> const ccpPath = '~/fabric-samples/bankchain/connection-banka.json';
> Transactionlistener();
> ```

Let's start writing the methods for our listener.

Writing the transaction listener method

The transaction listener will connect to the gateway and monitor it for any events created by our `corprem` contract by doing the following:

1. The transaction listener will first check our wallet to see whether an identity exists for connecting to the blockchain gateway. This is the `user1` identity that we created for Bank A earlier. If the user exists, we move on to the next steps, shown in the following code block:

    ```
    async function Transactionlistener (){

    try{
     const wallet = new FileSystemWallet('~/fabric-
    samples/bankchain/wallet-BankA');
     const userExists = await wallet.exists('user1');
    ```

```
if (!userExists) {
console.log('An identity for the user "user1" does not exist in
the wallet');
console.log('Run the registerUser-BankA.js application before
retrying');
return;
}
```

2. Next, we connect to the Hyperledger Fabric gateway with the user1 user, like this:

```
const gateway = new Gateway();
await gateway.connect(ccpPath, { wallet, identity: 'user1',
discovery: { enabled: true, asLocalhost: true } });
console.log("Gateway Connected");
const network = await gateway.getNetwork('bkchannel')
const contract = network.getContract('corprem');
```

- The network is set to our Bankchain channel, bkchannel.
- The contract object is set to corprem, which is our corporate remittance smart contract.
- The addContractListener method adds a new listener. This listener will listen to the txCreated event triggered by the corprem chaincode on the bkchannel chaincode, as follows:

```
const listener = await contract.addContractListener('contract-
listener', 'txCreated', (err, event, blockNumber, transactionId,
status) => {
if (err) {
        console.error(err);
        return;
    }
```

On the response from the listener, we check for errors.

In the case of no errors, the transaction payload is captured in the trans object, and the transaction block number and transaction ID are printed on the console, as shown in the following code block:

```
console.log(`Block Number: ${blockNumber} Transaction ID:
${transactionId} Status: ${status}`);

var trans=JSON.parse(event.payload.toString());
console.log(trans);
```

3. If the receiving bank in the transaction payload (`trans.Rbank`) is Bank A, we fetch the balance of the receiving customer in the `customers` table. To do so, we use the `pg` client and run a `SELECT` query on the table filtered by the customer's account, as follows:

```
if(trans.Rbank == 'Bank A')
 {

 client.query('SELECT balance from customers where account = $1',
[trans.Raccount], (error, results)=> {

 if (error) {
 throw error
 }
```

4. On a successful response, we add the transaction amount to the current balance of the customer and update the customer's new balance in the `customers` table, like this:

```
if(results)
 {
 var oldbal = results.rows[0].balance;
 var newbal = Number(oldbal) + Number(trans.amt);

 client.query('UPDATE customers set balance = $1 where account =
$2', [newbal, trans.Raccount], (error,  results) => {
```

5. After successfully updating the customer's balance, we insert the transaction into the `transactions` table. Notice in the following code block that we set the `transtype` flag to `Incoming`:

```
if (error) {
 throw error
 }

 client.query('INSERT INTO transactions(transaction_id,saddress,
saccount,sname, sbank, raddress, raccount, rname, rbank, amount,
currency, invhash, boehash, dochash, transtype) values ($1, $2, $3,
$4, $5, $6, $7, $8, $9, $10, $11, $12, $13, $14, $15)',
[trans.txid,trans.Saddr, trans.Saccount, trans.Sname, trans.Sbank,
trans.Raddress, trans.Raccount, trans.Rname,
trans.Rbank,trans.amt,trans.curr,trans.InvHash,trans.BOEHash,trans.
DocHash, 'Incoming'], (error, results) => {
```

6. After successfully updating the transaction to the `transactions` table, we call the `iread()` method to save the compliance files to the bank infrastructure's local storage. The `iread()` method takes the hash of the three compliance documents as input parameters, and fetches the documents from the IPFS network, as follows:

```
if (error) {
throw error
 }

iread(trans.InvHash,trans.BOEHash,trans.DocHash);
 })
```

That wraps up the transaction listener. Let's look at the `iread()` method.

Writing a method to fetch compliance documents from IPFS

The `iread()` method takes the invoice document hash (`invhash`), the BOE/BOL hash (`boehash`), and any other document hash (`dochash`) as input parameters, as shown in the following code block:

```
async function iread (invhash,boehash,dochash) {
try
{
```

Let's look at the logic for our code:

1. We fetch the invoice file from the IPFS network by using the invoice document hash (`invhash`). The file is saved to the local storage. In my case, I've stored the file in the `public` folder of my bank portal React app. We use the `fs` module to create a new file, and write the file contents to the file. The filename in the local storage follows the nomenclature `<File hash>.txt`.

   Let's look at how the file is fetched from IPFS using the hash value:

   ```
   const invfile = await ipfs.get(invhash)

   invfile.forEach((file) => {

   var url =
   '/home/ishan/CorpRemApp/CorpRemApp/public/uploads/'+invhash+'.txt';
   var writeStream = fs.createWriteStream(url);
   writeStream.write(file.content.toString('utf8'));
   ```

```
writeStream.end();
})
```

2. We follow the same flow for the other compliance documents, as shown in the following code block:

```
const boefile = await ipfs.get(boehash)
boefile.forEach((file) => {
var url =
'/home/ishan/CorpRemApp/CorpRemApp/public/uploads/'+boehash+'.txt';
var writeStream = fs.createWriteStream(url);
writeStream.write(file.content.toString('utf8'));
writeStream.end();
})

    const docfile = await ipfs.get(dochash)
docfile.forEach((file) => {
var url =
'/home/ishan/CorpRemApp/CorpRemApp/public/uploads/'+dochash+'.txt';
var writeStream = fs.createWriteStream(url);
writeStream.write(file.content.toString('utf8'));
writeStream.end();
})
```

A `catch` block catches any errors during execution, as shown in the following code block:

```
catch (error) {
 console.error(`Failed to write: ${error}`);
 }
}
```

That wraps up our transaction listener. The transaction listener for Bank B will follow the same steps. The changes that need to be made are mentioned in the next section.

Changes for transaction listener for Bank B

Duplicate the `TransListener-BankA.js` file for the transaction listener for Bank B, and rename it `TransListener-BankB.js`. Make the following changes to the code:

1. Change the `ipfs` client object to the client port for the Bank B IPFS node, as follows:

```
const ipfs = ipfsClient('http://localhost:5002')
```

2. Change the `conString` object, used to connect to `postgres`, to the following values for the `bankb` database:

```
const conString = "postgres://bankb:bankb@localhost:5432/bankb";
```

3. Set the `ccpPath` object to the location of the connection profile for Bank B, like this:

```
const ccpPath = '~/fabric-samples/bankchain/connection-bankb.json';
```

4. Substitute the location of the wallet with the user's identity for Bank B, like this:

```
const wallet = new FileSystemWallet('~/fabric-samples/bankchain/wallet-BankB');
```

5. Change the `if` clause for the listener to `Bank B`, to check for transactions where Bank B is the receiving bank, as follows:

```
 if(trans.Rbank == 'Bank B')
```

6. Change the wallet path for Bank B, like this:

```
        const wallet = new FileSystemWallet('~/fabric-
        samples/bankchain/wallet-BankB');
```

That wraps up both the transaction listeners.

Bring both the listeners online. Run the following command in separate Terminal windows:

```
$node TransListener-BankA.js
$node TransListener-BankB.js
```

`TransListeners` should both come online. The listeners will print the `Gateway Connected` message on the console to indicate that the listener is connected to the blockchain network and is listening for events.

That completes our backend infrastructure for both the banks. Next, we'll build a corporate remittance app frontend that will interact with the backend and allow users to submit transactions and view submitted transactions.

Creating the corporate remittance app frontend in React

We need to create a frontend that will interact with the backend server and allow users to submit transactions and view submitted transactions.

The app should render three screens:

The **Bank login** screen

The **Transfer** screen

The **View Transactions** screen

The user logs in using the **Bank login** screen. They can either log in as Acme Inc or Apex Corp, by clicking on the **Acme Inc.** button or the **Apex Corp** button.

After logging in, they land on the **Transfer** screen. Here, they can initiate a new transfer request by filling in the details of the remittance, including the receiver's name, account number, bank and address, and the transaction amount and currency. They also need to upload the compliance documents, which include the invoice document, BOE/BOL, and any other document they want.

On clicking on **Submit**, a new remittance transfer request is initiated and sent to the backend server for processing. After the backend confirms the success of the transaction, the user is notified of the **Tx Status** on the screen.

On clicking on **View Transactions**, the app fetches all of the user's transactions from the database and renders it on the screen. The user can view all incoming or outgoing transactions. By default, all incoming transactions are shown. The user can view all transaction details, including the compliance documents. The screen renders a separate link to view each document. On clicking on the link, the document is downloaded from the server's local storage.

The following are the main members of our app:

- There's main App.js file.
- There's following React components:
    - AppLogin.js
    - Transfer.js
    - ViewTransactions.js

Let's start building the app.

You can download the entire app code at the GitHub repository, at this link: `https://github.com/PacktPublishing/Blockchain-Development-for-Finance-Projects/tree/master/Chapter%204/CorpRemApp/src`.

Creating the React project environment

Before we can create our React app, we need to set the project directory and install the dependencies for our app, as follows:

1. Create a new React app called `CorpRemApp`, using `npx`, like this:

   ```
   npx create-react-app CorpRemApp
   ```

2. Update your `package.json` file to the following values:

   ```
   {
     "name": "CorpRemApp",
     "version": "1.0.0",
     "private": false,
     "dependencies": {
     "bulma-start": "0.0.2",
     "react": "^16.4.1",
     "react-dom": "^16.4.1",
     "react-scripts": "1.1.4"
     },
     "scripts": {
     "start": "react-scripts start",
     "build": "react-scripts build",
     "test": "react-scripts test --env=jsdom",
     "eject": "react-scripts eject"
     }
   }
   ```

3. Run `npm install` on the Terminal window to install the dependencies.
4. Next, within the `src` folder, create a `Components` folder for the app components.

Let's go through the components, one by one.

Building the container component

The container component has a fairly straightforward logic. It accepts the current state of the app from the app.js file. It checks the current value of the account state variable to see whether its value is not null, indicating the customer has successfully logged in to the app. If the value is null, the container renders the AppLogin.js component so that the user can log in.

If the account variable is not null, the container component next checks the ViewFlag state variable. If ViewFlag is set to 1, it indicates that the Transfer.js component needs to be rendered. If ViewFlag is set to 2, it indicates that the ViewTransactions.js component needs to be rendered.

Depending on the value of the ViewFlag state variable, the container component renders the Transfer.js or the ViewTransactions.js component and passes the required state and methods to the component.

The container component also renders the AddressBar component that shows the user's account number on the screen.

You can view the code for the container component at the GitHub repository, at this link: https://github.com/PacktPublishing/Blockchain-Development-for-Finance-Projects/blob/master/Chapter%204/CorpRemApp/src/Components/Container.js.

Building the AppLogin component

The AppLogin component renders a login screen with two buttons—**Log in as Acme Inc.** and **Log in as Apex Corp**. On clicking a button, the user is logged in to the app with the customer they select.

At the code level, the component calls the setAccount() method to set the bank customer account as Acme Inc or Apex Corp. The component passes the value 1 as an input parameter to the setAccount() method if the customer selected is Acme Inc. For Apex Corp, it sends the value 2, as shown in the following code block:

```
return (
  <div className="panel-block is-paddingless is-12" >
  <div className="column is-12" id="token-lists">

  <div className="column has-text-centered">
  <span className="button is-medium is-success" onClick={() =>
props.setAccount(1) }>
```

```
Login as Acme Inc.
</span >
</div>
<div className="column has-text-centered">
<span className="button is-medium is-info" onClick={() =>
props.setAccount(2)}>
Login as Apex Corp
</span >

</div>
</div>
</div>
)
```

Next, let's look at the `Transfer` component.

Building the Transfer component

The `Transfer` component allows the user to enter the remittance detail and initiate a new transaction. It submits the transaction request to the backend. On the response from the backend, it informs the user whether the transaction was successful or whether it failed.

Let's look at the code.

The `Transfer` component renders a screen with five text input fields and three file input fields. The fields include the following:

- Receiver's Name (Text)
- Receiver's Account (Text)
- Receiver's Bank (Text)
- Receiver's Address (Text)
- Proforma Invoice/Invoice (File)
- BOE/BOL (File)
- Any Other Document (File)
- Amount (In USD) (Text)

After clicking on the **Submit** button, the request is submitted to the backend server.

After successful transaction processing, the `Tx Status` tag informs the user whether the transaction went through or if it failed.

Lastly, the component renders a menu bar on the top. Users can cycle between the **Transfer** screen and the `ViewTransactions` screen by clicking on the **Transfer** button or the **View Transactions** button. The component calls the `TabView()` method, with the value 1 for the **Transfer** screen, and 2 for the `ViewTransactions` component. This value is then updated to the `ViewFlag` state variable.

You can view the code for the `Transfer` component at this GitHub repository link: `https://github.com/PacktPublishing/Blockchain-Development-for-Finance-Projects/blob/master/Chapter%204/CorpRemApp/src/Components/Transfer.js`.

Building the ViewTransactions component

The `ViewTransactions` component renders the customer's transaction details on the screen. It allows the customers to choose whether if they want to see their incoming or outgoing transactions by rendering a menu bar with the **Incoming** and **Outcoming** buttons.

On clicking the **Incoming** button, the `TransFlag` state variable is set to 1, and all incoming transactions are displayed on the screen. On clicking the **Outgoing** button, the `TransFlag` state variable is set to 2, and all outgoing transactions are displayed on the screen.

At the code level, the `ViewTransactions` component first renders a menu bar with the **Incoming Tx** and **Outgoing Tx** buttons. On clicking the buttons, the `TransSet()` method is called with the input parameter as 1 for incoming transactions, and 2 for outgoing transactions. The `TransSet()` method sets the value of the `TransFlag` state variable.

Next, the component renders the transactions on the screen. To do so, it maps the `trans` state variable on the screen. The `trans` state variable is an array that contains all of the transactions of the customer.

If `TransFlag` is set to 1, it indicates the user has requested to view only incoming transactions. The render function hides all transactions where the `transtype` value is `Outgoing`—that is, the transaction is an outgoing transaction.

If `TransFlag` is set to 2, it indicates the user has requested to view only outgoing transactions. The `render` function hides all transactions where the `transtype` value is `Incoming`— that is, the transaction is an incoming transaction.

Based on the preceding conditions, the `render` method prints all of the transaction details on the screen, including the following:

- `Transaction ID`
- Sender's Name
- Sender's Account
- Sender's Address
- Sender's Bank
- Receiver's Name
- Receiver's Account
- Receiver's Address
- Receiver's Bank
- Transaction Currency
- Transaction Amount
- Link to Invoice Document
- Link to BOE/BOL Document
- Link to Other Document

To generate the links to the compliance documents, we use the hash value of the documents. If you remember, when we built the transaction listener for Bank A and Bank B, we fetched the compliance documents from the IPFS network, after receiving a new transaction.

The documents were stored in the following location:

```
~/CorpRemApp/public/uploads/
```

Basically, this is the `public` folder of our app. The files were saved in the following format:

```
<Hash of the document>.txt
```

Hence, to retrieve the files from the frontend, we simply provide a link to this location. For example, to fetch the invoice document, we render the following link on the screen:

```
<a href={'uploads/' + tx.invhash+'.txt'} download>
```

This will basically generate a download link to the invoice document. The customer can click on the link to download and view the document.

You can view the code for the `ViewTransactions` component at the following GitHub repository link: `https://github.com/PacktPublishing/Blockchain-Development-for-Finance-Projects/blob/master/Chapter%204/CorpRemApp/src/Components/ViewTransactions.js`.

Let's look at the methods in our main `App.js` file.

Writing the methods in the App.js file

The `App.js` file defines the methods that are called by the components and passes them to the container component. It also sets the app initial state and passes it on to the container component.

You can view the `App.js` at the GitHub repository, at this link: `https://github.com/PacktPublishing/Blockchain-Development-for-Finance-Projects/blob/master/Chapter%204/CorpRemApp/src/App.js`.

Let's look at the methods defined by the `App.js` file.

Writing the constructor

The constructor is called when the app first loads, and it sets the app's initial state and defines the app's name, which is displayed by the `Description` container.

It sets the following state variables:

- `userID`: It sets the customer's `userID` to 1, which is the `userID` for both Acme Inc and Apex Corp in the Bank A and Bank B databases, respectively.
- `network`: It sets the network variable to `Private Testnet`.
- `server`: This is the default value of the listening port of the backend server of Bank A. This value is changed to `8001` when the Bank B customer (Apex Corp) logs in.
- `account`: This initializes the account variable as null.
- `balance`: This initializes the customer's balance to `0` before we fetch the actual balance from the backend.
- `name`: This initializes the customer name.
- `trans`: This initializes the `trans` object that stores the transactions after fetching it from the backend server.

- `ViewFlag`: This initializes the flag with the value 1.
- `TransFlag`: This initializes the flag with the value 1.
- `Fields`: This initializes the `rname` (Receiver's Name), `rbank` (Receiver's Bank), `raddress`(Receiver's Address), `raccount`(Receiver's Account), and `amount` (Transaction Amount) fields.

Next, let's look at how we set the user account.

Writing a method for setting the user account

The `setAccount()` method is called by the `AppLogin` component. Depending on whether the user clicks on Acme Inc or Apex Corp, the input parameter, 1 or 2, is sent to the method.

If the value of the input parameter is 2, indicating the customer is Apex Corp (a Bank B customer), the server state variable is set to `localhost:8001`, which is the listening port of the backend server of Bank B, as shown in the following code block:

```
if (flag == 2)
 {
 server = 'localhost:8001'
 };
```

Next, we fetch the customer's details from the backend server. We make a `fetch` call to the `/customerinfo` API endpoint, like this:

```
var url = 'http://'+ server +'/customerinfo';
 fetch(url, {
 method: 'POST',
 headers: {
 'Accept': 'application/json',
 'Content-Type': 'application/json',
 },
 body: JSON.stringify({
 userId : app.state.userId
 })
 }).then(function(response,error){
```

- On the response from the backend server, we parse the response object for the customer's name, account, address, and current balance. We set these values to the app state.
- Additionally, a `bank` variable is also added to the app state. The `bank` variable is to Bank A or Bank B, depending on whether the input parameter to the `setAccount()` method was 1 or 2. We also add the `server` variable with the listening port of the bank backend server, as follows:

```
then(function(data){

  var bank;

if(flag == 1)
  {
  bank = 'Bank A';
  }
  else
  {
  bank = 'Bank B';
  }

  app.setState({
  name: data.name,
  account: data.account,
  balance: data.balance,
  address: data.address,
  bank: bank,
  server: server
  });
```

Next, let's look at the view setters for the app.

Writing methods to toggle between app components

The `TabView()` and `TransSet()` methods allow us to toggle between the various screens available in the app, as follows:

- The `TabView` method is called when the user toggles between the `Transfer` screen and the `ViewTransactions` screen through the navigation.
- It expects an input parameter with the value 1 for rendering the `Transfer` screen and 2 for rendering the `ViewTransactions` screen. It sets the value of the `ViewFlag` state variable.

- If the value of the input parameter is 2, indicating the `ViewTransactions` screen, it calls the `TransSet` method to set the screen, to show the customer's outgoing transactions by default.
- It also calls `setTransactions()`, to populate the `trans` array object with the customer's transactions.

The `trans` object will be mapped and printed on the screen by the `ViewTransactions` component, as follows:

```
TabView = (flag) => {

if( flag == 2)
{
this.TransSet(2);
this.setTransactions();
}

this.setState({
ViewFlag: flag
});
}
```

The `TransSet` method is called when the user toggles between incoming and outgoing transactions on the `ViewTransactions` screen.

It simply accepts the value of the input parameter and sets the `TransFlag` state variable, and calls the `setTransactions()` method to update the `trans` array object with the user's transactions, as follows:

```
TransSet = (flag) => {

this.setState({
TransFlag: flag

});
this.setTransactions();
}
```

Next, let's look at the input change handlers.

Writing methods to handle input fields

We are handling two kinds of inputs in our app: text-based and file-based inputs.

The text-based inputs are handled by the `onInputChangeUpdateField` method. It tracks any changes in the text input fields and updates the values to the state fields array, where it can be accessed by the other methods of the app, as follows:

```
onInputChangeUpdateField = (name,value) => {
  let fields = this.state.fields;

  fields[name] = value;

this.setState({
  fields
  });
  };
```

The file-based inputs are handled by three change handlers, one for each type of file (invoice, BOE/BOL, and other document).

It listens to any file selection events. If a file is selected, it fetches the details of the file and adds it to the app state. It also updates the filename in the app state so that it can be displayed to the user.

The following is the change handler for the invoice document:

```
onChangeHandlerInv = event =>{

  console.log(event.target.files[0]);

  this.setState({
  InvFile: event.target.files[0],
  InvFname: event.target.files[0].name
  })

  }
```

The change handler for the BOE/BOL document and other documents follows a mechanism similar to this one.

Writing a method to submit payment requests

The `payment()` method will submit a new payment request to the backend infrastructure. It is called when the `Submit` button is clicked on the **Transfer** screen. Let's look at the `payment()` method:

1. We start the method by declaring a `FormData` object. The details for the transaction are added to the `FormData` object. These include the sender's details, the receiver's details, the transaction amount and currency, and the details of the compliance documents to be uploaded. We fetch the sender's details from the state and the receiver's details from the input fields. The currency is set to `USD` by default, as shown in the following code block:

```
payment = () => {
const data = new FormData();

data.append('sname',this.state.name);
data.append('saccount',this.state.account);
data.append('sbank',this.state.bank);
data.append('saddress',this.state.address);
data.append('rname',this.state.fields.rname);
data.append('raccount',this.state.fields.raccount);
data.append('rbank',this.state.fields.rbank);
data.append('raddress',this.state.fields.raddress);
data.append('amount',this.state.fields.amount);
data.append('currency','USD');
data.append('invfile',this.state.InvFile);
data.append('boefile',this.state.BOEFile);
data.append('docfile',this.state.DocFile);
```

2. Next, we add this `FormData` object to the request body, and submit the request to the `/payment` endpoint of our backend server, like this:

```
let app = this;
var url = 'http://'+ this.state.server +'/payment';
fetch(url, {
method: 'POST',
body: data}).
then(function(response,error) {
```

3. On receiving a response from the backend, we reset the fields and then set the user balance again, by calling the `resetApp()` and `setBalance()` methods respectively. The response data with the `Transaction successfully submitted` or `Transaction failed` message is updated to the `txstatus` state variable.

The `Transfer` component will display this message to the user, as follows:

```
if(response)
{
app.setBalance();
app.resetApp();
return response.json();
}
else
{
console.log(error);
}
}).then(function(data){
   console.log(data);
       app.setState({
           txstatus: data
       });
})
```

Next, let's look at the method that fetches the customer's transactions from the backend.

Writing a method to fetch customer transactions

The `setTransactions()` method fetches the customer's transactions by calling the `/gettrans` endpoint in the backend server.

It sends the customer's account in the request body, and all transactions to or from the customer account are returned in the response object, as follows:

1. We first call the `/gettrans` endpoint with the customer's account. We fetch the account from the app state, like this:

```
setTransactions()
{
let app = this;
 var url = 'http://'+ this.state.server +'/gettrans';
 fetch(url, {
 method: 'POST',
 headers: {
 'Accept': 'application/json',
 'Content-Type': 'application/json',
 },body: JSON.stringify({
 account : app.state.account
 })
 })
```

2. On receiving a response from the endpoint, we check for any errors. If there are no errors, we parse the JSON body to get the transaction data. The transaction data is then stored in the `trans` array in the app state, as follows:

```
.then(function(response,error){
if(response)
{
return response.json();
}
else
{
console.log(error);
}
}).then(function(data){
app.setState({
trans: data.tx
});
})
}
```

Let's look at the method used to set the user balance.

Writing a method to set the current user balance

The `setBalance()` method is called to set the current user balance. It is always invoked after a new transaction is submitted to the server. It calls the `/customerinfo` endpoint and updates the new balance to the app state, as follows:

1. We call the `/customerinfo` endpoint with the customer's `userID` from the app state, like this:

```
setBalance = () => {
let app = this;
var url = 'http://'+ this.state.server +'/customerinfo';
fetch(url, {
method: 'POST',
headers: {
'Accept': 'application/json',
'Content-Type': 'application/json',
},body: JSON.stringify({
userId : app.state.userId
})
}).then(function(response,error){
```

2. On receiving a response from the /customerinfo endpoint, we fetch the balance variable and update it to the app state, like this:

```
if(response)
{
return response.json();
}
else
{
console.log(error);
}
}).then(function(data){

app.setState({
balance: data.balance
});
})
}
```

That brings us to the end of our frontend and all of the components we need to develop for our project. In the next section, let's try out an end-to-end remittance transaction and see how the project works.

Running the corporate remittance app

Let's bring our blockchain network and application online. Make sure your Fabric network is up and running and the corprem chaincode is deployed. Also, ensure that identities have been created for writing to and reading transactions from the blockchain network for both the banks.

Also, ensure that the databases are set up with the test data. Do a quick check to see both the IPFS nodes are running. Bring the backend servers for both Bank A and Bank B online.

Let's start our React app, as follows:

1. Navigate to your React project environment. Start the React app with the following command:

   ```
   npm start
   ```

2. Open your browser and navigate to the home page for the app. The app should look like this:

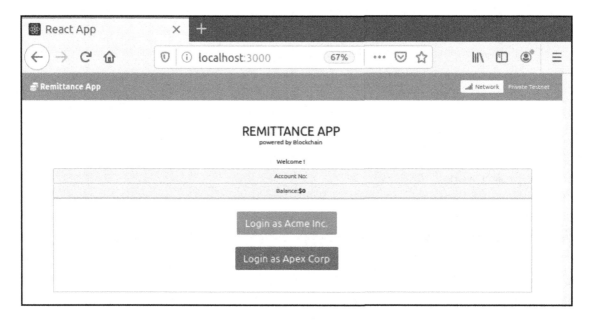

3. Let's log in to the app with the **Acme Inc** user. Click on the button that says **Login as Acme Inc**. A transfer screen like the following one should open:

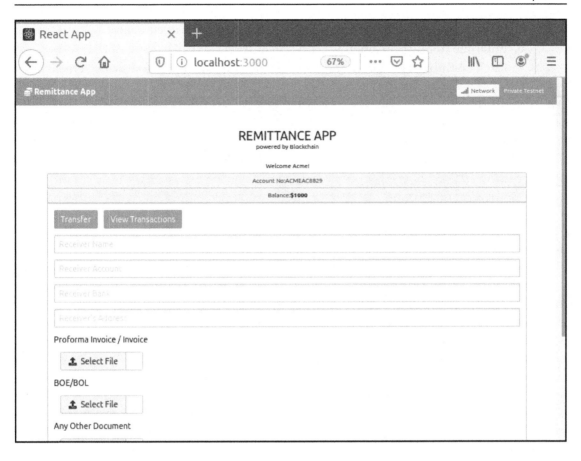

4. Let's try out a transaction. Enter the transaction details for an Apex Corp customer in Bank B. Enter the following details for the transaction:

- **Receiver Customer: Apex**
- **Receiver Account: APXAC09002**
- **Receiver's Address: Dubai**
- **Receiver's Bank: Bank B**

5. Upload a sample invoice file, BOE/BOL file, and other documents.
6. Enter the transaction amount. I am transferring 800 USD.
7. Click on **Submit** to submit the transaction, as shown in the following screenshot:

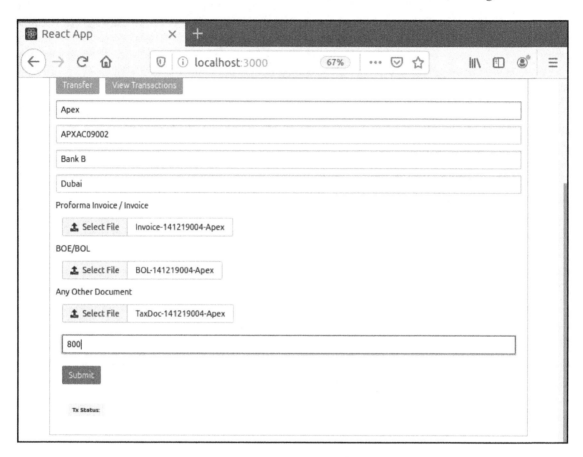

The transaction is now submitted to the backend, where it will be processed and forwarded to the blockchain network. The transaction documents will be uploaded and added to IPFS. After the successful processing of the transaction, the user's balance will be updated, the transaction will be added to the transactions table, and the control will return to the frontend.

At this point, the frontend **Tx Status** tag will show you a `Transaction successfully submitted` message, as follows:

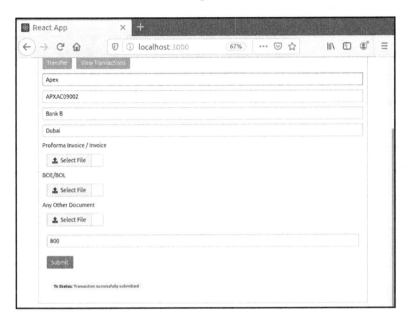

8. Click on the **View Transactions** button and then the **Outgoing Tx** button to view this transaction's details, as shown in the following screenshot:

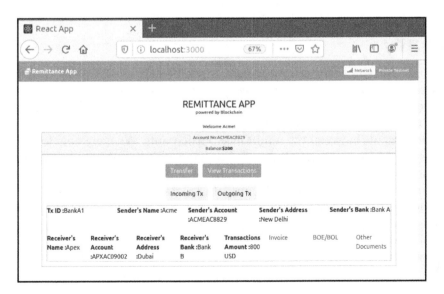

9. Next, log out of the **Acme Inc** user and log in to the **Apex Corp** user. Click on the **View Transactions** button, and then the **Incoming Tx** button to view this transaction in the Bank B user's portal, as shown in the following screenshot:

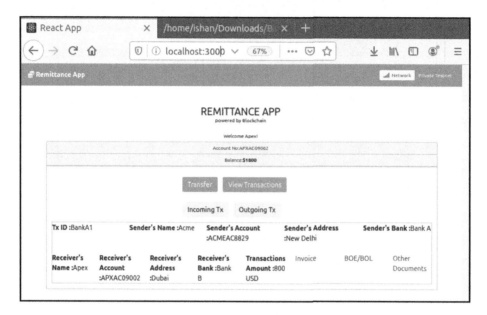

With this, we come to the end of the demonstration of our app.

Summary

That brings us to the end of the corporate remittance blockchain app project. This chapter gives you a good insight into using multiple tools to accomplish your end goal when building a blockchain app. In this specific case, we used Hyperledger Fabric for sharing transaction details on a shared ledger between participants, and we used IPFS to share transaction documents between the remittance participants. We were able to leverage both the platforms to build a real-time corporate remittance solution to circumvent a lot of the challenges faced by current remittance solutions, including reconciliation, visibility of transactions, exchange of compliance documents, creating a transparent and real-time workflow, and so on. Corporate remittance is probably one of the most important Blockchain use cases (if not the most important), and I hope this chapter will enable you to design complex products and workflows, adhering to the requirements of different corporate remittance use cases.

We started the chapter by understanding corporate remittances and how blockchain technology can help to make them better and more efficient. Next, we looked at an outline for our project and the different steps we would execute. Next, we set up a customer Hyperledger Fabric network called Bankchain between the Bank A and Bank B banks, created identities for the users of Bank A and Bank B on the network, and wrote and deployed our corporate remittance chaincode. We also set up a two-node IPFS network to share documents between the banks, and a backend database for storing customer and transaction details.

We built backend servers for Bank A and Bank B to provide an interface between the bank portal frontend and the blockchain network, the databases, and the IPFS network. Two transaction listeners were created, one for Bank A and one for Bank B, to listen for incoming transactions to the banks on the blockchain network, fetch the transaction details and documents, and save these to the bank's local infrastructure. Lastly, we built a bank portal in the frontend to allow the Acme Inc customer of Bank A and the Apex Corp customer of Bank B to log in, submit transactions, and view transaction details.

The main takeaway from this chapter is understanding how powerful the Hyperledger Fabric platform is and how it can be used to build complex banking and financial ecosystems and products that are more efficient and transparent than current processes. At the same time, I hope you were able to understand how to leverage IPFS for your blockchain projects. Another major takeaway is understanding how blockchain and distributed ledger technologies can be used to redesign and re-engineer current process flows, to build banking and financial systems of the future.

In the next chapter, we'll be looking at how the Stellar network can be used for retail remittances while enabling real-time **Know Your Customer** (**KYC**) and AML checks on a transaction.

5
Enabling Cross-Border Remittances with Real-Time KYC/AML Verification

In this chapter, we will be building a prototype cross-border blockchain retail remittance platform for banks. Cross-border remittances are a complex affair from a compliance and settlement point of view. Banks need to devise complex workflows to carry out compliance checks of the remitter and the beneficiary. The sending bank, receiving bank, and other partner banks need to agree on the compliance requirements of the sender and the receiver before remittance transactions can be executed or credited to the beneficiary. For carrying out a settlement, the sending and the receiving banks need to have an elaborate workflow where they have the visibility of incoming funds. Often, they might have to rely on partner banks—known as correspondence banks—to carry out the remittance process, which results in it taking a much longer time for funds to be paid out to the end beneficiary.

The following topics will be covered in this chapter:

- Technical requirements
- Designing a workflow for blockchain cross-border remittance
- Setting up a test network
- Creating user accounts
- Setting up bank domains
- Setting up the federation servers

- Setting up the compliance servers
- Setting up the bridge servers
- Setting up the callbacks server
- Building the bank portal
- Running the remittance platform

Technical requirements

You can access the code files of this chapter on the following GitHub link:

```
https://github.com/PacktPublishing/Blockchain-Development-for-Finance-Projects/
tree/master/Chapter%205/Cross%20Border
```

For this project, we'll be working with the Stellar/quickstart Docker container provided by the Stellar Foundation for trying out the Stellar platform. The details of the Docker image can be found at the following link: `https://hub.docker.com/r/stellar/quickstart/`.

I'm using Ubuntu 18.04.2 LTS for running the applications and deploying my blockchain. This project assumes that you are working on a UNIX operating system. Additionally, this project assumes you have **node.js** and **npm** installed. I'm using **node version 13.0.1** and **npm version 6.12.0.** You would also need the latest version of Docker and Docker Compose.

We'll be launching a Docker container with a single node, single client-server private instance of the Stellar platform.

To download the Docker image and launch the container, run the following command in a Terminal window:

```
docker run --rm -it -p "8000:8000" --name stellar stellar/quickstart --
standalone
```

This runs a standalone instance of the Stellar network with a single client and single node that will act as our development environment. It also runs a Postgres instance that stores transaction data that can be retrieved using the Horizon client.

We'll be configuring this network instance further in the *Setting up a Test Network* section.

Designing a workflow for blockchain cross-border remittance

For this project, you will attempt to build a prototype that seeks to eliminate inefficiencies in cross-border remittance. For the current project, we will be using the Stellar protocol, which comes with inbuilt modules that can be leveraged for KYC/AML workflows. For our project, we'll be building a remittance network with two banks, Bank A and Bank B. Each bank will have an in-house IT infrastructure with the following components:

- A user/customer database.
- A transactions database, which keeps a log of all incoming/received transactions and related metadata.
- A sanctions database, which holds sanction approvals for financial institutions and remitters.
- A compliance module, which will be used to carry out AML/KYC checks for payments.
- A federation module that allocates user-friendly payment addresses for customers to send and receive payments. These are similar to email IDs for payments.
- A bridge module, which will allow the bank to send payments on our blockchain network and listen for incoming payments to our account on the blockchain network.
- A bank portal, where users can log in and submit payment requests and the bank administration can view KYC/AML details of the received transactions.

The bank's IT infrastructure will connect to a private test Stellar network that we'll set up for our development activity. We'll be creating Stellar accounts for Bank A and Bank B on this network for sending and receiving payments. Finally, we'll be issuing the USD asset on the network, which will be the currency that's remitted between the banks.

Understanding how a payment request works

Before we start building our project, let's understand the journey of a payment request as it moves across our remittance platform. We'll also do a deep dive into the various components and modules. This will give you a good understanding of the functionality of each module when we are building our platform. For this example, consider Bank A to be the sending bank, that is, the bank that is sending the remittance and Bank B to be the bank that is receiving the payment.

The payment request begins with the customer logging into a banking portal. Typically, they'll enter the beneficiary's name, their account name, a beneficiary bank identifier code, such as a SWIFT BAN number, the amount to send, and the currency in which the payment will be credited to the beneficiary. In our blockchain remittance app, the customer's account number and SWIFT BAN number are replaced by a user-friendly ID that looks like an email ID. Thus, to send the payment to a customer called Stephen at Bank A, I only need to provide his friendly ID, which will look something like `Stephen*banka.com`. The first part of the ID is a unique identifier, while the second part after the asterisk indicates the domain, typically a domain controlled by the Bank A. When a payment request is to be sent, our remittance app automatically communicates with the `banka.com` domain and fetches Stephen's bank account number, customer number, and any other details that may be required for the payment to be processed.

After the remitter enters the beneficiary details, they need to enter the amount to be transferred and the destination currency, that is, the currency in which the beneficiary will be credited. Typically, banks and other FIs provide internal conversion rates for converting the source currency, that is, the currency in which the sender initiates a transaction to the destination currency. Sometimes, you can get a rate from an external market maker who does the conversion for the banks. In the Stellar network, you can actually set up a market maker of your own. (We'll be looking at this in `Chapter 9`, *Developing a Currency Trading Exchange for Market Making on Currency Exchanges*). In our project, to keep things simple, we'll assume the source and the destination currency are both US dollars, but you can easily integrate an API for conversion rates.

Lastly, they may need to provide identification details such as the name, address, date of birth, and so on for AML/KYC purposes. In our platform, we'll automatically fetch these details from the User Database. This means that the sender does not need to fill in these details explicitly. The customer clicks on submit to submit the payment request.

On clicking submit, the payment request is posted to the Bank A bridge server module. The Bank A bridge server carries out a series of steps:

1. First, it checks with Bank B and confirms whether a user exists with the beneficiary friendly ID that was entered in the payment request. If a user exists, Bank B returns the beneficiary's payment routing details (internal account number, internal customer number, Stellar account ID, and so on) to the bridge server. These details will be used to build the payment transaction that we will submit to the blockchain network. This metadata will help the receiving bank identify the customer that the payment is intended for.

2. Next, the bridge server of Bank A forwards the payment request to the compliance module of Bank A. The compliance module of Bank A checks the details of the sender and confirms if they are sanctioned to send a cross-border remittance – that is, the customer is not blacklisted – and fetches the KYC details of the sender from the internal user database. The compliance module of Bank A then communicates with the compliance module of Bank B, which is the receiving bank, and forwards the KYC details of the remitter/ sender.

3. The compliance module of Bank B receives the sender's details and carries out internal sanctions checks. Sanction checks are carried out to check whether the sender or the financial institution sending the transaction is blacklisted. It also verifies whether the beneficiary can receive the payment, that is, that the beneficiary is not blacklisted. If everything is in order, the compliance module of Bank B gives the go-ahead to Bank A to initiate the remittance transaction. If required, the compliance module of Bank A will also share the KYC details of the receiver/beneficiary with Bank A if required. These KYC details are typically the name, address, and date of birth of the beneficiary.

4. After the compliance module of Bank A gets the go-ahead from the compliance module of Bank B, it relays the go-ahead message to the bridge server of Bank A. The bridge server submits the payment request to the Stellar blockchain network. Typically, the request contains the sender's Stellar account ID, the receiver's Stellar account ID, the metadata to identify the customer (customer ID, account number, and so on), the currency being transferred, and the amount being transferred. Stellar account IDs are similar to Ethereum accounts or Bitcoin addresses. They are public keys and have a linked secret key that is used to sign the transactions that are being submitted to the network. In our remittance model, only the financial institution has a Stellar account ID, on the blockchain network. All the customers of a financial institution are mapped to this account ID. This is why we need to provide the metadata to identify the customer the payment is intended for. This model allows us to cut down on the cost of managing multiple public-private keys and tracking multiple accounts.

5. Once the payment has been submitted to the network, it is broadcasted to all the nodes in the network, including the node to which Bank B, the receiving bank, is connected. The bridge server of the receiving bank, Bank B, is constantly listening for payments to the bank's Stellar account. Upon receiving a payment, it carries out a series of steps. First, it checks whether the compliance handshake was carried out for the payment request. Next, it checks the beneficiary that the payment is intended for and if the beneficiary is sanctioned to receive the payment. If all the checks are passed, the amount is credited to the beneficiary's account. The beneficiary can now log into the bank portal and view the payment. The bank user can log into the portal and see the KYC/AML details of the received payment. That ends our payment flow.

This should give you an idea of how the end-to-end remittance flow works and how our app will function. Now, let's start working on the project. We'll be carrying out the following steps to set up and build the entire project:

1. Set up a private test Stellar network for development.
2. Create the USD asset, representing the US dollar asset that will be transferred.
3. Create the Stellar account IDs for Bank A and Bank B on the network and add a USD balance to them to try out remittances.
4. Set up local domain redirection for the `banka.com` and `bankb.com` domains so that we can try out the friendly ID resolution (federation) service for customers.
5. Set up the apache2 server that will host a `TOML` file. This `TOML` file will guide incoming requests to the bridge, compliance, and federation servers being run by the bank.
6. Set up the federation service or friendly ID resolution service for Bank A and Bank B.
7. Set up the compliance module for Bank A and Bank B that will handle all incoming and outgoing compliance requests.
8. Set up the bridge server for Bank A and Bank B that will be the bank portal's interface with the Stellar network.
9. Set up a callback server. As the name suggests, this will implement webhooks that can be invoked when a payment is received or when compliance data needs to be verified with the internal bank database.
10. Build a bank portal and backend service in React that will allow the customers and the bank to interact with the Stellar network and submit and receive payments. The bank user can also view the KYC details of received transactions.

We have a long road ahead of us! Let's get started with the network setup.

Setting up a test network

To build our project, we'll launch a simple Stellar network that contains a single blockchain node and a single client-server. The blockchain node in Stellar is called Stellar Core while the client-server is called **Horizon**. Horizon is a client-API server that extends a suite of handy endpoints that allow application developers to view transaction data and statistics and submit transactions to the core blockchain node. Similar to `web3-js`, Stellar has a Stellar Javascript SDK, which allows us to build requests that we can use to interact with Horizon.

Stellar provides a handy Docker image that can be used to quickly launch an ephemeral (temporary) or persistent (permanent) container so that we can implement the Stellar network. This docker container contains an instance of Stellar Core, an instance of Horizon, and the necessary installed dependencies, such as PostgreSQL and a Go environment:

1. To launch this docker image, simply run the following command in a Terminal window:

```
docker run --rm -it -p "8000:8000" --name stellar
stellar/quickstart --standalone
```

The preceding command downloads the Stellar/quickstart image from from Docker Hub and runs a container with Stellar Core and Horizon. Notice the docker proxy port at 8000. The docker proxy port extends the Horizon port inside the container. This means that any requests to Horizon can be submitted to the 8000 port of the host machine.

2. Wait for the container to come online. It will initiate a postgresql database, Stellar Core, and Horizon. After the container comes online successfully, you should be able to see the docker-proxy on port 8000 on your machine. Open a browser window and go http://localhost:8000.

You should be able to see the Horizon client-server, with the following client endpoints:

```
{
  "_links": {
    "account": {
      "href": "http://localhost:8000/accounts/{account_id}",
      "templated": true
    },
    "account_transactions": {
      "href":
"http://localhost:8000/accounts/{account_id}/transactions{?cursor,l
imit,order}",
      "templated": true
    },
    "assets": {
      "href":
"http://localhost:8000/assets{?asset_code,asset_issuer,cursor,limit
,order}",
      "templated": true
    },
    "metrics": {
      "href": "http://localhost:8000/metrics"
    },
```

```
      "order_book": {
        "href":
"http://localhost:8000/order_book{?selling_asset_type,selling_asset
_code,selling_asset_issuer,buying_asset_type,buying_asset_code,buyi
ng_asset_issuer,limit}",
        "templated": true
      },
      "self": {
        "href": "http://localhost:8000/"
      },
      "transaction": {
        "href": "http://localhost:8000/transactions/{hash}",
        "templated": true
      },
      "transactions": {
        "href":
"http://localhost:8000/transactions{?cursor,limit,order}",
        "templated": true
      }
    },
    "horizon_version": "v0.20.1",
    "core_version": "v11.4.0",
    "history_latest_ledger": 4,
    "history_elder_ledger": 2,
    "core_latest_ledger": 4,
    "network_passphrase": "Standalone Network ; February 2017",
    "current_protocol_version": 11,
    "core_supported_protocol_version": 11
}
```

Note the list of endpoints. Now, let's move on to account creation.

Creating user accounts

Before we can create the US dollar asset, we need to create our user accounts. Stellar accounts are similar to Ethereum accounts and they allow users to interact with the Stellar network through transactions. They contain a public key, which is referred to as an account ID, and a secret key or private key, which is used to sign transactions that are submitted to the ledger.

The stellar-sdk provides a utility called `Keypair.random` which generates a random `ed25519` public-private key pair. This can be used as a Stellar account. For a public-private key pair to be a valid account on the Stellar network, it needs a minimum balance of 20 lumens. Lumens is the native currency of the Stellar network. Thus, to create an account on our private network, we'll need to generate a new public-private key pair and fund it with a balance of more than 20 lumens.

To do so, we'll write a small Node.js application that will generate new key pairs and fund them.

Writing the createAccount utility

Now, let's create a new `nodejs` project directory:

1. Install the `stellar-sdk` JavaScript module by executing the following command in the directory:

   ```
   npm install --save stellar-sdk
   ```

2. Create a new project file called `CreateAccount.js` and import the `stellar-sdk`, as follows:

   ```
   const StellarSdk = require('stellar-sdk');
   ```

3. Next, we'll define a new instance of the `stellar-sdk` that points to our local Horizon instance:

   ```
   const server = new StellarSdk.Server('http://127.0.0.1:8000',
   {allowHttp: true});

   const passphrase = 'Standalone Network ; February 2017'
   ```

4. The passphrase only allows selected users to connect to our network. You can find the network passphrase by navigating to the Horizon landing page at `localhost:8000`. Locate the `network-passphrase` tag, as shown in the following code:

   ```
   "network_passphrase": "Standalone Network ; February 2017"
   ```

For the `quickstart` docker image, this passphrase is set to `"Standalone Network ; February 2017"` by default.

5. Next, we will identify our `MasterKey`. The master key is the root account that all the lumens are credited to when a new Stellar network is created. By default, the root account is issued 100 billion lumens at initialization. To fund new accounts, we'll need to transfer lumens from this account to the newly created accounts. As shown in the following code, the master key pair is fetched using the `Keypair.master` utility from the network passphrase:

```
const MasterKey = StellarSdk.Keypair.master(passphrase)
const MasterSecret = MasterKey.secret();
const MasterPublicKey = MasterKey.publicKey();

console.log ('Master Account',MasterSecret, MasterPublicKey);
```

From the preceding code, we can make the following observations:

- The `.secret()` and `.publicKey()` methods for a key pair give us its secret key and public key, respectively.
- In a production implementation of Stellar, you are expected to use a custom network phrase and transfer all the lumens or native currency from the master currency to another Stellar account that you control on the network.

6. Next, we will generate three random `ed25519` key pairs (public key and private key pairs) that will act as our accounts. We'll use the first account to issue the USD asset; the other two accounts will be for Bank A and Bank B. As shown in the following code, we will use the `Keypair.random` method in the `StellarSdk` to generate the public-private key pair:

```
const pair1 = StellarSdk.Keypair.random(passphrase);
const pair2 = StellarSdk.Keypair.random(passphrase);
const pair3 = StellarSdk.Keypair.random(passphrase);
```

7. For each of the three newly generated random keypairs, we will retrieve the public key and the private or secret key, as follows:

```
var SecretKey1 = pair1.secret();
var PublicKey1 = pair1.publicKey();
console.log ('Account1',SecretKey1, PublicKey1);

var SecretKey2 = pair2.secret();
var PublicKey2 = pair2.publicKey();
console.log ('Account2',SecretKey2, PublicKey2);

var SecretKey3 = pair3.secret();
var PublicKey3 = pair3.publicKey();
console.log ('Account3',SecretKey3, PublicKey3);
```

Make sure you log the newly generated keys and the master key to the console. We'll need these later.

Before we can use the newly generated keys, we need to fund them with lumens, which is the native currency of Stellar. Stellar does not allow users to send or receive transactions to any key pair with less than 20 lumens. This is done to avoid spamming the network. You can only send the `createAccount` transaction to newly generated key pairs to fund the account. The Stellar network also requires accounts to submit a "fee" to the network for every transaction, which is paid in lumens. So, to allow our accounts to create assets and trade, we'll transfer 100,000 lumens to each of the newly generated accounts.

8. Now, let's start building our `createAccount` transaction. We need to make asynchronous calls to fetch the transaction sequence number and fee, so we will start by declaring an asynchronous method, as follows:

```
(async function main() {

const account = await server.loadAccount(MasterPublicKey);
const fee = await server.fetchBaseFee();
```

From the preceding code, we can make the following observations:

- The `server.loadAccount` method fetches the current sequence number of the Stellar account.
- It is essential that transactions are submitted to the network in sequence to dictate the order in which they'll be processed and verified.
- Before submitting a transaction from an account, we fetch the current transaction sequence number for the account.
- The `server.fetchBaseFee` method fetches the minimum fee that's required for the transaction to go through on the network. You can think of it as being similar to fetching the current gas price in an Ethereum network.

9. Next, we will use the `TransactionBuilder` class to build a new `createAccount` transaction. Let's go through each part of the code, bit by bit. We'll start by creating a new transaction constant, as follows:

```
const transaction = new StellarSdk.TransactionBuilder(account, {
fee, networkPassphrase: passphrase})
```

This is returned by the `TransactionBuilder` class. First, we pass the source account (master key account), the network fee, and passphrase as input parameters. Now, we need to send the operations to be carried out by the transaction as input parameters:

```
.addOperation(StellarSdk.Operation.createAccount({
    source: MasterPublicKey,
    destination: PublicKey1,
    startingBalance: "100000"
}))
```

The first operation is `createAccount`. This will fund our newly created random key pair with a starting balance of 100,000 lumens. The source account is our master account public key, while the destination is the public key of the first random account we generated. In the following code, the same operation is repeated for the other two random key pairs we generated:

```
.addOperation(StellarSdk.Operation.createAccount({
    source: MasterPublicKey,
    destination: PublicKey2,
    startingBalance: "100000"
}))
.addOperation(StellarSdk.Operation.createAccount({
    source: MasterPublicKey,
    destination: PublicKey3,
    startingBalance: "100000"
}))
```

Notice how the `stellar-sdk` allows you to chain and link multiple operations in a single transaction? Lastly, we add the transaction timeout and call `build()` to build the transaction:

```
.setTimeout(30)
    .build();
```

The transaction timeout indicates that the transaction won't be valid for more than 30 seconds after the transaction object is created. `build()` instructs the `TransactionBuilder` class to create a new transaction object using the parameters we submitted. This object is stored in the `transaction` constant.

10. The transaction object is then signed using the master key pair, as shown in the following code:

```
transaction.sign(MasterKey);
```

11. Lastly, as shown in the following code, the transaction is posted to the transaction endpoint of the Horizon server:

```
try {
  const transactionResult = await
server.submitTransaction(transaction);
  console.log(transactionResult);
  } catch (err) {
  console.error(err);
  }
}) ()
```

This is done using `server.submitTransaction`. The result is logged to the console. This brings us to the end of the `CreateAccount` utility.

Running the createAccount utility

Now, let's run the `createAccount` utility, as follows:

1. Navigate back to the `nodejs` project in the Terminal window. Run the following command to run the utility:

   node CreateAccount.js

   First, the utility will log the master key to the console before logging the three newly created accounts. The string starting with S is the account's secret key. The following string, starting with G, is the public key, or account ID:

   Master Account
   SC5O7VZUXDJ6JBDSZ74DSERXL7W3Y5LTOAMRF7RQRL3TAGAPS7LUVG3L
   GBZXN7PIRZGNMHGA7MUUUF4GWPY5AYPV6LY4UV2GL6VJGIQRXFDNMADI

   Account1 SAEEE4UUP3DRYTEFHNFKCVB4ZCQT2W2KPFW7FLE6VLE7QABAAZATFZFD
   GAIHBCB57M2SDFQYUMANDBHW4YYMD3FJVK2OGHRKKCNF2HBZIRBKRX6E

   Account2 SDSQ5MJALF7VWDFEFETPGGWJK2UEQ5HU6HJBKMT5M5YDJ3WYKMC5RC3O
   GDW3IXTH3UFCU2KD6REURTLK7XVSUC4P4WDATMFPTW6YZFEAV7RWATAD

   Account3 SB6HTLWBKVY6KOGKFZE2EKH3ZFSIYHYXJOORGKIOHSMPHBCX4SS4PU6G
   GBETQAVAWJJIQ7CZPXWLXKZO6BELLACNR3E7BRD4WTYEANAGGR62VP6Q

2. Copy these accounts and store them safely for reference. We'll need these later when we set up our remittance app. Account 1 will be used to issue the USD asset. Accounts 2 and 3 will be used to map Bank A and Bank B to our remittance platform.

3. Wait for the utility to fire the `createAccount` transaction and print a response to the console. A successful response indicates that the three accounts have been created and funded as well. You can verify this by yourself. Open a new browser window. Paste the following link to view the newly created accounts: `http://localhost:8000/accounts/<Account ID>`.

Here is an example:
`http://localhost:8000/accounts/GAIHBCB57M2SDFQYUMANDBHW4YYMD3FJVK2OGHRK KCNF2HBZIRBKRX6E`.

You should be able to view the account. Scroll down and check out the balance for the native asset.

Keep the secret key and public key for these three accounts safe. Now, we will write a Node.js utility that will create the assets and extending trustlines.

Creating the USD asset

Now, we have to create the USD asset that we'll be remitting between the accounts. To create new assets on a network, we need to carry out the following steps:

1. Create a new asset object.
2. Extend trustlines to the receiving accounts.
3. Transfer the assets from the issuing account.

Let's look at these one by one.

Creating a new asset object

Creating an asset object on the Stellar network is an easy affair. All you need to do is use the `Asset` method of the Stellar SDK, as shown in the following code. The `Asset` method has two input parameters—Asset Code and Issuer Account. Asset Code is an alphanumeric code that's used to refer to the asset. The Issuer Account is the account that is used to create the asset:

```
Asset = new StellarSdk.Asset(<Code>,<Issuing Account>).
var USD = new StellarSdk.Asset('USD',
'GBUM3XRJKUVEQA4UF63CUCS3P72C5AZTRYI2VKELS7T7DVCCLV3DODNE');
```

The preceding code shows how we'll do this for the USD asset.

Extending trustlines to receive accounts

Trustlines are a concept unique to Stellar assets. They determine how much of a user-issued asset an account is willing to hold. Since assets on the Stellar network are supposed to be digital representations of fiat currency or other real-world assets, it is essential that the issuer issuing assets should be liquid.

Due to this, you should only hold 100 USD worth of assets that are issued by an issuer account if you know that they can exchange the Stellar USD tokens for 100 dollar bills. Trustlines are indicative of how many liquid assets you believe the asset issuer has and in turn is used to determine how much of the asset you would want your account to hold.

Now, we'll write a Node.js utility so that we can create new assets and extend trustlines to the receiving accounts.

Writing the utility

Follow these steps to write the Node.js utility:

1. Create a new `nodejs` app called `CreateTrustline.js`. Start by importing the `stellar-sdk` from `node-modules` and creating a new server object pointed at `localhost:8000` (the Horizon instance), as shown in the following code:

```
const StellarSdk = require('stellar-sdk');
 const server = new StellarSdk.Server('http://127.0.0.1:8000',
{allowHttp: true});
```

2. Next, we'll use the accounts we generated in the previous section. Here, the first account will be our issuing account, which issues assets. The second and third accounts will map to Bank A and Bank B, respectively. Use the secret key of the three accounts to extract their key pairs:

```
var issuingKeys =
StellarSdk.Keypair.fromSecret('SAEEE4UUP3DRYTEFHNFKCVB4ZCQT2W2KPFW7
FLE6VLE7QABAAZATFZFD');

 var receivingKeys1 =
StellarSdk.Keypair.fromSecret('SDSQ5MJALF7VWDFEFETPGGWJK2UEQ5HU6HJB
KMT5M5YDJ3WYKMC5RC3O');

  var receivingKeys2 =
StellarSdk.Keypair.fromSecret('SB6HTLWBKVY6KOGKFZE2EKH3ZFSIYHYXJOOR
GKIOHSMPHBCX4SS4PU6G');
```

The `issuingKeys` variable is the key pair for the issuing account. `receivingKeys1` and `receivingKeys2` are for the two receiving accounts, which represent Bank A and Bank B. These accounts will be holding the USD asset.

3. Now, we will create a new asset object for US dollar:

```
var USD = new StellarSdk.Asset('USD',
'GBUM3XRJKUVEQA4UF63CUCS3P72C5AZTRYI2VKELS7T7DVCCLV3DODNE');
```

Remember the public key for your issuing account that we saved when we created it? Paste it here and add a symbol that we'll use to refer to the asset. We use `StellarSdk.Asset` to create a new asset with these details.

Before we can transfer the USD asset, the receiving accounts need to extend a trustline for these assets. This is a transaction that's fired by the receiving account to itself. It indicates to the asset that the trustline needs to be extended for and the trustline limit.

4. Let's build our transaction. We will start by fetching the base network fee and the sequence number for the account. This is done using the server object we created earlier:

```
server.fetchBaseFee()
  .then(function(fee){
  console.log("Fee is",fee);

  server.loadAccount(receivingKeys1.publicKey())
  .then(function(account){
```

5. Since the transaction is to be fired from `receivingKeys1`, we will fetch the current sequence for this account. Let's take a look at our transaction:

```
var transaction = new StellarSdk.TransactionBuilder(account, { fee,
networkPassphrase:'Standalone Network ; February 2017'}
  .addOperation(StellarSdk.Operation.changeTrust({
  asset: USD,
  limit: '1000000',
  source: receivingKeys1.publicKey()
  })).setTimeout(100)
  .build();
```

6. Now, we will pass the account sequence number, fee, and the network passphrase, as follows:

```
var transaction = new StellarSdk.TransactionBuilder(account, { fee,
networkPassphrase:'Standalone Network ; February 2017'}
```

7. Next, we will add the `ChangeTrust` operation, as follows:

```
.addOperation(StellarSdk.Operation.changeTrust({
  asset: USD,
  limit: '1000000',
  source: receivingKeys1.publicKey()
  }))
```

The preceding operation indicates that we need to extend a trustline for the USD asset with a limit of $1,000,000. Since the transaction is to self, the source of the transactions is the public key of `receivingKeys1`.

8. Lastly, we add a transaction timeout after 100 seconds and invoke `build()` to build the transaction object:

```
.setTimeout(100)
  .build();
```

9. After building the transaction, we sign it using the public key for `receivingKeys1` and submit it to the Stellar network for processing. Add a catch block for catching any errors, as follows:

```
transaction.sign(receivingKeys1);

return server.submitTransaction(transaction);

})}).catch(function(error) {
  console.error('Error!', error);
});
```

10. Next, we will repeat the same for `receivingKeys2`. This is the second trading account that we created:

```
server.fetchBaseFee()
  .then(function(fee){
  console.log("Fee is",fee);

  server.loadAccount(receivingKeys2.publicKey())
  .then(function(account){
  var transaction = new StellarSdk.TransactionBuilder(account, {
fee, networkPassphrase:'Standalone Network ; February 2017'})
  .addOperation(StellarSdk.Operation.changeTrust({
  asset: USD,
  limit: '1000000',
  source: receivingKeys2.publicKey()
  }))
  .setTimeout(100)
  .build();

transaction.sign(receivingKeys2);

return server.submitTransaction(transaction);

})}).catch(function(error) {
  console.error('Error!', error);
});
```

That brings us to the end of our `CreateTrustline` utility. Now, let's run this utility.

Running the utility

Follow these steps to run the utility:

1. Navigate to your `nodejs` project repository in your Terminal window. Run the `CreateTrustline` utility by running the following command:

   node CreateTrustline.js

   A successful response from the Stellar network after the transaction has been submitted indicates that the trustlines have been created. Let's verify this.

2. Open a new tab in your internet browser. View any account on Horizon by going to the accounts link. You can do so by going to the following link:

   ```
   http://localhost:8000/accounts/<Account ID>
   ```

   For example, for `receivingKeys1(GDW3IXTH3UFCU2KD6REURTLK7XVSUC4P4WDATMFPTW6YZFEA V7RWATAD)` the link will be `http://localhost:8000/accounts/GDW3IXTH3UFCU2KD6REURTLK7XVSUC4P 4WDA TMFPTW6YZFEAV7RWATAD`

Scroll down and check the balances again. Notice how it shows balances for the USD asset and the native asset now?

Next, we'll write a Transfer utility to transfer these assets from the issuer account to the receiving account.

Funding the user accounts with USD

Now, we can transfer the USD assets from our issuing account to the receiving account. To do so, we'll write a small utility called Transfer and send the assets. We'll create two versions of this utility: one for receiving assests in account 1 and one for receiving assets in account 2.

Writing the utilities

We'll have to create two `nodejs` apps called `Transfer1.js` and `Transfer2.js`:

1. First, we'll write `Transfer1`. To do this, we need to import the Stellar SDK from the node modules, create the server object, and extract the public and private keys for the issuing account, as well as the two receiving accounts from their respective secret keys, as shown in the following code:

```
const StellarSdk = require('stellar-sdk');

const server = new StellarSdk.Server('http://127.0.0.1:8000',
{allowHttp: true});

var issuingKeys = StellarSdk.Keypair
.fromSecret('SAEEE4UUP3DRYTEFHNFKCVB4ZCQT2W2KPFW7FLE6VLE7QABAAZATFZ
FD');

var receivingKeys1 = StellarSdk.Keypair
.fromSecret('SDSQ5MJALF7VWDFEFETPGGWJK2UEQ5HU6HJBKMT5M5YDJ3WYKMC5RC
3O');

var receivingKeys2 = StellarSdk.Keypair
.fromSecret('SB6HTLWBKVY6KOGKFZE2EKH3ZFSIYHYXJOORGKIOHSMPHBCX4SS4PU
6G');

var USD = new StellarSdk.Asset('USD',
'GAIHBCB57M2SDFQYUMANDBHW4YYMD3FJVK2OGHRKKCNF2HBZIRBKRX6E');
```

2. Let's look at our transaction. We fetch the base fee and the account sequence number for the issuing account using the following code:

```
server.fetchBaseFee()
  .then(function(fee){
  console.log("Fee is",fee);
  server.loadAccount(issuingKeys.publicKey())
  .then(function(account){
```

3. Our transaction source account will be the issuing account that distributes the newly created asset:

```
var transaction = new StellarSdk.TransactionBuilder(account,{
fee,networkPassphrase:'Standalone Network ; February 2017'})
  .addOperation(StellarSdk.Operation.payment({
  destination: receivingKeys1.publicKey(),
  asset: USD,
```

```
    amount: '1000'
}))).setTimeout(100)
.build();
```

Asset transfer is a `payment` operation in Stellar. We need to provide the destination Stellar account (public key of `receivingKeys1`), the asset to be transferred (USD), and the amount to be transferred (1,000).

The transaction time is set to 100 seconds. We call `build()` to build and return the transaction object.

4. After the transaction object has been returned, we sign and submit the transaction. As shown in the following code, the transaction is signed using the issuing account's key pair since the source is the issuing account:

```
transaction.sign(issuingKeys);
return server.submitTransaction(transaction);
```

5. As shown in the following code, add a response block to log any errors and notify transaction success to the requestor by printing a message on the console:

```
.then(function(response,error){
  if (response)
  {
  console.log("Response",response);
  }
  else
  {
  console.log("Error",error);
  }})
});
```

That brings us to the end of `Transfer1`. Repeat the same steps for `Transfer2`, but replace the receiving account with `receivingKeys2`. Now, `Transfer1.js` will transfer the assets to the first receiving account, while `Transfer2` will transfer the assets to the second.

Now, let's run these utilities.

Running the utities

Follow these steps:

1. Navigate to your `nodejs` project directory. First, run `Transfer1` using the following command:

   node Transfer1.js

2. Wait for a successful transaction response. Then, run `Transfer2` using the following command:

   node Transfer2.js

3. After you get a successful transaction response, open a new browser window and check the balance of the two accounts. For example, for receiving account 1, use the following URL:

   ```
   http://localhost:8000/accounts/GDW3IXTH3UFCU2KD6REURTLK7XVSUC4P4WDA
   TMFPTW6YZFEAV7RWATAD
   ```

The balance should now be updated to 1,000 for the USD asset.

That brings us to the end of creating and issuing the USD asset. Now, we have two remitting accounts with USD assets ready. Let's set up the other components.

Setting up the bank domains

Before we can set up the individual components of the remittance platform, we need to have a developing and testing environment in place. As per Stellar's architecture, the components need to be linked to a public domain owned by the financial institution/bank. For our current project, we'll link the bank infrastructure to `banka.com` and `bankb.com` for Bank A and Bank B, respectively. To do so, we'll update the hosts file so that it routes requests to `banka.com` and `bankb.com` to our localhost. We'll also issue self-signed SSL certificates for these two domains. Stellar requires that the compliance information exchange between the two bank domains is signed and encrypted using an SSL certificate. Lastly, we'll host a `Toml` file in these two domains that will be used to route incoming requests to the bank infrastructure. Let's begin.

Updating the hosts file

Switch to the root user and navigate to your hosts file. By default, it should be at the
`/etc/hosts` location.

Open the file with a text editor such as nano or vim. Add the two `banka.com` and
`bankb.com` domain to the hosts file, as follows:

```
127.0.0.1               localhost
127.0.1.1               ishan-Inspiron-3537
127.0.1.1 banka.com banka
127.0.1.1 bankb.com bankb
# The following lines are desirable for IPv6 capable hosts
::1     ip6-localhost ip6-loopback
fe00::0 ip6-localnet
ff00::0 ip6-mcastprefix
ff02::1 ip6-allnodes
ff02::2 ip6-allrouters
```

This will route all outgoing requests to the `banka.com` and `bankb.com` domains to our
localhost.

Issuing the self-signed certificates for the domains

Follow these steps:

1. Now, we'll issue the self-signed certificates for the `banka.com` and
   `bankb.com` domains. To do so, we'll be using the `certutil` and `mkcert` utilities.

   To install `certutil`, run the following command:

   ```
   $ sudo apt-get install -y libnss3-tools
   ```

   To install `mkcert`, run the following commands:

   ```
   mkdir mkcert
   cd mkcert
   wget
   https://github.com/FiloSottile/mkcert/releases/download/v1.1.2/mkce
   rt-v1.1.2-linux-amd64
   mv mkcert-v1.1.2-linux-amd64 mkcert
   chmod +x mkcert
   ```

The preceding commands will create a directory called `mkcert`, download the binary from GitHub, and create an executable called `mkcert` for issuing self-signed certificates. Make sure you download the binary version for your OS. Since I'm using Ubuntu, I downloaded the Ubuntu version.

2. Run the following command to set up a local certificate store:

```
mkcert -install
```

Now, let's issue self-signed certificates for `banka.com` and `bankb.com`.

3. Run the following command to issue a certificate for `banka.com`:

```
./mkcert banka.com
```

Check the directory to see if the certificate files are generated. The `banka.com.pem` and `banka.com-key.pem` files should have been generated in your `mkcert` directory.

4. Repeat this for the `bankb.com` domain:

```
./mkcert bankb.com
```

We now have the self-signed SSL certificates for the `banka.com` and `bankb.com` domains. Now, let's set up the `http` server, which will accept and route all the incoming requests to the `banka.com` and `bankb.com` domains.

Setting up the http server and stellar.toml file

We'll start by configuring the `http` server for `banka.com` and `bankb.com`. I'm using `apache2`, but you can feel free to install and use any `http` server you find easy to use. Let's get started:

1. Configure the `apache2.conf` file, which is available under `/etc/apache2/` by default. Update the virtual host section in the `conf` file, as follows:

```
<VirtualHost *:80>
ServerAdmin admin@banka.com
DocumentRoot /var/www/banka
ServerName banka.com
ErrorLog logs/bankb.com-error_log
</VirtualHost>

<VirtualHost *:80>
```

```
ServerAdmin admin@bankb.com
DocumentRoot /var/www/bankb
ServerName bankb.com
ErrorLog logs/bankb.com-error_log
</VirtualHost>

<VirtualHost *:443>
DocumentRoot /var/www/banka
ServerName banka.com
ServerAdmin admin@banka.com
SSLEngine on
SSLCertificateKeyFile /etc/apache2/ssl/banka/banka.com-key.pem
SSLCertificateFile /etc/apache2/ssl/banka/banka.com.pem
ErrorLog logs/banka.com-error_log
</VirtualHost>

<VirtualHost *:443>
DocumentRoot /var/www/bankb
ServerName bankb.com
ServerAdmin admin@bankb.com
SSLEngine on
SSLCertificateKeyFile /etc/apache2/ssl/bankb/bankb.com-key.pem
SSLCertificateFile /etc/apache2/ssl/bankb/bankb.com.pem
ErrorLog logs/bankb.com-error_log
</VirtualHost>
```

This redirects incoming requests to ports 9080 and 443 to the relevant document root based on the domain that's requested, either banka.com or bankb.com.

2. Copy the self-signed certificate (banka.com.pem) and certificate key (banka.com-key.pem) we generated for banka.com to /etc/apache2/ssl/banka/. You need to create the directory and subdirectory before you copy these files.
3. Repeat this for bankb.com as well. Copy the bankb.com.pem and bankb.com-key.pem files to /etc/apache2/ssl/bankb/.

4. Next, we'll set up the `toml` file to redirect incoming requests. Stellar expects you to set up the `stellar.toml` file, which contains public information that your peers need to interact with and send payments to your account. By default, Stellar nodes look for the `stellar.toml` file in the following location:

```
http://<your domain name>/.well-known/stellar.toml
```

5. Now, we need to configure our `toml` file and put it in this location for both domains. Start by downloading a sample `stellar.toml` file. You can get it from Stellar's website here (`https://www.stellar.org/developers/guides/concepts/stellar-toml.html`). Update the file and replace its contents, as follows:

```
FEDERATION_SERVER=https://banka.com:8001/federation
AUTH_SERVER=https://banka.com:8003
SIGNING_KEY="GDW3IXTH3UFCU2KD6REURTLK7XVSUC4P4WDATMFPTW6YZFEAV7RWAT
AD"
ACCOUNTS=[
"GDW3IXTH3UFCU2KD6REURTLK7XVSUC4P4WDATMFPTW6YZFEAV7RWATAD"
]
DESIRED_BASE_FEE=100
DESIRED_MAX_TX_PER_LEDGER=400
[[CURRENCIES]]
code="USD"
issuer="GAIHBCB57M2SDFQYUMANDBHW4YYMD3FJVK2OGHRKKCNF2HBZIRBKRX6E"
display_decimals=2
```

This `toml` file indicates that we'll set up our federation service at port `8001`, where it can be accessed by other parties trying to send transactions to our domain. The `Auth` server indicates the compliance module service port. For compliance checks, requests need to be sent to port `8003`. We'll use these ports to set up our federation and compliance server later.

The `toml` file also provided information about the accounts controlled by our domain, which is the Bank A receiving account. It also provides a public key for inbound messages, which is basically the public key of our account. Lastly, the `toml` file specifies the currency assets that our account can receive and send, as well as the issuer account for the asset.

6. Similarly, create a `toml` file for the `bankb.com` domain as well:

```
FEDERATION_SERVER=https://bankb.com:8002/federation
AUTH_SERVER=https://bankb.com:8005
SIGNING_KEY="
GBETQAVAWJJIQ7CZPXWLXKZO6BELLACNR3E7BRD4WTYEANAGGR62VP6Q "
```

```
ACCOUNTS=[
" GBETQAVAWJJIQ7CZPXWLXKZO6BELLACNR3E7BRD4WTYEANAGGR62VP6Q "
]
DESIRED_BASE_FEE=100
DESIRED_MAX_TX_PER_LEDGER=400
[[CURRENCIES]]
code="USD"
issuer="GAIHBCB57M2SDFQYUMANDBHW4YYMD3FJVK2OGHRKKCNF2HBZIRBKRX6E"
display_decimals=2
```

7. Update access ports for the federation and compliance server for the `bankb.com` domain and the receiving account for Bank B.

8. Copy the `stellar.toml` file for the `banka.com` domain to `/var/www/banka/.well-known/stellar.toml`.

9. Copy the `stellar.toml` file for the `bankb.com` domain to `/var/www/bankb/.well-known/stellar.toml`.

10. In the web browser, navigate to `www.banka.com/.well-known/stellar.toml`. You should be able to view the `toml` file for `banka.com`.

11. Repeat the same for `www.bankb.com/.well-known/stellar.toml`. You should be able to view the `toml` file for `bankb.com` in the web browser as well.

Great! Now, we have everything set up for `banka.com` and `bankb.com`. We'll set up our internal infrastructure next.

Setting up the bank's internal databases

We need to set up the internal databases for both banks. These will be used to store user data and other requisite details. I will be using `postgresql`, but you can use any database you are comfortable with. Let's get started:

1. Create two users pertaining to Bank A and Bank B on the database. On my Ubuntu system, I am creating the `bankauser` and `bankbuser` users. Run the following commands:

   ```
   useradd bankauser
   useradd bankbuser
   ```

2. Next, set the password for the users with the following commands:

   ```
   passwd bankauser
   passwd bankbuser
   ```

   At the new password prompt, set the new password.

3. Log into the `postgres` user and open the PostgreSQL command line, as follows:

```
su - postgres
psql
```

4. Create a database for `banka` and `bankb` by running the following command on the `postgresql` command line:

```
CREATE DATABASE banka OWNER bankauser;
CREATE DATABASE bankb OWNER bankbuser;
```

5. Next, we need to create the requisite tables in the database and add some test data. Log out from the `postgres` command line and log in using the `bankauser` Unix login. Log into the `postgresql` command line for `banka` from `bankauser`, as follows:

```
su - bankauser
psql banka
```

First, we'll create the users table with test customer data:

```
CREATE TABLE users (
name VARCHAR,
address VARCHAR,
dob INTEGER,
friendlyid VARCHAR PRIMARY KEY,
sanction BOOLEAN,
balance INTEGER,
domain VARCHAR,
}
```

Next, we'll insert the following test data into the table:

```
INSERT INTO users(name, address, dob, friendlyid, sanction,
balance, domain)
VALUES
('John Doe', 'cityA', '01011988', 'johndoe', true, 1000,
'banka.com');
```

We add the customer's name, their address, date of birth, friendly ID for the account, sanction (true: allowed, false: not allowed), account balance, and the ID domain (`banka.com`).

6. Next, create the following sanctions table:

```
CREATE TABLE sanction (
domain VARCHAR,
```

```
bankname VARCHAR,
sanction BOOLEAN
}
```

7. Create the following entry for `bankb.com` in Bank A's sanction database:

```
INSERT INTO sanction(domain, bankname, sanction)
VALUES('bankb.com', 'Bank B',  true);
```

8. Lastly, create a transactions database where received transactions will be logged by the bridge server for the `banka` and `bankb` databases:

```
CREATE TABLE transactions (
txid VARCHAR,
sender VARCHAR,
receiver VARCHAR,
amount INTEGER,
currency VARCHAR,
kyc_info VARCHAR,
}
```

9. Create the table users, sanctions, and transactions for the `bankb` database as well. Log out and log in using `bankbuser` and connect to the `bankb` database like so:

```
su - bankbuser
psql bankb
```

10. Repeat the preceding steps and create the users, sanctions, and transactions database for `bankb` as well. Insert test values into the users table for `bankb` like so:

```
INSERT INTO users(name, address, dob, friendlyid, sanction,
balance, domain)
VALUES
('Jane Smith', 'cityB', '31031991', 'janesmith', true, 2000,
'bankb.com');
```

11. Also, insert these details into the sanction table, as follows:

```
INSERT INTO sanction(domain, bankname, sanction)
VALUES('banka.com', 'Bank A',  true);
```

We also need to create a database so that we can log our compliance requests and a database for all the transactions being handled by the bridge server.

Log out from `bankbuser` and log into `postgres` with the following command:

```
su - postgres
psql
```

Create the following databases:

```
CREATE DATABASE bridgea OWNER bankauser;
CREATE DATABASE bridgeb OWNER bankbuser;
CREATE DATABASE compliancea OWNER bankauser;
CREATE DATABASE complianceb OWNER bankbuser;
```

As its name suggests, `bridgea` corresponds to the bridge module of Bank A, `bridgeb` corresponds to the bridge module of Bank B, `compliancea` corresponds to the compliance module of Bank A, and `complianceb` corresponds to the compliance module of Bank B. We'll set up the individual databases later when we install the bridge and compliance module.

This should take care of the bank's internal database infrastructure. Let's move on to the other components.

Setting up the federation servers

The federation server will be used by the banks to resolve the customer's friendly IDs into their receiving Stellar account ID and the peripheral information required to process the received transaction. Follow these steps to set up the federation servers:

1. Download the federation server release from the Stellar website here (`https://github.com/stellar/go/releases/tag/federation-v0.2.1`).
2. Select the binary corresponding to your OS version and extract the binary file.
3. Copy the extracted folder and paste and create two copies of the extracted folders labeled `federationA` and `federationB`.
4. Open the `federation.cfg` file within the extracted folders in a text editor. Configure it like so for the federation for Bank A:

   ```
   port = 8001

   [database]
   type = "postgres"
   dsn =
   "postgres://bankauser:bankauser@localhost/banka?sslmode=disable"

   [queries]
   ```

```
federation = "SELECT '
GDW3IXTH3UFCU2KD6REURTLK7XVSUC4P4WDATMFPTW6YZFEAV7RWATAD ' as id,
friendlyid as memo, 'text' as memo_type FROM users WHERE friendlyid
= ? AND ? = 'banka.com'"

[tls]
certificate-file = "/home/.../mkcert/banka.com.pem"
private-key-file = "/home/.../mkcert/banka.com-key.pem"
```

As shown in the preceding code, we can make the following observations:

- Set the port where the federation server will run and set the database connection details. In my case, I'm connecting the banka database using the bankauser user. My password is also bankauser.
- Next, we set a query to fetch the user's details from the users table in the banka database and select what we will return. Thus, if the request is for johndoe*banka.com to the federation server, it will return the following parameters in the response:

```
id: GDW3IXTH3UFCU2KD6REURTLK7XVSUC4P4WDATMFPTW6YZFEAV7RWATAD
memo : johndoe
memotype: text
```

5. Lastly, set the certificate and the private key file location for encryption. Provide the location of the self-signed certificate for banka.com.
6. Repeat the steps for the Bank B federation server as well and configure the federaton.cfg file like so:

```
port = 8002

[database]
type = "postgres"
dsn =
"postgres://bankbuser:bankbuser@localhost/bankb?sslmode=disable"

[queries]
federation = "SELECT '
GBETQAVAWJJIQ7CZPXWLXKZO6BELLACNR3E7BRD4WTYEANAGGR62VP6Q ' as id,
friendlyid as memo, 'text' as memo_type FROM users WHERE friendlyid
= ? AND ? = 'bankb.com'"

[tls]
certificate-file = "/home/.../mkcert/bankb.com.pem"
private-key-file = "/home/.../mkcert/bankb.com-key.pem"
```

Now, we have our federation server set up.

7. Start the federation server by running the following command:

```
./federation
```

8. Test whether the server works by submitting a request in the browser:

```
Request -- https://banka.com:8012/federation?q=johndoe*banka.com
type=name
```

You should see the following response:

```
Response -
id: GDW3IXTH3UFCU2KD6REURTLK7XVSUC4P4WDATMFPTW6YZFEAV7RWATAD
memo : johndoe
memotype: text
```

Now, we will set up the compliance server.

Setting up the compliance server

The compliance server will be used by the banks to exchange the customer's KYC information before initiating a payment request. Follow these steps to set up the compliance server:

1. Download the compliance server release from the Stellar website here (`https://github.com/stellar-deprecated/bridge-server/releases`). Select the binary corresponding to your OS version.
2. Extract the binary file and copy the extracted folder. Paste and create two copies of the extracted folders labeled `complianceA` and `complianceB`.
3. Create a file called `compliance.cfg` inside the extracted folders and open it in a text editor. Configure it like so for the compliance server for Bank A:

```
external_port = 8003
internal_port = 8004
needs_auth = true
network_passphrase = "Standalone Network ; February 2017"

[database]
type = "postgres"
url =
"postgres://bankauser:bankauser@localhost/compliancea?sslmode=disab
le"

[keys]
```

```
# This should be the secret seed for your base account (or another
account that
# can authorize transactions from your base account).
signing_seed =
"SDSQ5MJALF7VWDFEFETPGGWJK2UEQ5HU6HJBKMT5M5YDJ3WYKMC5RC3O"
#encryption_key =
"SDSQ5MJALF7VWDFEFETPGGWJK2UEQ5HU6HJBKMT5M5YDJ3WYKMC5RC3O"

[callbacks]
sanctions = "http://localhost:5000/compliance/sanctions"
ask_user = "http://localhost:5000/compliance/ask_user"
fetch_info = "http://localhost:5000/compliance/fetch_info"

[tls]
certificate_file = "/home/ishan/mkcert/banka.com.pem"
private_key_file = "/home/ishan/mkcert/banka.com-key.pem"
```

From the preceding code, we can make the following observations:

- The external port is the TCP port where other banks or financial institutions need to submit requests for the exchange of compliance information.
- The internal port will be used by the bank's internal infrastructure to run compliance checks on its own customers while initiating a transaction.
- When the `needs_auth` flag is set to true, it means that the compliance server requires the KYC details of the beneficiary from the receiving bank when it is sending a payment.
- The Stellar network passphrase is the network's passphrase. The database will be used to log compliance requests. Notice how we provide the user details and compliance database details for `banka` that we set up earlier when we were setting up the bank's internal databases.
- The signing key that's used for the messages is the secret key of Bank A. We also specify the callbacks server for the compliance server.
- The compliance server will connect with these `webhooks` when it tries to fetch and validate the information from the bank's internal databases. We'll look at this in more detail when we set up the callback server.
- Lastly, we provide the certificate and key file for Bank A that we generated earlier to secure all the incoming and outgoing requests to the compliance server.

4. Set up the `compliance.cfg` file for Bank B:

```
external_port = 8008
internal_port = 8009
needs_auth = true
network_passphrase = "Standalone Network ; February 2017"
```

```
[database]
type = "postgres"
url =
"postgres://bankbuser:bankbuser@localhost/complianceb?sslmode=disab
le"

[keys]
# This should be the secret seed for your base account (or another
account that
# can authorize transactions from your base account).
signing_seed =
"SB6HTLWBKVY6KOGKFZE2EKH3ZFSIYHYXJOORGKIOHSMPHBCX4SS4PU6G"
#encryption_key =
"SB6HTLWBKVY6KOGKFZE2EKH3ZFSIYHYXJOORGKIOHSMPHBCX4SS4PU6G"

[callbacks]
sanctions = "http://localhost:5100/compliance/sanctions"
ask_user = "http://localhost:5100/compliance/ask_user"
fetch_info = "http://localhost:5100/compliance/fetch_info"

[tls]
certificate_file = "/home/ishan/mkcert/bankb.com.pem"
private_key_file = "/home/ishan/mkcert/bankb.com-key.pem"
```

From the preceding code, we can make the following observations:

- The external port is set to 8008, while the internal port is set to 8009.
- The database is set to complianceb for Bank B. The signing seed is the secret key for the Bank Stellar account.
- The callbacks server for Bank B will be running on port 5100.
- The certificate and key file are set to the relevant files for Bank B.

5. Next, let's bring our compliance server online. Navigate to the compliancea directory. First, we need to migrate the compliance database. Do so with the following command:

```
./compliance --migrate-db
```

6. Next, bring the server online with the help of the following command:

```
./compliance
```

Repeat the preceding steps for Bank B by navigating to the `complianceb` directory and executing the last two commands.

Now, we have set up the compliance server. Next, we'll set up the bridge server.

Setting up the bridge server

As the name suggests, the bridge server will 'bridge' the operations carried out by the federation server, the compliance server, the Horizon client-server and the Stellar Core. The requestor will submit payment requests to the bridge server and it will interface between these four components to ensure compliance checks are carried out and the transaction is submitted to the blockchain. Follow these steps to set up the bridge server:

1. Download the bridge server release from the Stellar website here (`https://github.com/stellar-deprecated/bridge-server/releases`). Select the binary corresponding to your OS version.
2. Extract the binary file and copy the extracted folder. Paste and create two copies of the extracted folder labeled `bridgeA` and `bridgeB`.
3. Create a file called `bridge.cfg` inside the extracted folders and open it in a text editor. Configure it like so for the bridge server for Bank A:

```
port = 8006
horizon = "http://localhost:8000"
network_passphrase = 'Standalone Network ; February 2017'

compliance = "http://banka.com:8004"

[[assets]]
code="USD"
issuer="GAIHBCB57M2SDFQYUMANDBHW4YYMD3FJVK2OGHRKKCNF2HBZIRBKRX6E"

[database]
type = "postgres"
url =
"postgres://bankauser:bankauser@localhost/bridgea?sslmode=disable"

[accounts]
base_seed =
"SDSQ5MJALF7VWDFEFETPGGWJK2UEQ5HU6HJBKMT5M5YDJ3WYKMC5RC3O"

receiving_account_id =
"GDW3IXTH3UFCU2KD6REURTLK7XVSUC4P4WDATMFPTW6YZFEAV7RWATAD"
```

```
authorizing_seed =
"SAEEE4UUP3DRYTEFHNFKCVB4ZCQT2W2KPFW7FLE6VLE7QABAAZATFZFD"

issuing_account_id =
"GAIHBCB57M2SDFQYUMANDBHW4YYMD3FJVK2OGHRKKCNF2HBZIRBKRX6E"

[callbacks]

receive = "http://localhost:5000/receive"
```

From the preceding code, we can make the following observations:

- `port` indicates the port that requests need to be submitted to on the bridge server.
- Horizon and network passphrases indicate the location of the Horizon client server and the network passphrase for our Stellar network.
- The compliance server is set to the internal port we set up while installing the compliance server in the previous section.
- `asset` indicates the assets we'll be listening for in our received payments. It is set to the USD asset we issued earlier.
- The database is set to the `bridgeA` database we set up when we were setting up our internal databases.
- The `accounts` tag specifies the default secret key that's used to sign transactions that are submitted from the bridge server, the receiving account for payments that the bridge server will listen to, the authorizing seed for the USD asset, and the issuing account for the USD asset.
- Lastly, we have set the callbacks server for receiving payments. This endpoint will be called whenever the bridge server receives a payment. We will look at this endpoint in more detail when we build our callbacks server.

4. Update the `bridge.cfg` file for Bank B's bridge server as well. Navigate to the `bridgeB` directory and make the following changes:

```
port = 8007
 horizon = "http://localhost:8000"
 network_passphrase = 'Standalone Network ; February 2017'

 compliance = "http://bankb.com:8009"

 [[assets]]
 code="USD"
 issuer="GAIHBCB57M2SDFQYUMANDBHW4YYMD3FJVK2OGHRKKCNF2HBZIRBKRX6E"

 [database]
```

```
type = "postgres"
url =
"postgres://bankbuser:bankbuser@localhost/bridgeb?sslmode=disable"

[accounts]
base_seed =
"SB6HTLWBKVY6KOGKFZE2EKH3ZFSIYHYXJOORGKIOHSMPHBCX4SS4PU6G"

receiving_account_id =
"GBETQAVAWJJIQ7CZPXWLXKZO6BELLACNR3E7BRD4WTYEANAGGR62VP6Q"

authorizing_seed =
"SAEEE4UUP3DRYTEFHNFKCVB4ZCQT2W2KPFW7FLE6VLE7QABAAZATFZFD"

issuing_account_id =
"GAIHBCB57M2SDFQYUMANDBHW4YYMD3FJVK2OGHRKKCNF2HBZIRBKRX6E"

[callbacks]

receive = "http://localhost:5100/receive"
```

From the preceding code, we can make the following observations:

- We update the client port to 8007 for our bridge server.
- We also update the compliance server port and the bridge server's database URL. Lastly, we update the signing key to the secret key for Bank B and the receiving account to the Stellar account ID for Bank B.
- Lastly, we set the callbacks server endpoint to 5100 where we will be hosting the callbacks server for Bank B.

5. Before we can bring the bridge server online, we need to set up the database. Navigate to the bridgeA directory and run the following command to set up the bridge database for Bank A:

```
./bridge --migrate-db
```

6. Next, run the following command to bring the bridge server online:

```
./bridge
```

Repeat the preceding steps for the bridge server for Bank B as well. Navigate to the bridgeB directory and run the last two commands. Now, we have set up the bridge servers for our remittance platform. We'll set up the callbacks server next.

Setting up the callbacks server

The callbacks server implements a set of endpoints that can be called by the other components of the bank infrastructure to fetch data from or update data to the bank's internal databases.

It implements the following endpoints:

- `/compliance/fetch_info`: Fetches the customer's name, address, and date of birth when provided the `friendlyID` of the customer from the users table
- `/compliance/sanction`: Validates whether the sender's financial institution is sanctioned to send transactions from the sanctions table
- `/compliance/ask_user`: Checks whether the receiving bank will send the beneficiary's KYC details to the sending bank (`fetch_info` is then called to fetch the details)
- `/receive`: Captures details about received payments and updates the beneficiary's balance

The first three are called by the compliance server for compliance checks. The last one is called by the bridge server whenever a payment is received. Let's get started:

1. Let's start by writing our `CallBack` server. First, we will write the callbacks server for Bank A. Create a `nodejs` app called `CallbacksA` and declare your dependencies, as follows:

```
const express = require("express");
const bodyParser = require("body-parser");
const app = express();
const pg = require('pg');
const conString =
"postgres://bankauser:bankauser@localhost:5432/banka";
const client = new pg.Client(conString);
```

We'll be using the `pg` client to connect with `postgres`. Notice how `conString` is set to the `banka` database URL. Make sure you install the dependencies in your `nodejs` environment.

2. The following lines set up `bodyParser` so that it parses requests that are sent to the app:

```
app.use(bodyParser.json());
app.use(bodyParser.urlencoded({ extended: true }));
```

3. Next, we will declare a middleware layer to allow **Cross-Origin Resource Sharing (CORS)**. This permits our other bank modules to interact with our callbacks server:

```
app.use(function (req, res, next) {

// Website you wish to allow to connect
 res.setHeader('Access-Control-Allow-Origin', '*');

// Request methods you wish to allow
 res.setHeader('Access-Control-Allow-Methods', 'GET, POST, OPTIONS,
PUT, PATCH, DELETE');

// Request headers you wish to allow
 res.setHeader('Access-Control-Allow-Headers', 'X-Requested-
With,content-type');

// Set to true if you need the website to include cookies in the
requests sent

// to the API (e.g. in case you use sessions)
 res.setHeader('Access-Control-Allow-Credentials', true);

// Pass to next layer of middleware
 next();
});
```

4. Set up the server and the port as follows. I'm running the `CallbacksA` server on port `5000`:

```
var server = app.listen(process.env.PORT || 5000, function () {
var port = server.address().port;
console.log("App now running on port", port);
});
```

5. We need to connect to the `pg` client to allow our services to interact with the database. To do so, use the following command:

```
client.connect();
```

6. First, let's write the `fetch_info` endpoint. The `fetch_info` endpoint carries out the following steps:

   1. Extracts the address of the bank customer from the request body.
   2. Splits the address into `'friendlyID'` and `'domain'`, delimited by `'*'`.
   3. Uses the `friendlyID` to run a select query on the users table and fetches the name, address, date of birth, and domain.
   4. Marshalls the results of the query into JSON and returns the response to the requestor:

```
app.post('/compliance/fetch_info', function (request, response)
{
var addressParts = request.body.address.split('*');
 var friendlyId = addressParts[0];

 // You need to create `accountDatabase.findByFriendlyId()`. It
should look
 // up a customer by their Stellar account and return account
information.

client.query('SELECT name,address,dob,domain from users where
friendlyid = $1', [friendlyId], (error, results) => {
if (error) {
 throw error
 }

 if(results)
 {
 response.json({
 name: results.rows[0].name,
 address: results.rows[0].address,
 date_of_birth: (results.rows[0].dob).toString(),
 domain: results.rows[0].domain
 });

 response.end();

 }});
});
```

The JSON response is sent to the requestor and is attached to the transaction when it is submitted to the blockchain network.

7. Next, let's look at the following sanctions endpoint. The sanctions endpoint carries out the following steps:

    1. Extracts the domain of the sender's address from the JSON request.

    2. Checks the sanction database to ensure the domain and the financial institution are allowed to send payments by running a select query against the sender's domain.

    3. If the domain owner, that is, the financial institution is sanctioned to send payments, send a 200 (OK) status in the response. If the entry does not exist, send an error 403 status with the message `FI not sanctioned`:

```
app.post('/compliance/sanctions', function (request, response) {
var sender = JSON.parse(request.body.sender)
client.query('SELECT * from sanction where domain = $1',
[sender.domain], (error, results) => {
if (error) {
 response.status(403).end("FI not sanctioned");
 }
if (results)
 {
 response.status(200).end();
 }
})
});
```

8. Next, we have the following `ask_user` endpoint, which is the last compliance endpoint. The `ask_user` endpoint is similar to the sanctions endpoint. It carries out one additional step – it checks whether the receiving bank will share KYC details of the beneficiary with the compliance server of the sending bank. If this value is set to true, the `fetch_info` endpoint is called to fetch the details of the beneficiary.

The `ask_user` endpoint carries out the following steps:

1. Fetches the sender's domain from the request.

2. Checks whether the domain is sanctioned to send payments in the sanctions database.

3. If it is not sanctioned, an error message with a 403 status is sent to indicate that the bank domain is not sanctioned. The message that's sent is `FI not sanctioned`.

4. If the domain is sanctioned, the endpoint checks the `'kyc'` column against the entry of the domain in the sanctions database. If it is set to true, that means that the receiving bank will share the `kyc` details of the beneficiary. Thus, a response status of 200 (OK) is returned.

5. If `kyc` is set to `false`, a response status of 403 with the message `KYC request denied` is returned to the requestor:

```
app.post('/compliance/ask_user', function (request, response) {
    var sender = JSON.parse(request.body.sender)


client.query('SELECT * from sanction where domain = $1',
[sender.domain], (error, results) => {
if (error) {
 response.status(403).end("FI not sanctioned");
 }
if (results)
 {

 if(results.rows[0].kyc == true)
 {
 response.status(200).end();
 }
 else
 {
 response.status(403).end("KYC request denied");
 }
 }
})
});
```

This brings us to the last endpoint of our callbacks server, which is `/receive`. This endpoint is called every time a payment is received by the bridge server. It carries out a series of steps:

1. Extracts the received amount and the identifier of the customer from the request. In our case, this is the `friendlyID`, which is unique for every customer, but it could be a bank account number or customer ID in the traditional banking system. This is available in the request as `request.body.route`. We also extract the `transactionid` and the sender's `friendlyID`, as well as the sender's KYC details from the attachment field in the request.

2. These details are captured in the transactions table in the Bank A database, which logs all received transactions.

3. After successfully logging the transaction to the transactions database, we need to update the balance of the beneficiary. We fetch the current balance from the users table in the Bank A database.

4. The user's current balance is then updated with the amount that was received in the transaction. After successfully updating the balance, we send a success (response 200 OK) message back to the user:

```
app.post('/receive', function (request, response) {
 var amount = parseInt(Number(request.body.amount).toFixed(2));
 var friendlyid = request.body.route;
 var SendObj = JSON.parse(request.body.data);
 var kycObj = JSON.parse(SendObj.attachment);
 client.query('INSERT INTO transactions(txid, sender, receiver,
amount, currency, kyc_info) VALUES ($1,$2,$3,$4,$5,$6)',
[request.body.transaction_id,SendObj.sender,request.body.route,amou
nt,request.body.asset_code,kycObj.transaction.sender_info], (error,
results) => {
 if (error) {
 console.log(error);
 response.status(500).end("Error inserting transaction");
 }
 if(results)
 {
 client.query('SELECT balance from users where friendlyid = $1',
[friendlyid], (error, results) => {
 if (error) {
 console.log(error);
 response.status(500).end("Not found");
 }
 if (results)
 {
 var balance = Number(results.rows[0].balance)
 balance = balance + + amount;

 client.query('UPDATE users set balance = $1 where friendlyid = $2',
[balance, friendlyid], (error, results) => {

 if (error) {
 console.log(error);
 response.status(500).end("Not found");
 }
 if (results)
 {
 response.status(200).end();
 }
 })
 }
```

```
})
}
})
});
```

That brings us to the end of the callbacks server for Bank A. Create a copy of this Node.js application for Bank B as well. Make sure that you change the port and the bank's internal database URL. For my callbacksB application, my port is `5100` and the database URL is `postgres://bankbuser:bankbuser@localhost:5432/bankb`.

That completes the backend infrastructure of our remittance platform. You can actually submit payment requests to the bridge server payment endpoint (`http://banka.com:8006/payment`) and follow the steps as payment is executed.

To try it out, simply submit a request with the following parameters:

- **id**: <Random transaction ID>
- **amount**: <Amount you want to send, such as 1000>
- **asset_code**: USD
- **asset_issuer**: <USD asset issuer account, such as GAIHBCB57M2SDFQYUMANDBHW4YYMD3FJVK2OGHRKKCNF2HBZIRBKR X6E>,
- **destination**: <receiver, such as janesmith*bankb.com>
- **sender**: <sender, such as johndoe*bankb.com>
- **use_compliance**: true

The request should go through. If you check the console for the compliance, bridge, and federation server, you should be able to observe that the following steps are carried out:

1. The bridge server for Bank A receives the payment request. It checks that the transaction request is syntactically correct and that the transaction is not a duplicate against the bridge database. Next, it checks the `stellar.toml` file hosted at the domain of the receiver (`www.bankb.com/.wellknown/stellar.toml`) to find the federation server for the receiving bank.
2. The bridge server for Bank A submits a request to the federation server of Bank B. The federation server of Bank B resolves the `janesmith*bankb.com` address into the receiving Stellar account (Bank B—GBETQAVAWJJIQ7CZPXWLXKZO6BELLACNR3E7BRD4WTYEANAGGR62VP6Q), the contents of the memo in the transaction (janesmith), and the `memotype('text')`, and returns to the bridge of Bank A.

3. Next, the bridge server of Bank A submits the payment request to the Bank A compliance server. The compliance server calls the `fetch_info` endpoint of the internal callbacks server for Bank A. Then, the `fetch_info` endpoint returns the details of the sender.

4. The compliance server of Bank A calls the compliance server of Bank B for a handshake. It checks the `stellar.toml` file of the receiving bank for the external endpoint of the compliance server of Bank B.

5. The compliance server of Bank A forwards the details of the transaction, including the sender's KYC, to the compliance server of Bank B.

6. The compliance server of Bank B calls the sanctions and the `ask_user` endpoints of the internal callbacks server of Bank B. It verifies whether the `banka.com` domain is sanctioned to send payments to Bank B and whether the KYC details of the beneficiary will be shared. If the KYC details of the beneficiary will be shared, it calls `fetch_info` to get the receiver's details.

7. The compliance server of Bank B sends its response to the compliance server of Bank A.

8. The compliance server of Bank A checks that it has received a go-ahead from Bank B and whether it has received the KYC details of the beneficiary. Then, it submits its response to the bridge server of Bank A.

9. Once the bridge server of Bank A gets the go-ahead, it creates a new payment transaction request with the requisite details, including the amount, currency, receiver's details, and sender's details. This transaction request is then submitted to the blockchain.

10. The bridge server of Bank B is constantly listening for incoming payments to Bank B's stellar account. On receiving payment, it will simply pick up the payment request and submit it to the `/receive` endpoint of the internal callbacks server of Bank B.

11. The `/receive` endpoint of the callbacks server will add the payment to the transactions table and update the beneficiary's balance.

That completes the end-to-end payment flow. Let's put a small bank portal on top that Bank A and Bank B customers can use to submit a payment request and that the admin can use to view the KYC details of the customer.

Building the bank portal

Next, we'll build a portal for Bank A and Bank B. Users can log in with their `friendlyID` and submit payment requests. Then, the Bank can log in and view the KYC details of transactions.

The portal will have two components:

- A Node.js backend that will post payments to the bridge server and fetch user details from the users table in the bank internal database.
- A React frontend that's used to submit requests and view status.

Let's start with the Node.js backend.

Building the bank portal backend

The bank portal backend server will carry out the following operations:

- Return the user's details (name and balance) based on the `'friendlyid'` unique identifier. These will be displayed to the user upon logging in. The `'/userdet'` server will be used for this.
- Return the user's currency balance based on the `'friendlyid'` unique identifier. The `'/userbal'` server will be used for this.
- Handle payment requests. It will submit a payment request that's forwarded by the customer to the bridge server endpoint. Before submission, it will check whether the user has a sufficient balance for the payment transaction. After the bridge server communicates that the transaction has been executed successfully, it will update the customer's account to reflect the new balance, minus the remitted amount. This is done by the `'/payment'` service.
- Lastly, it returns a list of received transactions with the sender's KYC details for the bank user to view. This is implemented by the `'/bankuser'` service.

Now, let's start building our backend server. I'm calling my backend server apps `DBServerA` and `DBServerB` for Bank A and Bank B, respectively:

1. Create a Node.js app called `DBServerA`. Start by declaring the dependencies shown in the following code. Make sure you have these installed in your `nodejs` environment:

   ```
   const express = require("express");
   const bodyParser = require("body-parser");
   ```

```
const app = express();
const pg = require('pg');
const conString =
"postgres://bankauser:bankauser@localhost:5432/banka";
const requestObj = require('request');
const client = new pg.Client(conString);
const USD = 'USD';
const issuer =
'GAIHBCB57M2SDFQYUMANDBHW4YYMD3FJVK2OGHRKKCNF2HBZIRBKRX6E';
var txid = 1001;
```

There are a few things you should observe here. Our `pg` client is pointed to the
`banka` database URL. Also, take note of the USD asset and its issuer being
mapped. We also set a counter variable to keep track of the current transaction ID.
We start with the transaction ID set to `1001` and increment it after every request.

2. Next, we set up `bodyparser` so that we can parse the incoming JSON requests,
   set up the CORS middleware, and initialize the app server at port `3600`, as
   follows:

```
app.use(bodyParser.json());
app.use(bodyParser.urlencoded({ extended: true }));

app.use(function (req, res, next) {

// Website you wish to allow to connect
 res.setHeader('Access-Control-Allow-Origin', '*');

// Request methods you wish to allow
 res.setHeader('Access-Control-Allow-Methods', 'GET, POST, OPTIONS,
PUT, PATCH, DELETE');

// Request headers you wish to allow
 res.setHeader('Access-Control-Allow-Headers', 'X-Requested-
With,content-type');

// Set to true if you need the website to include cookies in the
requests sent
 // to the API (e.g. in case you use sessions)
 res.setHeader('Access-Control-Allow-Credentials', true);

// Pass to next layer of middleware
 next();
});

var server = app.listen(process.env.PORT || 3600, function () {
 var port = server.address().port;
```

```
console.log("App now running on port", port);

});
```

Now, let's start writing the endpoints one by one.

3. Let's start with the '/userdet' service. This service fetches the customer's details based on the friendlyId of the customer from the internal users table of the banka database and returns the details in json format to the requestor:

```
app.post('/userdet', function (request, response) {

var idParts = request.body.friendlyid.split('*');
 var friendlyId = idParts[0];

client.query('SELECT name,balance from users where friendlyid =
$1', [friendlyId], (error, results) => {
if (error) {
 throw error
 }
 if(results)
 {
 response.json({
 name: results.rows[0].name,
 balance: results.rows[0].balance
 });
 response.end();
 }});
});
```

4. Next is the '/userbal' service, which is similar to '/userdet' except for the fact that it returns the current balance of the user. It fetches the customer's current balance based on the friendlyid of the customer from the internal users table of the banka database and returns the details in JSON format to the requestor:

```
app.post('/userbal', function (request, response) {
var idParts = request.body.friendlyid.split('*');
 var friendlyId = idParts[0];
 client.query('SELECT balance from users where friendlyid = $1',
[friendlyId], (error, results) => {
if (error) {
 throw error
 }

 if(results)
 {
```

```
response.json({
balance: results.rows[0].balance
});
response.end();
}});
});
```

5. Next, we have the `'/payment'` service, which posts incoming payment requests to the bridge server. Let's go through the steps one by one. First, we fetch the customer's `friendlyId` from the request body and split it into the customer ID and domain name, as follows:

```
app.post('/payment', function (request, response) {
var idParts = request.body.account.split('*');
var friendlyId = idParts[0];
```

Next, we use the customer's `friendlyId` to fetch their current balance and check whether the payment amount is greater than the customer's current balance. If the payment request amount is greater, an "Insufficient balance!" message is sent to the requestor:

```
client.query('SELECT balance from users where friendlyid = $1',
[friendlyId], (error, results) => {
if (error) {
response.json({
msg: "ERROR!",
error_msg: error
});
response.end();
}

if(results)
{
balance = results.rows[0].balance;

if(balance < Number(request.body.amount))
{
response.json({
msg: "ERROR!",
error_msg: "Insufficient balance!"
});
response.end();
}
```

If the transfer amount is less than or equal to the balance, we post a new request to the bridge server '/payment' endpoint at localhost:8006. The params posted are as follows:

- id: Current transaction ID. We fetch this from the txid variable we declared earlier and it is sent in string format.
- amount: Transaction amount. Received from the customer's request that's submitted to the bank portal.
- asset_code: Asset code (USD).
- asset_issuer: Asset issuer account for USD.
- destination: Friendly ID of the receiver. We get this from the customer's request that's submitted to the bank portal (for example, janesmith*bankb.com).
- sender: Friendly ID of the sender. We get this from the customer when they log into the bank portal (for example, johndoe*banka.com).
- use_compliance: This needs to be set to true if we wish to use the compliance server to exchange KYC information between remitting parties.

Let's take a look at the following code to understand how the code implements the request and response to the bridge server:

```
requestObj.post({
url: 'http://localhost:8006/payment',
form: {
id: txid.toString(),
amount: request.body.amount,
asset_code: USD,
asset_issuer: issuer,
destination: request.body.receiver,
sender: request.body.account,
use_compliance: true
}
},
function(err, res, body) {
if (err || res.statusCode !== 200) {
console.error('ERROR!', err || body);
response.json({
result: body,
msg: "ERROR!",
error_msg: err
});
response.end();
}
```

If we receive an error status code from the bridge server, the user is notified and an error message is printed to the console.

As shown in the following code, if the bridge server response is success, the following steps are carried out:

1. The user's current balance is fetched and updated. The transaction amount is deducted from the current balance.
2. The variable that stores the transaction ID, txid, is incremented by 1 to the next transaction ID.
3. After the preceding two steps, a success response is sent back to the requestor:

```
else {
 console.log('SUCCESS!', body);
 client.query('SELECT balance from users where friendlyid = $1',
 [friendlyId], (error, results) => {
 if (error) {
 console.log(error);
 response.status(500).end("User Not found");
 }
 if (results)
 {
 var balance = Number(results.rows[0].balance)
 balance = balance + - request.body.amount;
 client.query('UPDATE users set balance = $1 where friendlyid = $2',
 [balance, friendlyId], (error, results) => {
 if (error) {
 console.log(error);
 response.status(500).end("User Not found");
 }
 if (results)
 {
 response.json({
 result: body,
 msg: 'SUCCESS!'
 });
 txid++;
 console.log("Next txid",txid);
 response.status(200).end();
 }
 })
 }
 })
 }
 });
 }
```

```
})
});
```

We are left with one last service for our backend server: `'/bankuser'`. This service simply queries the transactions table in the `banka` database and fetches all the information about the received transactions, including the sender's KYC details. This is then sent back to the `requestor`:

```
app.get('/bankuser', function (request, response) {
client.query('SELECT * from transactions', (error, results) => {
if (error) {
 throw error
 }

 if(results)
 {
 response.json({
 tx: results.rows
 });
 response.end();
 }
})
});
```

That brings us to the end of the backend server for our bank portal for Bank A. Replicate and set up this server for Bank B as well. Make sure you change the database URL to `postgres://bankbuser:bankbuser@localhost:5432/bankb` and the port to `'3602'` or any other unused port. Also, make sure that you change the bridge server's internal port for Bank B in the `'/payment'` endpoint. In my case, this port is `8007`. This is highlighted in the following code:

```
requestObj.post({
 url: 'http://localhost:8007/payment',
 form: {
 id: txid.toString(),
 amount: request.body.amount,
 asset_code: USD,
 asset_issuer: issuer,
 destination: request.body.receiver,
 sender: request.body.account,
 use_compliance: true
 }
```

That completes creating the backend servers for Bank A and Bank B.

Building the bank portal frontend

We also need to build a frontend that our users will interact with. To do so, we'll build a simple interface in React. Our portal will have the following screens:

- A login screen, which will ask for the user's `friendlyId` to log in to the app. The user can also log in as a bank user to see the admin view.
- A payment screen, which is where customers can submit payments.
- A bank user screen, which will display received transactions and KYC details.

The major components for the React app are as follows:

- `Container.js`: This receives the current app state parameters from the `App.js` file and passes them to the child components. The child components are rendered on the basis of the current state of the app.
- `Assets.js`: This renders and initializes the USD asset.
- `AppLogin.js`: This renders a login screen where the user needs to submit their `friendlyId` mapped to the bank's domain. Alternatively, a bank admin user can log in.
- `Transfer.js`: A component that renders a form for accepting and submitting payment requests. The user asks for the receiver's friendly ID and the amount to be sent. The user is shown the **Tx Status** (Success/Failure) and **Tx Hash** after submitting the request to the blockchain network.
- `BankUser.js`: A component that renders a screen that maps all the received transactions, along with the sender's KYC information.

Creating the React project environment

Let's start creating our app environment:

1. Create a new React app called `cross-border` using the following `npx` command:

   ```
   npx create-react-app cross-border
   ```

2. Update your `package.json` file so that it contains the following values:

   ```
   {
   "name": "cross-border-app",
   "version": "1.0.0",
   "private": false,
   "dependencies": {
   ```

```
"bulma-start": "0.0.2",
"concat-stream": "^2.0.0",
"fs": "0.0.1-security",
"react": "^16.4.1",
"react-dom": "^16.4.1",
"react-scripts": "1.1.4",
"stellar-sdk": "^3.0.0",
},
"scripts": {
"start": "react-scripts start",
"build": "react-scripts build",
"test": "react-scripts test --env=jsdom",
"eject": "react-scripts eject"
}
}
```

3. Run `npm install` in a Terminal window to install the dependencies.
4. Finally, within the `src` folder, create a `Components` folder for the app components.

Let's take a look at our `USD.js`.

Mapping the USD asset

Create a file called `USD.js` to map the `USD` asset. Update it so that it contains the following values:

```
export default {
  code: "USD",
  issuer: "GAIHBCB57M2SDFQYUMANDBHW4YYMD3FJVK2OGHRKKCNF2HBZIRBKRX6E",
  symbol: "$"
}
```

The component sets the symbol, asset code, and asset issuer for the `USD` asset.

Writing the App.js file

Let's look at how the `App.js` file is written:

1. First, let's look at the following dependencies, which have to be imported:

```
import React, { Component } from 'react';
import StellarSdk from 'stellar-sdk';
import Nav from './Components/Nav';
import Description from './Components/Description';
```

```
import Container from './Components/Container';
import USD from './Components/USD';
var concat = require('concat-stream');
const requestObj = require('request');
const DBServer = 'localhost:3600';
```

From the preceding code, we can make the following observations:

- We import the React object and the `StellarSdk` into our app.
- The `StellarAsk` is used to create the `USD` asset interface for our app. `Nav`, `Description`, and `Container` are the navigation bar, description, and container component. These are rendered in the `App.js` itself. The `USD` asset is also imported.
- We set up the `concat` and `requestObj` objects so that we can send requests to our backend database server. Lastly, we set up the `DBServer` object, which specifies the `DBServer` the app is pointing to.
- Initially, this is set to `'localhost:3600'`, which is the `DBServer` for Bank A. To avoid multiple moving components, we'll use the same React app for Bank B as well. Just swap the `DBServer` here to `'localhost:3602'` and relaunch the app to use it for Bank B.

2. The constructor in the following code sets the app name and initializes the `USD` asset. It also initializes the state variables, including the network type, the account (`friendlyID`), the default balance value, and the name of the customer. It also initializes the fields so that it can capture the form values:

```
constructor(){
        super();
        this.appName = 'Remittance App';
    this.onInputChangeUpdateField =
this.onInputChangeUpdateField.bind(this);
    this.USDasset = USD;
    this.USD = new
StellarSdk.Asset(this.USDasset.code,this.USDasset.issuer);

    this.state = {
            network: 'Private Testnet',
            account: null,
            balance: 0,
            name: '',
            fields: {
            friendlyid: null,
            receiver: null,
            amount: null,
```

```
            sellprice: null,
            sellamount: null,
                        }
        }
    }
```

3. Next, we will check out the main App.js body. The methods that are implemented by App.js are as follows:

- setAccount
- setBalance
- setBank
- payment

Let's take a look at how these methods are implemented.

The following setAccount method is called to set the state account variable to the friendlyID the customer provides while logging into the app. It also calls the '/userdet' service in our backend server to get the user's details, including their name and current balance:

```
setAccount = () => {

var account = this.state.fields.friendlyid;
let app = this;
var url = 'http://'+ DBServer +'/userdet';

fetch(url,{
method: 'POST',
headers: {
'Accept': 'application/json',
'Content-Type':'application/json',
},
body: JSON.stringify({
friendlyid: account
})
}).then(function(response,error){
if(response)
{
return response.json();
}
else
{
console.log(error);
}
}).then(function(data){
```

```
app.setState({
account,
name: data.name,
balance: data.balance
});
})
}
```

The response from the '/userdet' service is used to set the name and balance state variables for our app.

The following setBalance method is called to update the state balance variable for the customer account. This method is typically called once a transaction credits or debits an amount to the user account:

```
setBalance = () => {
let app=this;
var account = this.state.account;
var url = 'http://'+ DBServer +'/userbal';
fetch(url,{
method: 'POST',
headers: {
'Accept': 'application/json',
'Content-Type':'application/json',
},
body: JSON.stringify({
friendlyid: account
})
}).then(function(response,error){
if(response)
{
return response.json();
}
else
{
console.log(error);
}
}).then(function(data){

app.setState({
balance: data.balance
});
})
}
```

This method calls the `'/userbal'` service in the backend server, which returns the user's current balance. This balance is set in the current app state.

The following `setBank` method fetches the details of the received transaction from the `'/bankuser'` service:

```
setBank = () => {

let app = this;
 var url = 'http://'+ DBServer +'/bankuser';
fetch(url).then(function(response,error){
 if(response)
 {
 return response.json();
 }
 else
 {
 console.log(error);
 }
 }).then(function(data){

 app.setState({
 receivedtx: data.tx
 });

 })
 }
```

The `receivedtx` state variable stores the array of the received transactions. These are mapped by the `BankUser` screen when the bank user logs in.

The following `payment` method is called whenever the submit button is clicked by the user. First, it posts the transaction request to the callback server's payment endpoint:

```
payment = () => {

 let app =this;
 var url = 'http://'+DBServer+'/payment';

 fetch(url,{
 method: 'POST',
 headers: {
 'Accept': 'application/json',
 'Content-Type':'application/json',
 },
 body: JSON.stringify({
```

```
receiver: this.state.fields.receiver,
amount: this.state.fields.amount,
account: this.state.account
})
```

4. The parameters that are sent for the request are fetched from the `field` variable values and the account variable we set earlier. As shown in the following code, upon receiving the request, the callbacks server forwards it to the bridge server and the entire payment flow is carried out:

```
}).then(function(response,error){
if(response)
{
return response.json();
}
else
{
console.log(error);
}
}).then(function(data){
```

In the preceding code, we wait for the response from the callbacks server. The response body is extracted and evaluated based on the response from the server.

5. In the following code, if the transaction response message is `'SUCCESS!'`, the `txstatus` in the state is set to `'Transaction Successful'` and the `txid` in the state is set to the transaction hash. If the transaction creates an error, the `txstatus` state variable is set to `'Transaction Failed'`:

```
if(data.msg == "SUCCESS!")
{
var disObj = JSON.parse(data.result);
app.setState({
txstatus: 'Transaction Successful',
txid: disObj.hash
});
app.setBalance();
}
else
{
console.log("Error",data);
app.setState({
txstatus: 'Transaction Failed',
});
}
});
}
```

That completes creating our `App.js` file. You can find the entire code and interface for the remittance app in this book's GitHub repository.

That wraps up all the components we need to build for our remittance app. Let's run the platform and see how it works.

Running the remittance platform

Before we run our remittance application, make sure the following actions have been carried out:

- The Stellar private network has been set up and is online.
- The USD asset has been issued and the Stellar accounts for the banks have been created and funded.
- The bank's internal databases have been created and test customer data has been entered.
- The federation servers have been set up.
- The compliance servers have been set up.
- The bridge servers have been set up.
- The callbacks servers have been set up.
- The app interface and backend server have been built.

If even one of these has not been completed, please ensure that you do so before going through this section. First, let's bring all the backend components and servers online:

1. Navigate to the `/federationA` and `/federationB` directories and bring the servers online using the `./federation` command.
2. Navigate to the `/complianceA` and `/complianceB` directories and bring the servers online using the `./compliance` command.
3. Navigate to the `/bridgeA` and `/bridgeB` directories and bring the servers online using the `./bridge` command.
4. Navigate to your `nodejs` project directory, specifically the apps for `CallbacksA` and `CallbacksB`, and bring the apps online with the `node CallbacksA.js` and `node CallbacksB.js` commands.
5. Next, bring the bank portal backend server online with the `node DBServerA.js` and `node DBServerB.js` commands.

Let's start our bank portal app. Navigate to the React `app` directory. Run the app with the following command:

```
npm start
```

The app should launch in the browser as follows:

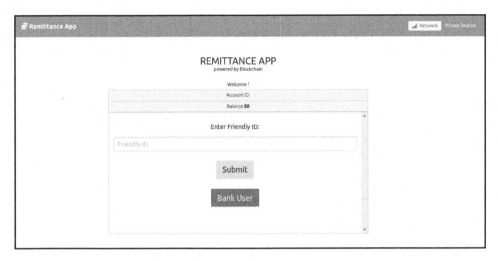

1. Enter the friendly ID of the customer to log in. As you may recall, we set the customer ID to `johndoe*banka.com` in our users table while entering test data:

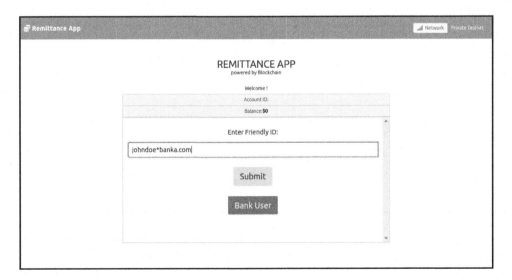

2. Click on **Submit** to log in. You should see the customer transfer screen:

3. Enter the details of the payment and click on the **Transfer** button. I'm transfering 10 USD to **janesmith*bankb.com**:

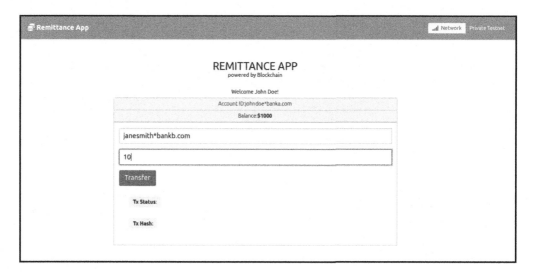

4. Once the transaction goes through, a message stating **Transaction Successful** and the **Tx Hash** from the blockchain will printed on the screen:

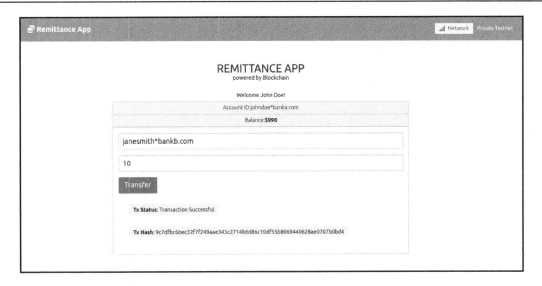

5. Now, let's configure our bank portal for Bank B. Simply swap the `DBServer` constant in `App.js` to the following value. You can find it at the top of the code where we imported our dependencies:

```
const DBServer = 'localhost:3602';
```

6. Now, refresh the app in the browser. Log into the app, this time using the friendly ID `janesmith*bankb.com`:

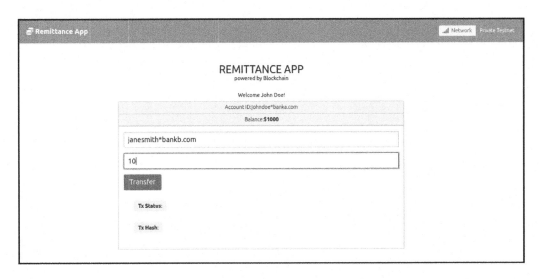

Notice how the balance has changed from $2,000 (which we set manually while entering the test data into our users table) to $2,010:

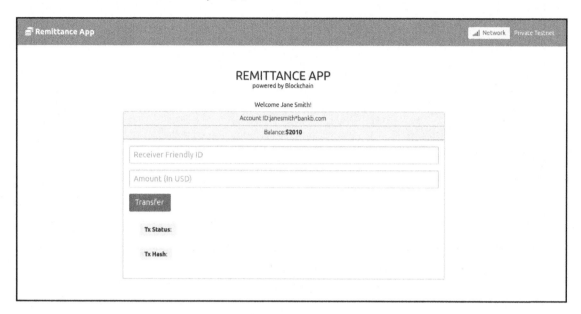

7. Now, refresh the app and log into the main page by clicking on the **Bank User** button. You should be taken to the Bank User screen, where you will be able to see the transactions details, including the sender's KYC details:

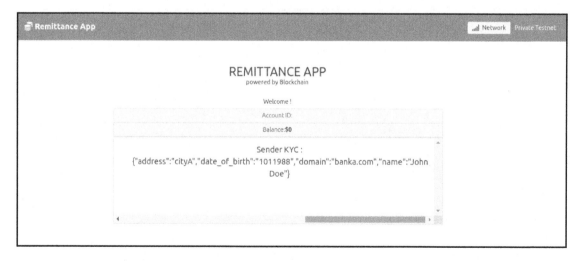

That brings us to the end of our demo for the remittance app.

If you rerun this demo, make sure you remove the logged transactions from the `bridgeA`, `bridgeB`, `complianceA`, and `complianceB` databases. Since transaction IDs need to be unique, the bridge and compliance server will disallow a transaction if they find that a transaction with the same ID already exists.

Summary

So, we finally finished building our remittance platform. This chapter gives you good insight into how to build off-chain workflows that can augment blockchain platforms to build new-age solutions for the banking and finance industry. An upgraded version of this platform can be used for transparent, faster, and secure cross-border remittances by banks and other financial institutions. You can also look at it to create global payment networks that participants can connect to and remit very easily while ensuring existing KYC/AML norms are met for such remittances.

We started this chapter by looking at what a blockchain cross-border remittance system looks like and how blockchain can help eliminate many of the lacunas in the existing system. Then, we built a platform to demonstrate these benefits by leveraging the Stellar network. We looked at and set up the various components that we needed to build for this. These included an ID resolution service (federation) for making remittances user-friendly for customers, a compliance service for exchanging AML/KYC information prior to the actual remittance, a callbacks server for allowing the bank components to interact with the internal database, and a bridge server for orchestrating the workflow across the components.

We also set up a private Stellar network with test accounts for Bank A and Bank B, a USD asset for remitting, and the frontend and backend portals for the bank. The user can submit payment requests and the admin can view KYC details of received transactions from this portal.

The main takeaway from this chapter is understanding how an ecosystem like this is built and how the components interact with each other while leveraging the blockchain. This also gives you an insight into how payment systems are changing. This particular system solves a huge problem in cross-border remittances where, even today, KYC/AML information is exchanged in several remittance corridors through less efficient means.

In the next chapter, we'll be looking at more complex financial products that leverage the blockchain to build transparent and efficient processes.

2

Section 2: Blockchain Workflows Using Smart Contracts

Inter-organizational and inter-departmental workflows are inefficient and time-consuming owing to high dependency on the reconciliation process. These workflows depend on the availability of data and information from a different organization or department for decision making or executing a process. Additionally, this data needs to be verified for any discrepancies before being processed. This further adds to the delay. Blockchain can help us to make these processes more efficient using smart contracts. Once the stakeholders have agreed to the conditions of a smart contract and deployed it to the blockchain, they cannot be modified. This makes them very handy for preventing fraud and promoting transparency.

We can build safe and secure workflows and business processes that span across organizations and departments and execute based on pre-determined conditions using smart contracts. In the next chapter, we'll be verifying this concept. To do so, we'll be building a blockchain-enabled LC issuing and settlement module.

This section comprises the following chapter:

- Chapter 6, *Building a Letter of Credit Workflow Module Using Smart Contracts*

6

Building a Letter of Credit Workflow Module Using Smart Contracts

Smart contracts are excellent tools for building automated and transparent workflows. In addition to this, the advantage that blockchain provides in terms of immutability and auditability gives architects the ability to design efficient smart contracts give architects and developers the ability to design efficient. enterprise-grade workflows that can integrate with legacy IT systems and business processes. An escrow is a great example of a use case where smart contracts provide value. An escrow is a financial product whereby a third party—such as a bank—will hold assets or money on behalf of two parties that are executing an agreement or a transaction. The third party acts as a facilitator to ensure that the parties in the agreement do not try to commit fraud or cheat each other. Financial organizations could, hypothetically, move management and operation of escrows completely to blockchains to save costs on backend processes, accounting, and reconciliation.

This chapter focuses on creating one such financial product that relies on escrow. We'll build a **Letter of Credit (LC)** module that can be used to create and issue smart contract-backed escrows on the fly. These smart contracts can also be used for viewing the live status of the escrows by all the participants, and for initiating settlement. By the end of this chapter, you will be able to create an LC/escrow using smart contracts. You will also learn to build and deploy enterprise workflows using DApps.

This chapter will cover the following topics:

- Understanding smart contracts and blockchain-based workflows
- Creating a **US dollar (USD)** token for accounting
- Deploying a USD token for accounting

- Creating an LC Master smart contract
- Creating an LC smart contract
- Deploying the LC Master smart contract
- Creating the LC module React app
- Running the LC module

Technical requirements

The code files for this chapter are available at the following link: `https://github.com/PacktPublishing/Blockchain-Development-for-Finance-Projects/tree/master/Chapter%206`.

To develop our project, we'll be using the following:

- **Ganache private blockchain server:** `https://trufflesuite.com/ganache/`
- **Trufflesuite:** `https://github.com/trufflesuite/truffle`
- **MetaMask plugin for Chrome/Firefox/Safari:** `https://metamask.io/`

For installing Ganache on Ubuntu, you might need to change some settings. Click on the drop-down menu next to the Ganache directory name in the Title bar of the file explorer. Select **Preferences**. Navigate to the **Behavior** tab. Under **Executable Text Files**, select the **Ask what to do** option. Navigate back to the file you downloaded from the Ganache download link. Right-click on the file, and click on **Properties**. Select the **Permissions** tab. Select the **Allow executing files as program** option. Now, double-click on the file. The Ganache blockchain should start smoothly. It's probably best to do a global installation of Truffle to avoid any conflicts. For example, create a directory workspace called `truffle` and install truffle using `sudo npm install truffle -g`.

I'm using Ubuntu 18.04.2 LTS to run the preceding applications and deploy my blockchain. This project assumes that you are working on a Unix operating system. Additionally, this project assumes you have `Node.js` and `npm` installed. I'm using Node version 13.0.1 and npm version 6.12.0.

Lastly, we'll be using the OpenZeppelin library of smart contracts to write our contracts. To use this library, create a project folder in your Truffle workspace. Let's call it `tokenwallet`. Create a `package.json` file in the `project` folder and update it with the following values:

```
{
  "dependencies": {
    "babel-register": "^6.23.0",
    "babel-polyfill": "^6.26.0",
    "babel-preset-es2015": "^6.18.0"
  },
  "devDependencies": {
    "openzeppelin-solidity": "^2.2.0"
  }
}
```

Run `npm install` to install the `OpenZeppelin` library, and `babel` for your truffle workspace.

Understanding smart contracts and blockchain-based workflows

Smart contracts are automated workflows written on top of the blockchain ledger that can read and write to the blockchain ledger and update the state of the blockchain system. What makes them special is that once they are deployed, they cannot be modified or controlled by external accounts (human-controlled accounts). They will always behave in accordance with the code written into them. This makes them perfect for creating time- or condition-based escrows that can operate without the involvement of a middleman.

Let's take an example. Alice wants to buy a car from Bob, but she will pay Bob the money and take possession of the car only if Bob gets a **no objection certificate** (NOC) issued for harmful emissions. Bob, on the other hand, doesn't want to spend more money on repairing his old car because he is worried that Alice might back out of the sale. To solve the conundrum, Alice and Bob could enter into a smart contract-based escrow. Alice puts her money on the blockchain into the escrow, and Bob puts an asset token that indicates ownership of the vehicle. This escrow is essentially a blockchain smart contract that will map the ownership of the vehicle to Alice and send the funds to Bob, only if he gets a copy of the NOC certificate from the relevant authority. The entire escrow logic is written using a smart contract platform (for example, Solidity). Since no one controls the escrow, neither Alice nor Bob needs to trust a middleman.

Scope of an LC workflow project

In this chapter, we'll be using a slightly more restrained approach, suited for financial application. We'll build an LC workflow. Our blockchain network will consist of three participants—the Buyer, the Seller, and GreenGables bank, which is the banker to the Buyer. The Buyer wants to purchase some goods (let's say, engine pistons) from the Seller. However, they do not have enough cash at hand to do so, but they'll have the money after they sell the final product with the pistons installed (let's say the final product is an engine). They then go to their bank, GreenGables, to extend a line of credit, which can be used for paying the Seller when the Seller delivers the pistons to them.

GreenGables bank does a credit analysis of the Buyer and comes to the conclusion that it is safe to extend the line of credit to the Buyer. However, the Seller needs to submit validating documents to show the pistons have been manufactured and shipped. These can include a **Bill of Lading (B/L)**, an invoice, a **Carry and Forwarding Agent (CFA)** document, and so on. The Buyer agrees, and the bank issues a document (called an LC) to formalize the process.

The Buyer can share this document with the Seller and ask them to start manufacturing their product. After the Seller has manufactured and shipped the goods, they send the supporting documents to the LC smart contract, to get paid. The bank settles with the Seller after validating the documents and other details. Finally, the Buyer repays their loan to the bank, ending the LC life cycle.

We'll be creating the following smart contracts:

- **USD (ERC20)**: The first contract will be a simple ERC20 standard token that will represent the USD in our system, for accounting purposes.
- **LC Master**: The second contract, called LC Master, will issue new LC agreements between parties and manage these agreements/contracts on the blockchain. It will be invoked by the bank entity each time it needs to issue a new LC. On being invoked to issue a new LC, the LC Master contract will create and deploy a new LC smart contract on the blockchain. The LC Master contract will also allocate the funds to the new LC contract on the blockchain. The newly minted LC will disburse these funds when the LC is settled. The LC Master also keeps track of all the LCs issued and their current status.

- **LC**: This contract will serve as an interface for issuing new LCs. Functionality-wise, it is a template that the bank will use for issuing LC contracts. For each contract, the bank will just need to change the contract parameters, and then use this template to create and float the new contract. With respect to the actual implementation, every time a new LC smart contract needs to be created, the LC Master smart contract will use this contract interface to create and deploy the new contract.

Setting up the LC workflow

To set up our LC module, we'll be following these steps:

1. Writing, compiling, and deploying our USD asset contract. Since we need a fungible asset to represent the USD, we'll be using the ERC20 contract standard to create this asset.
2. Capturing the address of the USD token and mapping it to our LC Master and LC smart contracts. This address will be used to invoke the USD smart contract when transferring funds.
3. Writing the LC Master and LC smart contracts. We'll deploy the LC Master contract to the blockchain. The LC smart contract will be used only as an interface by the LC Master. It will be imported as part of the LC Master code, and will not be actually deployed using truffle. All new LCs deployed will be created using this interface.
4. Deploying the LC Master smart contract.
5. Creating our React application for creating, viewing, and settling LCs.
6. Running and testing the application.

Creating a USD token for accounting

We need to create a USD currency token that will be used by us, simply for accounting purposes. In an enterprise application, this token will act as a dummy asset, mapped one to one to the actual funds owned by the bank. In our system, we'll use it to represent the funds allocated by the bank to the LC escrow account and track the movement of funds across the banking system.

Let's start writing our ERC20 smart contract, which will be used to issue and distribute this token, by following these steps:

1. Start by creating the USD.sol file. We first declare the compiler version, as shown in the following code snippet:

   ```
   pragma solidity ^0.5.2;
   ```

2. Next, import the contracts that we need to create our ERC20 token, as follows:

   ```
   import "openzeppelin-
   solidity/contracts/token/ERC20/ERC20Detailed.sol";
   import "openzeppelin-
   solidity/contracts/token/ERC20/ERC20Capped.sol";
   import "openzeppelin-solidity/contracts/ownership/Ownable.sol";
   ```

   We are using the OpenZeppelin contract suite for creating our ERC20 token. The OpenZeppelin contract suite provides us with sample smart contracts that can be quickly imported to create our own contracts. Here, we are using the following contracts from OpenZeppelin:

   - ERC20Detailed **contract**: Defines the ERC20 contract and essential methods such as transfer, balanceOf, approve, and so on.
   - ERC20Capped **contract**: Creates an ERC20 token with an upper cap on the number of tokens. It can also be used to assign a minter role to an address. The minter role is used to indicate an address that can mint tokens from this smart contract.
   - Ownable.sol: The ownable contract is used to implement the ownership modifier to public methods, extended by the ERC20 token.

3. Define the contract USD and inherit the aforementioned contracts, as shown in the following code snippet:

   ```
   contract USD is ERC20Detailed, ERC20Capped, Ownable {
   ```

4. Lastly, define the constructor contract, like this:

```
constructor()
ERC20Detailed("US Dollar", "USD", 2)
ERC20Capped(10000000000)
MinterRole()
payable public {}
}
```

From the preceding code, we can make the following observations:

- We called the constructor of the ERC20Detailed contract to set the name of the token (US Dollar), the token symbol (USD), and the number of decimal places after zero (2 decimal places).
- We called the ERCC20Capped constructor, to define the upper cap of the number of USD tokens that can be issued (**10000000000** tokens in total).
- Lastly, we called the MinterRole() contract constructor, which defines the address of the contract owner as the default minter of the token.
- The contract is payable, which allows it to receive and transfer assets.

Putting it all together, the following code block shows how USD.sol looks:

```
pragma solidity ^0.5.2;

import "openzeppelin-solidity/contracts/token/ERC20/ERC20Detailed.sol";
import "openzeppelin-solidity/contracts/token/ERC20/ERC20Capped.sol";
import "openzeppelin-solidity/contracts/ownership/Ownable.sol";

contract USD is ERC20Detailed, ERC20Capped, Ownable {

constructor()

ERC20Detailed("US Dollar", "USD", 2)
ERC20Capped(10000000000)
MinterRole()
payable public {}

}
```

In this section, we've successfully created a USD token for accounting. Now, let's proceed further, towards deploying it.

Deploying a USD token for accounting

Let's deploy the contract token we wrote in the previous section to our Ganache development blockchain, as follows:

1. Bring your Ganache blockchain online.
2. Start your truffle console and connect it to the local blockchain by using the following command:

   ```
   >>truffle console
   ```

3. Move the USD.sol file to the contracts directory in your truffle path. Navigate back to the truffle console and compile the contract from the truffle console, like this:

   ```
   (truffle development)>> compile
   ```

4. Next, create a migration file for USD.sol, like this:

   ```
   create migration USD
   ```

5. Check under the migration directory in your truffle path. You'll observe a new migration file for USD. Update it, as follows:

   ```
   const USD = artifacts.require("USD");

   module.exports = function(deployer) {
     deployer.deploy(USD);
   };
   ```

6. Navigate back to the console. Migrate the contract to the Ganache blockchain with the help of the following command:

   ```
   (truffle development)>> migrate
   ```

   Capture the contract address from the console, after the contract has been deployed. Keep this safe as we'll need it later. The contract address is highlighted in the following screenshot:

```
ishan@ishan-Inspiron-3537: ~/walletcontract/walletcontract
File  Edit  View  Search  Terminal  Help

  > Saving migration to chain.
  > Saving artifacts
  -------------------------------------
  > Total cost:            0.04209884 ETH


1564657566_usd.js
=================

  Replacing 'USD'
  ---------------
  > transaction hash:    0x4d629e42e34057d6e63159bde77db063188e11652b250866f2296769d320617c
  > Blocks: 0            Seconds: 0
  > contract address:    0x0357B7E560260945c62b99C002eFC4f5B149eC2a
  > block number:        7
  > block timestamp:     1564894981
  > account:             0x60f569790e9b87f93aB6bF9bBb3118f6E1C1598b
  > balance:             99.87926076
  > gas used:            1781163
  > gas price:           20 gwei
  > value sent:          0 ETH
  > total cost:          0.03562326 ETH


  > Saving migration to chain.
  > Saving artifacts
  -------------------------------------
  > Total cost:            0.03562326 ETH

Summary
=======
> Total deployments:   4
> Final cost:          0.11880988 ETH

truffle(development)> 
```

Creating an LC Master smart contract

The LC Master is the singular most important component of our project. It creates new LC smart contracts and keeps track of their current status.

Our smart contract will feature the following components:

- Struct array
    - LCDoc[]: To keep track of all LCs issued
- Methods
    - createLC: To create and deploy a new LC
    - lengthLC: To return the total number of LCs issued

- `viewLC`: To view an LC
- `modify LC`: To modify the status and current amount of an LC

- Events

  - `CreateLCSuccessful`: Event emitted on successful LC creation
  - `ModifyLCSuccessful`: Event emitted on successful LC modification

- Modifiers

  - `onlyOwner`: Allows only the owner access to the method

Writing the contract

Now, let's start writing our LC Master smart contract, which will contain the components we discussed in the previous section, as follows:

1. Create a file called `LCMaster.sol`.

2. Let's start writing the contract. We first need to define the version of the Solidity compiler we'll be using, as shown in the following code snippet:

```
pragma solidity ^0.5.2;
```

3. Next, we import our dependent contracts, like this:

```
import "./LC.sol";
import "openzeppelin-solidity/contracts/token/ERC20/ERC20.sol";
```

4. Since our contract transfers the USD ERC20 token, we implement the `ERC20Interface` by importing `ERC20.sol` from OpenZeppelin. This allows us to access the methods of the USD token contract from the LC Master contract. `LC.sol` is the interface used to define individual LCs deployed by `LCMaster`. (More on this later, when we write the LC smart contract interface.) Run the following code:

```
contract LCMaster {

struct LCData {
 uint LCNo;
 address BuyerAcc;
 address SellerAcc;
 uint Amount;
 bytes2 Status;
 uint DOIssue;
 uint DOExpiry;
```

```
    address LCAddress;
    }

LCData[] LCDoc;
```

In the preceding code, we started by defining the `LCMaster` contract. Next, we created the `LCData` structure and the `LCDoc[]` struct array. This structure and array are used to map and keep track of all LC contracts issued by `LCMaster`. They capture and store the following elements:

- LC number
- Buyer's Ethereum account address
- Seller's Ethereum account address
- Amount kept in escrow
- Current status of the LC (I—Issued, P—Partially Settled, S—Settled)
- **Date of issue (DOI)** of the LC
- **Date of expiration (DOE)** of the LC
- Ethereum address to where the LC smart contract is deployed

5. We define the parameters to capture the owner's address and the `ERC20Interface` from `ERC20.sol`, as follows:

```
    address owner;
    ERC20 public ERC20Interface;
```

6. Next, we define an event, `CreateLCSuccessful`, which is emitted whenever a new LC is created successfully, by running the following code:

```
    event CreateLCSuccessful(
    uint LCNum,
    address SAcc,
    address BAcc,
    uint Amt,
    bytes2 Stat,
    uint DOI,
    uint DOE,
    address LCAdd
    );
```

The event shown in the preceding screenshot prints the LC's details to the console, including the following parameters:

- LC number (LCNum)
- Seller's Ethereum account address (SAcc)
- Buyer's Ethereum account address (BAcc)
- Amount kept in escrow (Amt)
- Current status of the LC (**I**—Issued, **P**—Partially Settled, **S**—Settled)
- DOI of the LC (DOI)
- DOE of the LC (DOE)
- Ethereum address to where the LC smart contract is deployed (LCAdd)

7. The following event, ModifyLCSuccessful, is called whenever the LC is successfully modified externally. This is used mostly by the LC smart contracts to update the current status and amount of the LC. Run the following code:

```
event ModifyLCSuccessful(
uint LCNum,
address SAcc,
address BAcc,
uint Amt,
bytes2 Stat
);
```

8. We also implement the following modifier to ensure only the contract owner (which is the bank, in this case) is able to access certain methods. This modifier is called onlyOwner. This is done through the following code snippet:

```
modifier onlyOwner {
if (msg.sender!=owner) revert();
_;
}
```

When the onlyOwner modifier is added to a method, it enforces that only the contract owner can access it.

9. Our constructor in the following code block is a payable one to allow it to transfer and receive assets:

```
constructor () public payable
{
owner=msg.sender;
LCDoc.length = 1;
}
```

The constructor in the preceding code block sets the owner parameter to the contract deployer and initializes the length of the `LCDoc` array to 1.

10. Now, we define our first method, the `createLC()` method, like this:

```
function createLC(address BAcc, address SAcc,uint Amt, uint DOE)
public onlyOwner returns (uint)
{
```

The preceding function, `createLC`, accepts the Buyer's Ethereum address (`BAcc`), the Seller's Ethereum address (`SAcc`), the escrow amount (`Amt`), and the Date of Expiry (`DOE`), and creates the LC. It returns the LC number as a `uint` parameter. It is defined with the `onlyOwner` modifier, which indicates only the bank can access it.

11. The following code block shows the `createLC` function:

```
function createLC(address BAcc, address SAcc,uint Amt, uint DOE)
public onlyOwner returns (uint)
{
  LC newLC = new LC(LCDoc.length,BAcc,SAcc,Amt, now,DOE,owner);
  ERC20Interface =
ERC20(0x0357B7E560260945c62b99C002eFC4f5B149eC2a);
  ERC20Interface.transfer(address(newLC), Amt);
  LCDoc.push(LCData(LCDoc.length,BAcc,SAcc,Amt,'I', now
,DOE,address(newLC)));

  emit CreateLCSuccessful(LCDoc[LCDoc.length-1].LCNo,
  LCDoc[LCDoc.length-1].SellerAcc,
  LCDoc[LCDoc.length-1].BuyerAcc,
  LCDoc[LCDoc.length-1].Amount,
  LCDoc[LCDoc.length-1].Status,
  LCDoc[LCDoc.length-1].DOIssue,
  LCDoc[LCDoc.length-1].DOExpiry,
  LCDoc[LCDoc.length-1].LCAddress);

  return LCDoc[LCDoc.length-1].LCNo;
}
```

12. Here is a step-by-step explanation of the preceding code. The method first issues a new LC smart contract using the `LC.sol` contract interface that we imported earlier:

```
LC newLC = new LC(LCDoc.length,BAcc,SAcc,Amt, now,DOE,owner);
```

This will essentially create a new LC smart contract.

13. The `LCMaster` contract then transfers funds in USD to the newly minted contract. Remember the `USD.sol` smart contract address you copied earlier? Substitute it here, instead of `0x0357B7E560260945c62b99C002eFC4f5B149eC2a`. This address tells the interface where our USD token contract is deployed. After setting the interface, we call the `transfer` function on the USD token to transfer tokens equivalent to the escrow amount (`Amt`) from our `LCMaster` smart contract account to the new LC address (`address(newLC)`), as shown in the following code block:

```
ERC20Interface = ERC20(0x0357B7E560260945c62b99C002eFC4f5B149eC2a);
ERC20Interface.transfer(address(newLC), Amt);
```

14. Lastly, we push a new LC instance to our `LCDoc` struct array using the following line of code:

```
LCDoc.push(LCData(LCDoc.length,BAcc,SAcc,Amt,'I', now
,DOE,address(newLC)));
```

15. The following event, `CreateLCSuccessful`, is emitted once the preceding steps complete successfully:

```
emit CreateLCSuccessful(LCDoc[LCDoc.length-1].LCNo,
LCDoc[LCDoc.length-1].SellerAcc,
LCDoc[LCDoc.length-1].BuyerAcc,
LCDoc[LCDoc.length-1].Amount,
LCDoc[LCDoc.length-1].Status,
LCDoc[LCDoc.length-1].DOIssue,
LCDoc[LCDoc.length-1].DOExpiry,
LCDoc[LCDoc.length-1].LCAddress);
```

16. Finally, the contract returns the LC number of the newly minted LC to the requestor, as shown in the following line of code:

```
return LCDoc[LCDoc.length-1].LCNo;
```

17. Next, we define the `lengthLC()` method, to get the number of LCs issued by the LC Master for looping and counting, like this:

```
function lengthLC() public view returns (uint)
{
 return LCDoc.length;
}
```

18. The following method, `viewLC()`, is another important method. It returns the details of an LC, including the current status and amount for a specific `LCNo`, like this:

```
function viewLC(uint viewLCNo) public view returns (address,
address, uint, bytes2, uint, uint, address)
{

if(msg.sender == owner || msg.sender == LCDoc[viewLCNo].SellerAcc
|| msg.sender == LCDoc[viewLCNo].BuyerAcc)
{

return (
 LCDoc[viewLCNo].SellerAcc,
 LCDoc[viewLCNo].BuyerAcc,
 LCDoc[viewLCNo].Amount,
 LCDoc[viewLCNo].Status,
 LCDoc[viewLCNo].DOIssue,
 LCDoc[viewLCNo].DOExpiry,
 LCDoc[viewLCNo].LCAddress

);
}
}
```

On invocation, the preceding method first verifies if the `requestor` is the bank or the Buyer or Seller for whom the contract is issued. Only then does it return the details of the contract.

19. Lastly, we define the `ModifyLC` method, as follows:

```
function modifyLC(uint LCNum, uint SettleAmt, bytes2 Stat) public
 {
 LCData memory Temp;
 Temp = LCDoc[LCNum];
 Temp.Status = Stat;
 Temp.Amount = SettleAmt;
 delete LCDoc[LCNum];
 LCDoc[LCNum] = Temp;
```

```
emit ModifyLCSuccessful(
  LCDoc[LCNum].LCNo,
  LCDoc[LCNum].SellerAcc,
  LCDoc[LCNum].BuyerAcc,
  LCDoc[LCNum].Amount,
  LCDoc[LCNum].Status);
  }
  }
```

The `modifyLC` method is invoked by the individual LC smart contracts to update the status and amount of the LC after a successful settlement event. It accepts the LC number, the settled amount, and current status as input, and updates the same for the `LCDoc` array.

The method captures the initial value of the LC and stores it in a temporary variable. It updates the `Status` and `Amount` from the input parameters and then updates the new values to the `LCDoc` array.

20. After a successful modification, it fires the `ModifyLCSuccessful` event:

```
emit ModifyLCSuccessful(
  LCDoc[LCNum].LCNo,
  LCDoc[LCNum].SellerAcc,
  LCDoc[LCNum].BuyerAcc,
  LCDoc[LCNum].Amount,
  LCDoc[LCNum].Status);
  }
  }
```

And that's it. We have our `LCMaster` contract. Let's write the LC smart contract and deploy them both.

Creating an LC smart contract

The LC smart contract will serve as an interface for the LC Master contract so that we can create and deploy a new contract. The smart contract will consist of the following components:

- Data structure
    - LCNew: To capture and store the LC details
- Functions
    - `viewLCDetails`: To view the LC details
    - `settleLC`: To invoke a settlement request to the LC

- Modifiers
    - `onlyAuth`: Only permits buyer, seller, and the bank to access to the method
    - `onlySeller`: Only permits the seller to access the method
- Event
    - `SettleLCSuccessful`: Triggered after a successful settlement request

Now, let's start creating the LC smart contract by following these steps:

1. Start by creating a file called `LC.sol`.

2. We will first declare the compiler version and import our dependent contracts, as shown in the following code block:

```
pragma solidity ^0.5.2;

import "openzeppelin-solidity/contracts/token/ERC20/ERC20.sol";
import "./LCMaster.sol";
```

Our compiler version is `0.5.2`. We import the `ERC20.sol` contract from OpenZeppelin's suite. This interface will allow us to transfer tokens during settlement. We also import the `LCMaster` contract as we need to access the `ModifyLC` method in `LCMaster` during settlements.

3. Next, we will define the contract and the LC structure, as shown in the following code block:

```
contract LC {

struct LoC {
 uint LCNo;
 address BuyerAcc;
 address SellerAcc;
 uint Amount;
 uint IniAmount;
 bytes2 Status;
 uint DOIssue;
 uint DOExpiry;
 bytes32 DocHash;
 }

LoC LCnew;
```

The LoC struct in the preceding code is used to define the parameter of the LC contract. It captures and stores the following details:

- LC number (LCNo)
- Buyer's Ethereum account address (BuyerAcc)
- Seller's Ethereum account address (SellerAcc)
- Amount available in escrow (Amount)
- Initial amount stored to escrow (IniAmount)
- Current status of the LC (**I**—Issued, **P**—Partially Settled, **S**—Settled)
- DOI of the LC (DOIssue)
- DOE of the LC (DOExpiry)
- Hash of the document submitted by the Seller during settlement (DocHash)

The DocHash element is important. It is required to capture the hash of the supporting documents for settlement. Since the hash is unique and the blockchain is immutable, this makes the record tamperproof. In the case of suspicion of fraud, the hash of the documents can be easily calculated again and verified with the record stored in the blockchain for verification.

4. Next, we define instances for the ERC20 contract and the LC Master contract, and also define a parameter to hold the bank's address for modifiers and access controls, as follows:

```
LCMaster LCM;
 ERC20 public ERC20Interface;
address bank;
```

5. In the following code, we will define our constructor:

```
constructor (uint LCNum,address BAcc,address SAcc,uint Amt,uint
DOI,uint DOE,address bankadd) public
 {
bank = bankadd;
LCnew.LCNo = LCNum;
LCnew.BuyerAcc = BAcc;
LCnew.SellerAcc = SAcc;
LCnew.Amount = Amt;
LCnew.IniAmount = Amt;
LCnew.Status = 'I' ; // I - Issued, S - Settled, P - Partially
Settled
LCnew.DOIssue = DOI;
LCnew.DOExpiry = DOE;
LCnew.DocHash = 0x0;
```

From the preceding code, we can make the following observations:

- The constructor takes in the input parameters sent to it by the LCMaster contract and maps it to the LC struct LCNew object.
- These parameters now define our new contract. It also sets the default status as 'I' (Issued), the date of issue to now (current blockchain and system time), and DocHash to 0x0 (Default Hash value—No Document submitted yet).
- It also sets the bank Ethereum address as the address that initially calls the createLC method in the LC Master contract (bankadd). This parameter is sent as part of the input parameters from the LC Master.
- Initial amount and amount are set to the same value initially. This value (Amt) is the escrow amount.

6. We also need to define our imported contract dependencies. The LCMaster instance is sent to the msg.sender address because the new contract is deployed by the LC Master. This is held by the LCM object. The ERC20Interface instance is set to the USD token contract address that we stored earlier. Replace 0x0357B7E560260945c62b99C002eFC4f5B149eC2a with your USD token contract address. The code is shown here:

```
LCM = LCMaster(msg.sender);
 ERC20Interface =
ERC20(0x0357B7E560260945c62b99C002eFC4f5B149eC2a);
 }
```

7. Next, in the following code block, we define the modifiers for our methods. The onlyAuth modifier allows access only to the bank, Buyer, and Seller relevant to the LC:

```
modifier onlyAuth {
  if (msg.sender!=bank && msg.sender!=LCnew.BuyerAcc &&
msg.sender!=LCnew.SellerAcc) revert();
  _;
  }
```

8. The following modifier, onlySeller, is for the settlement method. It allows only the Seller's account address to invoke a settlement request on the LC:

```
modifier onlySeller {
  if (msg.sender!=LCnew.SellerAcc) revert();
  _;
  }
```

9. The following event, `SettleLCSuccessful`, is triggered when a settlement request is processed successfully and funds are transferred to the Seller's account:

```
event SettleLCSuccessful(
uint LCNum,
address SAcc,
uint Amt,
uint IAmt,
bytes2 Stat,
bytes32 DocH
);
```

The preceding event prints the LC number, the Seller's account from which the settlement request was made, the amount asked for settlement, the initial amount, the current status of the LC, and the document hash provided for verification during settlement.

10. Now, let's start writing our functions. We start with the `viewLCDetails` `()` function, shown in the following code block:

```
function viewLCdetails() public onlyAuth view returns (uint,
address, address, uint,uint, bytes2, uint, uint, bytes32)
{
```

The `onlyAuth` modifier in the preceding code block ensures only the bank, Buyer, and Seller accounts can access it. The return parameter types are defined as per the original declaration in our `LCnew` structure.

11. Next, we return the requisite data, as shown in the following code block:

```
return ( LCnew.LCNo,
LCnew.BuyerAcc,
LCnew.SellerAcc,
LCnew.Amount,
LCnew.IniAmount,
LCnew.Status,
LCnew.DOIssue,
LCnew.DOExpiry,
LCnew.DocHash
);
}
```

The method returns the LC details—specifically, the following parameters:

- LC number (`LCNo`)
- Buyer's Ethereum account address (`BuyerAcc`)
- Seller's Ethereum account address (`SellerAcc`)
- Amount available in escrow (`Amount`)
- Initial amount stored to escrow (`IniAmount`)
- Current status of the LC (**I**—Issued, **P**—Partially Settled, **S**—Settled)
- DOI of the LC (`DOIssue`)
- DOE of the LC (`DOExpiry`)
- Hash of the document submitted by the Seller during settlement (`DocHash`)

12. The following method, `settleLC`, is invoked by the Seller during a settlement request:

    ```
    function settleLC(uint SettleAmt, bytes32 DocH) public onlySeller
    {
    ```

    It takes the settlement amount (`SettleAmt`) and document hash (`DocH`) as input. The `onlySeller` modifier ensures only the Seller account can access it.

13. We start by putting two `require` statements in place to ensure that our LC contract is valid, as shown in the following code block:

    ```
    require(LCnew.DOExpiry >= now && now >= LCnew.DOIssue, "LC Expired
    or Invalid Date ofIssue");
    require(SettleAmt > 0 && SettleAmt <= LCnew.Amount , "Invalid
    Settlement Amount");
    ```

From the preceding code, we can make the following observations:

- The first `require` statement checks that the time at which the settlement request was sent is after the date of issue, and before or on the date of expiry of the LC.
- In the case of an invalid date of request or an expired LC, it presents the message `LC Expired or Invalid Date of Issue` to the console.
- The second `require` statement checks if the settlement amount sent by the seller for processing is greater than zero and if it is below the total amount available in the LC.

14. Next, we check if the settlement amount (**SettleAmt**) is less than or equal to the total amount available in the escrow account. In the case of the settlement amount being less, the Seller can still proceed with a partial settlement. They are paid the settlement amount from the LC escrow, and the LC escrow amount parameter is updated to reflect the currently available funds.

    If the settlement amount is equal to the total funds allocated to the LC, the entire amount is settled and transferred to the Seller's Ethereum account. The LC's status should update to `'S'`, indicating settled, and the amount in escrow will be set to zero.

15. We check the partial settlement case by verifying the settlement amount using an `if` clause, as shown in the following code block:

    ```
    if(SettleAmt == LCnew.Amount )
    {
    ERC20Interface.transfer(msg.sender, SettleAmt);
    LCM.modifyLC(LCnew.LCNo,0,'S');
    ```

From the preceding code, we can make the following observations:

- If the settlement amount (`SettleAmt`) is equal to the total amount available under the escrow (`LCNew.Amount`), we send a transaction worth the escrow amount to the Seller's address.
- This is done by calling the `ERC20` transfer method using the `ERC20Interface` we defined earlier. The `transfer` method transfers the settlement amount from the LC escrow account to the Seller's account.
- The Seller's account is identified here, through the `msg.sender` variable, as it holds the account of the Seller making the settlement request.

16. Next, we invoke the `modifyLC` method we created earlier in our LC Master smart contract. This invocation is done using the LC Master LCM instance we defined earlier.

    The input parameters that are set are the LC number, **0** (current amount in LC after settlement), and the **'S'** flag, indicating a full settlement of the LC.

17. The following code shows the `modifyLC` method from `LCMaster` that we wrote earlier:

```
function modifyLC(uint LCNum, uint SettleAmt, bytes2 Stat) public
{
LCData memory Temp;
Temp = LCDoc[LCNum];
Temp.Status = Stat;
Temp.Amount = SettleAmt;
delete LCDoc[LCNum];
LCDoc[LCNum] = Temp;
```

- The `modifyLC` method declares a temporary object called `Temp` and stores the existing values of the LC.
- It then updates the current amount (0 USD) and status (S) of the LC, as sent by the child LC contract, and updates it to the `LCDoc` struct array.
- It does so by deleting the old component and replacing the new one.

18. It then issues an event with the new LC details after successful modification, as shown in the following code block:

```
emit ModifyLCSuccessful(
LCDoc[LCNum].LCNo,
LCDoc[LCNum].SellerAcc,
LCDoc[LCNum].BuyerAcc,
LCDoc[LCNum].Amount,
LCDoc[LCNum].Status);
}
```

The preceding event prints the `LCNo`, the Seller's account, the Buyer's Account, current amount, and current status.

19. Back to our `settleLC()` method in the LC smart contract. After the successful execution of the transfer and update to the LC Master contract, we update the LC details in the LC smart contract, as shown in the following code block:

```
LCnew.Amount = 0;
LCnew.Status = 'S';
LCnew.DocHash = DocH;
}
```

In the preceding code, the current amount is set to **0**, the status to **'S'**, and the document hash sent as part of the request is stored. These details can be viewed any time using the `viewLCdetails()` method.

20. Lastly, the `SettleLCSuccessful` event is triggered, as follows:

```
emit SettleLCSuccessful(LCnew.LCNo,
  LCnew.SellerAcc,
  LCnew.Amount,
  LCnew.IniAmount,
  LCnew.Status,
  LCnew.DocHash);
```

It prints the following details to the console:

- The Seller's Ethereum account to which the funds were transferred (`SellerAcc`)
- The current funds in the escrow (`Amount`)
- The initial funds in the escrow (`IniAmount`)
- The current status of the LC (`Status`)
- The hash of the document submitted for settlement (`DocHash`)

If the settlement amount is less than the amount, the following `else` clause will be triggered:

```
else
 {
uint currAmt = LCnew.Amount - SettleAmt
ERC20Interface.transfer(msg.sender, SettleAmt);
LCM.modifyLC(LCnew.LCNo,currAmt,'P');
```

From the preceding code, we can make the following observations:

- We first calculate the current amount (`currAmt`), by deducting the settlement amount from the escrow amount.
- Next, we invoke the `ERC20` transfer method, using the `ERC20Interface` to send the settlement amount from our LC escrow account to the Seller's account. The Seller's account is identified from the system-defined `msg.sender` parameter.
- The LC Master instance (`LCM`) is used to invoke the `modifyLC` method within the LC Master smart contract. The input parameters are the LC number (`LCnew.LCNo`), the current amount in the LC escrow (`currAmt`), and the current status (`'P'`), to denote partial settlement.

As in the total settlement case, the `modifyLC` method updates the current status and current amount for the LC and triggers the `ModifyLCSuccessful` event. After a successful settlement, we update the LC details for our child LC contract. The new amount, the new status, and the hash of the document submitted for settlement is updated for our `LCnew` object, which holds the LC details, as follows:

```
LCnew.Amount = currAmt;
LCnew.Status = 'P';
LCnew.DocHash = DocH;
```

These can be viewed for recording purposes using the `viewLCdetails` method. Lastly, the `SettleLCSuccessful` event is triggered, as follows:

```
emit SettleLCSuccessful(LCnew.LCNo,
  LCnew.SellerAcc,
  LCnew.Amount,
  LCnew.IniAmount,
  LCnew.Status,
  LCnew.DocHash);
  }
  }
  }
```

The preceding code prints the following details to the console:

- The Seller's Ethereum account to which the funds were transferred (`SellerAcc`)
- The current funds in the escrow (`Amount`)
- The initial funds in the escrow (`IniAmount`)
- The current status of the LC (`Status`)
- The hash of the document submitted for settlement (`DocHash`)

With that, we come to the end of our `settleLC` method, and the LC smart contract.

Deploying the LC Master smart contract

To deploy the smart contract, first bring your Ganache blockchain online. Make sure your Ganache test server is running on `localhost:8545`. To do so, select the **New Workspace** option from the Ganache launch screen. Click on the **Server** tab on the **Workspace** screen. Set the port number to `8545`, as shown in the following screenshot:

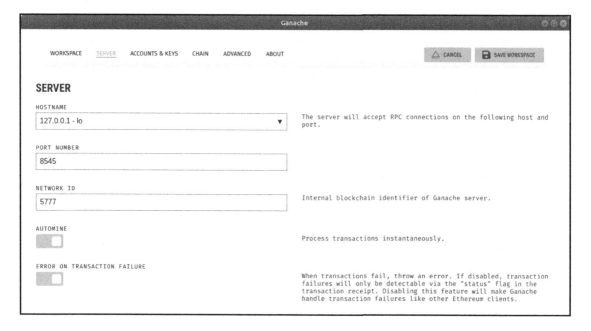

Click on **Save Workspace** in the upper-right corner. A blockchain network will be started, as follows:

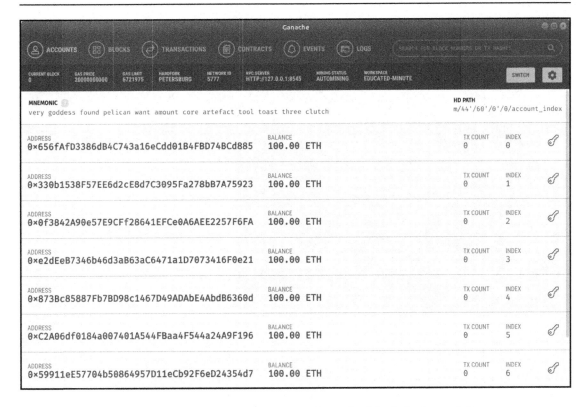

Let's deploy the contracts we built earlier to our Ganache blockchain, as follows:

1. Open a Terminal window and navigate to your truffle project directory. Bring the truffle console online by entering the following command:

```
truffle console
```

2. Copy and paste the LCMaster.sol and LC.sol contracts into the contracts directory in your truffle project.

3. As shown in the following screenshot, navigate back to the truffle console and compile both the contracts by entering the `compile` command:

4. After successful compilation, create a migration file for `LCMaster.sol`, like this:

```
(truffle development)>> create migration LCMaster
```

The preceding command will return the following output:

5. Within your File Explorer, navigate to your truffle directory. Open the `migration` folder.

6. Open the newly created migration file in a text editor and update it with the following code:

```
const LCMaster = artifacts.require("LCMaster");
module.exports = function(deployer) {
  deployer.deploy(LCMaster);
};
```

7. Now, navigate back to the truffle console and enter `migrate` on the Terminal window to migrate the `LCMaster` contract, as follows:

```
(truffle development)>> migrate
```

The console should deploy all the contracts again, as follows:

```
ishan@ishan-Inspiron-3537: ~/walletcontract/walletcontract
File  Edit  View  Search  Terminal  Help

    > Saving migration to chain.
    > Saving artifacts
    - - - - - - - - - - - - - - - - - - - - - - - - - - - - -
    > Total cost:              0.03562326 ETH


1564802152_l_c_m_aster.js
=========================

    Replacing 'LCMaster'
    - - - - - - - - - - - - -
    > transaction hash:       0x490bee2464851191399566644ac0408e7681008941583c17198a329579b1075f6
    > Blocks: 0               Seconds: 0
    > contract address:       0x26518b6a8E4f8B20413C1Cf70DC05B58Cb5171A0
    > block number:           9
    > block timestamp:        1564893066
    > account:                0x60f569790e9b87f93aB6bF9bBb3118f6E1C1598b
    > balance:                99.82747302
    > gas used:               2562167
    > gas price:              20 gwei
    > value sent:             0 ETH
    > total cost:             0.05124334 ETH


    > Saving migration to chain.
    > Saving artifacts
    - - - - - - - - - - - - - - - - - - - - - - - - - - - - -
    > Total cost:             0.05124334 ETH


Summary
=======
> Total deployments:    5
> Final cost:           0.17005322 ETH

truffle(development)> []
```

Note the address to which the LC Master contract is deployed. We'll need this later.

All right. So, now, we have all three of our contracts deployed. Let's create our React app, which will interact with these three smart contracts.

Creating the LC module React app

Our React app will have the following users and features. It will allow end users to interact with our smart contracts through a frontend layer, as follows:

- `Bank`: The bank user who logs in to the app. The user can create and view LCs.
- `Buyer`: The buying merchant who requests an LC from the bank. The Buyer can view all the LCs issued in their name by the bank.
- `Seller`: The selling merchant who will approach the bank for settlement, on the successful delivery of their goods to the buying merchant. The Seller can view the LCs that include them as a beneficiary and submit a settlement request.

Broadly, the app will have the following React components:

- `Address Bar`: Displays the account used to access the app in real time.
- `Description`: A component that provides a description of the app.
- `Nav`: A component that implements a navigation bar, with the bank's name and logo.
- `InputField`: A component that implements the input fields, used for getting inputs from the user.
- `Container`: The link between the main `App.js` file and the rest of the child components. It renders child components based on the current state. It receives all state variables and methods and forwards them to the child components, as and when required.
- `Bank Login`: A login screen for our bank. It will allow the Buyer, the Seller, and the bank to log in to the app and use it. It also redirects them to the lower screens, for using the app.
- `BankTabCreate`: The component that renders the Create LC screen for the bank user.
- `BankTabView`: The component that renders the View LC screen for the bank user.
- `BuyerTabView`: The component that renders the View LC screen for the Buyer.
- `SellerTabSettle`: The component that renders the Settle LC screen for the Seller.

- `SellerTabView`: The component that renders the View LC screen for the Seller.
- `LCView`: The component that renders a singular screen, with all the details of a single LC. It can be accessed by the bank user, the Buyer, or the Seller.

Apart from these components, the two `js` files in the contract folder will hold the following details:

- `LCMaster`: Holds the contract address and the `LCMaster` contract **application binary interface (ABI)**
- `LC`: Holds the ABI for the LC contract

Lastly, we'll have our regular React files, including the following:

- `App.js`
- `App.cs`
- `index.js`
- `package.json`

Some knowledge of React is expected for this part of the tutorial. If you want to skip the React part and directly get to executing the app, you can access the entire code base at the following GitHub link.

We'll be taking a look at only the important components in this section, and thus not all the components will be covered. However, you can access the entire code base at the following GitHub link: `https://github.com/PacktPublishing/Blockchain-Development-for-Finance-Projects/tree/master/Chapter%206/LCApp`.

Now, let's dive into creating our app.

Creating the React project environment

Let's set up our app environment, as follows:

1. Create a new React app called `LCApp` using `npx`, like this:

```
npx create-react-app LCApp
```

2. Update your `package.json` to the following values:

```
{
  "name": "lcapp",
  "version": "1.0.0",
  "dependencies": {
  "bulma-start": "0.0.2",
  "react": "^16.4.2",
  "react-dom": "^16.4.2",
  "react-scripts": "1.1.4",
   "web3": "^1.2"
  },
  "scripts": {
  "start": "react-scripts start",
  "build": "react-scripts build",
  "test": "react-scripts test --env=jsdom",
  "eject": "react-scripts eject"
  }
}
```

3. Run `npm install` on the Terminal window to install the dependencies.
4. Next, within the `src` folder, create a `Components` folder for the app components. Also, create a `contracts` folder within `src`. We'll be using this to map the contracts being used by the app.

Setting up the contract interfaces

Next, we will create the contract interface that will be used by our React app to invoke the contracts. Follow these steps:

1. Within the `contracts` folder, create the `LCMaster.js` and `LCabi.js` files.
2. Open the `LCMaster.js` file in a text editor.
3. With the file open, navigate to your truffle project environment, which you used to deploy the `LCMaster` and LC smart contracts.
4. In the truffle environment, locate the `builds` directory. Under `builds`, you'll find the `LCMaster.json` build file.

5. Open the file and locate the contract ABI. It should look like this:

```
1  {
2    "contractName": "LCMaster",
3    "abi": [
4      {
5        "inputs": [],
6        "payable": true,
7        "stateMutability": "payable",
8        "type": "constructor"
9      },
10     {
11       "anonymous": false,
12       "inputs": [
13         {
14           "indexed": false,
15           "internalType": "uint256",
16           "name": "LCNum",
17           "type": "uint256"
18         },
19         {
20           "indexed": false,
21           "internalType": "address",
22           "name": "SAcc",
23           "type": "address"
24         },
25         {
26           "indexed": false,
27           "internalType": "address",
28           "name": "BAcc",
29           "type": "address"
30         },
31         {
32           "indexed": false,
33           "internalType": "uint256",
34           "name": "Amt",
35           "type": "uint256"
36         },
37         {
38           "indexed": false,
39           "internalType": "bytes2",
40           "name": "Stat",
41           "type": "bytes2"
42         },
43         {
44           "indexed": false,
45           "internalType": "uint256",
46           "name": "DOI",
47           "type": "uint256"
48         },
49         {
50           "indexed": false,
51           "internalType": "uint256",
52           "name": "DOE",
53           "type": "uint256"
54         },
```

Copy this entire ABI and paste it into the `LCMaster.js` file as a parameter, as follows:

```
export default {

abi: ["constant": true,
 "inputs": [],
 "name": "ERC20Interface",
 "outputs": [
 {
 "name": "",
 "type": "address"
 }
 ], .............]}
```

6. Similarly, copy and paste the contract address we got for `LCMaster.js` during deployment. Add this as a parameter to `LCMaster` as well, like this:

```
export default {

address: "0x26518b6a8E4f8B20413C1Cf70DC05B58Cb5171A0",

abi: [.............]}
```

7. Save the file. We'll load this object in order to interact with the `LCMaster` contract we deployed to the blockchain.

8. Now, open the `LCabi.js` file in a text editor. Add the ABI for the LC smart contract as a parameter.

9. To do so, navigate back to the truffle build directory and open the `LC.json` build file.

10. Open the file and locate the ABI.

11. Copy the ABI and paste it into the `LCabi.js` file as a parameter, as follows:

```
export default {
 "abi": [
 {
 "constant": true,
 "inputs": [],
 "name": "ERC20Interface",
 "outputs": [
 {
 "name": "",
 "type": "address"
 }
 ], ......]}
```

So, now, we have our contract interfaces. Let's create our components.

Building the React components

We will build the following components in the proceeding subsections:

- `BankLogin.js`
- `BankTabCreate.js`
- `SellerTabSettle.js`
- `SellerTabView.js`
- `Container.js`

Let's start working on our React app components. We'll start with the `BankLogin.js` component.

Creating the BankLogin.js component

The `BankLogin.js` component is pretty standard. It renders a screen with three buttons that indicate the three user roles defined earlier. These are the Buyer, the Seller, and the Bank. On clicking on the button, the relevant user is logged in, as follows:

- For the Bank user, the default screen is the Create LC screen.
- For the Buyer, the default screen is the View LC screen.
- For the Seller, the default screen is the Settle LC screen.

Let's look at how the `Banklogin.js` component renders the login screen:

```
<div className="column has-text-centered">
 Login as:
 </div>

 <div className="column has-text-centered">
 <span className="button is-medium is-warning" onClick={() =>
props.BuyerSessionView()}>
 Buyer
 </span >
 </div>

 <div className="column has-text-centered">
 <span className="button is-medium is-primary is-6" onClick={() =>
props.BankSessionCreate()}>
 GreenGables Bank
```

```
   </span>
   </div>

   <div className="column has-text-centered">
   <span className="button is-medium is-danger is-6" onClick={() =>
props.SellerSessionSettle()}>
   Seller
   </span>
   </div>
```

More on
the `BuyerSessionView`, `BankSessionCreate`, and `SellerSessionSettle` methods late
r, when we write our `App.js` code.

Creating the BankTabCreate.js component

The `BankTabCreate.js` component renders a screen that can be used for capturing the
details for creating a new LC. On submitting the request, it calls the `createLC` method,
which generates a new LC contract on the blockchain. More on this method later, when we
write our `App.js` code. The code can be seen here:

```
   </div>
   <InputField onInputChangeUpdateField={props.onInputChangeUpdateField}
   fields={props.fields} name="BuyerAccount" placeholder="Buyer Account"/>

   <InputField onInputChangeUpdateField={props.onInputChangeUpdateField}
   fields={props.fields} name="SellerAccount" placeholder="Seller Account"/>

   <InputField onInputChangeUpdateField={props.onInputChangeUpdateField}
   fields={props.fields} name="Amount" placeholder="Amount"addon="USD"/>

   <InputField onInputChangeUpdateField={props.onInputChangeUpdateField}
   fields={props.fields} name="DOExpiry" placeholder="Date of Expiry
(YYYYMMDD)"/>
   </div>

   </div>
   <div className="panel-block is-paddingless is-12 ">
   <div className="column has-text-centered ">

   <div className="button" onClick={() => props.createLC()}>
   Submit
   </div>


   <div className="button" onClick={() => props.closeTab()}>
```

```
Back
</div>
```

The screen captures the Buyer's Ethereum account address, the Seller's Ethereum account address, the amount of the LC escrow, and the DOE of the LC through the input fields. By clicking on the **Submit** button, it calls the `createLC` method to invoke the `LCMaster` smart contract.

Creating the SellerTabSettle.js component

The `SellerTabSettle.js` component renders a screen for capturing and settling a settlement request from the Seller, as follows:

```
<InputField onInputChangeUpdateField={props.onInputChangeUpdateField}
  fields={props.fields} name="LCNo" placeholder="LC Number"/>

<InputField onInputChangeUpdateField={props.onInputChangeUpdateField}
  fields={props.fields} name="Amount" placeholder="Amount" addon="USD"/>

<InputField onInputChangeUpdateField={props.onInputChangeUpdateField}
  fields={props.fields} name="DocHash" placeholder="Document Hash"/>

</div>
</div>
<div className="panel-block is-paddingless is-12 ">
<div className="column has-text-centered ">

<div className="button" onClick={() => props.settleLC()}>
Submit
</div>

<div className="button" onClick={() => props.SellerSessionView()} >
Back
</div>
```

It renders a screen with the input fields to capture the LC number the seller wants to settle, the settlement amount, and the hash signature of the document submitted by the Seller for the settlement. On clicking the **Submit** button, the `settleLC` method is called. More on this method later, when we look at our `App.js` file.

Creating the SellerTabView.js component

The `SellerTabView.js` component maps an array, `LCNew`, containing the list of all LCs issued with the Seller as the beneficiary, and displays it to the user in a serialized manner. Additionally, it provides the **View Details** and **Settle LC** buttons next to each entry. On clicking on the **Settle LC** button, the user is redirected to the **Settle LC** screen, where the Seller can submit a settlement request. On clicking **View Details**, the Seller is redirected to the `LCView` screen, which shows all the details of the LC.

The `BankTabView.js` and `BuyerTabView.js` components are similar to the `SellerTabView.js` component in implementation, except they do not have the option to settle the LC.

One interesting point to note here is the implementation of the `DOI` and `DOE` parameters.

Since the Ethereum blockchain stores dates in **Universal Time Coordinated** (UTC) format (milliseconds from January 1, 1970), we first convert the date fetched from the blockchain into a standard ISO format string. The ISO format string is then spliced so that we only have the date of issue and expiry, and the time details are not shown to the user, as follows:

```
props.LCNew.map((LC,index) => {
  var DOI = (new Date(LC.DOI*1000)).toISOString();
  var DOE = (new Date(LC.DOE*1000)).toISOString();
  var DOIssue=DOI.split("T",1);
  var DOExpiry=DOE.split("T",1);
```

Creating the Container.js component

The `Container.js` component holds several other components, toggles a components' display as per state changes, and passes down their props to the components after it receives them from `App.js`.

The `Container.js` component mainly renders dependent on the `state.role` and `state.option` state variables that are sent to it by `App.js`. `state.role` indicates the role of the user (Bank, Buyer merchant, Seller merchant) currently logged in to the application. `state.option` indicates the option selected by the user (View LC, Create LC, Settle LC).

Based on the option selected, the container renders and toggles between the following components:

- `BuyerTabView.js`
- `BankTabCreate.js`
- `BankTabView.js`
- `SellerTabView.js`
- `SettlerTabSettle.js`
- `BankLogin.js`
- `LCView.js`

As their names suggest, the first five components indicate the role and the option selected. So, for example, when the Bank selects Create LC, `BankTabCreate.js` is rendered.

The sixth component in the list, `BankLogin.js`, is the default component rendered when no role or option is selected. Thus, it is the login page and the landing page for our app.

The `LCView.js` component is a common component that gives the details of a single LC, and it gets rendered whenever the option selected is `ViewSingleLC`, whichever the role might be.

A list of props is passed on while rendering the components. These include the following:

- `LCNew`, an array that maps a list of all LCs that the user can view/settle.
- `LC`, a struct variable that stores the details of the LC to be displayed in the `LCView` component.
- `createLC()` and `settleLC()` methods, which are called by their respective components on clicking the **Submit** button.
- A set of session setters, including `BuyerSessionView`, `BankSessionView`, `BankSessionCreate`, `SellerSessionSettle`, and so on, which set the current **role** and **option** when invoked. Thus, they are passed to the components while rendering to enable navigation between the `App` components.

So, now, we have completed building our components. Let's bring it all together with our main `App.js` file.

Writing the app methods and creating the App.js file

The `App.js` file will have the following methods defined under it:

- `constructor ()`: Initializes the state variables.
- `componentDidMount`: Checks if the MetaMask web3 provider is available and fetches the user's Ethereum account.
- A set of session `setters` that set the role and the `option` selected. These include the following:
  - `BuyerSessionView`
  - `BankSessionCreate`
  - `BankSessionView`
  - `SellerSessionView`
  - `SellerSessionSettle`
  - `SellerSessionVSettle`
- A set of utility methods for navigation and operation, which include the following:
  - `onInputChangeUpdateField`: For capturing and storing the input fields data to the state.
  - `closeTab`: To close the current tab and go back to the landing page.
  - `closeViewTab`: To close the view single LC tab.
  - `resetApp`: To reset the app, including the state variables and the form fields, after a transaction.
- The `createLC` method
- The `viewLC` method
- The `viewSingleLC` method
- The `settleLC` method
- `render`: Renders the `Component.js` file and passes it the props

Let's take a look at these.

Writing the constructor() method

Let's look at the constructor method of our `App.js` file and the preliminary state it initializes, as follows:

1. The constructor starts by instantiating the `LCMaster` and `LCabi` components we defined earlier, like this:

```
class App extends Component {

constructor(){
super();

this.LCMaster = LCMaster;
this.LCabi = LCabi;
```

2. Next, it sets the app name (`GreenGables Bank`) and binds our methods so that they can be accessed from the child components, as follows:

```
this.appName = 'GreenGables Bank';
this.closeTab = this.closeTab.bind(this);
this.resetApp = this.resetApp.bind(this);
this.viewLC = this.viewLC.bind(this);
this.viewSingleLC = this.viewSingleLC.bind(this);
this.onInputChangeUpdateField =
this.onInputChangeUpdateField.bind(this);
```

3. Lastly, it declares and defines our default state when the app is loading for the first time. Notice how the `role` and the `option` variables are set to null. It also declares a set of fields, including `BuyerAccount`, `SellerAccount`, `Amount`, `DOExpiry`, `DocHash`, and `LCNo`, which will be used by the child components to take inputs from the user. It also declares the `LCNew` array, which will store the dynamic list of LCs that will be used for further processing. The LC object will be used to store information when the user wants to view the details of a single LC:

```
this.state = {
role: null,
option: null,
LCNew: [],
LC: [],
fields: {
BuyerAccount: null,
SellerAccount: null,
Amount: null,
DOExpiry: null,
DocHash: null,
```

```
      LCNo: null
      },
    };
```

Using the componentDidMount method

We use our `componentDidMount` method to check if the MetaMask-injected `web3provider` is currently available within the browser window. This is done by checking if the `window.ethereum` object is available, as follows:

```
componentDidMount(){
  var account;

  if (window.ethereum) {
```

If `window.ethereum` is available, we instantiate our current `web3` instance so that it uses the MetaMask-injected `web3` instance, like this:

```
if (window.ethereum) {
  const ethereum = window.ethereum;
  window.web3 = new Web3(ethereum);
  this.web3 = new Web3(ethereum);
```

Next, we ask MetaMask for permission to access the user's accounts that are available in the MetaMask wallet. This is done by requesting access through `ethereum.enable()`, as follows:

```
ethereum.enable().then((accounts) => {
```

When we run our app, MetaMask will pop up a window to the user, asking if they want to grant the app access to their MetaMask accounts. If the user clicks on **Confirm**, the app is then able to access the MetaMask-injected `web3` instance and the user's accounts.

On approval, MetaMask returns an array of the accounts available in the wallet. The primary account is available at the zeroth position, `account[0]`. Our app captures this account and stores it as the default account for our `web3` instance, as follows:

```
ethereum.enable().then((accounts) => {
this.web3.eth.defaultAccount = accounts[0];
```

Additionally, we capture and update this account to our state as well, like this:

```
account = accounts[0];
let app = this;
this.setState({
account
 });
```

This ends our `componentDidMount` method.

Building the session setters

The session setters have a standard format, as follows:

```
BuyerSessionView = () => {
 this.setState({
 role: 'Buyer',
 option: 'View'
 })
 this.viewLC();
 };
```

On invocation, they set the state role and option, based on their functionality. So, in the preceding example, `BuyerSessionView` sets the role to `Buyer` and the option to `View`.

In the case of all the `View` setters, the session setter method also calls the `viewLC()` method to populate the `LCnew` array before rendering the view LC screen. The `viewLC()` method fetches the list of LCs relevant to the current session user from the `LCMaster` smart contract and populates it in the `LCnew[]` array.

Writing the createLC method

Now, we come to the primary methods of our app. We start with the `createLC` method, as follows:

1. We start the app by storing the current app state in the `app` variable, as shown in the following code block. This will allow us to refer to the current app state during asynchronous calls:

   ```
   createLC = () => {
    let app = this;
   ```

2. The contract variable is used to instantiate an `LCMaster` object, which points to the `LCMaster` smart contract we deployed earlier to our blockchain. We do so by using the `web3.eth.contract` method. The input parameter to this method is the contract ABI, and the second parameter is the contract address. Since we had mapped these earlier to the `LCMaster` object, we simply fetch these values and pass them to the method, like this:

```
var contract = new this.web3.eth.Contract(this.LCMaster.abi,
this.LCMaster.address);
```

3. Next, we fetch the user inputs while creating the LC. The date input by the user is spliced into year, month, and day, like this:

```
let dateExpiry = this.state.fields.DOExpiry;
let year = dateExpiry.slice(0,4);
let month = dateExpiry.slice(4,6)-1;
let day = dateExpiry.slice(6,8);
```

4. This value is then converted into UTC format, which Ethereum understands and interprets, like this:

```
var DateTemp = new Date(year, month, day, 23, 59, 59, 0)
var DOE = Math.floor(DateTemp.getTime()/1000.0)
```

5. We use our contract object to call the `createLC` method in `LCMaster`, as shown in the following code block. The transaction is sent from the `web3.defaultAccount` we set earlier:

```
contract.methods.createLC(this.state.fields.BuyerAccount,this.state
.fields.SellerAccount,
  this.state.fields.Amount,DOE).send({from:
app.web3.eth.defaultAccount}).then(function(response){
```

6. Lastly, we check the response from the smart contract method. The successful response, which is the contract LC number, is printed to the console, as follows:

```
if(response) {
console.log("LC No.");
console.log(response);
app.resetApp();
}
})
```

On to the next method, `viewLC`.

Writing the viewLC method

Next, let's look at the method that will fetch the details of the LCs issued by the bank on the blockchain. To do so, we'll fetch the LC details from the LC Master smart contract by invoking the smart contract `viewLC` method, as follows:

1. We start our `viewLC` method by defining the contract instance, similarly to the last method, as follows:

```
let app = this;
var lastLC;

var contract = new
this.web3.eth.Contract(this.LCMaster.abi,this.LCMaster.address);
```

2. The first contract call is to the `lengthLC` method. This method returns the number of LCs that have been created in the `LCMaster` contract. This number is the length of the `LCDoc` array. The code can be seen here:

```
contract.methods.lengthLC().call().then(function(response){
```

3. On a successful response, we store the length of the `LCDoc` array in the `lastLC` variable, like this:

```
if(response) {
lastLC = response;
```

4. If `lastLC` is greater than 1 (that is, LCs have been issued by the `LCMaster` contract), we perform the next set of steps, like this:

```
if (lastLC > 1)
{
app.setState({
LCNew: [],
})

for (let i = 1; i < lastLC ; i++)
{
contract.methods.viewLC(i).call().then(function(response){
```

We first reset the LCNew state variable and clean any previous data. Next, we run a loop and iterate from 0 to lastLC, and call the viewLC method in the LCMaster smart contract. For each function call to viewLC , we send the i loop counter as the LCNo input parameter.

The resultant output response is captured by a set of local variables. Notice how the value for Status is converted using a web3 utility from hex to ASCII. This is because Ethereum stores bytes values in hex representation. The code can be seen here:

```
if(response) {
  let LCNo = i;
  let SAcc = response[0];
  let BAcc = response[1];
  let Amount = response[2];
  let Status = app.web3.utils.hexToAscii(response[3]);
  let DOI = response[4];
  let DOE = response[5];
  let LCAdd = response[6];
```

5. LCNew is initialized as a local variable from the LCNew state variable. For each iteration of the loop, we push the viewLC response to the LCNew local variable and update the LCNew state variable, as follows:

```
let LCNew = app.state.LCNew;

LCNew.push({
LCNo,
BAcc,
SAcc,
Amount,
Status,
DOI,
DOE,
LCAdd
});
app.setState({
          LCNew
      })
```

That brings us to the end of the viewLC method in our App.js file.

Writing the viewSingleLC method

The `viewSingleLC` method is used to view the details of a single LC. Unlike `viewLC`, it returns the details of the LC from the LC smart contract instead of the LC Master smart contract. Let's look at the code for the method:

1. The method takes the LC address as the input parameter. It will fetch the details of a single LC and allow the app to render these details on the screen. It does so by invoking the `viewLCDetails` function on the LC.

   It first resets the `LC` state variable to blank, like so:

   ```
   viewSingleLC = (LCAdd) => {

   let app = this;
   app.setState({
   LC: [],
   });
   ```

2. Next, it instantiates the LC smart contract. To do so, it fetches the ABI from the `LCabi` object we created earlier. It takes the address from the input parameters, as follows:

   ```
   var contract = new this.web3.eth.Contract(this.LCabi.abi,LCAdd);
   ```

3. Next, a call is made to the `viewLCDetails` method in the LC smart contract, as follows:

   ```
   contract.methods.viewLCdetails().call().then(function(response){
   ```

4. On a successful response, the response is mapped to a set of local variables, like this:

   ```
   if(response) {
   let LCNo = response[0];
   let BuyerAcc = response[1];
   let SellerAcc = response[2];
   let Amount = response[3];
   let IniAmount = response[4];
   let Status = app.web3.utils.hexToAscii(response[5]);
   let DOI = response[6];
   let DOE = response[7];
   let DocHash = response[8];
   ```

5. The local variables are then pushed to the LC array, like this:

```
let LC = app.state.LC;

LC.push({
LCNo,
BuyerAcc,
SellerAcc,
Amount,
IniAmount,
Status,
DOI,
DOE,
DocHash
});
```

6. Finally, we update the app state with a new LC array. We also set the current option to `ViewSingleLC` so that the `LCView` component is rendered, as follows:

```
app.setState({
LC,
option: 'ViewSingleLC'
})
```

With that, we come to the end of the `viewSingleLC` method.

Writing the settleLC method

The `settleLC` method is called when the Seller wants to initiate a settlement. The method starts by instantiating the `LCMaster` contract.

Next, it calls the `viewLC` method in `LCMaster` with the LC number for which settlement is requested. It gets the LC number from the `fields` defined in the state, as follows:

```
settleLC = () => {
 let app = this;
 var contractMaster = new
this.web3.eth.Contract(this.LCMaster.abi,this.LCMaster.address);
contractMaster.methods.viewLC(app.state.fields.LCNo).call().then(function(r
esponse){
```

On a successful response, we capture the LC contract address for the LC number, from the response in the `LCAddress` local variable, as follows:

```
if(response) {
  let LCAddress = response[6];
```

We instantiate a new contract instance for the LC smart contract. After instantiating, the `settleLC` method is called in the LC smart contract. We pass the settlement amount and the document hash as input parameters, as follows:

```
var contractLC = new app.web3.eth.Contract(app.LCabi.abi,LCAddress);
contractLC.methods.settleLC(app.state.fields.Amount,app.state.fields.DocHas
h)
.send({from: app.web3.eth.defaultAccount})
                .then(function(response){
                  if(response) {
                                console.log(response);
                                app.resetApp;
                                }
```

The successful response is logged to the console and `resetApp` is called to reset the app state.

That brings us to the end of our `App.js` file. Let's run the app and see how it looks.

Running the LC module

Let's run the entire application and see how it works. If you have not already done so, start your Ganache blockchain and run a Quickstart blockchain at `localhost:8545`, as shown in the following screenshot:

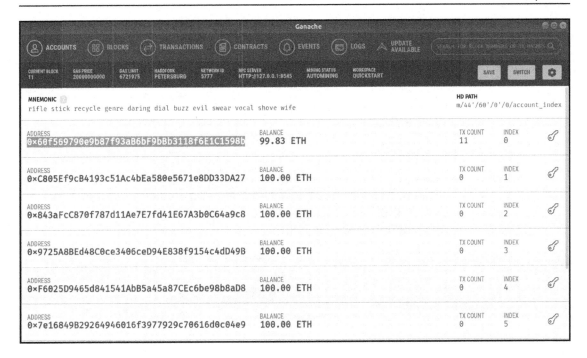

Make sure the USD token contract and LC Master contract are deployed. If you haven't already done so, you might want to revisit this again by looking at the previous steps.

Before we can deploy LCs, we need to provide funds to the LC Master smart contract. The LC Master will distribute these funds whenever it creates a new escrow—that is, a new LC smart contract.

To do so, we need to allocate some USD tokens to the LC Master smart contract. These tokens will act as the USD balance for the LC issuer. Take the following steps:

1. Navigate to the truffle console. In the command line, set your web3 default account to the first account in your Ganache HD wallet using the following command:

```
web3.eth.defaultAccount =
'0x60f569790e9b87f93aB6bF9bBb3118f6E1C1598b'
```

2. Next, enter the following command into the truffle console. It will mint (generate) a `10000000` USD token to the LC Master contract address. Your LC Master smart contract address is the one you get after deploying the contract through truffle:

```
USD.deployed().then(function(instance) { return
instance.mint("<Your LC Master contract address>",10000000);
}).then(function(responseb) {console.log("response",
responseb.toString(10));});
```

3. Before we can start, we also need to set up the MetaMask wallet so that we can use the application. We'll be using three Ethereum accounts for our demo. We need to import all three into MetaMask. Navigate back to the Ganache interface, as shown in the following screenshot:

We will be using the first account in the preceding list as the bank account, the second account as the buying merchant's account, and the third as the selling merchant's account.

4. To import an account, click on the **key** icon on the extreme right, next to the Index column. A screen will pop up with the secret key, like the one in the following screenshot:

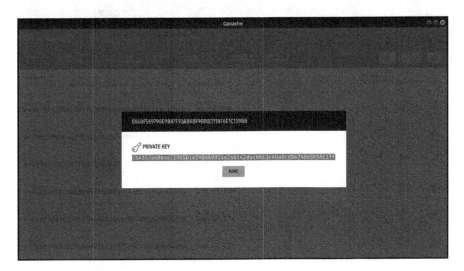

5. Copy this key and open your MetaMask wallet. Make sure you are connected to `localhost:8545` as your Ethereum network source.

6. Click on the circular pie icon at the top-right corner. Select **Import Account** from the menu that opens, as shown in the following screenshot:

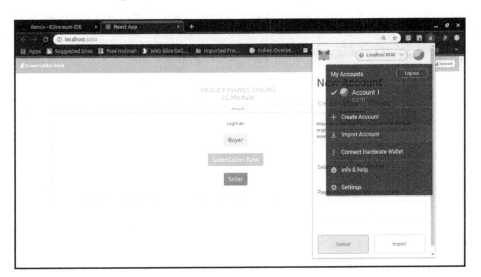

7. Make sure the **Import** tab is selected and that **Type** is selected as **Private Key**, as shown in the following screenshot:

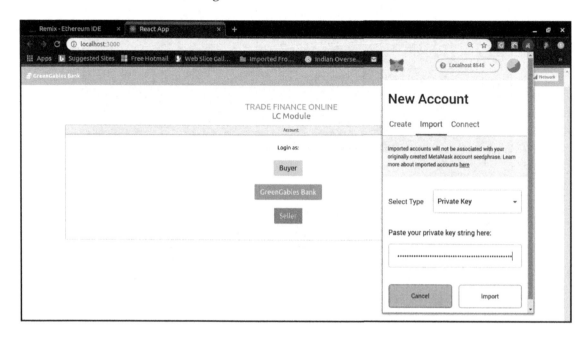

8. Paste the secret key you copied earlier and click on **Import**. The account should now appear in your wallet, as shown in the following screenshot:

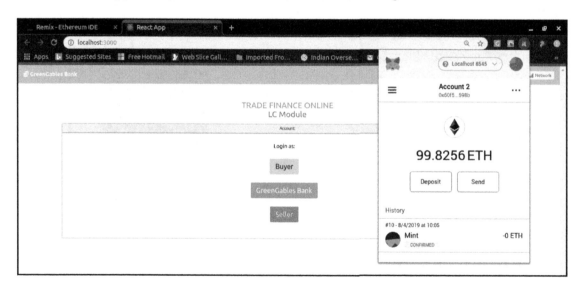

9. Do this for the first three accounts in the Ganache blockchain list. The accounts should appear in your Metamask wallet, as shown in the following screenshot:

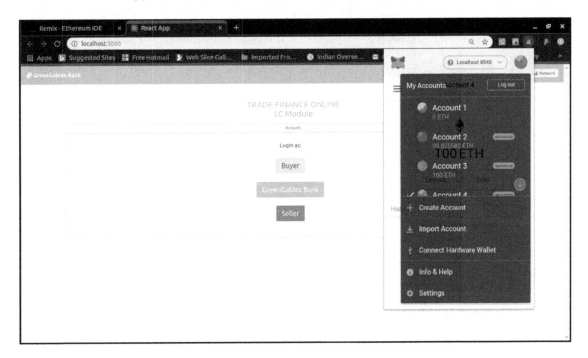

TIP

Addresses can be mapped to users and stored in a database for this screen. Then, the bank user only has to select the Buyer and the Seller from a drop-down list, and the account will get populated automatically.

OK. Now, we are ready to start our LC module.

Navigate to your React project directory and into the `LCApp` folder. Start the application by running the following command:

```
npm start
```

After a while, the app will open in the browser, as follows:

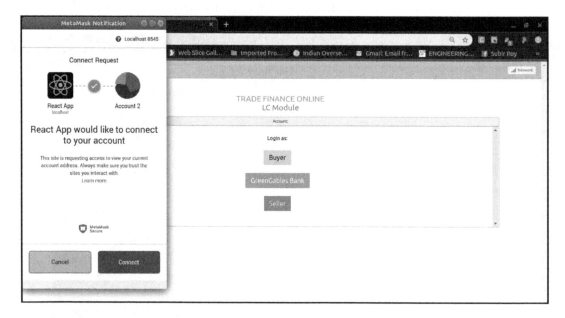

In the MetaMask popup that appears, select **Connect** to allow our React app to use MetaMask's injected web3 instance.

You might have to sign in to MetaMask if you have signed out. Sign in and repeat the preceding steps. You will then see the following screen:

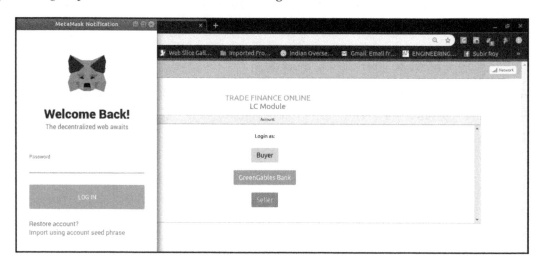

Now, we are ready to start with our demo, as follows:

1. First, we will go through the app as the bank user. Let's say a new LC has been requested by a customer to the bank. The bank verifies their credit rating and ascertains the customer is liquid. Then, they agree to issue an LC.

   Make sure the bank's Ethereum account is selected in MetaMask. If it's not, go back to MetaMask, and from the account dropdown, select the account. If you have followed the steps correctly, this should be **Account 2** in your MetaMask wallet, as shown in the following screenshot:

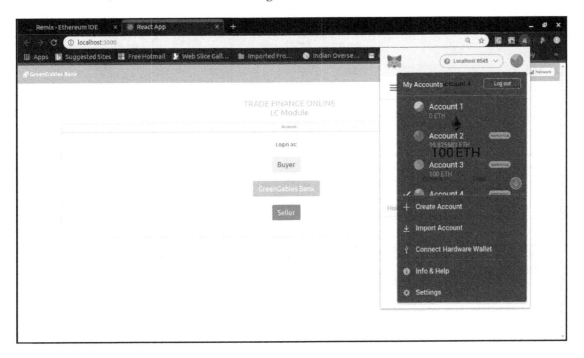

2. After selecting the current account, the app should look like the one shown in the following screenshot. Notice the **Account:** tab, with the bank's Ethereum account displayed:

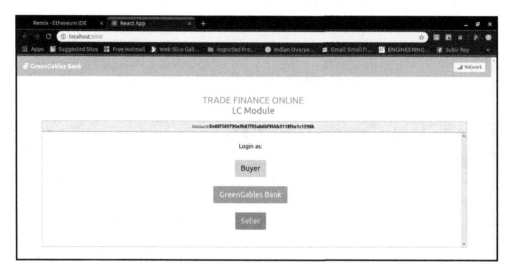

3. Click on the **GreenGables Bank** button to log in as a bank user. You'll be navigated to a new screen containing the **Create LC** and **View LC** buttons, as shown in the following screenshot:

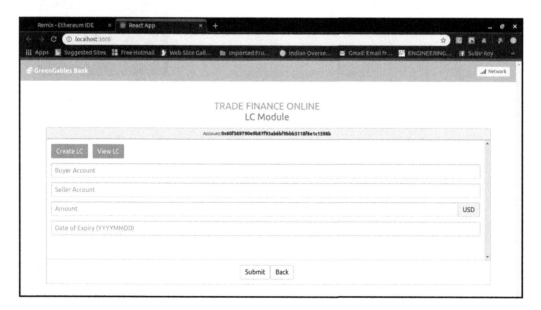

Let's start by creating a new LC.

4. Enter the details in the form in the **Create LC** screen. The Buyer account and the Seller account are the second and third accounts we imported from Ganache, respectively. Under the MetaMask wallet, these will be available as **Account 3** and **Account 4**. Paste these details into the MetaMask screen. Let's issue an LC with a small amount, around $1,000, due to expire on September 1, 2019, as follows:

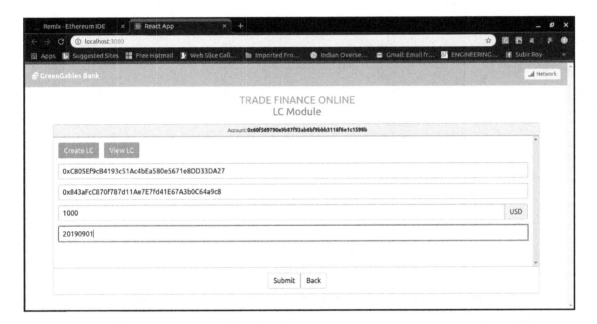

5. Click on the **Submit** button at the bottom of the screen to continue. On clicking on **Submit**, the `createLC` method is called. MetaMask will pop up with a notification, asking if you want to send the transaction, as shown in the following screenshot:

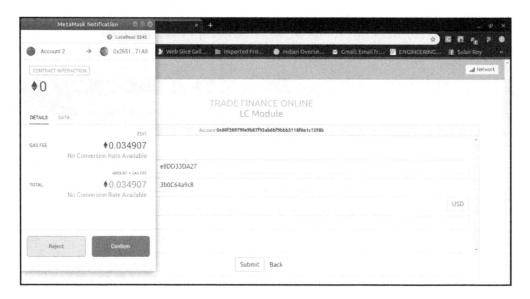

6. Click on **Confirm**. The transaction will be submitted and you'll get a notification at the top of your browser screen, as shown in the following screenshot:

7. Log in again as the bank user (**GreenGables Bank**). Click on **View LC**. You should be able to see the newly issued LC here, as follows:

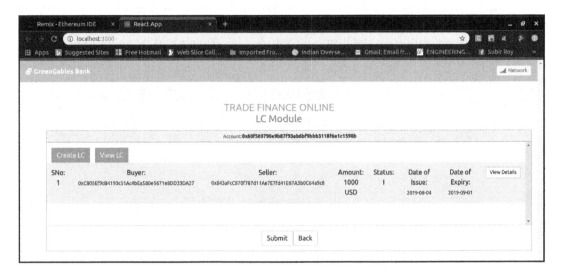

8. Click on **View Details**. This is a call to the `viewLCdetails` method in the newly deployed smart contract. It will show you the details of the LC, as shown in the following screenshot:

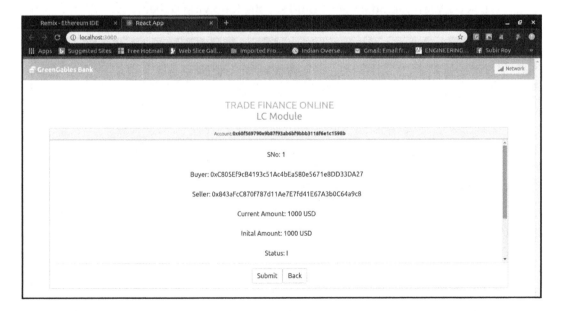

9. Now, let's log back into the app as a buyer. Go back to the app home screen by clicking the **GreenGables Bank** icon at the top left-hand side.

10. In your MetaMask wallet, switch to **Account 3**, which is the Buyer's account, and reload the app. The `Account` tag should now reflect the Buyer's address. Click on the `Buyer` button on the home page to log in. You should be able to see the **View LC** screen, as follows:

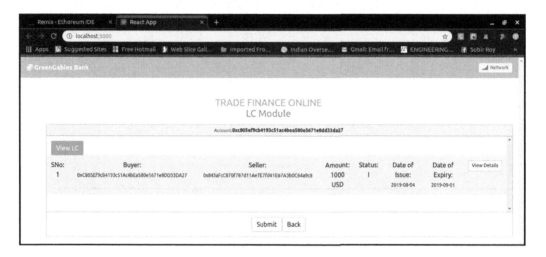

11. Click on **View Details**; you should see the following screen:

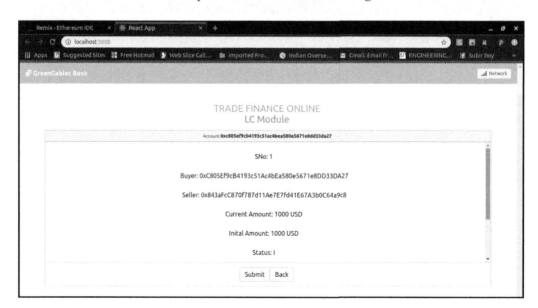

12. OK. Now, let's log in as the Seller merchant and try to view and settle the LC. Switch to the Seller's account in MetaMask (**Account 4**), as follows:

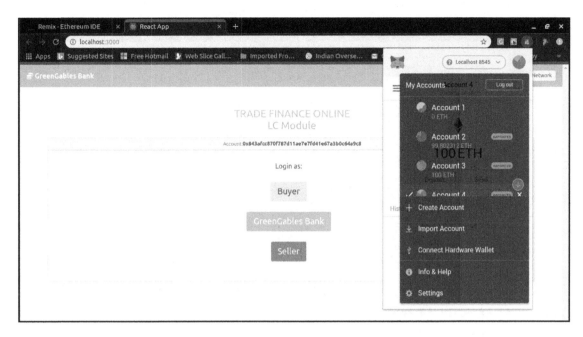

13. Navigate back to the app screen and reload the app. Log in as **Seller** and navigate to the **View LC** screen by clicking on the **View LC** button, as follows:

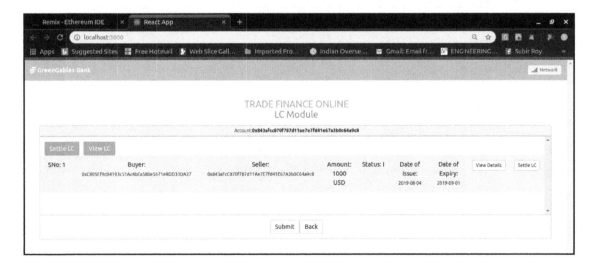

14. Now, let's try to settle this LC. Let's create a mock invoice document whose hash we'll be submitting for audit purposes, as follows:

15. Save the file. To calculate the hash, you can upload it to an online hash converter and convert the file into a SHA256 or SHA3 hash. Alternatively, you can build a hash connector Node.js utility to upload the file and return its hash.

16. Here, I am using an online hash converter to get the SHA256 hash. Now, you will have to upload the file, as follows:

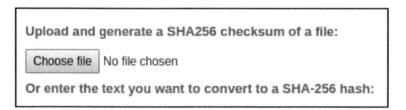

17. Browse and select the file, as follows:

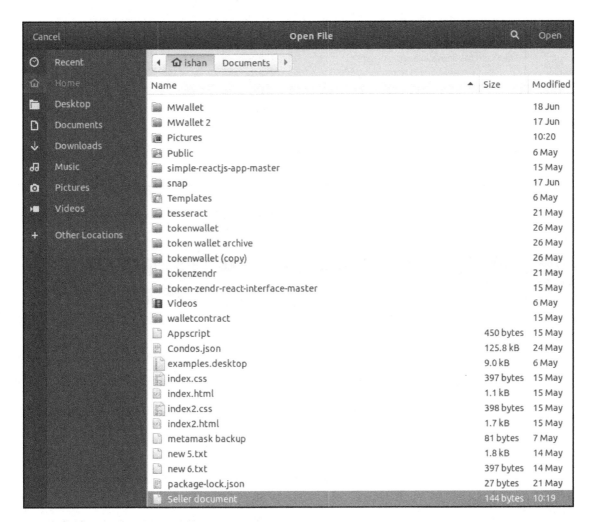

18. Click on **Convert** to get the hex hash representation, as follows:

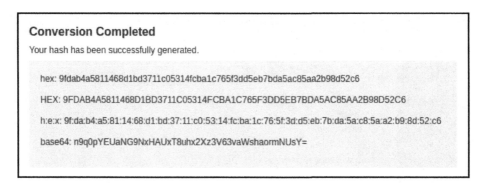

19. Now, go back to the Settle LC screen on our LC app. Click on the **Settle LC** button next to the LC you want to settle, as follows:

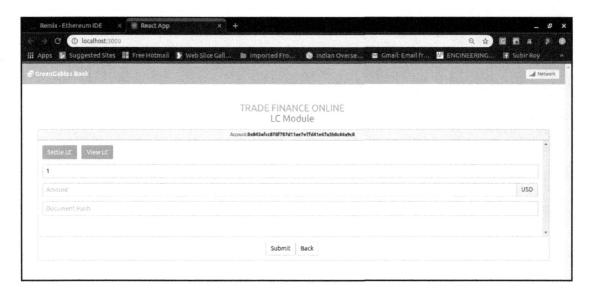

The **Settle LC** screen should pop up with the LC number populated, as shown in the following screenshot:

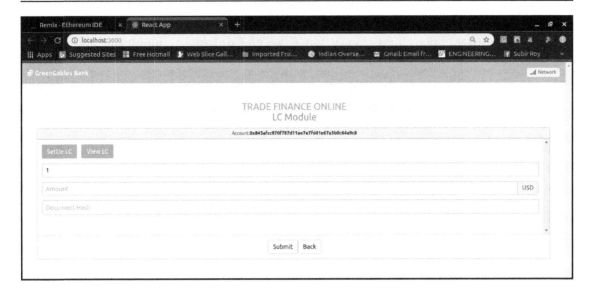

Let's try a partial settlement first. Let's raise a settlement claim for $500.

20. Put the amount as 500 USD and paste the SHA256 hash we generated. Make sure you add 0x at the front of the hash as Ethereum supports checksum hex, as follows:

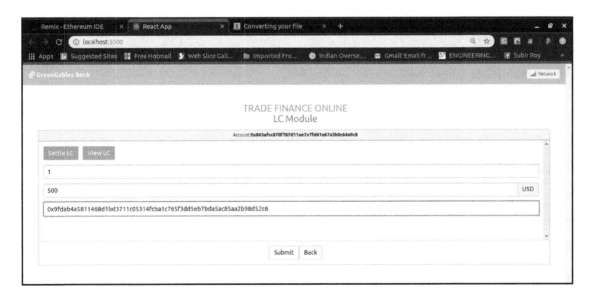

21. Click on the **Submit** button to continue. MetaMask will open a window, asking if you want to permit the transaction. Click on **Confirm** to continue, as follows:

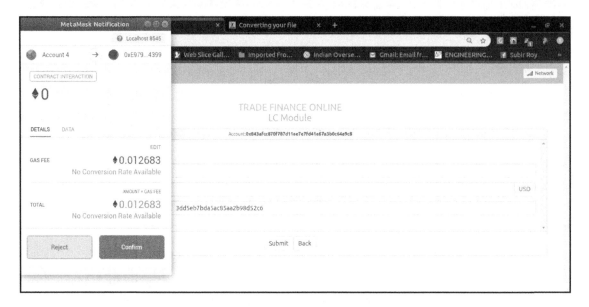

After a successful transaction submission, you'll get a notification in the browser at the top of the screen, as shown in the following screenshot:

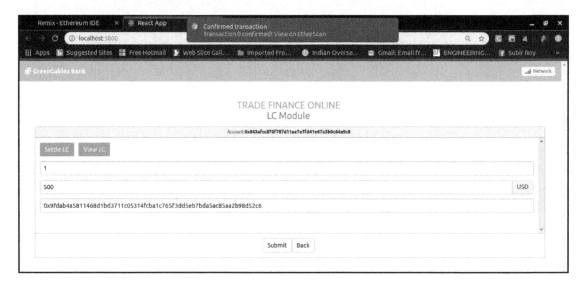

22. Navigate to the **View LC** screen. You'll see that the LC status has changed from **I** to **P**, indicating partial settlement. The amount available has gone down to **500 USD** from **1000 USD**, as shown in the following screenshot:

If you click on the **View Details** button, you should be able to see the initial amount as **1000 USD** and the current amount as **500 USD**. You should also be able to see the Document hash.

23. Now, transfer the rest of the amount. Create a new invoice and document hash. Go to the **Settle LC** screen and submit a new Settle LC request for 500 USD, as follows:

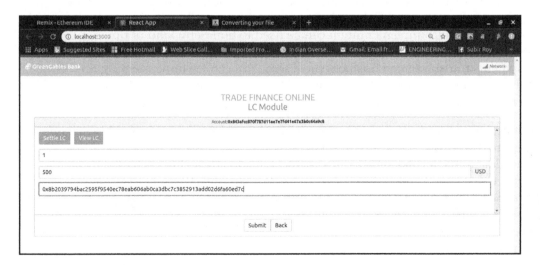

24. Allow MetaMask to submit the transaction by clicking on **Confirm**. After a successful transaction execution, you should see the LC status change to **S** and **Amount** change to **0 USD**, as shown in the following screenshot:

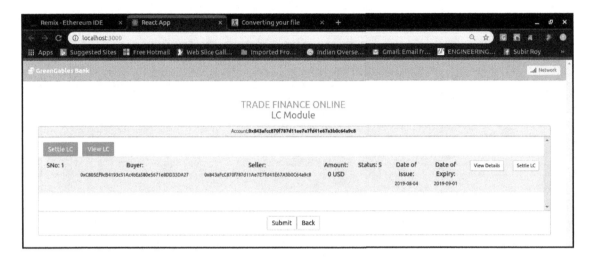

With that, we come to the end of our LC life cycle.

Summary

So, finally, we wrap up building our LC workflow. This chapter should help you design more complex smart contracts and give you a good understanding of how to leverage smart contracts as escrows and for designing workflows. While the use case we looked at is a very basic LC, this implementation can be used to build any kind of time- or condition-based escrow between two or more parties and can be used to build very efficient, transparent, and automated business processes. You can try implementing this setup within a private blockchain between organizations and see if you can tweak it to come up with more interesting workflows and use cases.

We started this chapter by looking at how escrows can be devices in the blockchain world, using smart contracts. We charted out a multi-smart contract design for building our application and determined how the contracts would connect to each other. Then, we leveraged our knowledge in order to build a React frontend and a Blockchain backend. While the Blockchain backend issued the new LCs and maintained the LCs, the React app allowed various user roles to access and interact with these contracts. Then, we ran our entire app and tracked an LC through its life cycle, from issue to view to—finally—settlement.

The main takeaway from this chapter is understanding how to build complex financial applications, including escrows, using blockchains and smart contracts. It also gives you an insight into how business processes can be automated using Blockchain. This particular system carries out the settlement and captures and stores a document hash as proof of settlement. Thus, it's a more robust system.

In the next chapter, we'll be looking at other financial applications of blockchain technology for **banking and financial services (BFSI)** enterprises.

3
Section 3: Securing Digital Documents and Files Using Blockchain

Organizations today generate and handle a huge volume of digital documents and files in a wide variety of formats. This makes it a difficult task for them to secure and protect these documents from tampering or modifications from internal and external threats. Blockchain can be useful in this regard. It can ensure the sanctity of digital documents and protect file repositories from attacks and threats.

In the next chapter, we'll be leveraging blockchain technology to build a solution that protects digital documents from tampering and prevents unauthorized modifications to filesystems.

This section comprises the following chapter:

- Chapter 7, *Building a Tamper-Proof Document Storage System*

7
Building a Tamper-Proof Document Storage System

Blockchain's inherent property of immutability makes it an excellent tool for securing information and records. Once stored in a blockchain, data cannot be modified or updated. This is due to the distributed nature of the and its use of hash functions and cryptography. In this chapter, we'll be leveraging this feature of blockchain to build a module that will secure the contents of a document repository. To achieve this, we'll be using Hyperledger Fabric 1.4. Our solution will record hash signatures for the documents within a repository on a private Hyperledger Fabric network. It will then monitor all the recorded files and check at fixed time intervals to see whether the files have been tampered with or modified. Additionally, it'll check whether any new files have been added or modified. If any changes have been made, it will throw a notification and inform the user.

In this chapter, we'll be covering the following topics:

- Tamper-proof document storage using blockchain
- Setting up a Hyperledger Fabric network
- Writing and deploying the DocsApp chaincode
- Building a node backend service
- Creating a React frontend for the app
- Running the tamper-proof application

Technical requirements

You can access the code files of this chapter at the following GitHub link:

```
https://github.com/PacktPublishing/Blockchain-Development-for-Finance-Projects/
tree/master/Chapter%207.
```

For this project, we'll be working with the Hyperledgic Fabric 1.4 binaries and Docker images provided in the Hyperledger Fabric GitHub repository.

You can find the step-by-step installation process at the following link:

```
https://hyperledger-fabric.readthedocs.io/en/release-1.4/prereqs.html.
```

Hyperledger Fabric assumes that you have the following dependencies installed:

- The latest version of the cURL tool
- The latest versions of Docker and Docker Compose
- Go version 1.12.x
- Node.js version 10.15.3 or higher
- Npm version 5.6.0 or higher
- Python 2.7

After downloading and installing the dependencies, we need to download and install the binaries, samples, and docker images for Hyperledger Fabric. For this, we'll be using `Curl` to download the images from the Fabric repository:

```
curl -sSL http://bit.ly/2ysbOFE | bash -s 1.4.0
```

This will take up to 15 minutes to complete, depending on your network connectivity.

Tamper-proof document storage using blockchain

The consensus algorithm of blockchains makes it virtually impossible to alter any data once it is stored in the blockchain. The consensus algorithm of a blockchain is an elaborate mechanism that ensures that the data captured on all the nodes in the blockchain network (the participating computers or servers that store a copy of the blockchain ledger) is uniform. This means that the data stored on each node, as well as the sequence in which the data is organized, is the same throughout all the nodes in the network.

This also means that once data is written or captured in a blockchain, it is virtually immutable—that is, it cannot be modified as long as the blockchain network remains unchanged. If the recorded data on one of the nodes is altered, the consensus algorithm prevents the altered data from being written to the other nodes in the network, thereby maintaining the original data.

We will be using this property of blockchains to build a tamper-proof document management system. We'll build a software utility that captures and stores the following details in a private Hyperledger Fabric network:

- The hash of each document in our document management system (**document hash**)
- The hash of the file tree diagram of the entire document management system (**file tree hash (FTH)**)
- The hash of the **last modified time (MTH)** of all the documents we are monitoring

The utility will calculate the FTH and the last **modified time hash (MTH)** for our document storage system every 5 seconds. It'll then check whether the FTH and the last MTH match the original entry that was stored in the blockchain. If there is a mismatch, it means that one or more documents in our document storage have been modified, added, or removed. The utility will then throw a notification to the user. It will also calculate and validate the hash of each individual file in our document storage to identify the tampered files and display these to the user.

To build our utility and integrate it with the blockchain, we'll go through the following steps:

1. Bring the Hyperledger Fabric sample first network online to create a test development network
2. Deploy the chaincode DocsApp with the methods to capture and retrieve individual document hashes, the FTH, and the MTH, to and from the blockchain network. A chaincode is essentially the Hyperledger Fabric equivalent of a smart contract.
3. Create a backend server in Node.js that will use the Hyperledger Fabric SDK to make requests to the DocsApp chaincode to write new hash signatures and retrieve already written hash signatures.
4. Create a DocsApp frontend in React that will allow the user to submit the directory path that is to be secured using the utility. This frontend will notify the user of the current status of the documents (tampered/not tampered) that are being captured using the utility.

Broadly, our project will contain the following components:

- The Hyperledger Fabric private network: We'll be using the default fabric `first-network` sample. It will contain the organizations, `org1` and `org2`. Each organization has two peers, `peer0` and `peer1`. It also contains the orderer organization, `orderer`. The network will be using the *solo* consensus mechanism. The solo consensus mechanism runs a single orderer node that orders transactions. In an enterprise setup, you would probably want to spread the nodes across several departments and subdepartments in order to preserve their data.
- The backend utility: This is used to calculate hashes, submit hashes to the blockchain ledger, and check hashes that have already been recorded to the blockchain.
- React frontend: This allows the user to select a directory that will be protected and view the current status of the files that are being monitored by the application.

Let's start by setting up our Hyperledger Fabric network.

Setting up the Hyperledger Fabric network

For this project, we'll be working with the Hyperledger Fabric samples provided in the Hyperledger Fabric GitHub repository.

You need to have Docker and Docker Compose installed to carry out the setup. To install all the dependencies, go to `https://hyperledger-fabric.readthedocs.io/en/release-1.4/install.html` and follow the instructions.

After downloading and installing the dependencies, we need to download and install the binaries, samples, and Docker images for Hyperledger Fabric. To do this, we'll be using `curl` to download the images from the Fabric repository, as follows:

```
curl -sSL http://bit.ly/2ysbOFE | bash -s 1.4.0
```

This will take up to 15 minutes to complete, depending on your network connectivity. Once this is complete, move on to the next step.

Bringing the first network sample online

To keep things simple, we'll be using the `first-network` Hyperledger Fabric sample for our project:

1. Navigate to the `first-network` directory under the `fabric-samples` directory. The default location should be as follows:

   /fabric-samples/first-network/

2. Start the network by running the following command in the `first-network` directory. It executes the `byfn.sh` script that brings the Hyperledger network online with two organizations (`org1` and `org2`) and two nodes for each organization (`peer0` and `peer1`). It also starts an ordering service:

   ```
   ./byfn.sh up -a -n -s couchdb
   ```

   In total, we will have five nodes:

- peer0 - org1
- peer1 - org1
- peer0 - org2
- peer1 - org2
- The orderer node

   The nodes are participants of a single channel called `mychannel`. We also use `couchdb` as our backend state database, indicated by the `-s` flag in the command.

3. Wait for the network to come online. This might take a few minutes.

Next, we'll create identities for the `org1` organization that can be used to submit transactions to the network.

Creating the admin and user identities

Before we can submit any transactions, we need to create an admin identity and a user identity. To do so, we'll be running the node utilities in the GitHub repository at `https://github.com/PacktPublishing/Blockchain-Development-for-Finance-Projects/tree/master/Chapter%207`.

The `enrollAdmin` utility will be used to create a new admin identity and the `registerUser` utility to register a new user:

1. Create a new folder in the `fabric-samples` directory called `DocsApp`. Within the directory, create a subfolder called `wallet`. You can find these utilities in the Github link mentioned above

2. Copy the `enrollAdmin` and `registerUser` utilities in to the `DocsApp` directory.

3. First, run the utility `enrollAdmin` to register the admin user:

```
node enrollAdmin
```

A new identity for the admin should have been added to the `wallet` directory

4. Next, run the utility `registerUser`:

```
node registerUser
```

A new identity for `user1` should have been added to the `wallet` directory.

Now, we should be ready to submit transactions to our blockchain network.

Writing and deploying the DocsApp chaincode

Now that our network is online, the next step we need to do is write and deploy our chaincode contract. The chaincode DocsApp consists of the following methods:

- `addDocHash`: This method adds a new document hash to the blockchain. Document hashes are indexed by the hash of the file path.
- `addParamHash`: This method adds the FTH and the MTH to the blockchain indexed by a timestamp. The timestamp indicates the time at which the FTH and MTH were calculated and stored to the blockchain.
- `queryDocHash`: This method retrieves the last updated hash for a document using the hash of the file path.
- `queryParamHash`: This method retrieves the FTH and the MTH stored in the blockchain at a particular time using the timestamp indicating the time that it was stored.

We'll also have to install the chaincode for all the nodes that are part of our network and instantiate it. Let's start writing the contract.

Writing the DocsApp smart contract

Let's write our DocsApp chaincode:

1. Create a new file called `DocsApp.js`. We start writing the contract by declaring the dependent `fabric-contract-api` library, which is used to define our contract object:

   ```
   const { Contract } = require('fabric-contract-api');
   class docsapp extends Contract {
   ```

2. Next, we'll write the `addDocHash` method. The `addDocHash` method will add a new document's hash signature to the Hyperledger Fabric network. It takes `PathHash` (the hash of the file path of the document) and the `DocHash` (the hash of the document). The `ctx` object is the context object that is used to index information in the ledger. We also set a `console.info` statement to print a checkpoint to the console indicating the start of the `DocHash` method:

   ```
   async addDocHash(ctx, PathHash, DocHash) {
     console.info('============= START : Register Document Hash
   ===========');
   ```

   The document object is defined next. It takes `DocHash` and `PathHash` as input parameters. It also sets the `docType` parameter equal to the `document` flag:

   ```
   const document = {
     DocHash,
     PathHash,
     docType: 'document'
     };
   ```

3. Lastly, we use `putState` to add our document object to the blockchain ledger as a JSON object and print a message on the console to indicate the end of the `addDocHash` method:

   ```
   await
   ctx.stub.putState(PathHash,Buffer.from(JSON.stringify(document)));
   console.info('============= END : Register Document
   Hash===========');
     }
   ```

4. The `addParamHash` method adds the MTH (the hash of the array of the last-modified time of all the documents in a secured directory) and the FTH (the hash of the file tree path of all the secured documents in the secured document). It takes the context object, the MTH, the FTH, and the timestamp of when the hash was calculated:

```
async addPathHash(ctx, Time, MTimeHash, TreeHash) {
  console.info('============= START : Register M Time Hash
===========');

const TH = {
  Time,
  MTimeHash,
  TreeHash,
  docType: 'TimeHash'
  };
```

The `TH` object captures the time, the MTH, and the FTH. The method then calls `putState` to write the `TH` object in the blockchain ledger. The timestamp acts as the context for the ledger entry; it'll be used to retrieve entries from the blockchain ledger:

```
await ctx.stub.putState(Time,Buffer.from(JSON.stringify(TH)));
  console.info('============= END : Register Time Hash ===========');
  }
```

The `queryDocHash` method queries and retrieves document hashes stored in the blockchain and indexed by `PathHash`. It takes the file path hash as input and returns the last recorded `DocHash` from the blockchain state database:

```
async queryDocHash(ctx, PathHash) {
  const DocHashBytes = await ctx.stub.getState(PathHash); // get the
document hash from chaincode state
```

We use the `getState` API to get the document hash linked to `PathHash` from the blockchain state database.

The method will return the marshaled JSON string received from the state database as a string object if it finds a linked document object to the input `PathHash`:

```
if (!DocHashBytes || DocHashBytes.length === 0) {
  throw new Error('Invalid ${PathHash}.Document not registered');
  }
console.log(DocHashBytes.toString());
return DocHashBytes.toString();
  }
```

5. Similarly, we write the `queryParamHash` method, which will retrieve the last MTH and the FTH stored at the blockchain state database using the timestamp:

```
async queryPathHash(ctx, Time) {
  const TimeHashBytes = await ctx.stub.getState(Time); // get the
  document hash from chaincode state
```

We use the `getState` API to get the MTH and FTH hash linked to a timestamp from the blockchain state database.

The method will return the marshaled JSON string received from the state database as a string object if it finds a linked document object to the input timestamp:

```
if (!TimeHashBytes || TimeHashBytes.length === 0) {
  throw new Error('Invalid ${Time}. Time not registered');
  }
console.log(TimeHashBytes.toString());
return TimeHashBytes.toString();
  }
}

module.exports = docsapp;
```

This brings us to the end of our DocsApp chaincode contract. Now, let's install it in the nodes and deploy it.

Deploying the DocsApp smart contract

We need to set up a new chaincode directory for our contract. In your Hyperledger Fabric `fabric-samples` directory, navigate to the `chaincode` directory. It will be at the following location by default:

```
/fabric-samples/chaincode/
```

We will use the following steps to deploy our DocsApp smart contract:

1. In the `chaincode` folder, create a new folder with the name `docsapp`.
2. In the `docsapp` folder, create an `index.js` file with the following values:

```
/*
 * SPDX-License-Identifier: Apache-2.0
 */

'use strict';

const docsapp = require('./lib/docsapp');

module.exports.docsapp = docsapp;
module.exports.contracts = [ docsapp ];
```

   This will declare the `docsapp` object, which will be used by our `peer chaincode install` and `peer chaincode instantiate` tools for deploying our chaincode within the blockchain.

3. Next, create a `lib` folder in the `docsapp` directory. By default, your `lib` folders filepath should look as follows:

   /fabric-samples/chaincode/docsapp/lib

4. Copy and paste the `docsapp.js` file along with the DocsApp smart contract code that we wrote in the previous section.
5. Now, we need to install this smart contract for all our peers, `peer0.org1.example.com`, `peer1.org1.example.com`, `peer0.org2.example.com`, and `peer1.org2.example.com`, which comprise our Hyperledger Fabric network. To do this, we'll be using the `peer chaincode install` command.

   The `peer chaincode` utility is a tool that is available in the **command-line interface** (CLI) Docker container, which is available by default as a Docker image in the Hyperledger Fabric repository. It allows us to interact with and carry out operations on chaincodes (a chaincode is the Hyperledger Fabric equivalent of a smart contract).

   Let's look at the `peer chaincode install` statement that we will be using to deploy our chaincode for `org1` on `peer1`:

   ```
   docker exec
   -e CORE_PEER_LOCALMSPID=Org1MSP
   ```

```
-e CORE_PEER_ADDRESS=peer0.org1.example.com:7051
-e
CORE_PEER_MSPCONFIGPATH=/opt/gopath/src/github.com/hyperledger/fabr
ic/peer/crypto/peerOrganizations/org1.example.com/users/Admin@org1.
example.com/msp
-e
CORE_PEER_TLS_ROOTCERT_FILE=/opt/gopath/src/github.com/hyperledger/
fabric/peer/crypto/peerOrganizations/org1.example.com/peers/peer0.o
rg1.example.com/tls/ca.crt
cli peer chaincode install -n docsapp -v 1.0
-p /opt/gopath/src/github.com/chaincode/docsapp -l node
```

Let's go through the different parts of the command one by one. The docker exec command is used to execute a command within the Docker container. The -e is used to set environment variables inside the Docker container before executing a command.

The CORE_PEER_LOCALMSPID environment variable indicates the membership service provider for the node. The membership service provider is used to define the Root Certificate Authorities and Intermediate Certificate Authorities that will be used to issue identities for a trusted domain/organization on the blockchain network. Here, we set it to Org1MSP, which is the MSP service for Org1.

The CORE_PEER_ADDRESS environment variable indicates the external client port for peer 1 (node 1 in our Hyperledger Fabric network) to which requests need to be submitted. We set it here to peer0.org1.example.com:7051, which is our node's client port.

The CORE_PEER_MSPCONFIGPATH environment variable indicates the configuration path for the membership policy for peer 1 within peer 1's Docker container.

The CORE_PEER_TLS_ROOTCERT_FILE environment variable indicates the location of the root certificate (the certificate authority certificate) for the digital signature used by peer 1.

The cli phrase indicates the container name in which we are executing peer chaincode commands. This, as we discussed earlier, is the command-line interface Docker container.

Lastly, we use the -n tag to indicate the chaincode name, -v, to indicate the version of the chaincode, -p, to indicate the path where the smart contract code is available, and -l to indicate the scripting language of the smart contract, which is node (Node.js) in our case.

6. Run the command with a Linux user with Docker privileges in the Terminal. It should print a message similar to the following one on successful execution. This message is from the command-line container:

```
2019-10-29 05:56:55.357 UTC [chaincodeCmd] install -> INFO 003
Installed remotely response:<status:200 payload:"OK" >
```

7. Now, craft a `peer chaincode install` statement for all the other nodes in our network:

```
//chaincode install statement for peer1 org1

docker exec -e CORE_PEER_LOCALMSPID=Org1MSP -e
CORE_PEER_ADDRESS=peer1.org1.example.com:8051 -e
CORE_PEER_MSPCONFIGPATH=/opt/gopath/src/github.com/hyperledger/fabr
ic/peer/crypto/peerOrganizations/org1.example.com/users/Admin@org1.
example.com/msp -e
CORE_PEER_TLS_ROOTCERT_FILE=/opt/gopath/src/github.com/hyperledger/
fabric/peer/crypto/peerOrganizations/org1.example.com/peers/peer0.o
rg1.example.com/tls/ca.crt cli peer chaincode install -n docsapp -v
1.0 -p /opt/gopath/src/github.com/chaincode/docsapp -l node

//chaincode install statement for peer0 org2

docker exec -e CORE_PEER_LOCALMSPID=Org2MSP -e
CORE_PEER_ADDRESS=peer0.org2.example.com:9051 -e
CORE_PEER_MSPCONFIGPATH=/opt/gopath/src/github.com/hyperledger/fabr
ic/peer/crypto/peerOrganizations/org2.example.com/users/Admin@org2.
example.com/msp -e
CORE_PEER_TLS_ROOTCERT_FILE=/opt/gopath/src/github.com/hyperledger/
fabric/peer/crypto/peerOrganizations/org2.example.com/peers/peer0.o
rg2.example.com/tls/ca.crt cli peer chaincode install -n docsapp -v
1.0 -p /opt/gopath/src/github.com/chaincode/docsapp -l node

//chaincode install statement for peer1 org2

docker exec -e CORE_PEER_LOCALMSPID=Org2MSP -e
CORE_PEER_ADDRESS=peer1.org2.example.com:10051 -e
CORE_PEER_MSPCONFIGPATH=/opt/gopath/src/github.com/hyperledger/fabr
ic/peer/crypto/peerOrganizations/org2.example.com/users/Admin@org2.
example.com/msp -e
CORE_PEER_TLS_ROOTCERT_FILE=/opt/gopath/src/github.com/hyperledger/
fabric/peer/crypto/peerOrganizations/org2.example.com/peers/peer0.o
rg2.example.com/tls/ca.crt cli peer chaincode install -n docsapp -v
1.0 -p /opt/gopath/src/github.com/chaincode/docsapp -l node
```

8. Run them in the Terminal. You should get a successful peer installation message after each peer install command, as follows:

```
INFO 003 Installed remotely response:<status:200 payload:"OK" >
```

9. Next, we need to instantiate the chaincode across the nodes. We'll use the following command for instantiating the chaincode:

```
docker exec
-e CORE_PEER_LOCALMSPID=Org1MSP
-e
CORE_PEER_MSPCONFIGPATH=/opt/gopath/src/github.com/hyperledger/fabr
ic/peer/crypto/peerOrganizations/org1.example.com/users/Admin@org1.
example.com/msp cli peer chaincode instantiate
-o orderer.example.com:7050
-C mychannel
-n docsapp
-l node
-v 1.0
-c '{"Args":[]}'
-P 'AND('\''Org1MSP.member'\'','\''Org2MSP.member'\'')'
--tls
--cafile
/opt/gopath/src/github.com/hyperledger/fabric/peer/crypto/ordererOr
ganizations/example.com/orderers/orderer.example.com/msp/tlscacerts
/tlsca.example.com-cert.pem --peerAddresses
peer0.org1.example.com:7051
--tlsRootCertFiles
/opt/gopath/src/github.com/hyperledger/fabric/peer/crypto/peerOrgan
izations/org1.example.com/peers/peer0.org1.example.com/tls/ca.crt
```

Let's look at the environment variables, which are denoted by the -e tag.

The CORE_PEER_LOCALMSPID environment variable indicates the membership service provider for the node. The membership service provider is used to define the Root Certificate Authorities and Intermediate Certificate Authorities, which will be used to issue identities for a trusted domain/organization on the blockchain network. Here, we set it to Org1MSP, which is the MSP service for Org1.

The CORE_PEER_MSPCONFIGPATH environment variable indicates the configuration file path for the Membership Service Provider for peer 1 within peer 1's Docker container.

- The -C tag indicates the Hyperledger Fabric network channel to which this chaincode will be instantiated. In Hyperledger Fabric, channels are private blockchain ledgers that can be read or written to only by the approved participants of the channel. We set it to the default mychannel channel.
- The -n tag indicates the name of the chaincode being instantiated. Here, we set it to docsapp.
- The -l tag indicates the scripting language, which in our case is a node.
- The -v tag is the version number of the chaincode.
- The -c tag indicates the constructor arguments for the contract, if there are any.
- The -P tag indicates the member participants of the network.
- The --tls tag indicates that messages will be SSL encrypted. The tags --cafile and --tlsRootCerFiles tags indicate the certificate file for orderer and peer0.org1.

Run the command in the Terminal window. If instantiation is successful, you will not get any message on the Terminal window.

That completes writing and deploying of our docsapp chaincode (smart contract). Let's move on to writing the backend node server.

Building the backend services

We need to build backend services that our frontend can access to write the hashes to the Fabric blockchain and read the hashes from the Fabric blockchain.

We'll be creating the Node.js utility using and building the following services:

- /api/hashwrite: This endpoint exposes a service that is used for calculating the hash of all the artifacts in a directory root, the hash of the file path of all the artifacts, and the hash of the modified timestamp of all the artifacts then submitting them to the blockchain.

- `/api/hashread`: This endpoint exposes a service that is used for re-calculating the hash of all the artifacts in a directory root, the hash of the file path of all the artifacts, and the hash of the modified timestamp of all the artifacts then verifying whether they match the hash values recorded in the blockchain. If there is a mismatch, then it indicates that one or more documents have been tampered with.

Let's start writing our Node.js utility.

Writing the backend server

Create a new Node.js app called `hashcheck.js` in your project directory by going through the following steps:

1. We first start by declaring the dependencies:

```
var fs = require('fs');
var path = require('path');
const { Keccak } = require('sha3');
const { FileSystemWallet, Gateway } = require('fabric-network');
var express = require("express");
var bodyParser = require("body-parser");
```

The following list describes the dependencies -

- `fs` is the file stream node module, which will allow us to parse a file and other metadata associated with a file
- `path` is used to resolve and create Unix filepaths.
- The `sha3` node module can be used to generate SHA3 hashes from input data
- `fabric-network` is the Fabric SDK that is used to interact with services exposed by the deployed chaincodes on the blockchain.
- `express` is the Node.js web application framework that is used to define our services.
- `body-parser` is a middleware used to parse the body of a request submitted to an endpoint.

2. Next, we start defining our app. We define a new app object using the `express` framework:

- `bodyParser.json()` ensures that the middleware parses requests of the JSON type.
- `bodyParser.urlencoded()` ensures that the middleware parses request bodies of the form-data type into key–value pairs that can be easily read by the app.
- `ccpPath` stores the local storage path for the network configuration for `org1`:

```
var app = express();
app.use(bodyParser.json());
app.use(bodyParser.urlencoded({ extended: true }));
const ccpPath = '/home/ishan/fabric-samples/first-
network/connection-org1.json';
```

3. Next, we add some middleware to enable cross-origin requests between our Node.js app and the React frontend.

The middleware adds a header to indicate that requests from all sources (*) and methods are welcome (`GET`, `POST`, and so on). It allows all content types and credentials. This is set for testing purposes:

```
app.use(function (req, res, next) {
  res.setHeader('Access-Control-Allow-Origin', '*');
  res.setHeader('Access-Control-Allow-Methods', 'GET, POST, OPTIONS,
PUT, PATCH, DELETE');
  res.setHeader('Access-Control-Allow-Headers', 'X-Requested-
With,content-type');
  res.setHeader('Access-Control-Allow-Credentials', true);
  next();
});
```

4. Next, we define a server object that we will use to bring our app online. The app will listen on port `3600` for incoming requests:

```
var server = app.listen(process.env.PORT || 3600, function () {
  var port = server.address().port;
  console.log("App now running on port", port);
});
```

5. Our backend server will have the following methods.

- `walkDir()`: This takes a directory path as an input parameter and returns an array with the list of files in the directory path.
- `bWrite()`: This writes the hash of a file to the blockchain.
- `pWrite()`: This writes the hash of the last modified time and the hash of the directory file tree to the blockchain.
- `bRead()`: This reads the recorded hash of a file from the blockchain. It takes the hash of the directory path of the file as input and returns the document hash.
  - `pRead()`: This returns the last MTH and FTH that were stored at a particular time. The time is written in UTC format.

Our backend server will have the following services:

- `/api/hashwrite`: This takes a directory path as input and records the hash of all the member files of the directory, the hash of the last modified time, and the hash of the file tree path to the blockchain.
- `/api/hashread`: This takes a directory path and the modified time as input and fetches the hash of the last modified time and the hash of the file tree path from the blockchain.
- `/api/hashreadfile`: This takes a directory path and an array with a list of files recorded in the blockchain as input parameters. It then fetches the hash of each file from the blockchain and checks whether the hash has been modified or is the same. If there is a mismatch between the hash of a document in the directory and the hash of the same document that was recorded for the blockchain, it indicates that the version in the directory has been tampered with.

Let's start writing the methods for our backend server.

Building a method for listing files in a directory

The `walkDir()` method is a recursive function. It takes a directory path, `dir`, as an input parameter and returns a list of all the files in the director. It's written as follows:

```
var walkDir = function(dir, done) {
 var results = [];
 fs.readdir(dir, function(err, fList) {
 if (err) return done(err);
 var maxLength = fList.length;
 if (!maxLength) return done(null, results);
 fList.forEach(function(file) {
```

```
file = path.resolve(dir, file);
fs.stat(file, function(err, stat) {
if (stat && stat.isDirectory()) {
walkDir(file, function(err, res) {
results = results.concat(res);
if (!--maxLength) done(null, results);
});
} else {
results.push(file);
if (!--maxLength) done(null, results);
}
});
});
});
};
```

Let's take a look at each line of `walkDir` and understand how it works:

1. The method accepts the absolute path of a directory as an input parameter:

   ```
   var walkDir = function(dir, done) {
     var results = [];
   ```

2. It then uses the `readdir` method in the `fs` module to read the directory contents in the directory path, `dir`:

   ```
   fs.readdir(dir, function(err, fList) {
   ```

3. If it gets an error while reading, then that indicates either that the directory path is invalid or that the directory is empty. In this case, `walkDir()` will return the error message `(err)` to the requester and terminate the execution of the `walkDir()` method:

   ```
   if (err) return done(err);
   ```

4. If there is no error, it means that `readdir` has successfully read and returned the directory's contents (the files and subfolders in the `dir`) in the `fList` array.

5. Next, we'll next iterate through each member of the `fList` array and check whether it's a file or a directory:

   ```
   var maxLength = fList.length;
     if (!maxLength) return done(null, results);

     fList.forEach(function(file) {
         file = path.resolve(dir, file);
   ```

6. For each file path stored in the `fList` array, we use `fs.stat()` to check whether the member at the directory path is a file or a subdirectory.

7. Let's first look at what happens when the member is a file. This is covered in the `else` clause:

```
fs.stat(file, function(err, stat) {
.........
else {
  results.push(file);
  if (!--maxLength) done(null, results);
  }
})
```

8. If the member is a file, then the file path is pushed into our `results` array, which `walkDir()` will return. After each push, the method checks whether `maxLength` (that is, the length of the `fList` array) has been reached. This indicates that all the members of the `fList` array have been processed. The `walkDir()` method returns the `results` array with the list of files and ends the execution.

9. Next, we look at what happens when the member is a subdirectory. If on calling `fs.stat` we realize that our member is a subdirectory, then `walkDir()` will recursively call itself, sending the subdirectory's path as the input parameter. If there is subdirectory within our subdirectory, then a new recursive call will be made to `walkDir()` with the sub-subdirectory as the input parameter to fetch its members. This process will continue until we reach is a subdirectory that has only files as members. Each iteration of the `walkDir()` method call returns the list of all the files, including the files in all the subdirectories to the requester in the `results` array.

10. In our case, when we receive the list of files in our subdirectory, they are added to the `results` array using `results.concat()`. After adding the new elements to the `results` array, we check whether we have reached the `maxLength` of the `fList` array (the end of the `fList` array). On reaching the end of the fList array, the loop ends and we return control to the invoker with the results:

```
fs.stat(file, function(err, stat) {
    if (stat && stat.isDirectory())
      {
      walkDir(file, function(err, res) {
      results = results.concat(res);
      if (!--maxLength) done(null, results);
      });
```

This completes our walkthrough of the `walkDir()` method, which is used to list all the files in a directory path. It returns the `results` array, which contains all the files, including the files in the subdirectories listed.

Building a method to write a file hash to the blockchain

The asynchronous `bwrite` method writes a file hash to the blockchain. It takes the hash of the directory path of the file (`pHash`) and the document hash (`dHash`) as input and writes to the blockchain.

1. Before writing to the blockchain, we need access to a registered identity that has permission to write to our blockchain. We'll use the `user1` user that we registered in our wallet earlier. Using the Hyperledger Fabric SDK `FileSystemWallet` method, we'll create a new wallet object pointing to the wallet we created for DocsApp. We check whether the `user 1` user is registered in the wallet. Execution of the method will proceed only if the `user 1` user exists:

```
async function bWrite (pHash,dHash) {

  try {
  const wallet = new FileSystemWallet('/home/ishan/docsapp/wallet');
  const userExists = await wallet.exists('user1');
  if (!userExists) {
  console.log('An identity for the user "user1" does not exist in
  the wallet');
  console.log('Run the registerUser.js application before
  retrying');
  return;
  }
```

2. Next, we define a new `Gateway` object to connect to our blockchain:

```
const gateway = new Gateway();
  await gateway.connect(ccpPath, { wallet, identity: 'user1',
  discovery: { enabled: true, asLocalhost: true } });
  const network = await gateway.getNetwork('mychannel');
  const contract = network.getContract('docsapp');
```

3. The `Gateway` object is configured with the wallet (DocsApp wallet location), user identity (`user 1`), blockchain channel (`mychannel`), and chaincode contract (`docsapp`)) to point it to our chaincode in our blockchain. We use `getNetwork` to set the channel and `getContract` to set the chaincode:

```
await contract.submitTransaction('addDocHash',pHash,dHash);
console.log("Transaction Doc has been submitted");
await gateway.disconnect();
```

4. Next, we invoke our contract and submit a new transaction. We submit a call to the contract `addDocHash` method and submit the file path hash (`pHash`) and file hash (`dHash`) as input parameters to the contract method. You will remember from the previous section that this method creates a `document` object, which it then writes to the blockchain state database indexed by the file path hash (`PathHash`). After successful transaction submission, a message is printed to the console and the gateway is disconnected:

```
} catch (error) {
console.error(`Failed to submit transaction: ${error}`);
process.exit(1);
}
};
```

5. A `catch` statement is added to catch any errors during transaction submission.

This ends our analysis of the `bWrite` method. Next, we'll take a look at the `pWrite` method.

Building a method to write the MTH and the FTH to the blockchain

The `pWrite` method takes the last MTH and FTH as input and writes them to the blockchain. The hashes are indexed in the blockchain by the timestamp at which the hashes where calculated. This is done so as to create a timestamped audit log of all the times that a new entry was recorded for the secured directory in the blockchain.

1. The `pWrite` function is similar in structure to `bWrite`. It first defines a new wallet object and a gateway to connect to our `docsapp` chaincode:

```
async function pWrite(FTH,MTH) {

try {
const wallet = new FileSystemWallet('/home/ishan/docsapp/wallet');
const userExists = await wallet.exists('user1');
```

```
if (!userExists) {
console.log('An identity for the user "user1" does not exist in
the wallet');
console.log('Run the registerUser.js application before
retrying');
return;
}

const gateway = new Gateway();
await gateway.connect(ccpPath, { wallet, identity: 'user1',
discovery: { enabled: true, asLocalhost: true } });
const network = await gateway.getNetwork('mychannel');
const contract = network.getContract('docsapp');
```

It uses the user 1 identity and connects to the mychannel channel. The wallet object points to the wallet we created for DocsApp. The contract object is set to docsapp.

2. As we've already discussed, the hashes, MTH and FTH, are indexed by the time in which they were recorded. So, we need to fetch the current UTC timestamp. This is done using the following steps. The UTC timestamp is captured to the dateTime variable:

```
var today = new Date();

var dateTime = Date.UTC(today.getFullYear(), today.getMonth()+1,
today.getDate(),
today.getHours(),today.getMinutes(),today.getSeconds());
```

3. Now, we submit the transaction to our DocsApp chaincode contract:

```
await
contract.submitTransaction('addPathHash',dateTime.toString(),MTH,FT
H);
console.log("Transaction PathHash has been submitted");
await gateway.disconnect();
return dateTime.toString();
```

Note how this time, we call the chaincode addPathHash method to write the MTH and FTH hashes. The input parameters are dateTime, MTH, and FTH.

4. A message is logged to the console upon successful submission and the gateway is disconnected. The dateTime variable is returned to the requester and can be used in the future for retrieving the MTH and FTH.

5. A `catch` statement is added to catch any errors during transaction submission:

```
catch (error) {
 console.error(`Failed to submit transaction: ${error}`);
 process.exit(1);
 }
 }
```

This ends our analysis of the `pWrite` method. Let's look at the methods we'll use to read from the blockchain next.

Building a method to read MTH and FTH from the blockchain

The `pRead()` method fetches the last MTH and FTH from the blockchain and compares them with the current MTH (`ModTH`) and FTH (`FileTH`):

1. It takes the time at which the hash has recorded on the blockchain (`dateTime`), the current MTH of the directory (`ModTH`), and the current FTH of the directory (`FileTH`) as input parameters.

2. We start the `pRead()` method by first defining the `wallet` object and connecting to the gateway in a similar way to the last two functions:

```
async function pRead (dateTime,ModTH,FileTH) {

 try {

 const wallet = new FileSystemWallet('/home/ishan/docsapp/wallet');
 const userExists = await wallet.exists('user1');
 if (!userExists) {
 console.log('An identity for the user "user1" does not exist in
the wallet');
 console.log('Run the registerUser.js application before
retrying');
 return;
 }

 const gateway = new Gateway();
        await gateway.connect(ccpPath, { wallet, identity: 'user1',
discovery: { enabled: true, asLocalhost: true } });
    const network = await gateway.getNetwork('mychannel');
    const contract = network.getContract('docsapp');
```

The identity that's used for connecting is user 1. The wallet object is set to the wallet we created for DocsApp. The gateway connects to the mychannel channel and the docsapp chaincode.

3. Next, we use the evaluateTransaction method to call the read-only queryPathHash method in our docsapp chaincode. You might remember from the previous section that the queryPathHash method in the docsapp chaincode fetches the MTH and the FTH, which are indexed by the timestamp at which they were recorded:

```
const resultFT = await
contract.evaluateTransaction('queryPathHash',dateTime);
```

4. The MTH and FTH returned by the queryPathHash method are captured in the resultFT variable:

```
var MTH = resultFT.toString('ascii',14,78);
 var FTH = resultFT.toString('ascii',115,179);
 console.log("Transaction has been evaluated");
 await gateway.disconnect();
```

5. The MTH and FTH are fetched from the blockchain and stored in the MTH and FTH variables. Since the result is returned in marshaled JSON format, we need to slice the result and separate the MTH and the FTH from the resultFT variable. The gateway is disconnected and a message is printed to the console.

6. Next, we verify whether the hashes fetched from the blockchain match the hash that is calculated and sent as an input parameter to the pRead() method:

```
var result;

if(MTH != ModTH || FTH != FileTH)
{
result = 'Tampered'
}
else
{
result = 'Not Tampered'
}

return result;
```

7. If the hashes match, then this indicates that the directory has not been tampered with. If they do not match, then this indicates that the file directory has been tampered with. The result (tampered/not tampered) is returned to the requester.

8. A `catch` statement is added to catch any errors during transaction evaluation:

```
} catch (error) {
 console.error(`Failed to submit transaction: ${error}`);
 return error;
 process.exit(1);
 }
 };
```

This brings us to the end of our walkthrough of the `pRead()` method. The `pRead()` method is called when our application is verifying whether the directory under observation has been tampered with. We'll look at the `bRead()` method next, which fetches individual document hashes.

Building a function to compare the current hash signature of a file with the hash recorded in the blockchain

The `bRead()` function is called to compare the hash of a file in the monitored directory with the hash signature recorded previously in the blockchain. It takes the hash of the directory path of a file (p) and the current hash of the file (d) as input parameters:

1. Let's take a look at the function. Like the `pRead` methods, we start `bRead` by defining our `wallet` object and gateway connection. We point the connection to the `docsapp` smart contract and `mychannel` network channel. We'll be using the `user1`, to submit our evaluation transaction:

```
async function bRead (p,d) {

 try {
 const wallet = new FileSystemWallet('/home/ishan/docsapp/wallet');
 const userExists = await wallet.exists('user1');
 if (!userExists) {
 console.log('An identity for the user "user1" does not exist in
the wallet');
 console.log('Run the registerUser.js application before
retrying');
 return;
 }

 const gateway = new Gateway();
 await gateway.connect(ccpPath, { wallet, identity: 'user1',
discovery: { enabled: true, asLocalhost: true } });
```

```
const network = await gateway.getNetwork('mychannel');
const contract = network.getContract('docsapp');
```

2. We'll be connecting and submitting an `evaluateTransaction` request to the `docsapp` method, `queryDocHash`. The `queryDocHash` method returns the file hash signature recorded in the blockchain. It takes the hash of the directory path of the file as input and returns the hash of the file recorded in the blockchain:

```
const result = await
contract.evaluateTransaction('queryDocHash',p);
```

3. The response is returned in marshaled JSON format. We convert the response in to a string and splice the string to get the file hash from the response:

```
const data = result.toString('ascii',12,76);
console.log(`Transaction has been evaluated, result is:
${result.toString('ascii',12,76)}`);
```

4. Next, the method checks whether the hash we receive in the response (`data`) is the same as the current file hash (`d`) that is sent as an input parameter. If there is a mismatch, it means that the file has been tampered with. If there is not a mismatch, then this means that the file has not been tampered with:

```
var status;
 if (data == d)
 {
 console.log("File not tampered");
 status = 'Not Tampered';
 return status;
 }
 else
 {
 console.log("File tampered");
 status= 'Tampered';

 return status;
 }
```

5. The result (Tampered/Not Tampered) is returned to the requester in the output parameter, `status`.

6. A `catch` statement catches any errors during transaction evaluation:

```
} catch (error) {
 console.error(`Failed to submit transaction: ${error}`);
 process.exit(1); }
 };
```

That ends our walkthrough of the bRead() method. The bRead() method is called when we realize that our directory has been tampered with from the result of the pRead() method. It is called for each file member in the directory to identify which files have been tampered with.

Next, let's take a look at the services that our backend server will expose for our frontend React interface to consume.

Writing a backend service for securing a directory by recording hashes in the blockchain

The /api/hashwrite service performs the very important task of calculating the hash of each individual file in a directory, the hash of the last modified time of all the files in the directory, and the hash of the file tree of the directory, and then storing them in the blockchain. It takes the directory path as an input parameter.

The following are the steps that are carried out by the service:

1. Extract the directory path to be secured from the request body.
2. Call the walkDir function to list all the files in the directory.
3. Iterate through all the files in the directory, calculate the hash for each file, and call the bWrite method to write the hash to the blockchain, indexed by the hash of the directory path of the file. For each iteration created, add the last modified time of the file to an array object and the file path to an array object.
4. At the end of the iteration, call the pWrite function to write the hash of the arrays with the last modified time and file path to the blockchain indexed by the current timestamp.
5. Return the array of the list of files secured by the blockchain, the last MTH and FTH, and the timestamp at which the hashes were recorded in the response object to the requester.

Let's start writing the service:

1. The request body to the service has the directory path that is to be secured under the DirPath key:

```
app.post("/api/hashwrite", function(request , response){
var directory = request.body.DirPath;
var timestamp = [];
var modtime;
var jsonString;
```

2. We store the directory path in the `directory` variable.

3. Next, we call the `walkDir` method. The `directory` variable is sent as an input parameter:

```
walkDir(directory,function(err,res){
  if (res)
  {
  var files = res;
```

4. The `walkDir` method returns the `res` array with the list of files in our directory path. Upon a successful response from `walkDir`, we iterate through all the members of the files array, this is basically all the directory paths for all the files in our directory:

```
var counter = 1;
files.forEach(function (file) {
```

5. For each file in our array, we calculate the hash of the file path and the file data.

6. First, we calculate the SHA3 hash digest of the file path and store it in the p variable:

```
var hashPath = new Keccak(256);
hashPath.update(file);
var p = hashPath.digest('hex');
```

7. Next, we fetch the last modified time of the file using the `fs statSync` method and store it in the `timestamp` array. The `timestamp` array will store the last modified time for all the files:

```
var stats = fs.statSync(file);
timestamp.push(stats.mtime);
```

8. Lastly, we use the `fs ReadStream` method to read the file and calculate the SHA3 hash digest of the file's contents. The hash of the file's contents is stored in the d variable:

```
var hashFile = new Keccak(256);
var s = fs.ReadStream(file);
s.on('data', function(d) { hashFile.update(d);});
s.on('end', function() {
var d = hashFile.digest('hex');

console.log("File path hash",p);
console.log("File Hash",d);

bWrite(p,d);
```

9. At the end of the hash digest calculation the file, the hash of the file path and the file's contents are printed to the console.

10. We call the `bWrite` method with the input parameters `p` and `d` to write the file's hash to the blockchain, indexed by the file path hash.

11. When we reach the end of the file list in our directory, we calculate the FTH (`FTH`) using the `files` array and the MTH (`MTH`) using the `timestamp` array. The file list, `MTH`, and `FTH` are printed to the console for reference:

```
var CounterT = counter;
if ( CounterT == files.length)
{
console.log("Files",files);
var FileTreeHash = new Keccak(256);
FileTreeHash.update(files.toString());

var FTH = FileTreeHash.digest('hex');
console.log("FTH ");
console.log(FTH);

var MTimeHash = new Keccak(256);
MTimeHash.update(timestamp.toString());
var MTH = MTimeHash.digest('hex');
console.log("MTH ");
console.log(MTH);
```

12. The `pWrite` method is called to write the hashes, MTH and FTH, to the blockchain. A JSON response is sent to the requester with the `files` array, MTH, FTH, and the time at which the hash was recorded (`modtime`):

```
pWrite(FTH,MTH).then(function(modtime){
jsonString = JSON.stringify({files: files,MTH: MTH,FTH: FTH,
modtime: modtime});
response.send(jsonString);
});
}
});

counter++;
});
```

13. The counter is incremented at the end of each iteration.

14. An `else` block catches any errors that occurred while fetching the list of files using `walkDir()`:

```
else
{
 console.log(err);
 jsonString = JSON.stringify({Error: err});
 response.send(jsonString);
}
});
})
```

That ends our walkthrough of the `/api/hashwrite` service. This service is called the first time our app is launched. It asks the user for the directory to be secured and sends it to the service as a request. Next, we'll write the services that are used to read the hashes that are recorded in the blockchain and compare them with the real-time hash signatures of files, the real-time hash of the modified time of the files and the real-time file tree structure hash. In the case of a mismatch, it indicates that the files and the directory have been tampered with.

Writing a service to verify the last modified time and the file tree structure

Since it is impractical to inspect every file to verify whether it has been tampered with, we'll only be verifying whether the file tree structure of the directory or the last modified time of any of the files has changed. This will indicate whether a file has been added or removed from our directory or any file has been tampered with since our app recorded the hashes. The individual files will be checked and verified only when we find that the MTH (MTH) has changed. We will check these files to locate the actual file(s) that were tampered with.

In this section, we'll write the `/api/hashread` service to check whether there is a mismatch between the current MTH (MTH) and the FTH (FTH) of the directory and the MTH and FTH captured in the blockchain by the `/api/hashwrite` service. In the next section, we'll write the `/api/hashreadfile` service to inspect and compare the hashes of the individual files in our directory.

Let's start writing the `/api/hashread` service:

1. The request body that's sent to the `/api/hashread` service from the frontend contains the timestamp at which the MTH and FTH hashes were recorded in the blockchain and the directory path. The timestamp is under the `modtime` key and the directory path is under the key `DirPath`, in the request body:

```
app.post("/api/hashread", function(request , response){

var modtime = request.body.modtime;
var jsonString;
var directory = request.body.DirPath;
var timestamp = [];
```

2. Next, we call the `walkDir` method to get the current file tree structure of the directory and the **last modified time** of the files in the directory:

```
walkDir(directory,function(err,res){
  if (res)
  {
  var files = res;
  var counter = 1;
```

3. Next, we iterate through the file list returned by the `walkDir` method:

```
files.forEach(function (file) {
```

4. For each iteration, we fetch the last modified time of the file using the `fs.statSync` method and push it into the `timestamp` array:

```
var stats = fs.statSync(file);
timestamp.push(stats.mtime);
```

5. At the end of the iteration, we calculate the hash of the `timestamp` array with the last modified time (MTH) and the hash of the `files` array with the file tree structure (FTH):

```
var CounterT = counter;

 if ( CounterT == files.length)
 {
 var FileTreeHash = new Keccak(256);
FileTreeHash.update(files.toString());
 var FTH = FileTreeHash.digest('hex');
 var MTimeHash = new Keccak(256);
 MTimeHash.update(timestamp.toString());
 var MTH = MTimeHash.digest('hex');
```

6. The newly calculated MTH and FTH are sent as input parameters to the `pRead()` method, along with the `modtime` parameter. The `pRead` method will fetch the prerecorded hashes from the blockchain and compare them to see whether there is a mismatch. If there is a mismatch with the MTH, then it indicates that one or more files in the directory have been tampered with. If there is a mismatch with the FTH, then this indicates that a file has been added to or removed from the directory:

```
pRead(modtime, MTH, FTH).then(function(err,res){
  if (res)
  {
  jsonString = JSON.stringify({result: res,files: files });
  response.send(jsonString);
  }
  else
  {
  jsonString = JSON.stringify({result: err, files: files});
  response.send(jsonString);
  }
})}
  counter++;
  })}})});
```

The response from the `pRead` method (tampered/not tampered) that's received from the `pRead` function is sent to the response body in the `result` key and the files array is returned in the `files` key. After each iteration, the counter is incremented.

Writing a service to inspect and identify tampered files

The `/api/hashreadfile` service will be called by the frontend if the response from the `/api/hashread` service indicates that the MTH (`MTH`) or FTH (`FTH`) has changed, indicating that our secure directory has been tampered with. The `/api/hashreadfile` service will then help us identify which files have been tampered with.

Let's start writing our service:

1. The request body to the `hashreadfile` service will contain the directory path under the `DirPath` key and the list of files to be inspected under the `files` array:

```
app.post("/api/hashreadfile", function(request , response){

x`var directory = request.body.DirPath;
```

```
var files = request.body.files;

var responseObject = [];
var timestamp = [];
var jsonString;
var counter = 1;2.
```

2. Next, we iterate through the list of files in the `files` array. For each file, we'll calculate the SHA3 hash of the file path and the file's contents. The file path hash is stored in the `p` variable and the file content hash is stored in the `d` variable. We use the `ReadStream` method to calculate the hash of the file's contents. At the end of the hash digest creation, we will call the `bRead` method. The hashes are printed to the console for reference:

```
files.forEach(function (file) {

var hashPath = new Keccak(256);
hashPath.update(file);
var p = hashPath.digest('hex');

var hashFile = new Keccak(256);
var s = fs.ReadStream(file);
s.on('data', function(d) { hashFile.update(d);});
s.on('end', function() {
var d = hashFile.digest('hex');

console.log("File path hash",p);
console.log("File Hash",d);
```

3. The `bRead` method is called with the input parameters `p` (the file path hash) and `d` (the file hash) for each iteration of the loop:

```
bRead(p,d).then(function(res){
  if(res)
  {
  responseObject.push({file: file, status: res});
  if( responseObject.length == files.length)
  {
  jsonString = JSON.stringify({res: responseObject});
  response.send(jsonString);
  }
  }
});
});
```

4. The `responseObject` object array captures the status of each file. For each iteration of the loop, we call the `bRead` method for checking whether the file has been tampered with. After getting the status of the file from the `bRead` method (tampered or not tampered), we push the file name and the status of the file into the `responseObject` array. At the end of the iteration, we send a response object back to the requester with the file list and status of each object in JSON format.

This brings us to the end of our walkthrough of the backend service. Next, we will create our DocsApp frontend, which the user will use to interact with our backend server and blockchain network.

Creating a React frontend for the app

Our frontend will be a React app with which the user can register a directory to secure our blockchain. After registering the directory, the app will iterate every 5 seconds and call the `/api/hashread` service to check whether the directory has been tampered with.

In the case the directory has been tampered with, the app will show the message `Tampered!` in the header; otherwise, it will say `Not Tampered`. It will then call the `/api/hashreadfile` service in the backend server to fetch a list of tampered files, added files, and removed files. These are then listed in the app.

The following are the constituent parts of the app:

- The main `App.js` file
- The following React components:
    - `Container.js`
    - `PathMapper.js`
    - `FolderBlock.js`
    - `FolderBlockChkStatus.js`
    - `GlowBar.js`

The following is a brief description of these components:

- `App.js`: The main `App.js` file implements the methods that interact with the backend server, submit requests, and interpret responses. It invokes `Container.js` for rendering the child components and forwards the current state to `Container.js`.

- **React components**: These components render the DocsApp frontend:
  - `Container.js`: This receives the current state from `App.js` and passes it to the child components.
  - `PathMapper.js`: This is the landing screen for the app that asks the user for the root of the directory they want to secure.
  - `FolderBlock.js`: This is the component that renders the list of files in the directory and their current status (tampered/not tampered).
  - `FolderBlockChkStatus.js`: This is the component that renders the list of files in the directory and their current status (tampered/not tampered). If the directory has been tampered with, it shows the list of tampered files, added files, and removed files in the directory.
  - `GlowBar.js`: This is the component that shows the message `Tampered` with a red highlight if the directory is found to have been tampered with or `Not Tampered` with a green highlight if the directory has not been tampered with.

Let's start creating the frontend.

Creating the React project environment

Before we can create our React app, we need to set the project directory and install the dependencies for our app:

1. Create a new React app called `DocsApp` using `npx`:

   ```
   npx create-react-app DocsApp
   ```

2. Update your `package.json` to the file so that it has following values:

   ```
   {
     "name": "DocsApp",
     "version": "1.0.0",
     "private": false,
     "dependencies": {
     "bulma-start": "0.0.2",
     "react": "^16.4.1",
     "react-dom": "^16.4.1",
     "react-scripts": "1.1.4"
     },
     "scripts": {
   ```

```
"start": "react-scripts start",
"build": "react-scripts build",
"test": "react-scripts test --env=jsdom",
"eject": "react-scripts eject"
}
}
```

3. Run npm install on a Terminal window to install the dependencies.
4. Next, within the src folder, create a Components folder for the app components.

Let's go through the components one by one.

Building the container component

The container component has fairly simple logic. It renders the PathMapper component on the first launch of the app, which prompts the user for a root directory path to be secured.

After the directory have been registered and the hashes are captured in the blockchain, the value of DirPath (the root of the directory that is to be secured) is set in the app state. At this point, the container renders the FolderBlock component.

After this, the app checks whether there is a mismatch between the values of MTH and FTH and the recorded hash values in the blockchain. Every 5 seconds, it reiterates and checks whether there is a mismatch between the directory and the values in the blockchain. The container component renders the FolderBlockChkStatus component. This component renders the list of all the files in the directory under inspection and their current status (Tampered/not Tampered). In the case that the directory has been tampered with, it lists all the tampered, added, and removed files:

```
render(){

return (
.............
{
this.props.DirPath == null?
<div>
<PathMapper setDir={this.props.setDir}
fields={this.props.fields}
PathMap={this.props.PathMap}
onInputChangeUpdateField={this.props.onInputChangeUpdateField}/>
</div> :

this.props.vstatus == true?
```

```
<div>
<PanelHeader DirPath={this.props.DirPath} />
<GlowBar fstatus={this.props.fstatus} />
<FolderBlocknew verfile={this.props.verfile}
addFile={this.props.addFile}
remFile={this.props.remFile}
BView={this.props.BView}
changeBView={this.props.changeBView}
DirPath={this.props.DirPath} />
</div>:

<div>
<PanelHeader DirPath={this.props.DirPath} />
<GlowBar fstatus={this.props.fstatus} />
<FolderBlock files={this.props.files}
DirPath={this.props.DirPath}
startTimer ={this.props.startTimer} /> />
</div>
}
. . . . . . . . . . . . . . .
. . . . . . . . . . . . . . .
```

The container is rendered by App.js, which passes the current state of the app and the methods to the container, which then passes it to the child components as and when they are rendered based on the conditional clause statement.

Building the PathMapper component

The PathMapper component renders a single panel with an input field for entering the directory path to be secured and a **Submit** button. On clicking the **Submit** button, the PathMap() method is called, which sets the DirPath state variable. This variable holds the root directory path for the lifecycle of the app:

```
<div>
 Enter Root of directory path to be secured
 </div>
 <InputField onInputChangeUpdateField={props.onInputChangeUpdateField}
 fields={props.fields} name="DirPath" Placeholder="Directory Path"/>
 <p className="control">
 <a className="button is-success"
 onClick={() => props.PathMap()}>
 Submit
 </a>
 </p>
 </div>
```

The `PathMapper` component is rendered the first time the app is launched. It captures and sets the `DirPath` state variable.

Building the FolderBlock component

The `FolderBlock` component is rendered after we write the file hashes, the MTH, and the FTH to the blockchain. It lists the files in the directory that are written to the blockchain and the directory path for each file:

```
{
props.files.map((file,index) => {

var splitString = file.split("/");
var reverseArray = splitString.reverse();

return (
<div className="panel-block is-multiline">
<div className="column">

<div key={index} className="columns token">
<div className="column">
<strong>FileName </strong>
: {reverseArray[0]}
</div>
<div className="column">
<strong> Path</strong>
: {file}
</div>
</div>
</div>
</div>
)
})
}
```

Since the `file` array contains just the directory location of each file, we iterate through each member and split it from the end, delimited by `"/"` to get the file name. The file location and file name are then rendered on the screen.

The `FolderBlock` component is rendered only for about the first 5 seconds after the app writes all the hashes to the blockchain. When the app runs the first interval to compare and look for mismatches between the current hash signatures of the directory and the hash signatures written to the blockchain, the `FolderBlock` component is replaced by the `FolderBlockChkStatus` component.

The `FolderBlockChkStatus` component also shows the current status of the file (Tampered/Not Tampered) based on the result of the comparison returned by the backend server. Let's look at the `FolverBlockChkStatus` component next.

Building the FolderBlockChkStatus component

The `FolderBlockChkStatus` component is probably the most complex component. It carries out the following tasks:

- Displays whether the current status of the directory is `Directory is Tampered`/`Not Tampered`
- Displays whether the current status of the file is `Tampered` or `Not Tampered`
- In the case that the directory is tampered with, displays the list of tampered files, added files, and removed files

Go through the following steps to build the `FolderBlockChkStatus` component:

1. We start by rendering a simple menu bar to allow the user to navigate between the different categories of files:

```
<div className="panel-block">
<div className="columns ">
<p className="column control">
<a className="button is-light"
onClick={() => props.changeBView(1)}>
All Files
</a>
</p>
<p className="column control">
<a className="button is-light"
onClick={() => props.changeBView(2)}>
Added Files
</a>
</p>
<p className="column control">
<a className="button is-light"
onClick={() => props.changeBView(3)}>
Removed Files
</a>
</p>
<p className="column control">
<a className="button is-light"
onClick={() => props.changeBView(4)}>
Tampered Files
```

```
</a>
</p>
</div>
```

2. The `props.changeBView` method changes the `BView` state variable in to a value between 1 and 4. Each value indicates a screen type, as follows:

```
1 - All Files Screen
2 - Added Files Screen
3 - Removed Files Screen
4 - Tampered Files Screen
```

3. A conditional statement iterates through the values of the state variable `BView` and renders the screen accordingly. When `BView` is 1, the **All Files** screen is rendered. It lists all the files with their directory location. If a file is tampered with, the background is highlighted in red using the `warning` color tag for the `bulma` framework. The `verfile` array contains a list of all files that are currently located in the directory. Any files that have been removed are not present in this array and by extension are not displayed on this screen:

```
props.BView == 1?

  <div className="panel-block">
  <div className="panel-block is-paddingless is-12" >
  <div>
  {
  props.verfile.map((f,index) => {

  var splitString = f.file.split("/");
  var reverseArray = splitString.reverse();

  return (
  <div className={f.status == 'Tampered' ? "has-background-danger" :
  "has-background-white"}>
  <div className="panel-block is-multiline">
  <div className="column">

  <div key={index} className="columns token">
  <div className="column">
  <strong>FileName </strong>
  : {reverseArray[0]}
  </div>
  <div className="column">
  <strong> Path</strong>
  : {f.file}
  </div>
  <div className="column">
```

```
<strong>Status </strong>
: {f.status}
</div>
```

4. When `BView` is 2, this indicates that the user has clicked on the **Added Files** button. The app will render a screen with a list of all the files that have been added since the hash was last captured in the blockchain. The `addFile` array contains a list of all files that have been added since the hash of the directory was recorded to the blockchain. When the `BView` state variable is set to 2, the app will map the `addFile` array and display all the newly added files on the screen:

```
props.BView == 2?

<div className="panel-block">
<div className="panel-block is-paddingless is-12" >
<div>
{
props.addFile.map((file,index) => {

var splitString = file.split("/");
var reverseArray = splitString.reverse();

return (
<div className="panel-block is-multiline">
<div className="column">
<div key={index} className="columns token">
<div className="column">
<strong>FileName </strong>
: {reverseArray[0]}
</div>
<div className="column">
<strong> Path</strong>
: {file}
</div>
```

5. When `BView` is 3, this indicates that the user has clicked on the **Removed Files** button. The app will render a screen with a list of all the files that have been added since the hash was last captured in the blockchain. The `remFile` array contains a list of all the files that have been removed since the hash of the directory was recorded to the blockchain. When the `BView` state variable is set to 3, the app will map the `remFile` array and display all of the removed files on the screen:

```
props.BView == 3?

<div className="panel-block">
```

```
<div className="panel-block is-paddingless is-12" >
<div>
{
props.remFile.map((file,index) => {

var splitString = file.split("/");
var reverseArray = splitString.reverse();

return (
<div className="panel-block is-multiline">
<div className="column">
<div key={index} className="columns token">
<div className="column">
<strong>FileName </strong>
: {reverseArray[0]}
</div>
<div className="column">
<strong> Path</strong>
: {file}
</div>
```

6. When the value of BView is not equal to 1, 2, or 3, the user has selected option 4. This indicates that the user has clicked on the **Tampered Files** button. The app will render a screen with a list of all the files that have been tampered with since the hash was last captured in the blockchain. The verFile array contains a list of all the files with their current status (Tampered/Not Tampered). Only files with the status of Tampered are displayed on the screen:

```
props.verfile.map((f,index) => {

var splitString = f.file.split("/");
var reverseArray = splitString.reverse();

return (
<div className={f.status == 'Not Tampered' ? "is-hidden" :
"has-background-white" }>
<div className="panel-block is-multiline">
<div className="column">

<div key={index} className="columns token">
<div className="column">
<strong>FileName </strong>
: {reverseArray[0]}
</div>
<div className="column">
<strong> Path</strong>
: {f.file}
```

```
</div>
<div className="column">
<strong>Status </strong>
: {f.status}
</div>
```

This brings us to the end of the components for the app. We'll look at the methods for our app next.

Writing the app methods

Our `App.js` file will define the methods that will be called by the child components. It'll also render the container component and pass it the state of the app, in which the container component will then transfer to the child components when they are rendered.

The app will use the following methods:

- `startTimer`: Sets an interval of 5 seconds and calls the `pathcheck()` method every 5 seconds to see whether there is a mismatch in the last modified time or file tree structure compared to the version recorded in the blockchain.
- `hashFile`: The method that calls the backend `/api/hashwrite` service to write hash signatures to the blockchain and updates the app state with the list of files being monitored, the FTH, the MTH, and the time that the hash was captured.
- `pathCheck`: The method that calls the backend `/api/hashread` service to check whether there is a mismatch in the MTH and FTH that was recorded to the blockchain and the current last MTH and FTH of the directory. In the case of a mismatch, it stops the interval loop and sets `fstatus` state variable to `Tampered` to indicate that the directory has been tampered with.
- `fileCheck`: The method that calls the backend `/api/hashreadfile` service to identify the tampered files in the directory. After a response from the service, it updates the state variables with the current status of the files.
- `compFiles`: The method that compares the list of files being monitored by the app with the latest file list of the directory. It adds the list of removed files, added files, and the files that still exist in the directory to the app state.
- `changeBView`: Cycles between the various views of the app by modifying the `BView`.

Let's start by looking at the constructor and the app state that is defined by it.

The app starts by declaring the `appName` app member and setting it to `DocsApp`, which is the name of our application:

```
constructor(){
  super();
  this.appName = 'DocsApp';
```

The state of the app contains the following variables, which we'll be using in our methods. We'll look at the purpose of these state variables when we write our methods:

```
this.state = {
DirPath: null,
fstatus: null,
vstatus: false,
modtime: null,
files : [],
verfile: [],
remFile: [],
addFile: [],
MTH : null,
FTH: null,
tflag: true,

fields: {
DirPath: null,
},
 };
```

We also add the `DirPath` field variable, which will capture and store the `root` directory path that is to be secured. This will be entered by the user on the screen. Let's start writing the methods.

Creating a method to set the timer interval

The `startTimer` method sets the timer interval that calls the `hashread` method every 5 seconds to see whether there is a mismatch between the MTH and FTH hashes recorded in the blockchain and the current MTH and FTH hashes:

1. The method checks whether the `tflag` state variable is set to `true`. You might remember that this value is set to `true` in the constructor. This is to avoid multiple firing when the app is rendered multiple times because of changes in state:

   ```
   startTimer = () =>{
     if(this.state.tflag == true)
   ```

```
{
console.log ("Started Timer");
this.intervalHandle = setInterval(this.pathCheck,5000);
```

2. The interval set is `intervalHandle`. It calls the `pathCheck` method every 5 seconds (5,000 milliseconds). Next, we set the app state variable `tflag` to `false` to ensure that the interval is not set multiple times:

```
this.setState({
tflag: false
});
}
}
```

This wraps up the `startTimer` method. Let's move on to the next method.

Creating a method to write the hashes to the blockchain

Next, let's look at the `hashFile` method. The `hashFile` method is called after the user submits the directory path to be secured for hashing and writing the directory components and parameters to the blockchain:

1. We first capture the local state and methods of the app from the `this` object. We also fetch the directory path submitted by the user and store it in the `DirPath` variable:

```
hashFile = () => {

let app = this;
var DirPath = this.state.fields.DirPath;
```

2. Next, we call the `hashwrite` API in our backend server with the directory path (`DirPath`) as the input parameter:

```
fetch('http://localhost:3600/api/hashwrite', {
method: 'POST',
headers: {
'Accept': 'application/json',
'Content-Type': 'application/json',
},
body: JSON.stringify({
DirPath: DirPath})
}).then(function(response,error) {
```

3. Next, we check for a successful response from the `hashwrite` services:

```
if(response)
{
return response.json();
}
else
{
console.log(error);
}
}).then(function(data){
```

4. The data in the response JSON object is parsed to fetch the `DirPath`, the list of monitored files, the MTH, the FTH, and the time when the hash was captured (`modtime`):

```
app.setState({
  DirPath: DirPath,
  status: 'Idle',
  files : data.files,
  MTH : data.MTH,
  FTH: data.FTH,
  modtime: data.modtime
  });
  });
  }
```

The following app state variables are set:

- `DirPath`: Directory root path
- `status`: Current state of the app
- `files`: Array with the list of files
- `MTH`: MTH of the files in the directory path
- `FTH`: FTH of the directory
- `modtime`: Time when hashes were recorded in the blockchain

That wraps up our `hashFile` method. Let's move on to the next method, which we will use to compare the current `last modified time` and the `file tree structure` of the secured directory with the values stored in the blockchain.

Creating a method to check for a mismatch between the last modified time and the file tree structure

Next, we will look at the `pathCheck()` method. After writing the hash signatures to the blockchain, the app renders the `FolderBlock` component. This component triggers the 5-second interval timer by calling the `startTimer` method. The `startTimer` method, in turn, calls the `pathCheck` method, every 5 seconds to verify whether there is a mismatch between the hash signature of the MTH (`MTH`) and FTH (`FTH`) written in the blockchain and the actual hash value of the MTH and FTH when calculated from the directory under observation. A mismatch indicates that some data in our directory has been tampered with.

Let's see how the `pathCheck` method achieves this:

1. We start by capturing the app state and the `DirPath` state variable(directory path), `modtime` (the time when the hashes were captured in the blockchain), and files locally (the `files` array with the list of files being observed):

```
pathCheck = () =>{

  let app = this;

  var DirPath = this.state.fields.DirPath;
  var modtime = this.state.modtime;
  var files = this.state.files;

  this.setState({
          status: 'Verifying'
      });
```

2. We also change the status variable to `Verifying`.
3. Next, we call the `hashread` service on our backend server. Remember that the `hashread` service takes `DirPath` and `modtime` as input parameters so that it can fetch the MTH and FTH recorded in the blockchain, calculate the present values of `MTH` and `FTH` from our directory, and see whether there is a mismatch between the two. A mismatch indicates that one or more files have been tampered with or have been added/removed.
4. We then use `fetch` to call the `hashread` service on port `3602` of our backend server and provide the `DirPath` and `modtime` input parameters in the request body:

```
fetch('http://localhost:3602/api/hashread', {
  method: 'POST',
  headers: {
```

```
'Accept': 'application/json',
'Content-Type': 'application/json',
},

body: JSON.stringify({
DirPath: DirPath,
modtime: modtime,
})
}).then(function(response,error) {
```

5. Upon a successful response from the backend, we parse the data in the `response.json`:

```
if(response)
{
return response.json();
}
else
{
console.log(error);
}
}).then(function(data){
```

6. The result of the check (`Tampered`/`Not Tampered`) is stored in the `fstatus` state variable, where it can be accessed by the other components of the app. The list of files currently present in the directory is returned by the `hashread` service in the response key `files`. We store these in the `filesNew` array:

```
then(function(data){
 app.setState({
 fstatus: data.result,
 });
 var filesNew = data.files;
 if(data.result == "Tampered")
 {
 clearInterval(app.intervalHandle);

 var params = {files,filesNew};
 app.compFiles(params);
 }
 });
}
```

Next, we check whether the status returned by the backend service is `Tampered`. If the directory has been tampered with, we stop the iterating interval and call the `compFiles` method with the parameters `files` and `filesNew` (the original list of files in the directory and the list of files currently in the directory). The `compFile` method will allow us to identify whether any files have been added or removed from the directory. This wraps up our `pathCheck` method.

Writing a method to check whether any files have been added or removed from the directory

The `compFile` method compares the old and new list of files to see whether there is a mismatch between the two. It iterates through the old and new list of files of the directory under observation to check whether any new files have been added or removed. The `addFile` variable stores the added files and the `remFile` variable stores the removed files. The files that were present both during the initial hashing and during the verification are stored in the array,`extFile` . You can find the code for the `compFile` method in the `App.js` file at https://github.com/PacktPublishing/Blockchain-Development-for-Finance-Projects/blob/master/Chapter%207/Docs%20App/src/App.js.

At the end of the execution, the method sets the arrays `extFile`, `remFile`, and `addFile` to the app state. It then calls the `fileCheck` method to check which of the individual files have been tampered.

Writing a method for identifying tampered files from the list of files

The `fileCheck` method identifies the list of tampered files from the `extFile` file array. To do this, it calls the backend `hashreadfile` service:

1. We start by locally capturing the list of files in the `extFile` variable. As you might remember, this is the list of files present during the initial hashing and the verification check. We want to identify which files among these may have been tampered with:

```
filecheck = () =>{

  const files = this.state.extFile;
  const DirPath = this.state.fields.DirPath;
  let app = this;
```

2. Next, we call the `hashreadfile` service in our backend node server. As you might remember, the input parameters are `DirPath` (directory path) and `files` (the list of files present in the directory):

```
fetch('http://localhost:3602/api/hashreadfile', {
method: 'POST',
headers: {
'Accept': 'application/json',
'Content-Type': 'application/json',
},

body: JSON.stringify({
DirPath: DirPath,
files: files
})
}).then(function(response,error) {
```

3. Upon a successful response, we parse the `response.json` object to fetch the data returned by the backend:

```
if(response)
{
console.log(response);
return response.json();
}
else
{
console.log(error);
}
}).then(function(data){
```

4. The backend `hashreadfile` service returns the file array to us with the status of the files. This list is stored in the state variable `verfile`. At the same time, the `vstatus` flag is set to `true` to notify the app to render the `FolberBlockChkStatus` component with the list of tampered files:

```
app.setState({
verfile : data.res,
vstatus: true
})
});
}
```

This ends the `fileCheck` method for our `App.js` file .This also concludes the development of our app. Now let's run the components together to see how the app looks and functions.

Running the tamper-proof application

Let's run our application.

Make sure that the Hyperledger Fabric network is running:

1. Bring the backend server online:

   ```
   node hashcheck
   ```

2. Next, bring the React app online. Navigate to the react directory and enter the following command:

   ```
   npm start
   ```

3. The app should now open up in your browser, as shown in the following screenshot:

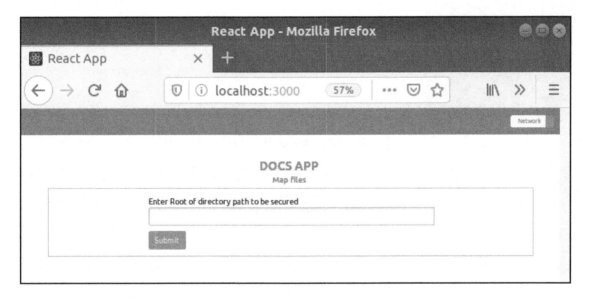

4. We need to provide a test directory that we'll be monitoring with our app.

I've created a mock test directory, as shown in the following screenshot. Feel free to create your own directory or use a preexisting one:

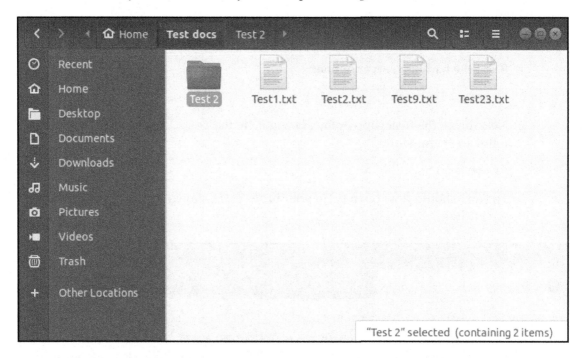

5. Next, we will enter the absolute path of the directory in our app to secure it:

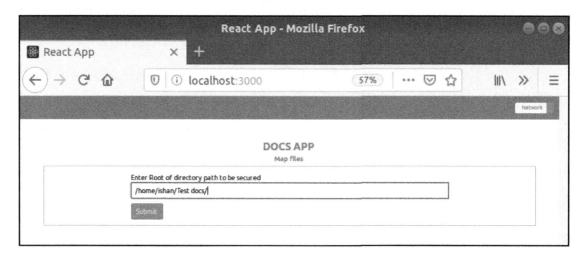

6. Click on **Submit** to proceed. The app will next hash the files in our directory and capture them to the blockchain. The app will then monitor each of the files in the directory:

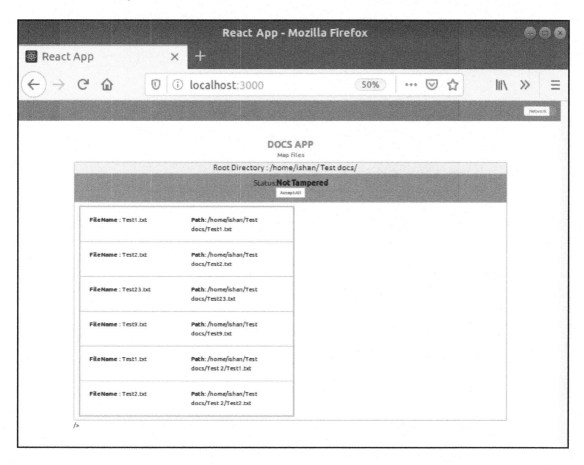

7. The green banner and the **Not Tampered** status indicates that the directory has not been tampered with. Let's try to remove a file from the directory and see how the app works.

The app banner should become red with the message **Tampered**:

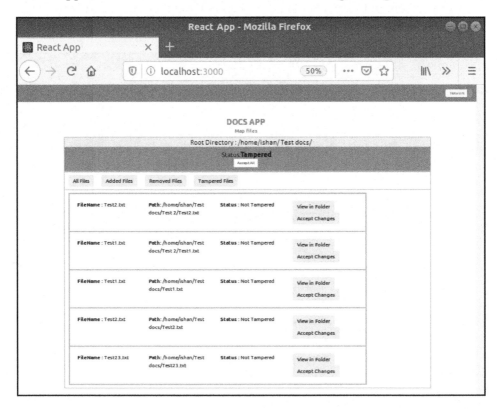

8. Click on **Removed Files** to see the removed file:

That ends our demo. You can try out the app to see how it works with cases where a file has been modified or added to the directory.

Summary

That wraps up our tamper-proof Blockchain app. In an enterprise scenario, you can use this app to detect any tampering and then replace the files from a backup, such as a disaster recovery site, if required. This is a simple prototype, and I'm sure that you can figure out multiple applications for this workflow in the different business processes of a financial organization, such as managing digital copies of customers' private documents, confidential files and business information, transaction data, and so on.

We started this chapter with the intention of leveraging the tamper-proof property, or immutability, of blockchains to build an app that will notify us when a record-keeping or document storage system has been tampered with. To that end, we set up a private Hyperledger Fabric network with two nodes, two organizations, and one channel. On the network, we deployed a chaincode smart contract that would be used to record hashes and retrieve hashes from the blockchain for comparison. We also built an app with a node backend that would interact with the chaincode contract and a React frontend that would be used by a user to submit a directory that can be secured by the app. Lastly, we ran our app and used it to see how the app works when the directory is tampered with.

The main take away from this chapter should be how the tamperproof property can be used and extended to build complex applications that secure data and information. In the next chapter, we'll be leveraging these features to build a trading exchange.

The next chapter will introduce you to the concept of decentralized exchanges. We'll be implementing a trading exchange using the Ethereum platform.

4
Section 4: Decentralized Trading Exchanges Using Blockchain

Decentralized trading exchanges are probably one of the best financial applications of blockchain technology. In recent years, commodity and asset trading exchanges around the world have been susceptible to scams and frauds arising from orderbook manipulation and inflated trading volumes. Additionally, reconciliation and settlement is an expensive and time-consuming affair for most exchanges. Decentralized trading exchanges look to solve both of these issues by replicating the orderbook across the network participants in real time and using a blockchain ledger to settle trades between the traders. The distributed nature of the orderbook means that it cannot be tampered with or modified by an individual or a single party. All trades are posted instantly to the ledger and settled. Exchange participants can validate these trades simply by checking the ledger.

In the next two chapters, we'll be building decentralized trading exchanges of our own. We'll be building an asset exchange platform and a multi-currency exchange platform that uses blockchain technology for securing the trading process.

This section comprises the following chapters:

- Chapter 8, *Building a Decentralized Trading Exchange on Blockchain*
- Chapter 9, *Developing a Currency Trading Exchange for Market Making*
- Chapter 10, *Looking into the Future*

8
Building a Decentralized Trading Exchange

This chapter deals with building a decentralized trading exchange using a private Ethereum blockchain. Traditionally, trading exchanges require an authority who will facilitate the trade between the buyers and the sellers. This authority will post the buy offers and sell offers from all the traders in a single platform, where they are visible to all the participants. This platform is referred to as the orderbook. Traders can trade against the offers that are posted on the orderbook.

In this chapter, we attempt to *decentralize* or basically remove the authority that manages the orderbook from the picture. The decentralized exchange will still have an orderbook, except it will be managed by a smart contract and will be available for all the participants to view and trade against in real time. We will be building an exchange on top of this orderbook that allows traders to trade US dollars for gold.

In this chapter, we will cover following topics:

- Technical requirements
- Decentralized trading exchanges
- Issuing the trading assets
- The orderbook smart contract
- Building the exchange app
- Running the exchange app

Technical requirements

The code files of this chapter are available at `https://github.com/PacktPublishing/Blockchain-Development-for-Finance-Projects/tree/master/Chapter%208`.

We'll be using the following sources to develop our project:

- Ganache private blockchain server—`https://trufflesuite.com/ganache/`
- Trufflesuite—`https://github.com/trufflesuite/truffle`
- Metamask plugin for Chrome/Firefox/Safari—`https://metamask.io/`

To install Ganache on Ubuntu, you might need to change some settings. Click on the drop-down menu next to the directory name. Select **Preferences**. Navigate to the **Behavior** tab. Under **Executable Text Files**, set the option to **Ask what to do**. Navigate back to the file downloaded from the Ganache download link. Right-click on the file and click on **properties**. Select the **Permissions** tab. Select the **Allow executing files as program** option. Now, double-click on the file. The Ganache blockchain should start smoothly. It's probably best to do a global installation of Truffle to avoid any conflicts. For example, create a directory workspace called `truffle` and install Truffle using `sudo npm install truffle -g`.

I'm using Ubuntu 18.04.2 LTS to run the preceding applications and to deploy my blockchain. This project assumes that you are working on a Unix operating system. Additionally, this project assumes that you have **node.js** and **npm** installed. I'm using **node version 13.0.1** and **npm version 6.12.0**.

Lastly, we'll be using the **OpenZeppelin** library of smart contracts to write our contracts. To use this library, create a project folder in your Truffle workspace. Let's call it `tokenwallet`. Create a `package.json` file in the `project` folder and update it with the following values:

```
{
  "dependencies": {
    "babel-register": "^6.23.0",
    "babel-polyfill": "^6.26.0",
    "babel-preset-es2015": "^6.18.0"
  },
  "devDependencies": {
    "openzeppelin-solidity": "^2.2.0"
  }
}
```

Run `npm install` in order to install the OpenZeppelin library and Babel for your Truffle workspace.

Decentralized trading exchanges

Blockchains can play an important role in the disintermediation of financial systems. Most financial systems today include a number of middlemen and organizations that facilitate the smooth working of the entire ecosystem. Obviously, this means placing your trust with these intermediary players, and believing that they will not try to carry out any fraudulent activity, or relay incorrect information to you. This chapter is an example of a system that attempts to reduce the number of middlemen and authorities in the existing model, in order to build a faster and more transparent system. A decentralized trading exchange is one where the orderbook is not controlled by a central authority.

As the name suggests, the entire trading process is decentralized, meaning it is without a central authority or organization to facilitate the trades. Removing a central authority means that traders do not have to place their trust in an intermediary for trading. The orderbook is not maintained by such an authority, thus, the scope for fraud or tampering with the orderbook is reduced. You also do not have to pay transaction or trading fees, since the middleman is absent. Additionally, since the system is built on top of a blockchain platform, trades are reconciled and settled between traders that are almost instantaneous when compared to a traditional trading exchange.

The exchange would consist of the following components:

- A decentralized orderbook that records all offers, and is managed by a smart contract on the blockchain
- A US-dollar ERC20 token, and a gold ERC20 token to keep a track of our trading assets
- A frontend app that displays the orderbook to users in real time, and matches a trading request submitted by the user against the available offers on the orderbook

Basic components of a trading exchange

Trading exchanges consist of the following important components:

- **Orderbook**: A platform where a central authority posts buy and sell offers for different assets from all the traders that are interacting with the exchange. These assets can be anything ranging from shares of a company to currencies such as US dollars and UK pounds, to commodities such as gold, silver, crude oil, and so on. The orderbook is visible to all trade participants in real time, and it updates as new offers are submitted, or trades are carried out. To buy or sell an asset, the trader simply needs to look at the current price and then submit a new offer. If there is a matching offer, a trade is carried out.

- **Matching engine**: The matching engine matches incoming trade requests as offers against the existing offers on the orderbook. So, let's say you submitted an offer to buy a gram of gold for $50, the matching engine will scout the orderbook to see if a trader is selling a gram of gold for $50. If an offer exists, it will debit $50 from your account and credit a gram of gold. This $50 will be credited to the trader who had posted the sell request that your offer matched against. If the matching engine is unable to find a matching offer for you, it will simply forward your offer to the orderbook, where it will wait until someone makes a matching sell request against your offer.

- **Accounts**: User accounts hold the base asset and the counter asset. The asset that you use to buy or sell is called a **base asset**. Thus, if you buy or sell gold using US dollars, then US dollars is the base asset. The commodity to be bought or sold is called the **counter asset**. Thus, in the example, gold is a counter asset.

The term '*Price*' in the orderbook reflects the amount of US dollars that you will have to pay to buy a gram of gold, or the amount of US dollars that you will receive on selling a gram of gold. Price is always per unit cost. The term '*Quantity*' refers to the total grams of gold that are available at that price.

Scope of the decentralized exchange project

In our project, we'll be building an exchange that allows the user to trade gold for US dollars. Unlike the traditional model, where the central authority builds and maintains the orderbook platform, in our model the orderbook is built and managed using a smart contract. It will be available to all traders who connect to our private blockchain platform to trade, and it will be stored in all the nodes that are hosted as part of our blockchain

We'll be building and deploying the following components:

- Two ERC20 token smart contracts called `Gold` and `USD`. The ERC20 gold token represents our gold asset (the counter asset), and the ERC20 USD token represents the amount of US dollars (the base asset) that are used to buy or sell gold.
- A smart contract called **Orderbook.** This contract will allow users to trade gold for USD. It will keep a track of all the incoming buy and sell offers, and will allow traders to view and execute a trade against an existing offer that is stored in the contract.
- A frontend React app called **Exchange**. This app will serve two purposes. First, it will display the orderbook in real time to the user. Second, it will show the user their current base asset and counter asset balance. Lastly, and most importantly, when the user submits a buy or sell request, it will run a matching algorithm to verify if there are any matching trades against the user's offer. If yes, it will execute a trade against that offer by invoking the orderbook smart contract. If no, it will add the offer to the orderbook by invoking the smart contract.

Alright then, let's get started.

Issuing the trading assets

In our exchange, we'll allow the user to buy or sell the gold asset using US dollars. Thus, gold will be our counter asset, that is, the asset that is being bought or sold. US dollars will be our base asset, that is, the asset that is being used to buy or sell.

Before we can build a trading exchange around these assets, we need to create these assets on our blockchain. To do so, we'll create an ERC20 token that represents gold, and an ERC20 token that represents USD. The tokens are fungible and fixed in nature, and can go up to two decimal places. One gold token represents one gram of gold, and one USD token represents one dollar.

Writing the contracts

We'll be using the OpenZeppelin suite of smart contract templates for writing our contracts. Let's start by writing the USD token contract:

1. We start writing the code by declaring the Solidity compiler version:

```
pragma solidity ^0.5.2;
```

2. Next, we import the requisite OpenZeppelin contract templates, which we will use to build our token:

```
import "openzeppelin-
solidity/contracts/token/ERC20/ERC20Detailed.sol";

import "openzeppelin-
solidity/contracts/token/ERC20/ERC20Capped.sol";

import "openzeppelin-solidity/contracts/ownership/Ownable.sol";
```

The first contract template is ERC20Detailed. The ERC20Detailed contract allows you to set the parameters of the ERC20 token using a constructor such as the token name, token symbol, and the number of decimals after zero. It also implements the ERC20 standard contract interface, which is extended by our contract.

The second contract template is ERC20Capped. This contract allows us to create an ERC20 token with a capped supply. Basically, we are fixing the upper limit for the total number of tokens that can be issued.

Lastly, we have the ownable contract. This contract essentially sets the contract owner parameter to the Ethereum address that deploys the contract.

3. Next, we define our contract name:

```
contract USD is ERC20Detailed, ERC20Capped, Ownable {
```

The USD contract inherits the ERC20Detailed, ERC20Capped, and Ownable contracts that we imported before using the 'is' keyword. This allows us to define and access the members of these contracts.

4. Lastly, we define the constructor for our token contract:

```
constructor()
ERC20Detailed("US Dollar", "USD", 2)
ERC20Capped(10000000000)
MinterRole()
payable public {}
}
```

Within our constructor, we call the constructors for our inherited contracts. The `ERC20Detailed` contract constructor is called, and it sets the token name, token symbol, and the number of decimal places after zero as US dollars, USD, and 2, respectively. The `ERc20Capped` contract constructor is called to set the total number of tokens in circulation as 10,000,000,000 USD tokens. Lastly, we call the MinterRole contract constructor to set the Minter address, that is, the address that will create and issue new tokens. This is set to the address that is deploying the contract. MinterRole is a contract that is inherited by the `ERC20Capped` contract. We can also open these contracts within OpenZeppelin and see how the constructors are defined within them. You can observe these at the OpenZeppelin GitHub repository, at `https://github.com/OpenZeppelin`.

This is how the constructor for `ERC20Detailed` is defined:

```
constructor (string memory name, string memory symbol, uint8
decimals) public {
 _name = name;
 _symbol = symbol;
 _decimals = decimals;
 }
```

This is how constructor for `ERC20Capped` is defined:

```
constructor (uint256 cap) public {
 require(cap > 0, "ERC20Capped: cap is 0");
 _cap = cap;
 }
```

This is how constructor for `MinterRole` is defined:

```
constructor () internal {
 _addMinter(_msgSender());
 }
```

5. Lastly, we define our contract as payable in order to receive ethers and define the scope as public. Putting it all together, this how our USD token contract looks:

```
//USD.sol
pragma solidity ^0.5.2;

import "openzeppelin-
solidity/contracts/token/ERC20/ERC20Detailed.sol";
import "openzeppelin-
solidity/contracts/token/ERC20/ERC20Capped.sol";
import "openzeppelin-solidity/contracts/ownership/Ownable.sol";
```

```
contract USD is ERC20Detailed, ERC20Capped, Ownable {

constructor()
ERC20Detailed("US Dollar", "USD", 2)
ERC20Capped(10000000000)
MinterRole()
payable public {}
}
```

The `Gold` token contract is similar to the `USD` token contract. The only difference is in the token name and symbol. I am calling my token `Gold`, and the symbol that I am using is `Au`. You can change the total number of tokens or decimal places if you want. This is how my `Gold` token contract looks:

```
//Gold.sol
pragma solidity ^0.5.2;

import "openzeppelin-
solidity/contracts/token/ERC20/ERC20Detailed.sol";
import "openzeppelin-
solidity/contracts/token/ERC20/ERC20Capped.sol";
import "openzeppelin-solidity/contracts/ownership/Ownable.sol";

contract Gold is ERC20Detailed, ERC20Capped, Ownable {

constructor()
ERC20Detailed("Gold", "Au", 2)
ERC20Capped(10000000000)
MinterRole()
payable public {}
}
```

Now that we have our two assets, let's compile them using the Truffle framework and the Solidity compiler.

Compiling the contracts

We will be using the Truffle framework and the Ganache blockchain for this project:

1. Begin by creating a quickstart blockchain using Ganache.
2. Copy and paste the `USD` and `Gold` contract files to the `contract` folder in your Truffle workspace.

3. Now, bring the Truffle console online. Navigate to the path containing your `truffle—config.js`.

4. Enter `truffle console` on the Terminal window in order to access the Truffle console.

5. Compile both the contracts by entering the `compile` command in the Truffle command line.

6. Provided there are no errors, your contracts should now be compiled and ready to migrate. Hold the compiled builds for now.

7. We'll be migrating and deploying these contracts, along with our orderbook smart contract.

This completes the creation and issuing of the trading assets on our blockchain. Next, we'll write our orderbook smart contract.

Orderbook smart contract

The orderbook smart contract is the core component of our entire project.

It carries out the following functions:

- Records incoming buy/sell offer requests from the frontend and moves the base or counter asset from the user's Ethereum account to the smart contract account.
- Allows traders to view the recorded buy/sell offers on the smart contract.
- Accepts trade requests against already recorded buy/sell offers and executes the trade. As part of the trade, the orderbook updates the available amount in an offer, and transfers the base or counter asset both from the trader's account and to the trader's account.
- Emits an event to indicate when a new buy or sell offer is updated, or a new trade is carried out. This event will be subscribed to by our frontend app to update and display the orderbook in real time.

Now, let's write our orderbook contract.

Writing the contract

Let's begin writing the orderbook smart contract with the functions that we discussed in the previous section:

1. Start by creating a smart contract file called `Orderbook.sol`.

2. We begin by defining first the Solidity compiler version:

   ```
   pragma solidity ^0.5.2;
   ```

3. Next, we import the `open-zeppelin` contract template (`ERC20.sol`):

   ```
   import "openzeppelin-solidity/contracts/token/ERC20/ERC20.sol";
   ```

   Importing the `ERC20` contract allows our smart contract to transfer the `Gold` and `USD` `ERC20` tokens to and from the trader's Ethereum accounts, using the `Transfer` method in the `ERC20` contract.

4. Next, we define the contract name as `Orderbook`:

   ```
   contract Orderbook {
   using SafeMath for uint;
   ```

   We also use the `using` keyword to declare that we'll be using the `SafeMath` library for all integer arithmetic calculations.

5. Start by declaring a data structure for the orders or the offers that will be managed by our orderbook. To do so we define the `Order` struct:

   ```
   struct Order
   {
    uint Amount;
    uint Price;
    uint TimeStamp;
    address Trader;
    bytes2 Status;
   }
   ```

   The `Order` struct has five members, namely `Amount`, `Price`, `TimeStamp`, `Trader`, and `Status`. `Amount` indicates the amount of gold in grams that is being bought or sold in the order.

   `Price` indicates the price in US dollars per gram of gold that the buyer is willing to pay, or that the seller is expecting as payment.

`TimeStamp` stores the time at which the order was placed in **Universal Time Coordinated (UTC)**.

`Trader` stores the Ethereum address of the trader who placed the order.

`Status` shows the current status of the order ('A'—Available, 'T'—Traded).

6. We define two struct arrays using our `Order` structs called Buys and Sells. As the name suggests, the `Buy[]` array will capture buys and `Sells[]` will capture sells:

```
Order[] Buys;
Order[] Sells;
ERC20 public ERC20Base;
ERC20 public ERC20Counter;
address owner;
```

We also define two contract instances using the `ERC20` contract. The `ERC20Base` instance will point to our `USD` token and the `ERC20Counter` instance will point to our `Gold` token.

7. Lastly, we define an address variable to capture the contract owner's address:

```
modifier onlyOwner {
  if (msg.sender!=owner) revert();
  _;
}
```

A modifier `onlyOwner` is also created. It checks if the contract invoker is the contract owner.

8. When the contract is first loaded, our constructor is fired. The constructor takes the address of the `Base` and `Counter` tokens as input parameters. For our project, these will be the `USD` token address and the `Gold` token address, respectively. We also set the owner address variable to the address that deploys the contract (`msg.sender`):

```
constructor (address Base,address Counter) public
{
ERC20Base = ER20(Base);
ERC20Counter = ERC20(Counter);
owner = msg.sender;
}
```

9. There are three types of events that will be emitted by our contract. The events are namely BuyAdded, SellAdded, and TradeAdd:

```
event BuyAdded(
 uint indexed Order_No,
 uint Amt,
 uint Price,
 address trader
 );

event SellAdded(
 uint indexed Order_No,
 uint Amt,
 uint Price,
 address trader
 );

event TradeAdd(
 uint indexed Order_No,
 uint Amt,
 uint Price,
 address maker,
 address taker
 );
```

All three emit the order and trade details, including the OrderNo, Amount, Price, and the address of the trader who placed the order. In the case of TradeAdd, the maker is the trader who placed the order that is being traded, and the taker is the trader who matches against the order.

10. Now, we come to the interesting part. The addBuy method accepts an order from the user, and adds it to the buys[] array that we declared earlier:

```
function addBuy(uint Amt, uint BuyPrice) public returns (uint)
{
 ERC20Base.transferFrom(msg.sender,
address(this),Amt.mul(BuyPrice));
 Buys.push(Order(Amt,BuyPrice,now,msg.sender,'A'));
 emit BuyAdded(Buys.length,Amt,BuyPrice,msg.sender);
 return Buys.length;
}
```

- The `addBuy` function takes the order amount (`Amt`) and price (`BuyPrice`) as input parameters.
- On invoking the `addBuy` method, it first transfers the equivalent USD tokens for the order from the trader's Ethereum address to the smart contract's address. So, let's say if you wanted to buy 10 grams of gold for $50 per gram, `addBuy` would transfer -> *10 grams * $50 = $500* from your Ethereum account to the smart contract's address.
- The smart contract's address here is represented by `address(this)`.
- `addBuy` invokes the `transferFrom` method in the Base asset `ERC20` interface to transfer the USD tokens from the trader's account to the smart contract address. This method will only work successfully if the trader has approved the contract to move funds from its address.
- After a successful transfer, it pushes a new buy order with the details to the buys array (`Buys[]`). Lastly, it emits the `BuyAdded` event, and returns the new length of the Buys array to the contract invoker.

11. The `addSell` method also works similar to the `addBuy` method:

```
function addSell(uint Amt, uint SellPrice) public returns (uint)
{
  ERC20Counter.transferFrom(msg.sender, address(this),Amt);
  Sells.push(Order(Amt,SellPrice,now,msg.sender,'A'));
  emit SellAdded(Sells.length,Amt,SellPrice,msg.sender);
  return Sells.length;
}
```

- It takes the order amount (`Amt`) and price (`SellPrice`) as input parameters. It uses the `ERC20Counter` contract instance that points to the `Gold` token to transfer gold tokens from the trader's address to the contract address.
- After the successful transfer, a new sell order is added to the orderbook sell array (`Sells[]`).
- Lastly, it emits the `SellAdded` event with the order details. It then returns the new length of the `Sells` array to the contract invoker.

12. The `viewLengthBuy()` and `viewLengthSell()` methods return the current length of the `Buys` and `Sells` arrays, respectively, to the contract invoker:

```
function viewLengthBuy() public view returns (uint)
{
  return Buys.length;
}
```

```
function viewLengthSell() public view returns (uint)
{
 return Sells.length;
}
```

13. The `viewBuy` method returns an already recorded buy order to the contract invoker:

```
function viewBuy(uint OrderNo) public view returns (uint,uint,uint,
address)
{
 return (
 Buys[OrderNo-1].Amount,
 Buys[OrderNo-1].Price,
 Buys[OrderNo-1].TimeStamp,
 Buys[OrderNo-1].Trader
 );
}
```

It takes `OrderNo` as an input parameter. It returns the order `Amount`, `Price`, `Timestamp`, and the address of the `Trader`.

14. The `viewSell` method is similar to the `viewBuy` method:

```
function viewSell(uint OrderNo) public view returns
(uint,uint,uint,address)
{
 return (
 Sells[OrderNo-1].Amount,
 Sells[OrderNo-1].Price,
 Sells[OrderNo-1].TimeStamp,
 Sells[OrderNo-1].Trader
 );
}
```

It takes `OrderNo` as an input parameter and returns the sell order details.

15. Next, we come to the trade function. This method is invoked whenever you need to trade against an existing order:

```
function trade(uint OrderNo, uint Amt, uint TradePrice, uint
trade_type) public returns ( uint, uint , address)
{
 // 1 is Buy trade , 2 is Sell Trade
```

Let's look at this method in detail:

- The trade function takes `OrderNo` to be traded against, and trading amount (`Amount`), trading price (`TradePrice`), and `trade_type` as input parameters. `trade_type` can have a value of 1 for buy trades, and 2 for sell trades.
- When an order is sent to the `trade` method, it checks whether the order consumes the matching order fully or partially. It also checks if the incoming request is for a buy order or a sell order. Accordingly, it handles the trading request.

16. Thus, if the incoming request is for a `Buy` trade and the trade amount is equal to the order amount, the snippet of code does the following:

```
if (trade_type == 1 && Sells[OrderNo-1].Amount == Amt)
{
require(TradePrice >= Sells[OrderNo-1].Price, "Invalid Price");
ERC20Base.transferFrom(msg.sender,
Sells[OrderNo-1].Trader,Amt.mul(Sells[OrderNo-1].Price));
Sells[OrderNo-1].Amount = 0;
Sells[OrderNo-1].Status = 'T';
ERC20Counter.transfer(msg.sender, Amt);
emit TradeAdd(OrderNo, Amt,
Sells[OrderNo-1].Price,Sells[OrderNo-1].Trader,msg.sender);
return (
OrderNo,
Amt,
msg.sender
); }
```

17. The method starts by first checking that the trading price (buy price) is greater than or equal to the sell order that it is matching against. This is enforced using a `require` statement, and in the case of a mismatch, a `revert()` statement is thrown with the message `"Invalid Price"`:

```
require(TradePrice >= Sells[OrderNo-1].Price, "Invalid Price");
```

18. Next, it uses the `ERC20Base` contract instance to transfer the equivalent US dollars from the taker's Ethereum address to the maker's Ethereum address. The taker here is the trader who submits the trading offer to the `trade` method. The maker is the trader who had placed the order that the method is matching against. The `trade` method assumes that the traders have already approved the smart contract address to move USD tokens from their Ethereum address:

```
ERC20Base.transferFrom(msg.sender,
Sells[OrderNo-1].Trader,Amt.mul(Sells[OrderNo-1].Price));
```

19. Next, the `trade` method updates the Sell order. The amount is set to 0, and the status to `'T'` for traded:

```
Sells[OrderNo-1].Amount = 0;
Sells[OrderNo-1].Status = 'T';
```

20. After updating the matching order, the counter asset, which is gold in our case, is transferred to the trader who invoked the `trade` method. This completes the exchange of the gold and US dollar assets between the two buyers:

```
ERC20Counter.transfer(msg.sender, Amt);
emit TradeAdd(OrderNo, Amt,
Sells[OrderNo-1].Price,Sells[OrderNo-1].Trader,msg.sender);
```

Lastly, an event is emitted with the trade details.

21. Finally, the method returns the order number that is traded against (`OrderNo`), the trading amount (`Amt`), and the trader's address to the contract invoker:

```
return (
OrderNo,
Amt,
msg.sender
);
```

22. The alternative buy case when the trading amount is less than the order amount is similar to this case. The difference is that the status of the order of the trade is still kept as `A` for available, and the order amount is updated to show the amount available in the order after a successful trade:

```
else if (trade_type == 1 && Sells[OrderNo-1].Amount > Amt)
{
ERC20Base.transferFrom(msg.sender,
Sells[OrderNo-1].Trader,Amt.mul(Sells[OrderNo-1].Price));
require(TradePrice >= Sells[OrderNo-1].Price, "Invalid Price");
Sells[OrderNo-1].Amount = Sells[OrderNo-1].Amount - Amt;
Sells[OrderNo-1].Status = 'A';
ERC20Counter.transfer(msg.sender, Amt);
emit TradeAdd(OrderNo, Amt,
Sells[OrderNo-1].Price,Sells[OrderNo-1].Trader,msg.sender);
return (
OrderNo,
Amt,
msg.sender
);
}
```

Both the sell cases are similar to buy. The only difference is that the `trade_type` input parameter should be set to 2, and the trading price in the sell case should be less than or equal to the buy order that it is matching against. Putting it all together, this how the trading method looks.

23. In the case where none of the conditions are met, a revert statement is thrown by the `trade` method with the message, `"Invalid trade parameters"`.

24. One last method that we are left with in our orderbook contract is the decommission method. The `decommission` method is invoked by the contract owner to decommission the orderbook. It returns the assets held against the orders that are waiting in the orderbook to the traders:

```
function decommission() public onlyOwner
{
 uint i = 0;
 while ( i <= Buys.length || i <= Sells.length)
 {
 if( i <= Buys.length)
 {
 uint Amt = Buys[i].Amount;
 Amt = Amt.mul(Buys[i].Price);
 ERC20Base.transfer(Buys[i].Trader,Amt);
 delete Buys[i];
 }

 if( i <= Sells.length)
 {
 ERC20Counter.transfer(Sells[i].Trader,Sells[i].Amount);
 delete Sells[i];
 }
 i++;
 }
```

This method uses the `onlyOwner` modifier to ensure that only the contract owner can invoke it. It iterates against the `buys[]` and `sells[]` arrays, and transfers the equivalent base or counter amount back to the trader who placed the order. After a successful transfer, it deletes the buy or sell request from the orderbook.

Great, so that was our `Orderbook` smart contract. Let's compile and deploy this contract, along with the contracts that we compiled previously.

Migrating all the contracts to the blockchain

Now that we have written the contract, we need to migrate the contracts to our blockchain where we can execute them:

1. Copy and paste the orderbook smart contract file to the `contracts` folder in your Truffle workspace.

2. Navigate to the Truffle console Terminal that you had opened earlier for compiling the USD and Gold token contracts. If you closed the console, you can bring it online again by entering `truffle console` in your Truffle workspace:

3. Compile all the contracts by entering the `compile` command in the Truffle command line.

4. Provided there are no errors, your contracts should now be compiled and ready to migrate.

5. Now, create a migration file for the orderbook contract. Enter the following command in the Truffle console:

```
create migration orderbook
```

6. Navigate to the migration folder in your Truffle workspace. A new migration file should have been created for your `Orderbook` contract.

7. Open the file and replace the contents of the file with the following code:

```
const Orderbook = artifacts.require("Orderbook");
const Gold = artifacts.require("Gold");
const USD = artifacts.require("USD");

module.exports = function(deployer) {

  deployer.deploy(USD).then(function(){
  return deployer.deploy(Gold);}).then(function(){
  return deployer.deploy(Orderbook,USD.address,Gold.address);})
};
```

Let's understand the migration script:

- The preceding migration script deploys three contracts back to back. It first deploys the USD token contract, followed by the gold token contract.
- It uses the blockchain addresses of the USD and Gold tokens as input parameters to the constructor for the orderbook contract.

8. This is required because our Orderbook contract constructor takes the address of the Gold and the USD contract as input and uses it to instantiate the Gold and USD contract:

```
//orderbook smart contract constructor.

constructor (address Base,address Counter) public
{
ERC20Base = ERC20(Base);
ERC20Counter = ERC20(Counter);
owner = msg.sender;
}
```

9. Now, navigate back to the Truffle console and enter `migrate` in order to migrate all the contract to the blockchain.

10. Make sure you note down the contract address for the USD token, the Gold token, and the Orderbook contract, because we'll require these again soon enough:

11. Copy the contract address for all the contracts:

```
ishan@ishan-Inspiron-3537: ~/walletcontract/walletcontract
File  Edit  View  Search  Terminal  Help
> gas price:           20 gwei
> value sent:          0 ETH
> total cost:          0.03562326 ETH


Replacing 'Gold'
----------------
> transaction hash:    0xda6582ecc52730e6d8bd1e275942d1b11d287b768a42d4b2e00779814f3ae85d
> Blocks: 0            Seconds: 0
> contract address:    0x662D0a4B006914016A2Cb5CD351DD170E81af252
> block number:        8
> block timestamp:     1567735454
> account:             0x60f569790e9b87f93aB6bF9bBb3118f6E1C1598b
> balance:             99.84364518
> gas used:            1780779
> gas price:           20 gwei
> value sent:          0 ETH
> total cost:          0.03561558 ETH


Replacing 'Orderbook'
---------------------
> transaction hash:    0x996548860b02f342c655ab603f4d053dbc7773b12c052adf5e8782c234c35b2c
> Blocks: 0            Seconds: 0
> contract address:    0x26518b6a8E4f8B20413C1Cf70DC05B58Cb5171A0
> block number:        9
> block timestamp:     1567735455
> account:             0x60f569790e9b87f93aB6bF9bBb3118f6E1C1598b
> balance:             99.79096218
> gas used:            2634150
> gas price:           20 gwei
> value sent:          0 ETH
> total cost:          0.052683 ETH


> Saving migration to chain.
> Saving artifacts
-------------------------------------
```

That brings us to the end of our smart contracts. Now, let's build the browser app that the user will interact with.

Building the exchange app

The exchange app that we're going to build needs to perform the following functions:

1. Keep a track of the Gold and USD token balance for the user.
2. Allow the user to view orders on the orderbook contract.

3. Update the orderbook in real time by listening to any buy/sell/trade events that are triggered by the orderbook smart contract.

4. Allow the user to submit buy and sell requests.

5. Match the buy/sell requests against existing orders in the orderbook if matching orders are available.

6. If no matching orders are available, submit a new buy/sell order to the orderbook.

Alright, now let's start building our app. This section assumes basic-to-intermediate knowledge of React.js from the user. The entire React interface can be downloaded from the GitHub repository as follows:

```
https://github.com/PacktPublishing/Blockchain-Development-for-Finance-Projects/
tree/master/Chapter%209/React
```

Building the app

Our exchange app will constitute the following:

- The main `App.js` file
- The following react components:
  - `Container.js`
  - `AddressBar.js`
  - `Orderbook.js`
  - `TradePanel.js`
- The following contract interfaces:
  - `Gold.js`
  - `USD.js`
  - `OrderbookABI.js`

Here is a brief description of the components:

- **App.js**: The main `App.js` file that implements the methods that interact with our smart contract and sets the initial state. It invokes `Container.js` for rendering the child components and forwards the current state to `Container.js`.

- **React components**: These components render our exchange app:
    - `Container.js`: It receives the current state from the `App.js` file, and passes it to the child components.
    - `AddressBar.js`: It implements an address bar which shows the user's Ethereum account and current Gold and USD balance.
    - `OrderBook.js`: This component renders the current orderbook in the app. It maps the `buys[]` and `sells[]` state arrays, which contain the current buy and sell requests and displays it to the user. The `buy[]` and `sell[]` arrays are populated with orders from our orderbook smart contract.
    - `TradePanel.js`: It renders a `Buy` and `Sell` panel that permits the user to enter the `Amount` and `Price` and submit a `Buy` or `Sell` request to the app.
- **Contract interfaces**: These are used to instantiate our gold, USD, and orderbook contracts within the app. They contain the contract **Application Binary Interface (ABI)** and contract address. As the name suggests, `Gold.js` and `USD.js` are for the Gold and USD contracts. `OrderbookABI.js` is for the orderbook smart contract.

Creating the React project environment

Before we can start building our app, we need to set up the `project` directory and install the dependencies:

1. Create a new React app called Exchange using `npx`:

   ```
   npx create-react-app Exchange
   ```

2. Update your `package.json` to the following values:

   ```
   {
   "name": "Exchange",
   "version": "1.0.0",
   "dependencies": {
   "bulma-start": "0.0.2",
   "react": "^16.4.2",
   "react-dom": "^16.4.2",
   "react-scripts": "1.1.4",
    "web3": "^1.2"
   },
   "scripts": {
   ```

```
"start": "react-scripts start",
"build": "react-scripts build",
"test": "react-scripts test --env=jsdom",
"eject": "react-scripts eject"
}
}
```

3. Run `npm install` on the Terminal window in order to install the dependencies.

Next, within the `src` folder, create a `Components` folder for the app components. Also, create a `contracts` folder within `src`. We'll be using this to map the contracts that are being used by the app.

Setting up the contract interfaces

We need to set up interfaces that our app will use in order to interact with the smart contracts that will be deployed to our blockchain:

1. Within the `contracts` folder, create the `Gold.js`, `USD.js`, and `OrderbookABI.js` files.
2. Open the `Gold.js` file in a text editor.
3. With the file open, navigate to your Truffle project environment that you used to deploy the smart contracts.
4. In the Truffle environment, locate the `build` directory. Under `build`, you'll have the `Gold.json` build file.
5. Open the file, and locate the ABI contract . It should look like the code that follows.
6. Copy this entire ABI, and paste it in `OrderbookABI.js` as a parameter, as follows:

```
export default {

abi: [
    {
      "constant": true,
      "inputs": [],
      "name": "name",
      "outputs": [
        {
          "name": "",
          "type": "string"
        }
      ],
```

```
        "payable": false,
        "stateMutability": "view",
        "type": "function"
    },
],..............]}
```

7. Similarly, copy and paste the contract address that we got for the Gold token contract during deployment. Add this as a parameter to the interface as well:

```
export default {

address: "0x662D0a4B006914016A2Cb5CD351DD170E81af252",

abi: [..............]}
```

8. Save the file. We'll load this object to interact with the Gold contract that is deployed to the blockchain.
9. Repeat these steps for the OrderbookABI.js file and the USD.js file as well.

Now, we have our contract interfaces. Let's take a look at the important methods in our App.js file.

Writing the App.js file

Let's go through the sections of our App.js file one by one:

1. We start by importing the requisite dependencies, components, and contract interfaces:

```
import React, { Component } from 'react';
import Web3 from 'web3'
import Nav from './Components/Nav';
import Description from './Components/Description';
import Container from './Components/Container';
import OrderbookABI from './Contracts/OrderbookABI';
import Gold from './Contracts/Gold';
import USD from './Contracts/USD';
```

2. Within our constructor section, we initialize the state of the app:

```
constructor(){
 super();
 this.appName = 'Exchange';
 this.watchweb3 = new Web3(new
Web3.providers.WebsocketProvider('ws://localhost:8545'))
```

```
this.OrderbookABI = OrderbookABI;
this.Gold = Gold;
this.USD = USD;
this.onInputChangeUpdateField =
this.onInputChangeUpdateField.bind(this);
this.setBalance = this.setBalance.bind(this);
this.state = {


network: 'Checking...',
account: null,
buys: [],
sells: [],
AuBalance: 0,
USDBalance: 0,
lastBlock: 0,
fields: {
buyprice: null,
buyamount: null,
sellprice: null,
sellamount: null
}
};
```

Notice the `watchweb3` parameter. We initialize a `web3` provider that connects to our blockchain through a web socket (`ws://localhost:8545`). This is required in order to watch the events as they happen on our blockchain. We'll be initializing a separate `web3` object by accessing Metamask's injected `web3`. This separate `web3` object will give us access to the user's MetaMask account for submitting transactions to the contracts.

Also, observe how the contracts are instantiated into the app state.

3. Next, let's take a look at the `componentDidMount` section. This section carries out two important tasks.

Firstly, it requests access to MetaMask's injected `web3` object. On submitting this request, the user should see a pop-up notification, asking if he wants to grant access to the app to access his MetaMask wallet. On granting permission, MetaMask returns an array of accounts, where the primary account is at the zeroth position of the array.

This account is captured by our `componentDidMount` section, and is then updated to the state. It is also set as the default `web3` account:

```
componentDidMount(){

  var account;

  if (window.Ethereum) {
  const Ethereum = window.Ethereum;

  this.web3 = new Web3(Ethereum);

  Ethereum.enable().then((accounts) => {

  account = accounts[0];
  this.web3.eth.defaultAccount = account ;

  let app = this;

  this.setState({
  account
  });

  this.setNetwork();
  this.setBalance();
  this.setOrderbook();
  this.watchOrderbook();
  })
  }
}
```

The second task that is carried out by this section is setting the user balances and the orderbook when the app loads. It does so by calling the `setBalance` and `setOrderbook` methods.

4. The `watchOrderbook` method is called next. It initializes a listener that tracks our orderbook smart contracts for any events.
5. Lastly, this app renders the container component and forwards the current state to the container component. It also renders the title bar and description using `Nav.js` and `Description.js`:

```
render() {

  return (
  <div>
  <Nav appName={this.appName} network={this.state.network} />
```

```
<Description />
<Container
onInputChangeUpdateField={this.onInputChangeUpdateField}
account={this.state.account}
buys={this.state.buys}
sells={this.state.sells}
setBalance={this.setBalance}
AuBalance={this.state.AuBalance}
USDBalance={this.state.USDBalance}
Buy={this.Buy}
Sell={this.Sell}
fields={this.state.fields}/>
</div>
)
}
```

Now, we are good to look at the methods that make our app tick.

Let's start by looking at the setOrderbook method.

Displaying the orderbook

The setOrderbook method, as the name suggests, pulls and relays the information that is required to display the orderbook to the user. It does so by invoking the viewBuy() and viewSell() methods on our orderbook smart contract, and populating the buys[] and sells[] arrays in the app state:

1. We start writing the method by initializing a new contract instance that points to our Orderbook smart contract:

    ```
    setOrderbook = () =>
     {
     let app = this;
     var lastBuy;
     var lastSell;
     var contract = new
    this.watchweb3.eth.Contract(this.OrderbookABI.abi,this.OrderbookABI
    .address);
    ```

2. We will first populate the buy orders in the buys[] array, and then the sell orders in the sells[] array.

3. We first call our smart contract `viewLengthBuy` method to find the total number of buy orders on our decentralized orderbook in the orderbook smart contract:

```
contract.methods.viewLengthBuy().call().then(function(response){
  if(response) {
  lastBuy = response;
```

4. If there are buy orders in the orderbook smart contract, then we proceed to populate these buy orders to our app's `buys[]` array:

```
if (lastBuy >= 1)
  {
  app.setState({
  buys: [],
  })

  for (let i = 1; i <= lastBuy ; i++)
  {
```

5. We do so by iterating between all the order numbers, from 1 until `lastBuy`.

6. For each `OrderNo`, we call the `viewBuy` contract method. The input parameter is the order number (`i`), and the output parameters are order amount (`Amount`), order price (`Price`), and the timestamp when the order was placed:

```
contract.methods.viewBuy(i).call().then(function(response){
  if(response) {

  let OrderNo = i;
  let Amount = Number(response[0]);
  let Price = Number(response[1]);
  let TimeStamp = Number(response[2]);
```

7. The response from `viewBuy` is captured in our local variables. If the order is still active, meaning it has trading units available, only then it is pushed to the orderbook:

```
if ( Amount > 0)
  {
  let buys = app.state.buys;
  buys.push({
  OrderNo,
  Amount,
  Price,
  TimeStamp
  });

  app.setState({
```

```
buys
})
```

8. The `buys[]` array is updated with the new buy order, and the app state is set after each iteration.

9. When we reach the end of the buy records on the orderbook, we sort the buy orders by price and timestamp:

```
if (i == lastBuy)
{
let buys = app.state.buys
buys.sort(function (a, b) {
if(a.Price == b.Price)
{
return (a.TimeStamp < b.TimeStamp) ? 1 : (a.TimeStamp <
b.TimeStamp) ? -1 : 0;
}
else
{
return (a.Price < b.Price) ? 1 : -1;
}
});
app.setState({
buys
})
}
```

The higher the buy price, the greater the preference it gets in the orderbook. Thus, it is closer to the top of the orderbook. Buy orders are sorted in descending order, and then displayed to the user. If two buy orders have the same price, the buy order with the older timestamp gets preference.

After the sorting operation has been carried out, the buys array is again updated to the app state. This brings us to the end of the orderbook buy side. The orderbook sell side flows in a similar way to the buy side:

```
contract.methods.viewLengthSell().call().then(function(response){
if(response) {
lastSell = response;

if (lastSell >= 1)
{
app.setState({
sells: [],
})

for (let i = 1; i <= lastSell ; i++)
```

```
{

contract.methods.viewSell(i).call().then(function(response){
if(response) {

let OrderNo = i;
let Amount = Number(response[0]);
let Price = Number(response[1]);
let TimeStamp = Number(response[2]);

if ( Amount > 0)
{

let sells = app.state.sells;
sells.push({
OrderNo,
Amount,
Price,
TimeStamp
});

app.setState({
sells
})

if (i == lastSell)
 {
 let sells = app.state.sells
 sells.sort(function (a, b) {
 if(a.Price == b.Price)
 {
 return (a.TimeStamp < b.TimeStamp) ? -1 : (a.TimeStamp < b.TimeStamp) ? 1
: 0;
 }
 else
 {
 return (a.Price < b.Price) ? -1 : 1;
 }
 });
 app.setState({
 sells
 })
}
```

The only difference is that the sell side of the orderbook sorts orders in descending order, instead of ascending, so that the lowest sell price is at the top of the orderbook. This brings us to the end of the `setOrderbook` method. Next, let's set our listener for orderbook events.

Watching orderbook events

Next let's write a method which will track events as they happen on the orderbook:

1. The `watchOrderbook` method tracks the orderbook smart contract for any event. When a new event is received, that is, a new offer is submitted to the orderbook, it refreshes the orderbook to add the new event:

```
watchOrderbook() {
  let app = this;

var contractOB = new
app.watchweb3.eth.Contract(this.OrderbookABI.abi,this.OrderbookABI.
address);
```

We start by instantiating our orderbook contract through the `watchweb3` web3 object.

2. Next, we get the latest block number from the blockchain. `watchOrderbook` starts watching for events after the orderbook is initialized and set for the first time. Thus, it starts watching from the block, after which the app is initialized:

```
app.watchweb3.eth.getBlockNumber(function(error,response){
  if(response)
  {
  let lastBlock = response;
```

3. Next, we use the `web3` object to track all the events on our orderbook contract instance:

```
contractOB.events.allEvents({
  fromBlock: lastBlock+1 },
function(error, event){
  console.log("Event",event);
  app.setOrderbook();
  }).on('error', console.error);
```

We track all events from the orderbook contract after the block where the listener is first initialized. Any time there is a new event, the listener logs a new event to the console and calls the `setOrderbook` method in order to set the orderbook again.

Initiating a buy order

The next method(s) will accept a buy request from the user. It will first check in the orderbook to see if there is a matching order. If it is unable to find a matching order, it adds the order to the orderbook. The `Buy()` method handles the buy request and the `Sell()` method handles the sell request.

Let's look at the `Buy()` method:

```
Buy = () => {
let app = this;
  let amount = this.state.fields.buyamount;
  let price = this.state.fields.buyprice;
  var contractUSD = new this.web3.eth.Contract(app.USD.abi,app.USD.address);
  var contractOB = new
this.web3.eth.Contract(app.OrderbookABI.abi,app.OrderbookABI.address);
  var sells = app.state.sells;
```

1. We start by initializing and capturing the amount and the price of the order that is submitted by the user. Next, we instantiate the USD token contract and the orderbook contract by using the parameters in `OrderbookABI.js` and `USD.js`.

2. Next, we check if the `sells` array is empty, which means there are no sell orders. If the sells array is empty, we skip the next steps. We do not need to look for matching orders in the orderbook, as the sell side of the orderbook is empty. We can simply submit our buy order to the orderbook:

```
if(sells.length == 0 )
  {

contractUSD.methods.approve(app.OrderbookABI.address,amount*price*1
00)
    .send({from:
app.web3.eth.defaultAccount}).then(function(response){

  if(response) {
```

If the sell side is empty, we first use the USD contract interface's `approve` method. The `approve` method will approve the orderbook contract to move USD tokens that are worth the same as the order amount from the user's account.

The approval amount is *amount*price*100*. This is because the amount entered by the user is the amount of gold to buy, and the price is per unit of gold. So, we need to multiply them both to get the amount of USD tokens that a buyer needs to submit for the order. This amount is multiplied by 100, because Ethereum and the ERC20 contract standard consider the smallest unit during token operations.

Since the USD token has two decimal places, we need to multiply by $10^2 = 100$ to get the actual value that we want to approve. The same will apply for the Gold token.

3. Following a successful response to our `approve` method, we call the orderbook contract to add a new buy method:

```
if(response) {
contractOB.methods.addBuy(amount,price)
.send({from:
app.web3.eth.defaultAccount}).then(function(response){
console.log(response);
app.setBalance();
app.resetApp();
})
}
})
}
```

Let's understand the preceding code:

- We invoke the `addBuy` method and send the amount and the price as parameters. Following a successful response, we call the `setBalance` method in order to reflect the updated balance to the user on the screen and `resetApp` to clear the fields.
- Remember our `watchOrderbook` method? On successful response, `watchOrderbook` will register an event from the contract. It will thus call the `setOrderbook` method to refresh the `buys[]` array and display the new orderbook including the new buy to the user.

4. Our `else` block is fired. The first thing that it checks is whether our price is less than the first sell price in the orderbook. If our buy order price is less, it'll simply add our buy order to the orderbook, because no matching orders will exist against our order:

```
else
{
var i = 0;
let OrderPrice = sells[i].Price;

if (OrderPrice > price)
{
contractUSD.methods.approve(app.OrderbookABI.address,amount*price*1
00)
        .send({from:
```

```
app.web3.eth.defaultAccount}).then(function(response){
        if(response) {
        contractOB.methods.addBuy(amount,price)
        .send({from:
app.web3.eth.defaultAccount}).then(function(response){
            console.log(response);
            app.setBalance();
            app.resetApp();
        })
        }
    })
    }
```

Let's understand the preceding code:

- It will approve the order amount for the orderbook contract address using the USD token contract interface, and then call the orderbook contract to add a buy trade.
- If the `sells` array in the orderbook is not empty, then the `Buy` method needs to check for matching sells request for our buy order.

5. Thus, the `else` block is fired:

```
else
{
contractUSD.methods.approve(app.OrderbookABI.address,
amount*price*100)
.send({from:
app.web3.eth.defaultAccount}).then(function(response){
```

The first thing that the `else` block does is approve our orderbook smart contract to transfer USD tokens that are equivalent in size to our buy order. If our price is not less than the first order in the orderbook, this indicates that there are matching orders available for our order in the orderbook.

6. Following a successful response from the `approve` method, it iterates a loop for the sell side of our orderbook, until our counter is equal to the total length of the `sells` array:

```
contractUSD.methods.approve(app.OrderbookABI.address,
 amount*price*100)
 .send({from:
app.web3.eth.defaultAccount}).then(function(response){
 if(response) {
 while ( i < sells.length )
 {
```

7. Each iteration does two things. First, it checks whether the matching order in the orderbook can be consumed fully by our order, or whether some amount will be left after our buy order matches. Next, it checks whether our buy order still matches the next order in the loop. If it matches, the loop continues, otherwise the loop is stopped by setting our counter equal to `sells.length` so that the `while` loop exits:

```
while ( i < sells.length )
  {
  var counter = i;
  OrderPrice = sells[i].Price;
  var OrderAmount = sells[i].Amount;

  if (amount >= OrderAmount)
  {
  contractOB.methods.trade(sells[counter].OrderNo,OrderAmount
  ,OrderPrice, 1)
  .send({from:
  app.web3.eth.defaultAccount}).then(function(response){
  console.log(response);
  app.setBalance();
  app.resetApp();
  })
  amount = amount - OrderAmount;

  }
```

If the amount of gold assets to be bought in our buy order is more than the amount available in the matching order in the orderbook, it means that our order will fully consume the matching order. Thus, we call the `trade` method in the orderbook smart contracts, and accordingly send the trading parameters. The orderbook price and the orderbook amount are sent, since we want to give the best possible price to the trader, and the total amount that is available in the order. The input parameter 1 represents a buy trade to the orderbook smart contract.

Following a successful `trade`, the response is printed, and the balances and the app are reset. The `watchOrderbook` method registers an event and resets the orderbook.

8. Lastly, we update the buy order amount by removing the matching order amount.

If the required amount in our buy order is less than or equal to the available amount in the matching sell order, then our order's requirement is fully met and we can stop iterating the orderbook:

```
else
 {
contractOB.methods.trade(sells[counter].OrderNo,amount
 ,OrderPrice, 1)
 .send({from:
app.web3.eth.defaultAccount}).then(function(response){
 console.log(response);
 app.setBalance();
 app.resetApp();
 })

 amount = 0;
 }

 i++;
```

Thus, if our order's amount is less than the amount available in the matching sell order, the `else` clause is fired. It calls the `Orderbook` contract `trade` method. The input parameters sent here contain the amount as the trading amount, since our complete buy order will be met by this order. Following a successful response, we print a console log, set the balances, and reset the app. Again, the `watchOrder` listener tracks a new event and resets the orderbook. The `amount` parameter is set to zero, in order to indicate that our buy order is fully traded and no amount is left.

At the end of the matching, the loop counter is incremented by one.

9. Before the next iteration of the loop, we first check whether there is still an amount available in the loop, which can be traded if our order's price is still greater than the next buy order. If our order's price is less than the next sell price in the orderbook, it means that no more matching orders exist. So, we simply add our order to the buy side of the orderbook with the rest of the amount, and we end the loop. We also end the loop if the amount that is available to be traded in our `amount` parameter is zero:

```
if ( i < sells.length )
 {
OrderPrice = sells[i].Price;
 if (OrderPrice > price && amount > 0 )
 {
```

```
contractOB.methods.addBuy(amount,price)
 .send({from:
app.web3.eth.defaultAccount}).then(function(response){
 console.log(response);
 app.setBalance();
 app.resetApp();
 })
 }

 if (amount == 0 || OrderPrice > price)
 {
 i = sells.length ;
 }
 }
 }
if (amount > 0)
    {
        contractOB.methods.addBuy(amount,price)
        .send({from:
app.web3.eth.defaultAccount}).then(function(response){
        console.log(response);
        app.setBalance();
        app.resetApp();
    })
 }
```

To end the loop, we simply set our counter to the last value in the orderbook sell side, so that the loop terminates. That brings us to the end of the Buy() method.

Initiating a sell order

Sell requests that are submitted by the user are processed by the Sell() method. The Sell() method works similarly to the Buy() method that we discussed earlier. The only difference is that in the case of processing and executing a sell request, we check if the current sell price is less than, or equal to, the buy orders in the buys[] array. If this criterion is met, only then are there matching orders available.

The input parameter in the trade method for sell is 2. Thus, anytime the trade method is called for a sell trade, we need to send the trade_type input parameter as 2 to the orderbook smart contract:

```
contractOB.methods.trade(buys[counter].OrderNo,OrderAmount
 ,OrderPrice, 2)
 .send({from: app.web3.eth.defaultAccount}).then(function(response){
```

As with the buy side, every time an order is added or a successful buy trade is carried out, the watchOrderbook listener captures the event and sets the orderbook.

Setting the user asset balances

Next, Let's look at the method we'll use to update the user's Gold and USD balance after successful trades in the orderbook:

1. The setBalance method checks the Gold and USD tokens for the current asset balance for the user, and updates them to the frontend. We instantiate the USD token contract, and call the balanceOf method to get the user's USD token balance. Following a successful response, this balance is updated to the state in the USDBalance parameters, and is displayed in the address bar component:

    ```
    setBalance = () => {

     let app = this;

      var contractUSD = new
     this.web3.eth.Contract(app.USD.abi,app.USD.address);
     contractUSD.methods.balanceOf(app.web3.eth.defaultAccount).call().t
     hen(function(response){

      if(response)
      {
      let USDBalance = response;
      app.setState({
      USDBalance
      })
      }
      })
    ```

2. Next, let's look at how we fetch the balance for the Gold asset:

    ```
    var contractGold = new
    this.web3.eth.Contract(app.Gold.abi,app.Gold.address);

    contractGold.methods.balanceOf(app.web3.eth.defaultAccount).call().
    then(function(response){

     if(response)
     {
     let AuBalance = response;
     app.setState({
     AuBalance
     })
    ```

Similarly, the gold token contract is instantiated, and fetches the user balance for the gold token. Following a successful response, this balance is captured to the app state as `AuBalance`, and is displayed in the address bar component. That brings us to the end of building our exchange app. Now, let's run our app, and see how it looks and works.

Running the exchange app

Alright, so now that our exchange is complete, let's try running the app and see how it works:

1. Make sure that your Ganache blockchain and Truffle console are online. If not, bring your Ganache blockchain online, and connect your Truffle console to the blockchain.
2. Navigate to your Truffle project workspace, and enter `truffle console` in the Terminal in order to bring the console online.
3. Enter the `migrate` command in order to migrate all your contracts to the Ganache test blockchain:

   ```
   truffle(development)> migrate
   ```

4. Once the contracts are deployed, note the contract address and keep them safe.
5. Make sure that the contract address for the Gold, USD, and orderbook contracts are mapped correctly to the `Gold.js`, `USD.js`, and `OrderbookABI.js` contract interfaces in the exchange app code.
6. Next, set up MetaMask to work with our project.
7. Navigate to the main Ganache blockchain page. Click on the key icon next to the first account:

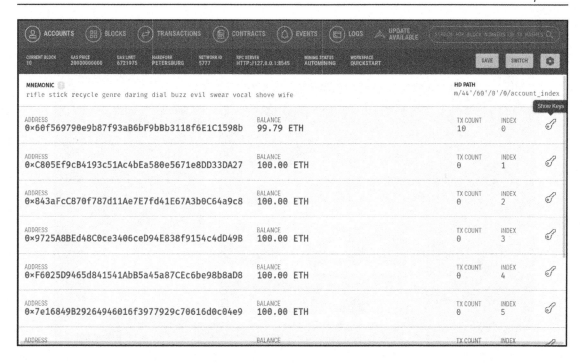

8. Copy the private key for the first account from the pop up that appears:

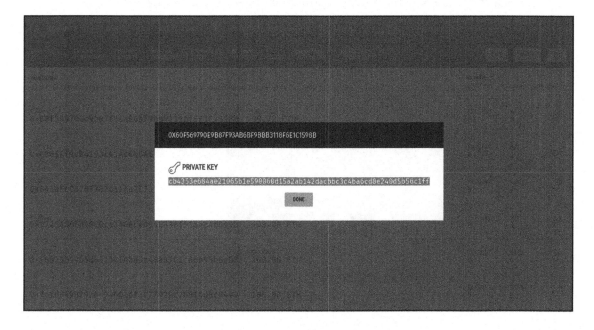

9. Now log into your **MetaMask** wallet. Click on the pie icon on the right-top side:

10. From the menu that appears, select **Import** account.
11. Select **Private Key** from the dropdown in the screen that appears:

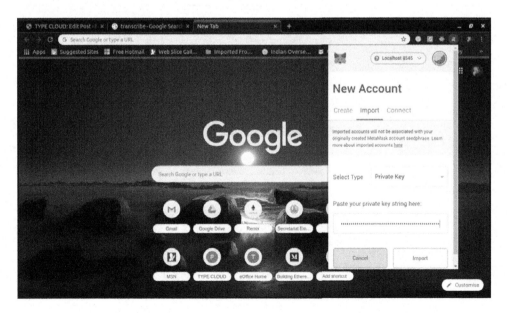

12. Paste the private key and click on **Import**.

13. You should now be able to see this account in MetaMask:

14. OK, now let's bring our app online. Navigate to the Exchange app project directory.

15. Run npm start in the Terminal window to bring the project online:

```
ishan@ishan-Inspiron-3537: ~/Exchange
File  Edit  View  Search  Terminal  Help
ishan@ishan-Inspiron-3537:~$ cd Exchange/
ishan@ishan-Inspiron-3537:~/Exchange$ npm start

> token-wallet@1.0.0 start /home/ishan/Exchange
> react-scripts start

```

16. The app should open in the browser, as follows:

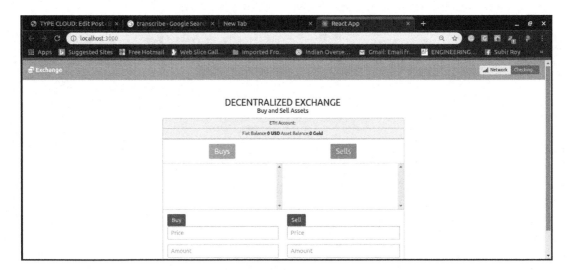

17. You'll also get a popup from MetaMask, asking if you want to permit the app to access your account and the injected web3. Click on **Connect** to give the app access to your account:

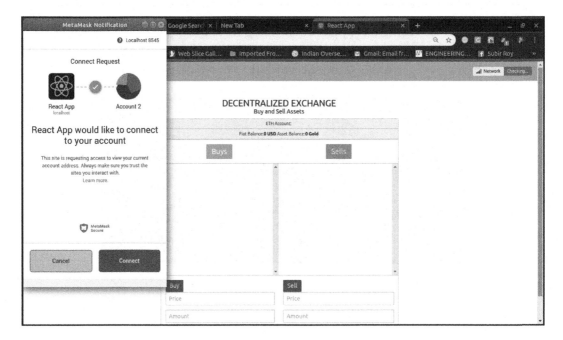

18. The app should now have access to your account, and the account address will be displayed in the address bar:

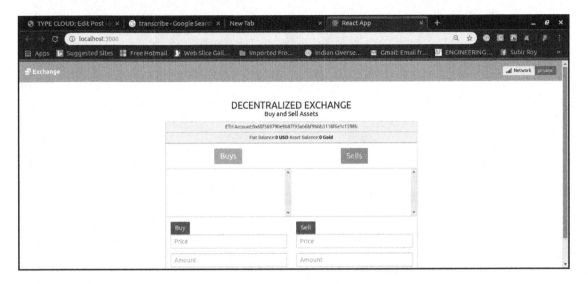

19. Before we can trade, we need to flood our account with funds. Navigate back to the Truffle console to transfer USD and Gold tokens to our account.

20. In the command line, set your `web3` default account to the first account in your Ganache HD wallet using this command:

```
web3.eth.defaultAccount =
'0x60f569790e9b87f93aB6bF9bBb3118f6E1C1598b'
```

21. Next, enter the following command in the Truffle console. It will mint (generate) 10,000,000 USD tokens to our address:

```
USD.deployed().then(function(instance) { return
instance.mint('0x60f569790e9b87f93aB6bF9bBb3118f6E1C1598b',10000000
); }).then(function(responseb) {console.log("response",
responseb.toString(10));});
```

22. Repeat the same for the Gold token. Enter the following command to the Truffle console. It will mint (generate) 10,000 Gold token to our address:

```
Gold.deployed().then(function(instance) { return
instance.mint('0x60f569790e9b87f93aB6bF9bBb3118f6E1C1598b',10000);
}).then(function(responseb) {console.log("response",
responseb.toString(10));});
```

23. The app screen should now look like this:

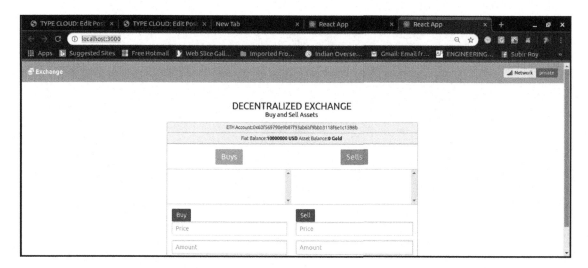

24. Observe the token balance in the address bar for Gold and USD tokens. Now, let's submit a buy trade. Let's submit a trade for 100 gold at $50 per unit:

25. Enter the amount and price values and click on **Submit**.
26. MetaMask will pop a notification, asking if you want to approve the movement of 5,000 USD tokens from your account. Click on **Confirm** to proceed:

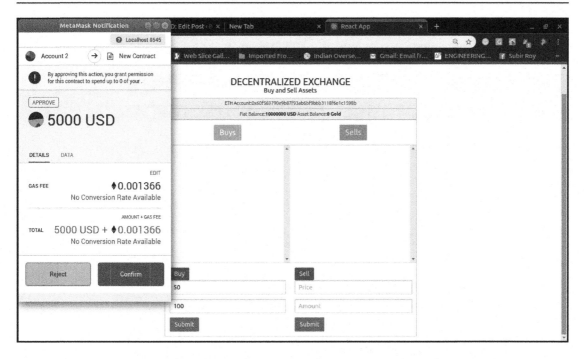

27. Next, MetaMask will pop a notification, asking if you want to send a transaction to the orderbook contract. Click on **Confirm** to proceed:

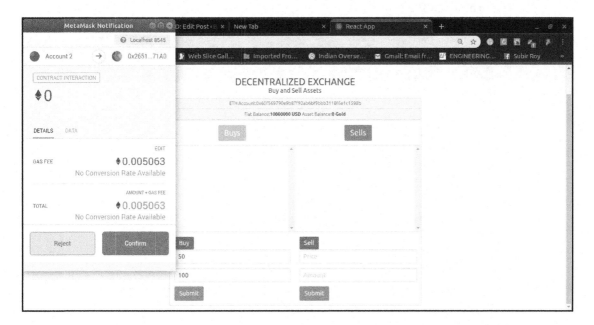

28. The order should go through, and you should be able to view it in the orderbook.

29. Also, notice that your balance for USD tokens has decreased by 5,000:

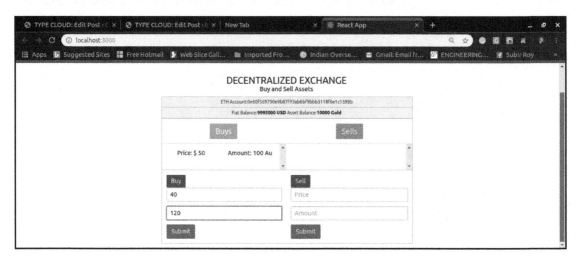

30. Let's enter a second order in the buy side. This time, let's enter a buy order for 120 gold at a price of $40 per unit.

31. Confirm the requisite permissions for MetaMask. You'll notice that the new order gets submitted to the orderbook, and the orderbook sorts itself to ensure that the $50 order is at the top:

32. Now, let's submit two sell orders for 90 gold at $60 per unit, and 70 gold at $70 per unit.

33. You'll notice this time the confirmation request that MetaMask pops is for transferring the Gold token from our account:

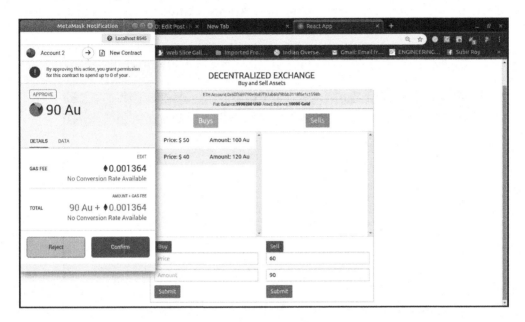

34. After the orders go through, the orderbook should look like this:

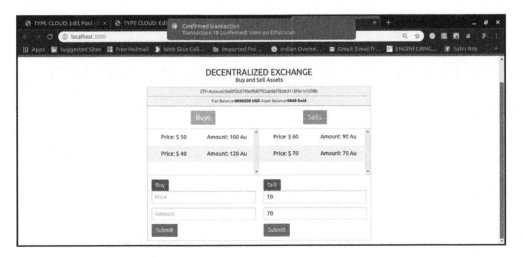

35. Now, let's try a trade. Let's try to match the buy order at $50. Submit a sell order for 10 gold at $50. See what happens.

36. Confirm the request notifications from MetaMask. Notice that the orderbook contract method that is invoked this time is **trade**.

37. Once the order goes through, the new **Amount** value for the buy order should be 90 gold. Also, notice that 10 gold has been added to your gold balance.

38. Let's try to match multiple orders. Submit a buy request for 160 gold at a price of $70. The buy order should match against both the offers on the sell side:

39. Notice how MetaMask requests your permission for every trade, since every trade is a new transaction to the contract.

40. The orderbook should have no more sell orders left after the successful trades, and the USD balance should have increased:

That brings us to the end of our decentralized exchange project.

Summary

That brings us to the end of this chapter. This chapter should help you design decentralized trading exchanges, or exchanges on a distributed blockchain network in general. It should also help you to port concepts of trading, such as orderbooks and matching engines, to blockchain very easily. The example case that we looked at uses only a single orderbook pair, gold versus US dollars, but it can be very easily expanded to support multiple orderbook pairs and assets, and can be scaled into a full-sized exchange with additional components and security checks in place. You can run this on a private blockchain for an enterprise, or deploy it on a public blockchain. Bear in mind that public blockchains will require gas for each transaction, and you might want to club transactions together. Also, your orderbook will be visible to everyone on the public blockchain.

We started the chapter by looking at decentralized exchanges and some basic trading concepts. We deployed our trading assets, gold and USD, as ERC20 tokens. We charted out an orderbook smart contract in order to manage buy and sell orders and execute trades. Since anyone can access the contract and view the orderbook, it is a transparent orderbook. Lastly, we created an exchange app to allow the user to access and view the orderbook , submit buy/sell trades, and view their token balance. The exchange app also matches submitted buy and sell orders against existing orders in the orderbook, and adds new orders to the orderbook. Lastly, we ran our app to see how it functions.

The main takeaway from this chapter is understanding how to build decentralized systems, such as exchanges, using blockchain. Such systems remove the need to trust a third party for executing trades.

In the next chapter, we'll be building a currency swap exchange that builds on this decentralized trading concept, and allows trading of currency assets on the Stellar blockchain network.

Developing a Currency Trading Exchange for Market Making

9

This chapter extends the idea of a decentralized exchange from the previous chapter and shows you how to build a market maker. Market makers are intermediaries that facilitate cross-border and cross-currency transactions, by allowing remittors to convert the remitting amount into a different currency. Let's say you are working in Europe and want to remit money back to your family in India: a market maker will convert the remitting amount into **Indian Rupees (INR)** from **Euros (EUR)**. Market makers are interesting, in the context of decentralized payment and remittance networks (such as Stellar and Ripple), because these networks gather the exchange rates from all the market makers on the network and allow the remittor to view them in a single platform. This platform is called the **distributed exchange**. This promotes competitive conversion rates and transparency. In this chapter, we'll be building a similar distributed exchange that trades **US Dollars (USD)**, **UK Pounds (GBP)**, and **EUR**. It will record offers from multiple market makers and display them in a single window.

We will cover the following topics:

- Introducing the distributed currency trading exchange
- Building the private test Stellar network
- Creating the user accounts
- Creating trading currency assets
- Building the currency trading exchange
- Running the currency exchange

Technical requirements

You can access the code files for this chapter through the following GitHub link: `https://github.com/PacktPublishing/Blockchain-Development-for-Finance-Projects/tree/master/Chapter%209`.

For this project, we'll be working with the `stellar/quickstart` Docker container, provided by the Stellar Development Foundation for trying out the Stellar platform. Details of the Docker image can be found at the following link: `https://hub.docker.com/r/stellar/quickstart/`.

I'm using Ubuntu 18.04.2 LTS for running the applications and deploying my blockchain. This project assumes that you are working on a Unix operating system. Additionally, this project assumes you have `node.js` and `npm` installed. I'm using node.js version 13.0.1 and npm version 6.12.0. You will also need the latest versions of Docker and Docker Compose.

We'll be launching a Docker container with a single node, single client-server private instance of the Stellar platform.

To download the Docker image and launch the container, run the following command in a Terminal window:

```
docker run --rm -it -p "8000:8000" --name stellar
stellar/quickstart --standalone
```

This runs a standalone instance of the Stellar network, with a single client and a single node that will act as our development environment. It also runs a `postgres` instance that stores transaction data that can be retrieved using the Horizon client server.

We'll be configuring this network instance further in the *Building the private test Stellar network* section.

Introducing the distributed currency trading exchange

Blockchains are facilitating much more transparent, faster, and efficient cross-border remittance transactions. This is due to the much faster reconciliation that the technology offers when compared to traditional payment systems. However, cross-border transactions are incomplete without cross-currency transactions.

Cross-currency transactions convert the starting or initiating currency of a cross-border remittance into a different currency, suited to the beneficiary receiving the remittance transaction. Thus, if an importer in India is paying an exporter in Germany, they may initiate the transaction in INR but may want the exporter to be paid in EUR. In traditional remittance transactions, the remittance enablers—that is, the remittance exchanges or banks themselves—provide an exchange rate to the remittor. This rate is, typically, a bit higher than the network. If I choose a specific remittance exchange or bank for my remittance transaction, I'm married to the exchange rate provided by them.

Distributed payment networks go a bit further than the traditional remittance models. They provide a transparent exchange, whereby any market maker can post their exchange rates. The user can then choose the best rate suitable for their transaction. All the buy-and-sell offers for a currency pair are recorded in a single platform, called an orderbook. Each currency trading pair has a unique orderbook. While facilitating a transaction, the user can choose their starting and destination assets, and the network will automatically choose the best rates from these exchanges and facilitate the transaction for them. Alternatively, these exchanges can also be used as trading exchanges, to buy and sell currency.

Each currency offer being submitted to the trading exchange has a base asset and a counter asset. The price of buying or selling a single unit is represented using the base asset. The amount to be bought or sold in a single offer is represented using the counter asset. Each asset is issued by an issuer account. This is simply an account that creates an asset on the network. To hold, send, and trade an asset, accounts need to extend a **trustline**. A trustline indicates how much of the asset they are willing to hold. It allows a user of the asset to declare how liquid they believe the issuer of the asset is, and then hold a proportional amount of the asset in their Stellar accounts. In simple terms, if you want to hold 100 USD in your account, the issuing account of the USD asset needs to extend a trustline of 100 USD to your account. If someone tries to transfer 101 USD to your account, the network will throw an error. Since assets on Stellar are a virtual representation of physical fiat currency, the trustline concept is important.

To build our market maker, we need to complete the following steps:

1. Create a private test Stellar network with the Stellar Core blockchain node and Horizon client/server that will allow us to interact with the blockchain node.
2. Create three test accounts. One is an issuing account, while the other two are receiving accounts. The issuing account will issue our trading assets, while the receiving account will trade them on the exchange.
3. Issue USD, GBP, and EUR assets on our private Stellar network using our issuing account.

4. Extend trustlines and transfer a "testing" amount of the assets to our receiving/trading accounts.

5. Build a frontend that will allow the trading user to log in with their account, view the available offers, and submit buy/sell offers. These offers will be recorded on the in-built distributed exchange that the Stellar network provides to us. The frontend will also show us successful trades.

The exchange would have the following components:

- The assets USD, GBP, and EUR, which are issued on a private Stellar network.
- Two user accounts that will act as market makers and hold the preceding currency.
- A trading exchange that connects to Stellar fetches offers for each trading currency pair and displays them to the user, accepts offers from the user, and displays the completed trades.

Let's start going through the steps, one by one.

Building the private test Stellar network

For building our project, we'll launch a simple Stellar network that contains a single blockchain node and a single client/server. The blockchain node in Stellar is called Stellar Core, while the client-server is called Horizon. Horizon is a client API server that extends a suite of handful endpoints, allowing application developers to view transaction data and statistics, and to submit transactions to the core blockchain node. Similar to web3-js, Stellar has a JavaScript SDK that allows us to build requests in order to interact with Horizon.

Stellar provides a handy Docker image that can be used to quickly launch an ephemeral (temporary) or persistent (permanent) container for implementing the Stellar network. This Docker container contains an instance of Stellar Core, an instance of Horizon, installed dependencies such as PostgreSQL, and a Go environment.

To launch this Docker image, simply run the following command on a terminal window:

```
docker run --rm -it -p "8000:8000" --name stellar stellar/quickstart --
standalone
```

This command downloads the Stellar/QuickStart image from the Docker repository and runs a container with Stellar Core and Horizon. Notice the Docker proxy port at 8000. The Docker proxy port extends the Horizon port inside the container. Thus, any requests to Horizon can be submitted to the 8000 port of the local machine.

Wait for the container to come online. It will initiate a PostgreSQL database, Stellar Core, and Horizon. After the container comes online successfully, you should be able to see the `docker-proxy` on port 8000 on your machine. Open a browser window and go to `http://localhost:8000`.

You should be able to see Horizon and the API endpoints and application details. Notice the list of endpoints for submitting requests to the client/server.

OK. Now, let's move on to account creation.

Creating the user accounts

Before we can create our assets and exchange, we need to create our user accounts. Stellar accounts are similar to Ethereum accounts, and they allow users to interact with the Stellar network through transactions. They contain a public key (which is referred to as an account ID) and a secret key or private key, which is used to sign transactions submitted to the ledger.

The `stellar-sdk` provides a utility called `Keypair.random`, which generates a random `ed25519` public-private key pair that can be used as a Stellar account. For a public-private key pair to be a valid account on the Stellar network, it needs a minimum balance of 20 lumens.

To create an account on our private network, we'll generate a new public-private key pair and fund it with a balance of more than 20 lumens.

To do so, we'll write a small `node-js` application that will generate a new key pair, and fund it.

Lumens is the native currency of the Stellar network. By default, the private instance issues 100 billion lumens and assigns it to a root account on the network. It is referred to by the symbol **XLM**. The minimum Stellar amount is referred to as *stroop*. It is one ten-millionth, 1/10000000, or 0.0000001. The term *stroop* is used as a convenient way to refer to these small measurements of amounts. The plural form is stroops (for example, 100 stroops).

Writing the CreateAccount utility

Let's start writing our Node.js create account utility, as follows:

1. Create a new nodejs project directory. Install the stellar-sdk JavaScript module by executing the following command in the directory:

   ```
   npm install --save stellar-sdk
   ```

2. Create a new project file called CreateAccount.js.
3. Start by importing the stellar-sdk, as follows:

   ```
   const StellarSdk = require('stellar-sdk');
   ```

4. Next, we'll define a new instance of the stellar-sdk, pointed to our local Horizon instance:

   ```
   const server = new StellarSdk.Server('http://127.0.0.1:8000',
   {allowHttp: true});

   const passphrase = 'Standalone Network ; February 2017'
   ```

5. The passphrase allows only selected users to connect to our network. You can find the network passphrase by navigating to the Horizon landing page at localhost:8000 in the browser. Locate the network-passphrase tag, as follows:

   ```
   "network_passphrase": "Standalone Network ; February 2017"
   ```

   For the quickstart Docker image, this passphrase is set to "Standalone Network ; February 2017", by default.

6. Next, we identify our MasterKey. The master key is the root account to which all lumens are credited when a new Stellar network is created. By default, the root account is issued 100 billion lumens at initiation.
7. To fund new accounts, we'll need to transfer lumens from this account to the newly created accounts.
8. The master key pair is fetched using the Keypair.master utility from the network passphrase, as follows:

   ```
   const MasterKey = StellarSdk.Keypair.master(passphrase)
   const MasterSecret = MasterKey.secret();
   const MasterPublicKey = MasterKey.publicKey();

   console.log ('Master Account',MasterSecret, MasterPublicKey);
   ```

9. The `.secret()` and `.publicKey()` methods for a key pair give us its secret key and public key, respectively.

> In a production implementation of Stellar, you are expected to use a custom network phrase and transfer all the lumens or native currency from the master currency to another Stellar account that you control on the network.

10. Next, we generate three random `ed25519` key pairs (public and private key pairs) that will act as our accounts. To do so, we use the `Keypair.random` method in the `StellarSdk`, as follows:

```
const pair1 = StellarSdk.Keypair.random(passphrase);
const pair2 = StellarSdk.Keypair.random(passphrase);
const pair3 = StellarSdk.Keypair.random(passphrase);
```

11. For each of the three newly generated random key pairs, we retrieve the public key and the private, or secret, key, as follows:

```
var SecretKey1 = pair1.secret();
var PublicKey1 = pair1.publicKey();
console.log ('Account1',SecretKey1, PublicKey1);

var SecretKey2 = pair2.secret();
var PublicKey2 = pair2.publicKey();
console.log ('Account2',SecretKey2, PublicKey2);

var SecretKey3 = pair3.secret();
var PublicKey3 = pair3.publicKey();
console.log ('Account3',SecretKey3, PublicKey3);
```

Make sure you log the newly generated keys and the master key to the console. We'll require these later.

Before we can use the newly generated keys, we need to fund them with lumens, which is the native currency of Stellar. Stellar does not allow users to send or receive transactions to any key pair with a lumens balance of less than 20. This is done to avoid spamming the network. You can only send the "Create Account" transaction to newly generated key pairs, to fund the account. The Stellar network also requires accounts to submit a "fee" to the network for every transaction, which is paid in lumens. Thus, to enable our accounts to create assets and trade, we'll transfer 100,000 lumens to each of the newly generated accounts.

Now, let's start building our `CreateAccount` transaction by following these steps:

1. We need to make asynchronous calls to fetch the transaction sequence number and fee, so we start by declaring an asynchronous method, like this:

```
(async function main() {

const account = await server.loadAccount(MasterPublicKey);
const fee = await server.fetchBaseFee();
```

- The `server.loadAccount` method fetches the current sequence number of the Stellar account. It is essential that transactions are submitted to the network in sequence, to dictate the order in which they'll be processed and verified. Before submitting a transaction from an account, we fetch the current transaction sequence number for the account.
- The `server.fetchBaseFee` method fetches the minimum fee required for the transaction to go through on the network. You can think of it as being similar to fetching the current gas price in an Ethereum network.

2. Next, we use the `TransactionBuilder` class to build a new create account transaction, like this:

```
const transaction = new StellarSdk.TransactionBuilder(account, {
fee, networkPassphrase: passphrase})
 .addOperation(StellarSdk.Operation.createAccount({
source: MasterPublicKey,
destination: PublicKey1,
startingBalance: "100000"
}))
 .addOperation(StellarSdk.Operation.createAccount({
source: MasterPublicKey,
destination: PublicKey2,
startingBalance: "100000"
}))
 .addOperation(StellarSdk.Operation.createAccount({
source: MasterPublicKey,
destination: PublicKey3,
startingBalance: "100000"
}))
 .setTimeout(30)
 .build();
```

Let's go through each step, one by one:

```
const transaction = new StellarSdk.TransactionBuilder(account, {
fee, networkPassphrase: passphrase})
```

3. We start by creating a new transaction constant. This is returned by the `TransactionBuilder` class. We first pass the source account (master key account), the network fee, and passphrase as input parameters. Next, we send the operations to be carried out by the transaction as input parameters, like this:

```
.addOperation(StellarSdk.Operation.createAccount({
source: MasterPublicKey,
destination: PublicKey1,
startingBalance: "100000"
}))
```

4. The first operation is `createAccount`. It'll fund our newly created random key pair with a starting balance of 100,000 lumens. The source account is our master account public key, and the destination is the public key of the first random account we generated. The same operation is repeated for the other two random key pairs we generated, as follows:

```
.addOperation(StellarSdk.Operation.createAccount({
source: MasterPublicKey,
destination: PublicKey2,
startingBalance: "100000"
}))
.addOperation(StellarSdk.Operation.createAccount({
source: MasterPublicKey,
destination: PublicKey3,
startingBalance: "100000"
}))
```

Notice how `stellar-sdk` allows you to chain and link multiple operations in a single transaction.

5. Lastly, we add the transaction timeout and call `build()` to build the transaction, as follows:

```
.setTimeout(30)
.build();
```

The transaction timeout indicates that the transaction won't be valid more than 30 seconds after the transaction object is created. `build()` instructs the `TransactionBuilder` class to create a new transaction object using the parameters we submitted. This object is stored in the `transaction` constant.

The transaction object is then signed using the master key pair, like this:

```
transaction.sign(MasterKey);
```

Lastly, the transaction is posted to the transaction endpoint of the Horizon server, as follows:

```
try {
 const transactionResult = await
server.submitTransaction(transaction);
 console.log(transactionResult);
 } catch (err) {
 console.error(err);
 }
}) ()
```

This is done using `server.submitTransaction`. The result is logged to the console.

This brings us to an end of the `CreateAccount` utility.

Running the CreateAccount utility

Now, let's run this utility. Navigate back to the `Node.js` project on the terminal window.

Run the following command to run the utility:

```
node CreateAccount.js
```

The utility will first log the master key to the console, and then the three newly created accounts. The string starting with S is the account's secret key. The string starting with G is the public key or account ID, as shown in the following code block:

```
Master Account SC5O7VZUXDJ6JBDSZ74DSERXL7W3Y5LTOAMRF7RQRL3TAGAPS7LUVG3L
GBZXN7PIRZGNMHGA7MUUUF4GWPY5AYPV6LY4UV2GL6VJGIQRXFDNMADI

Account1 SDHH7CAELIMPNZPRFEBJHSFP24B7UEAAJVW2PMR5AZP5OESHH435DZFC
GBUM3XRJKUVEQA4UF63CUCS3P72C5AZTRYI2VKELS7T7DVCCLV3DODNE

Account2 SCUN3DL3OCSU6SQ6K4BU3SIG7OHPKKUGFAR25CJG2JUSNIGGU3OCSVAS
GDM3ACVBVHZXPYHQYTMQFS42DSIU7AVIZS4ARWNQGUNGL55BPCBUJV6C

Account3 SDOE7ICIYRSH74VWUTO52T24BDZBYHRYSYAPS5V73Z37WLYQNA6B4PP4
GCCHNGQFPZOSCT2FKVZGMCK5OTVMJEKMUTDLHKV22J5XKF3ROUSECBXC
```

Copy these accounts and store them safely for reference. We'll need these later.

Wait for the utility to fire the `createAccount` transaction and print a response to the console. A successful response indicates the three accounts have been created—and funded, as well.

You can verify this by yourself. Open a new browser window. Paste the following link to view the newly created accounts: `http://localhost:8000/accounts/<Account ID>;` For example, `http://localhost:8000/accounts/GBUM3XRJKUVEQA4UF63CUCS3P72C5AZTRYI2VKEL S7T7DVCCLV3DODNE.`

You should be able to view the account. Scroll down and check out the balance for the native asset, as follows:

```
"balances": [
    {
        "balance": "100000.0000000",
        "buying_liabilities": "0.0000000",
        "selling_liabilities": "0.0000000",
        "asset_type": "native"
    }
```

Keep the secret key and public key for these three accounts safe. Now, let's write a `nodejs` utility in order to create the assets and extend the trustlines.

Creating trading currency assets

We have to create three currency assets on our private network for trading. These are USD, GBP, and EUR. To create new assets on a network, we need to carry out the following three steps in order:

1. Create a new asset object
2. Extend trustlines to the receiving accounts
3. Transfer the assets from the issuing account

Let's look at these, one by one.

Creating a new asset object

Creating an asset object on the Stellar network is an easy affair. You simply need to use the `Asset` method of the Stellar SDK. The `Asset` method has two input parameters—asset code and issuer account. The asset code is an alphanumeric code, used to refer to the asset. The issuer account is the account used to create the asset. The code is shown in the following code snippet:

```
Asset = new StellarSdk.Asset(<Code>,<Issuing Account>)
```

We'll use this to create all three of our assets, as part of our `Nodejs` utility, by running the following code:

```
var USD = new StellarSdk.8520Asset('USD',
'GBUM3XRJKUVEQA4UF63CUCS3P72C5AZTRYI2VKELS7T7DVCCLV3DODNE');
var GBP = new StellarSdk.Asset('GBP',
'GBUM3XRJKUVEQA4UF63CUCS3P72C5AZTRYI2VKELS7T7DVCCLV3DODNE');
var EUR = new StellarSdk.Asset('EUR',
'GBUM3XRJKUVEQA4UF63CUCS3P72C5AZTRYI2VKELS7T7DVCCLV3DODNE');
```

Extending trustlines to receiving accounts

Trustlines are a concept unique to Stellar assets. They determine how much of a user-issued asset an account is willing to hold. Since assets on the Stellar network are supposed to be digital representations of fiat currency or other real-world assets, it is essential that the issuer issuing assets should be liquid. Thus, you should only hold 100 USD worth of assets issued by an issuer account if you know that the issuer can exchange the stellar USD tokens for a 100-dollar bill. Trustlines are indicative of how much liquid you believe the asset issuer is and, in turn, are used to determine how much of the asset you would want your account to hold.

Writing the utility

Let's write a `Nodejs` utility in order to create new assets and extend trustlines to the receiving accounts, as follows:

1. Create a new `nodejs` app called `CreateTrustline.js`.
2. Start by importing the `stellar-sdk` from node-modules and creating a new server object pointed at `localhost:8000` (Horizon instance), as follows:

   ```
   const StellarSdk = require('stellar-sdk');
   const server = new StellarSdk.Server('http://127.0.0.1:8000',
   {allowHttp: true});
   ```

2. Next, we'll use the accounts we generated in the previous section. Let the first account be our issuing account, which issues assets. The second and third accounts will be the receiving accounts, which trade the assets on the exchange. Use the secret key of the three accounts to extract their key pair, as follows:

   ```
   var issuingKeys =
   StellarSdk.Keypair.fromSecret('SDHH7CAELIMPNZPRFEBJHSFP24B7UEAAJVW2
   PMR5AZP5OESHH435DZFC');
   ```

```
var receivingKeys1 =
StellarSdk.Keypair.fromSecret('SCUN3DL3OCSU6SQ6K4BU3SIG7OHPKKUGFAR2
5CJG2JUSNIGGU3OCSVAS');

 var receivingKeys2 =
StellarSdk.Keypair.fromSecret('SDOE7ICIYRSH74VWUTO52T24BDZBYHRYSYAP
S5V73Z37WLYQNA6B4PP4');
```

3. The `issuingKeys` variable is the key pair for the issuing account. `receivingKeys1` and `receivingKeys2` are for the two receiving accounts.

4. Next, we create the asset object. We create a new asset object for US Dollar and UK Pound, as well as for Euro, like this:

```
var USD = new StellarSdk.Asset('USD',
'GBUM3XRJKUVEQA4UF63CUCS3P72C5AZTRYI2VKELS7T7DVCCLV3DODNE');
var GBP = new StellarSdk.Asset('GBP',
'GBUM3XRJKUVEQA4UF63CUCS3P72C5AZTRYI2VKELS7T7DVCCLV3DODNE');
var EUR = new StellarSdk.Asset('EUR',
'GBUM3XRJKUVEQA4UF63CUCS3P72C5AZTRYI2VKELS7T7DVCCLV3DODNE');
```

Remember the public key for your issuing account that we saved when we created it? Paste it here and add a symbol that we'll use to refer the asset. Use `StellarSdk.Asset` to create a new asset with these details.

5. Before we can transfer the assets, the receiving accounts need to extend a trustline for these assets. This is a transaction that's fired by the receiving account to itself. It indicates the asset that will be held by the account and the maximum volume that can be held.

Let's write the transaction that will extend the trustline limit. We start by fetching the base network fee and the sequence number for the account. This is done using the server object we created earlier, as follows:

```
server.fetchBaseFee()
 .then(function(fee){
 console.log("Fee is",fee);

server.loadAccount(receivingKeys1.publicKey())
 .then(function(account){
```

Since the transaction is to be fired from `receivingKeys1`, we fetch the current sequence for this account.

6. Let's take a look at our extend trustline transaction, shown here:

```
var transaction = new StellarSdk.TransactionBuilder(account, { fee,
networkPassphrase:'Standalone Network ; February 2017'}
.addOperation(StellarSdk.Operation.changeTrust({
asset: USD,
limit: '1000000',
source: receivingKeys1.publicKey()
}))
.addOperation(StellarSdk.Operation.changeTrust({
asset: GBP,
limit: '1000000',
source: receivingKeys1.publicKey()
}))
.addOperation(StellarSdk.Operation.changeTrust({
asset: EUR,
limit: '1000000',
source: receivingKeys1.publicKey()
})).setTimeout(100)
.build();
```

Let's try to understand this transaction. We start by passing the account sequence number, fee, and the network passphrase, like this:

```
var transaction = new StellarSdk.TransactionBuilder(account, { fee,
networkPassphrase:'Standalone Network ; February 2017'}
```

Next, we add the ChangeTrust operation, as follows:

```
.addOperation(StellarSdk.Operation.changeTrust({
asset: USD,
limit: '1000000',
source: receivingKeys1.publicKey()
}))
```

The operation indicates that we need to extend a trustline for the asset USD, with a limit of 1 million USD. Since the transaction is to "self", the source of the transactions is the public key of receivingKeys1.

We also add the same operation for GBP and EUR, as follows:

```
.addOperation(StellarSdk.Operation.changeTrust({
asset: GBP,
limit: '1000000',
source: receivingKeys1.publicKey()
}))
.addOperation(StellarSdk.Operation.changeTrust({
asset: EUR,
```

```
limit: '1000000',
source: receivingKeys1.publicKey()
}))
```

Lastly, we add a transaction timeout after 100 seconds and invoke `build()` to build the transaction object, like this:

```
.setTimeout(100)
.build();
```

7. After building the transactions, we sign it using the public key for `receivingKeys1` and submit it to the Stellar network for processing. Add a catch block for catching any errors, as follows:

```
transaction.sign(receivingKeys1);

return server.submitTransaction(transaction);

})}).catch(function(error) {
console.error('Error!', error);
});
```

8. Next, we repeat the same for `receivingKeys2`—that is, the second trading account we created—as follows:

```
server.fetchBaseFee()
.then(function(fee){
console.log("Fee is",fee);

server.loadAccount(receivingKeys2.publicKey())
.then(function(account){

var transaction = new StellarSdk.TransactionBuilder(account, { fee,
networkPassphrase:'Standalone Network ; February 2017'})
.addOperation(StellarSdk.Operation.changeTrust({
asset: USD,
limit: '1000000',
source: receivingKeys2.publicKey()
}))
.addOperation(StellarSdk.Operation.changeTrust({
asset: GBP,
limit: '1000000',
source: receivingKeys2.publicKey()
}))
.addOperation(StellarSdk.Operation.changeTrust({
asset: EUR,
limit: '1000000',
```

```
    source: receivingKeys2.publicKey()
    })).setTimeout(100)
    .build();

transaction.sign(receivingKeys2);

return server.submitTransaction(transaction);

})}).catch(function(error) {
    console.error('Error!', error);
    });
```

That brings us to the end of our `CreateTrustline` utility. Now, let's run this utility.

Running the utility

Navigate back to the `nodejs` project repository on your terminal window. Run the `CreateTrustline` utility by executing the following command:

```
node CreateTrustline.js
```

A successful response from the Stellar network after the transaction is submitted indicates the trustlines have been created. You can verify this on your own.

Navigate to your internet browser and open a tab. View any account on Horizon by going to the accounts link. You can do so by going to the following link: `http://localhost:8000/accounts/<Account ID>`.

For example, for `receivingKeys1`, the public key we saved earlier is `GDM3ACVBVHZXPYHQYTMQFS42DSIU7AVIZS4ARWNQGUNGL55BPCBUJV6C`.

So, open the following link:

`http://localhost:8000/accounts/GDM3ACVBVHZXPYHQYTMQFS42DSIU7AVIZS4ARWNQ
GUNGL55BPCBUJV6C`.

Now, scroll down and check the balances again. Notice how it shows balances for four assets, including the native asset now. This can be seen in the following code block:

```
"balances": [
  {
    "balance": "0.0000000",
    "limit": "1000000.0000000",
    "buying_liabilities": "0.0000000",
    "selling_liabilities": "0.0000000",
    "last_modified_ledger": 503,
```

```
        "is_authorized": true,
        "asset_type": "credit_alphanum4",
        "asset_code": "USD",
        "asset_issuer":
"GBUM3XRJKUVEQA4UF63CUCS3P72C5AZTRYI2VKELS7T7DVCCLV3DODNE"
      },
      {
        "balance": "0.0000000",
        "limit": "1000000.0000000",
        "buying_liabilities": "0.0000000",
        "selling_liabilities": "0.0000000",
        "last_modified_ledger": 503,
        "is_authorized": true,
        "asset_type": "credit_alphanum4",
        "asset_code": "GBP",
        "asset_issuer":
"GBUM3XRJKUVEQA4UF63CUCS3P72C5AZTRYI2VKELS7T7DVCCLV3DODNE"
      },
      {
        "balance": "0.0000000",
        "limit": "1000000.0000000",
        "buying_liabilities": "0.0000000",
        "selling_liabilities": "0.0000000",
        "last_modified_ledger": 503,
        "is_authorized": true,
        "asset_type": "credit_alphanum4",
        "asset_code": "EUR",
        "asset_issuer":
"GBUM3XRJKUVEQA4UF63CUCS3P72C5AZTRYI2VKELS7T7DVCCLV3DODNE"
      },
      {
        "balance": "99999.9999700",
        "buying_liabilities": "0.0000000",
        "selling_liabilities": "0.0000000",
        "asset_type": "native"
      }
}
```

Next, we'll write a transfer utility, to transfer these assets from the issuer account to the receiving account.

Transferring the assets from the issuing account

Now, we can transfer the USD, GBP, and EUR assets from our issuing account to the receiving account. To do so, we'll write a small utility called **Transfer** and send the assets. We'll create two versions of this utility for receiving account 1 and receiving account 2.

Writing the utilities

All right. Now, let's write the `Node.js` utilities, to transfer the assets from the issuing account to the accounts we'll use for trading, as follows:

1. Create two `nodejs` apps called `Transfer1.js` and `Transfer2.js`.

2. Let's write `Transfer1`. We import the `StellarSDK` from `node_modules`, create the server object, and extract the public and private keys for the issuing account and the two receiving accounts from their respective secret keys, as follows:

```
const StellarSdk = require('stellar-sdk');

const server = new StellarSdk.Server('http://127.0.0.1:8000',
{allowHttp: true});

var issuingKeys = StellarSdk.Keypair
.fromSecret('SDHH7CAELIMPNZPRFEBJHSFP24B7UEAAJVW2PMR5AZP5OESHH435DZ
FC');

var receivingKeys1 = StellarSdk.Keypair
.fromSecret('SCUN3DL3OCSU6SQ6K4BU3SIG7OHPKKUGFAR25CJG2JUSNIGGU3OCSV
AS');

var receivingKeys2 = StellarSdk.Keypair
.fromSecret('SDOE7ICIYRSH74VWUTO52T24BDZBYHRYSYAPS5V73Z37WLYQNA6B4P
P4');

var USD = new StellarSdk.Asset('USD',
'GBUM3XRJKUVEQA4UF63CUCS3P72C5AZTRYI2VKELS7T7DVCCLV3DODNE');
var GBP = new StellarSdk.Asset('GBP',
'GBUM3XRJKUVEQA4UF63CUCS3P72C5AZTRYI2VKELS7T7DVCCLV3DODNE');
var EUR = new StellarSdk.Asset('EUR',
'GBUM3XRJKUVEQA4UF63CUCS3P72C5AZTRYI2VKELS7T7DVCCLV3DODNE');
```

3. Lastly, we create the three asset objects. Now, let's look at our transaction.

4. Fetch the base fee and the account sequence number for the issuing account, like this:

```
server.fetchBaseFee()
 .then(function(fee){
 console.log("Fee is",fee);
server.loadAccount(issuingKeys.publicKey())
.then(function(account){
```

5. Our transaction source account this time will be the issuing account, which distributes the newly created asset, as follows:

```
var transaction = new StellarSdk.TransactionBuilder(account,{
fee,networkPassphrase:'Standalone Network ; February 2017'})
 .addOperation(StellarSdk.Operation.payment({
destination: receivingKeys1.publicKey(),
asset: USD,
amount: '1000'
}))
```

Asset transfer is a payment operation in Stellar. We need to provide the destination Stellar account (with a public key of receivingKeys1), the asset to be transferred (USD), and the amount to be transferred (1,000).

6. We repeat the same for the other two assets as well, like this:

```
.addOperation(StellarSdk.Operation.payment({
destination: receivingKeys1.publicKey(),
asset: GBP,
amount: '1000'
}))
 .addOperation(StellarSdk.Operation.payment({
destination: receivingKeys1.publicKey(),
asset: EUR,
amount: '1000'
})).setTimeout(100)
.build();
```

7. The transaction timeout is set at 100 seconds. We call build() to build and return the transaction object.

8. After the transaction object is returned, we sign and submit the transaction. The transaction is signed using the issuing account's key pair since the source is the issuing account, as follows:

```
transaction.sign(issuingKeys);
 return server.submitTransaction(transaction);
```

9. Add a response block for logging any errors and notifying transaction success, like this:

```
.then(function(response,error){
if (response)
{
console.log("Response",response);
}
else
```

```
            {
            console.log("Error",error);
            }})
        });
```

That brings us to the end of `Transfer1`. Repeat the same steps for `Transfer2`, except replace the receiving account with `receivingKeys2`. Thus, `Transfer1.js` will transfer the assets to the first receiving account, and `Transfer2.js` to the second.

Now, let's run these utilities.

Running the utilities

Navigate to your `nodejs` project directory. First, run `Transfer1`, like this:

```
node Transfer1.js
```

Wait for a successful transaction response. Then, run `Transfer2`, like this:

```
node Transfer2.js
```

After you get a successful transaction response, open a new browser window and check the balance of the two accounts. For example, for receiving account 1, run the following code:

```
http://localhost:8000/accounts/GDM3ACVBVHZXPYHQYTMQFS42DSIU7AVIZS4ARWNQGUNG
L55BPCBUJV6C
```

The balance should now be updated, as follows:

```
    "balances": [
        {
        "balance": "1000.0000000",
        "limit": "1000000.0000000",
        "buying_liabilities": "0.0000000",
        "selling_liabilities": "0.0000000",
        "last_modified_ledger": 836,
        "is_authorized": true,
        "asset_type": "credit_alphanum4",
        "asset_code": "USD",
        "asset_issuer":
"GBUM3XRJKUVEQA4UF63CUCS3P72C5AZTRYI2VKELS7T7DVCCLV3DODNE"
        },
        {
        "balance": "1000.0000000",
        "limit": "1000000.0000000",
        "buying_liabilities": "0.0000000",
        "selling_liabilities": "0.0000000",
```

```
      "last_modified_ledger": 836,
      "is_authorized": true,
      "asset_type": "credit_alphanum4",
      "asset_code": "GBP",
      "asset_issuer":
"GBUM3XRJKUVEQA4UF63CUCS3P72C5AZTRYI2VKELS7T7DVCCLV3DODNE"
    },
    {
      "balance": "1000.0000000",
      "limit": "1000000.0000000",
      "buying_liabilities": "0.0000000",
      "selling_liabilities": "0.0000000",
      "last_modified_ledger": 836,
      "is_authorized": true,
      "asset_type": "credit_alphanum4",
      "asset_code": "EUR",
      "asset_issuer":
"GBUM3XRJKUVEQA4UF63CUCS3P72C5AZTRYI2VKELS7T7DVCCLV3DODNE"
    },
    {
      "balance": "99999.9999700",
      "buying_liabilities": "0.0000000",
      "selling_liabilities": "0.0000000",
      "asset_type": "native"
    }
  ],
```

That brings us to the end of creating and issuing the assets.

Now, we have two trading accounts, with assets ready to trade. Let's start building our exchange.

Building the currency trading exchange

Our currency exchange app will constitute of the following:

- The main `App.js` file
- The following React components:
  - `Container.js`
  - `AppLogin.js`
  - `AddressBar.js`
  - `TradePanel.js`

- Orderbook.js
- Trades.js
- The following asset interfaces:
  - Assets.js
  - USD.js
  - GBP.js
  - EUR.js

The following is a brief description of the components:

- App.js: The main App.js file that implements the methods that interact with the Stellar network and submits transactions to the network. It invokes Container.js for rendering the child components and forwards the current state to Container.js.
- React components: These components render our currency exchange app:
  - Container.js: It receives the current state from App.js and passes it to the child components.
  - AppLogin.js: A login screen that asks for the user's secret key, to set the default user account. All transactions are submitted from this account. The secret key is held within the app, and not stored permanently.
  - AddressBar.js: It implements an address bar that shows the user's Stellar account ID and current USD, GBP, and EUR balance.
  - TradePanel.js: It renders a buy-and-sell panel that permits the user to enter the amount and price, and submit a buy or sell request to the app.
  - OrderBook.js: This component renders the orderbook in the app for a selected trading pair. It maps the bids and asks arrays for each asset pair, and displays it to the user. The bids[] and asks[] arrays are populated with buy-and-sell orders from Stellar's distributed exchange.
  - Trades.js: This component renders and displays the successful trades in the exchange.
- Asset interfaces: These are used to instantiate the asset object within the app. They contain the asset code, issuer account, and symbol. There is one interface for each asset. The master interface, Assets.js, exports all three assets as an array within the app.

Creating the React project environment

Before we can create our React app, we need to set the project directory and install the dependencies for our app, as follows:

1. Create a new React app called `Currency-Exchange` using `npx`, like this:

```
npx create-react-app Currency-Exchange
```

2. Update your `package.json` to the following values:

```
{
  "name": "Currency-Exchange",
  "version": "1.0.0",
  "private": false,
  "dependencies": {
  "bulma-start": "0.0.2",
  "react": "^16.4.1",
  "react-dom": "^16.4.1",
  "react-scripts": "1.1.4",
  "stellar-sdk": "^3.0.0",
  },
  "scripts": {
  "start": "react-scripts start",
  "build": "react-scripts build",
  "test": "react-scripts test --env=jsdom",
  "eject": "react-scripts eject"
  }
}
```

3. Run `npm install` on the terminal window to install the dependencies.

Next, within the `src` folder, create a `Components` folder for the app components. Also, create an `Assets` folder within `src`. We'll be using this to map the assets being used by the app.

Setting up the asset interfaces

We need to import the asset interfaces that our app will use to interact with the assets deployed in the Stellar network, as follows:

1. Create a file called `Assets.js` in the `Assets` folder.

2. Update it with the following lines of code:

```
import USD from './USD';
import GBP from './GBP';
import EUR from './EUR';

const assets = [
  USD,
  GBP,
  EUR
];

export default assets;
```

3. The `Assets.js` file will create the assets array object with details of the three assets—USD, GBP, and EUR. This object will be used to instantiate the individual asset objects within the app.

4. Next, let's define the parameters for the individual assets, as follows:

```
//USD.js
export default {
  balance: 0,
  code: "USD",
  issuer:
"GBUM3XRJKUVEQA4UF63CUCS3P72C5AZTRYI2VKELS7T7DVCCLV3DODNE",
  symbol: "$"
}

//GBP.js
export default {
  balance: 0,
  code: "GBP",
  issuer:
"GBUM3XRJKUVEQA4UF63CUCS3P72C5AZTRYI2VKELS7T7DVCCLV3DODNE",
  symbol: "£"
}

//EUR.js
export default {
  balance: 0,
```

```
code: "EUR",
issuer:
"GBUM3XRJKUVEQA4UF63CUCS3P72C5AZTRYI2VKELS7T7DVCCLV3DODNE",
symbol: "€"
}
```

Each asset has the following: a default balance set to zero, the asset code, the asset issuer account, and the appropriate currency symbol.

The issuer account is the one we used to create our assets.

Writing the App.js file

Let's go through the sections of our App.js file one by one, as follows:

1. We start by importing the requisite dependencies, components, and asset interfaces, like this:

```
import React, { Component } from 'react';
import StellarSdk from 'stellar-sdk';
import Nav from './Components/Nav';
import Description from './Components/Description';
import Container from './Components/Container';
import assets from './Assets/Assets';
```

2. Within our constructor section, we initialize the state of the app, as follows:

```
class App extends Component {

constructor(){
super();
this.appName = 'Currency Exchange';
this.onInputChangeUpdateField =
this.onInputChangeUpdateField.bind(this);
this.assets = assets;
```

We set the name of the app, bind the methods that change the app state, and map the asset interfaces to the this object.

3. Next, we instantiate the asset objects using the asset interfaces. We use `StellarSdk.Asset` to instantiate the asset objects. The input parameters (which are the asset code and the issuer account) are fetched from the asset interfaces, like this:

```
this.USD = new
StellarSdk.Asset(this.assets[0].code,this.assets[0].issuer);

this.GBP = new
StellarSdk.Asset(this.assets[1].code,this.assets[1].issuer);

this.EUR = new
StellarSdk.Asset(this.assets[2].code,this.assets[2].issuer);
```

4. Next, we set the initial state of our `Currency-Exchange` app by running the following code:

```
this.state = {

network: 'Private Testnet',
account: null,
```

The network is set to Private Testnet, and the default user account is set to `null`.

5. Next, we define a set of bids and asks state arrays for each asset pair. Each array will hold the orderbook bids (buys) and asks (sells), and will be updated whenever a new offer is added to the orderbook. The code for this is as follows:

```
bidsUSDGBP: [],
asksUSDGBP: [],
bidsGBPEUR: [],
asksGBPEUR: [],
bidsUSDEUR: [],
asksUSDEUR: [],
```

6. The `tradesList` array stores the successful trades on the network. The initial counter variable for the state is set to the USD asset, while the initial base variable is set to the GBP asset, like this:

```
tradesList: [],
counter: this.USD,
base: this.GBP,
```

7. Lastly, we set the individual user balances for each asset to zero and initialize the fields used to capture information from the user/trader, like this:

```
GBPBalance: 0,
USDBalance: 0,
EURBalance: 0,
fields: {
secretkey: null,
buyprice: null,
buyamount: null,
sellprice: null,
sellamount: null,
}
}
}
```

8. Next, let's take a look at the componentDidMount() section, as follows:

```
componentDidMount(){

this.server = new StellarSdk.Server('http://127.0.0.1:8000',
{allowHttp: true});
 this.passphrase = 'Standalone Network ; February 2017';

}
```

The componentDidMount() section points the server to the local Horizon instance and instantiates the server object for interacting with the Stellar network. We also set the network passphrase in the this object.

9. Lastly, this app renders the Container component and forwards the current state to the Container component. It also renders the title bar and description using Nav.js and Description.js, like this:

```
render() {

return (
<div>
<Nav appName={this.appName} network={this.state.network} />
<Description />
<Container
onInputChangeUpdateField={this.onInputChangeUpdateField}
account={this.state.account}
base={this.state.base}
counter={this.state.counter}
setBalance={this.setBalance}
assets={this.assets}
```

```
tradesList={this.state.tradesList}
GBPBalance={this.state.GBPBalance}
USDBalance={this.state.USDBalance}
EURBalance={this.state.EURBalance}
bidsUSDGBP={this.state.bidsUSDGBP}
asksUSDGBP={this.state.asksUSDGBP}
bidsUSDEUR={this.state.bidsUSDEUR}
asksUSDEUR={this.state.asksUSDEUR}
bidsGBPEUR={this.state.bidsGBPEUR}
asksGBPEUR={this.state.asksGBPEUR}
setOrderbookPair = {this.setOrderbookPair}
Buy={this.Buy}
Sell={this.Sell}
fields={this.state.fields}
setAccount={this.setAccount}/>

</div>
)
}
}
export default App;
```

OK. Now, we are ready to look at the methods that make our app tick.

Let's start by looking at the `setAccount` method.

Setting the default user account

Before our trader can submit orders to the network, they need to have a valid Stellar account, funded with the trading assets. We created the trader's accounts using the `nodejs` utility in the previous section.

To load the user's account and balances and submit orders from their account, we need to map the user's secret key to the app. This secret key is kept on the client side in the ephemeral storage, and is not sent to the server side.

The `AppLogin.js` component renders a single field called **secret key**, to capture the user's secret key.

The `setAccount()` method is called to map this secret key and the public key to the app state, like this:

```
setAccount = () => {

var account =
StellarSdk.Keypair.fromSecret(this.state.fields.secretkey).publicKey()
```

```
this.setState({
account
});
this.setBalance(account);
this.setOrderbook();
this.setTrades();
};
```

The public key is derived using the `Keypair` class in the `StellarSdk`. We set the account to the app state.

Within this method, we also call the `setBalance` method to set the account balance, the `setOrderbook` method to set event streams for each asset pair `orderbook`, and the `setTrades` method to set up an event stream in order to receive trades whenever a new trade takes place. Let's take a look at these methods.

Setting the account balance

The `setBalance` method is invoked any time we need to update the user balance in the app. The `setBalance` method fetches the user balance for each asset from the Stellar network and updates the app's state variables, as follows:

```
setBalance = (account) => {
  let app=this;

var d = new URL(account,'http://127.0.0.1:8000/accounts/');
```

The `setBalance` method takes the user public key (account ID) as an input parameter. It captures the `this` object in the app parameter.

We also set the URL for fetching the account information for Horizon to `http://127.0.0.1:8000/accounts/<account public key>`.

Next, we call the account URL asynchronously. The response is captured and parsed into JSON as follows:

```
(async function main(){
await fetch(d)
.then(response => response.json())
.then(data => {
var balance = data.balances
```

The asset balances are returned in an array.

We map the balances array and update the balance variables for each asset in the current app state, like this:

```
balance.forEach((balance) => {
  if(balance.asset_code == 'GBP')
  {

  let GBPBalance = Number(balance.balance).toFixed(2);
  app.setState({
  GBPBalance
  });
  }
  else if(balance.asset_code == 'EUR')
  {
  let EURBalance = Number(balance.balance).toFixed(2);
  app.setState({
  EURBalance
  });
  }
  else if(balance.asset_code == 'USD')
  {
  let USDBalance = Number(balance.balance).toFixed(2);
  app.setState({
  USDBalance
  });
  }
  else
  console.log("Native Asset");
  })

  });
  })();
  }
```

Each asset balance is terminated to two decimal places. That brings us to the end of the setBalance method. The AddressBar component renders and displays the balance for all three assets.

Displaying the orderbook

The setOrderbook method is invoked to set event streams, one for each trading asset pair. The event streams are triggered every time a new order is submitted to the orderbook.

Start writing the `setOrderbook` method by capturing the `this` instance in the local app parameter, like this:

```
setOrderbook = () => {
let app = this;
```

The `orderbookHandler` method is an internal method invoked any time there is a new message on the `orderbook` event streams. The method checks the asset code of the base asset and counter asset of the new offer to determine which `orderbook` needs to be updated. The state variables holding the bids and asks are updated accordingly, as follows:

```
var orderbookHandler = function (orderbookResponse) {

if (orderbookResponse.base.asset_code == 'USD' &&
orderbookResponse.counter.asset_code == 'GBP')
{
var bidsUSDGBP = orderbookResponse.bids;
var asksUSDGBP = orderbookResponse.asks;
app.setState
({
bidsUSDGBP,
asksUSDGBP
});
}

else if (orderbookResponse.base.asset_code == 'USD' &&
orderbookResponse.counter.asset_code == 'EUR')
{
var bidsUSDEUR = orderbookResponse.bids;
var asksUSDEUR = orderbookResponse.asks;
app.setState
({
bidsUSDEUR,
asksUSDEUR
});
}

else if (orderbookResponse.base.asset_code == 'GBP' &&
orderbookResponse.counter.asset_code == 'EUR')
{
var bidsGBPEUR = orderbookResponse.bids;
var asksGBPEUR = orderbookResponse.asks;
app.setState
({
bidsGBPEUR,
asksGBPEUR
});
```

```
    }

    else
    {
    console.log("Invalid orderbook pair");
    }
    };
```

Next, we set the three event streams, that is, es1, es2, and es3. Each event stream checks the current status of the orderbook member within the server object. On a new message, the internal orderbookHandler method is called, as follows:

```
var es1 = this.server.orderbook(app.USD,app.GBP)
 .cursor('now')
 .stream({
 onmessage: orderbookHandler
 })

var es2 = this.server.orderbook(app.GBP,app.EUR)
 .cursor('now')
 .stream({
 onmessage: orderbookHandler
 })

var es3 = this.server.orderbook(app.USD,app.EUR)
 .cursor('now')
 .stream({
 onmessage: orderbookHandler
 })

 };
```

Individual event streams exist for the three orderbook pairs—USD-GBP, GBP-EUR, and USD-EUR. To set the orderbook object, we send the selling asset and the buying asset as the input parameter.

That brings us to the end of the setOrderbook method.

The bids and asks arrays for the currency pairs—namely, bidsUSDGBP, asksUSDGBP, bidsUSDEUR, asksUSDEUR, bidsGBPEUR, and asksGBPEUR—are stored in the app state. The Orderbook.js app component checks the current base and counter for trading and renders the relevant orderbook, as follows:

```
//Orderbook.js

if(props.counter.code == 'USD' && props.base.code == 'GBP')
 {
```

```
bids = props.bidsUSDGBP;
asks = props.asksUSDGBP;
Asymbol = props.assets[0].symbol;
Psymbol = props.assets[1].symbol;

}
else if(props.counter.code == 'USD' && props.base.code == 'EUR')
{
bids = props.bidsUSDEUR;
asks = props.asksUSDEUR;
Asymbol = props.assets[0].symbol;
Psymbol = props.assets[2].symbol;
}
else if(props.counter.code == 'GBP' && props.base.code == 'EUR')
{
bids = props.bidsGBPEUR;
asks = props.asksGBPEUR;
Asymbol = props.assets[1].symbol;
Psymbol = props.assets[2].symbol;
}
else
{
console.log ("Invalid Pair");
}
```

Depending on the currently selected counter and base asset, the bids and asks arrays are set for mapping. The asset symbols are also fetched from the asset interfaces. With that, we come to the end of the orderbook section.

Displaying successful trades to the user

Similar to the orderbook, we need to set an event stream for the successful trades in the network.

To do so, we use the following setTrades method:

```
setTrades = () => {

let app = this;

var tradeHandler = function (traderesponse) {
var tradesList = app.state.tradesList;
tradesList.push(traderesponse);


app.setState
```

```
({
tradesList
});

};


var es = this.server.trades()
 .cursor('now')
 .stream({
 onmessage: tradeHandler
 })
};
```

The internal `tradeHandler` method is called any time a new message is published to the trades event stream. The `tradeHandler` function updates the list of trades stored in the state variable, `tradesList`.

The `tradesList` array is mapped and rendered by the `Trades.js` component and displayed to the user in real time.

Buying and selling assets

Let's write the `Buy()` and `Sell()` methods for submitting buy-and-sell offers to the blockchain network:

1. Let's take a look at the `Buy` method, shown in the following code block:

   ```
   Buy = () => {

   let app = this;
   let amount = this.state.fields.buyamount;
   let price = this.state.fields.buyprice;
   ```

   We start by capturing the current app `state` in the local `app` variable. We also capture the buy amount and price from the `buyamount` and `buyprice` fields submitted by the user.

   Let's start writing the transaction for submitting the buy offer to the blockchain network.

2. Start by fetching the network base fee and the sequence number for the user's account. We fetch the user's account from the app state, as follows:

```
app.server.fetchBaseFee()
  .then(function(fee){

app.server.loadAccount(app.state.account)
  .then(function(account){
```

3. Stellar uses the `manageBuyOffer` operation type to submit buy offers. To create a new buy offer, we need to pass the selling currency asset, the buying currency asset, the buying amount, price, and `offerId`. `offerId` is set to 0 for new offers. The buy offer price and amount for the offer are fetched from the fields submitted by the user, as follows:

```
var transaction = new StellarSdk.TransactionBuilder(account,{ fee,
networkPassphrase: app.passphrase})
  .addOperation(StellarSdk.Operation.manageBuyOffer({
selling: app.state.base,
buying: app.state.counter,
buyAmount: amount,
price: price,
offerId : 0
}))
  .setTimeout(100)
  .build();
```

The transaction is set to time out 100 seconds after it is built. We call the `build()` method to build the transaction using `TransactionCallBuilder`.

4. After building the transaction, we sign it using the key pair for the user's account, like this:

```
let keypair = StellarSdk.Keypair.fromSecret(app.state.fields.secretkey);

transaction.sign(keypair);

return app.server.submitTransaction(transaction)}).
```

The transaction is then submitted to the private network using `server.submitTransaction`.

As a response from the server, the successful response or the error response is logged to the console, and the displayed balance is updated, like this:

```
then(function(response,error)
  {
```

```
if(response)
{
console.log("Transaction response", response);
app.setBalance(app.state.account);
}
else
{
console.log("Error",error);
}
})});
```

This brings us to the end of the Buy method.

The Sell method is similar to the Buy method. The only difference is that the operation type is manageSellOffer, as can be seen in the following code block:

```
Sell = () => {
  let app = this;
  let amount = this.state.fields.sellamount;
  let price = this.state.fields.sellprice;
app.server.fetchBaseFee()
  .then(function(fee){

  app.server.loadAccount(app.state.account)
.then(function(account){
  console.log(app.state.base);
  console.log(app.state.counter);
  console.log(app.passphrase);
  var transaction = new StellarSdk.TransactionBuilder(account,{
fee, networkPassphrase: app.passphrase})
            .addOperation(StellarSdk.Operation.manageSellOffer({
                selling: app.state.counter,
              buying: app.state.base,
                amount: amount,
                price: price,
              offerId : 0
                }))
            .setTimeout(100)
                .build();
            let keypair =
StellarSdk.Keypair.fromSecret(app.state.fields.secretkey);
            console.log(transaction);
            transaction.sign(keypair);
              return app.server.submitTransaction(transaction)}).
            then(function(response,error)
      {
        if(response)
        {
```

```
                    console.log("Transaction response", response);
                    app.setBalance(app.state.account);
        }
        else
        {
        console.log("Error",error);
        }
        })});


        }
```

That wraps up the `Buy` and `Sell` methods. Let's look at the last method in `app.js`.

Setting the active trading asset pair

Our exchange has three `orderbook` asset pairs upon which traders can trade.

The user can switch between the `orderbook` pairs by clicking the buttons for the respective currency pair on top of the `orderbook`.

The `setOrderbookPair` method is invoked every time the `orderbook` pair is changed.

 The method accepts the pair number as an input parameter. The pair number is mapped to the asset pair, as follows:

- USD-GBP
- GBP-EUR
- USD-EUR

So, if pair is set to `1`, it indicates the trading pair of USD-GBP.

The method checks the value of the pair input parameter and updates the base and counter asset in the app state accordingly, as follows:

```
setOrderbookPair = (pair) => {

if(pair == 1)
  {

  this.setState
  ({
  counter: this.USD,
  base: this.GBP
  });
  }
```

```
else if (pair == 2)
{

this.setState
({
counter: this.GBP,
base: this.EUR
});
}
else if (pair == 3)
{

this.setState
({
counter: this.USD,
base: this.EUR
});
}

else
{
console.log("Invalid Orderbook Pair");
}
this.setOrderbook();
}
```

After setting the `Orderbook` pair, we call the `setOrderbook` method to create the event stream for the `Orderbook`.

That brings us to the end of building our currency exchange app.

Now, let's run our app and see how it works.

Running the currency exchange

Make sure you have completed the following steps before you complete this section:

1. Bring the private Stellar network online.
2. Create user accounts and fund them with native currency.
3. Create the currency assets USD, GBP, and EUR and fund the trading accounts.
4. Extend the trustlines.

If you haven't completed the preceding steps, you can go back and finish those, come to this section, and proceed as follows:

1. To start the currency exchange, navigate to the React project direct and run the following command:

```
npm start
```

2. The app should open in the browser and should look like the following screenshot:

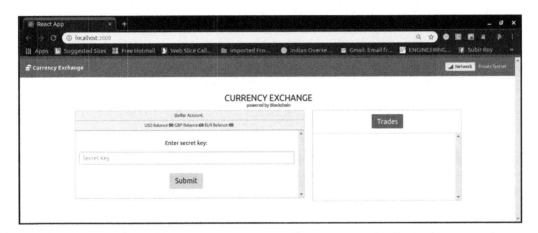

3. Copy the secret key for one of the trading accounts. Paste it in the box and click on **Submit**:

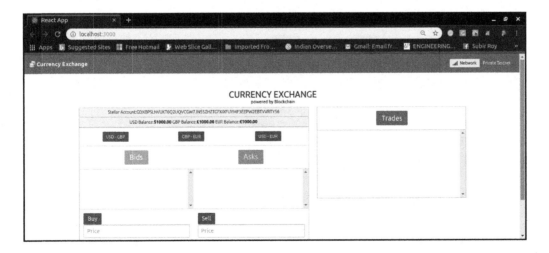

4. Notice the Stellar account and the asset balances. Now, let's submit a new buy order. Let's submit a buy order for $1 at £0.8.

5. Click on **Submit**. After the order is updated to the `orderbook`, it should be displayed on your screen as well, like this:

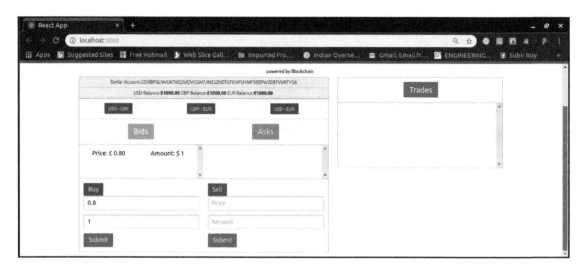

6. Let's try a few more buy-and-sell orders for the USD-GBP asset pair, as follows:

7. Now, let's try to match these orders using a different trader. Log in using the secret key for the other trading account, as follows:

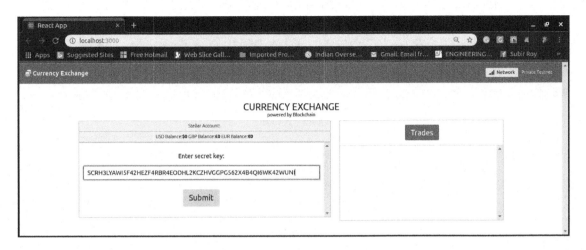

8. Let's try to match the Buy orders. Submit a sell request for $3 at £0.78, as follows:

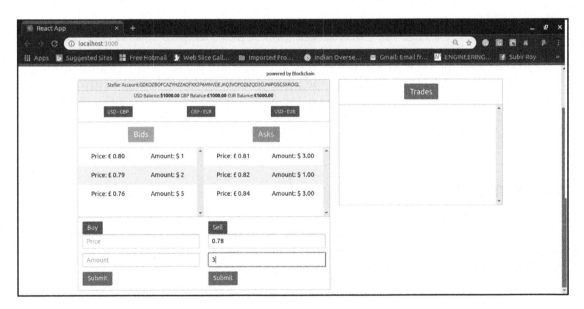

9. It should consume the first and second buy order fully, and the second buy offer partially. Also, try matching a sell offer. The completed trades should appear under the **Trades** tab, as shown in the following screenshot:

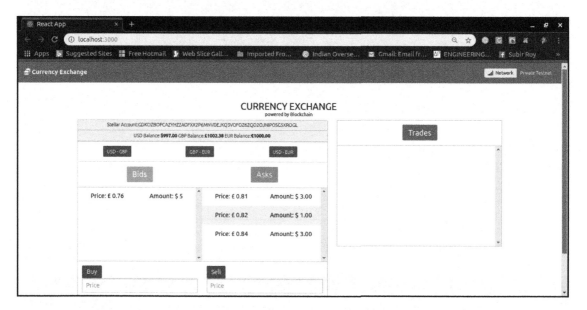

10. Click on the **GBP-EUR** button to change the trading asset pair. Try submitting buy-and-sell orders from both the trading accounts to see how the currency exchange works.

That brings us to the end of our demo and to the topic of currency exchange.

Summary

That brings us to the end of this chapter. This chapter should help you design complex currency asset exchanges and market makers on the Stellar payments network. You can run this on a private blockchain network or on a public instance of the Stellar network. It's a great tool to inboard traditional market makers to blockchain payment networks.

We started this chapter by looking at Stellar's distributed exchange and the concept of market makers. We set up a private Stellar network instance with Horizon and Stellar Core. We then created user accounts for trading and issuing assets. We created three trading assets—namely, US Dollar (USD), Pound (GBP), and Euro (EUR)—and funded our trading account with these assets. Lastly, we created our currency exchange on top of the private Stellar network and ran the entire currency exchange end to end.

The main takeaway from this chapter is understanding how we could onboard market makers to blockchain payment networks and build currency trading exchanges using blockchain. Such systems remove the need to trust a third party for executing cross-currency remittances and provide faster, more efficient payments.

In the next chapter, we'll see what is on the horizon for fintech applications for blockchain, and how we see the technology evolving to serve the domain better.

10
Looking into the Future

That brings us to the end of our journey of learning to implement financial services using blockchain technology. I hope it's been an interesting and informative journey for you. The projects covered in this book are meant to give you a fleshed-out idea of how different distributed ledger technology platforms can be leveraged when you are trying to build a financial product using blockchain. You could obviously build these projects and deploy them as is within the development environment setup of your organization, but ideally, I would recommend you modify the projects to meet your organizations' specific requirements and use cases. Building the projects as they are described in this book should get you 70% of the way.

In this chapter, we'll briefly summarize the projects we covered in this book. We'll look at the major takeaways and how you can apply them for building applications beyond those covered in this book. Lastly, we will discuss some blockchain concepts that you might want to look at. It will help to supplement the knowledge you get from this book. The topics covered in this chapter are as follows:

- Summarizing our journey
- Extending concepts to other applications
- The road ahead – some additional blockchain concepts

Summarizing our journey

We started this book by understanding how the banking and financial services industry operates today. We looked at blockchain technology and how it can make a difference in the financial sector. We looked at how to approach building financial applications using blockchain. We wrapped up our first chapter by taking a look at some of the popular blockchain platforms being used for financial applications. These include Ethereum, Hyperledger Fabric, and Stellar.

In Chapter 2, *Building a blockchain Wallet for Fungible and Non-Fungible Assets*, we worked on a blockchain wallet for holding both fungible and non-fungible tokens. This chapter looks at the concept of fungibility and how Ethereum smart contracts can be used to issue fungible and non-fungible tokens. Next, we built a wallet app that allows us to send and receive tokens. Additionally, you can approve other Ethereum accounts to mint new tokens from your address using the wallet.

The wallet is one of the most common blockchain application components. It is almost impossible to build a blockchain application without one. They serve as a tool for managing the user's private and public key pairs. Typically, they have a frontend that shows the number of tokens or assets the user is currently holding.

In Chapter 3, *Designing a Payment Gateway for Online Merchants*, we built a payment gateway that could be used by merchants to receive payments in ethers. To do so, we built a mock e-commerce website and a merchant Ethereum wallet for receiving payments. Customers could pay using their MetaMask Ethereum wallet or any other wallet to send a payment. The merchant's wallet was implemented using the BIP44 HD (Hierarchical Deterministic) wallet. This is a hierarchical system of deriving public-private key pairs from a single set of seed words. The BIP44 system allows us to generate a new receiving address for the merchant while receiving payments.

This ensures that the merchant's privacy on a public blockchain network is maintained. Our merchant wallet is built to track all of the receiving addresses generated by the BIP44 system for the merchant. Since Ethereum has a probabilistic consensus protocol, the merchant's wallet tracks the number of blocks added to the ledger after each transaction. After around 40 blocks, we can confirm the transaction.

This payment gateway model can be used across blockchain platforms for payments with slight modifications. For example, you could use this model for receiving payments on the bitcoin network or for ERC20 Ethereum tokens. The block confirmation feature would only be useful for blockchain platforms with probabilistic consensus protocols.

Chapter 4, *Corporate Remittances and Settlement*, focuses on corporate remittance. We build a permissioned Hyperledger Fabric network between the banks, Bank A and Bank B, for facilitating corporate remittances. We also set up a private IPFS network with a node for Bank A and a node for Bank B for sharing compliance documents between the banks. Lastly, we set up a bank portal where our corporate customer can log in and submit transactions and view transactions that have been submitted.

Corporate remittances are probably one of the most popular financial services offered by the banking and finance industry. They are also more susceptible to fraud compared to other financial services owing to the large ticket size of the transactions and the fact that the remitting customer is an organization instead of an individual. Hence, compliance checks and provenance for secure, efficient, faster, and fraud-resilient workflows are extremely important. This can be easily achieved using blockchain as seen in this chapter.

Chapter 5, *Enabling Cross-Border Remittances with Real-Time KYC/AML Verification,* uses the stellar distributed ledger platform to build a cross border remittance solution between retail customers aka individuals. The project uses the built-in Federation and Compliance modules of Stellar for exchanging KYC and AML information about the remittance participants as part of the transaction request. We set up a two-bank network with Bank A and Bank B. Each bank had its own infrastructure, including a database server, a backend server, a stellar node, and a frontend.

Customers could log in to the frontend and submit a payment request. Before submitting the request to the blockchain, the infrastructure first does a compliance handshake between Bank A and Bank B. The transaction is submitted to the blockchain only after the system gets a signoff from the remitting organization and the receiving organization.

Retail remittances have spiked in volumes significantly, especially remittances from the west to South Asian countries such as India and Bangladesh. A customer receiving payments in these countries from abroad still pays a hefty transaction processing cost for receiving money owing to a large number of intermediaries. Additionally, the payment might get delayed due to bureaucratic workflows. A cross-organization application similar to the one we described earlier will help to solve these problems and improve the customer experience

In Chapter 6, *Building a Letter of Credit Workflow Module Using Smart Contracts,* we looked at building automated workflows using smart contracts. Specifically, we looked at automating Letter of Credit (LC) workflows. We built an LC portal where Bank A and a buyer and seller can log in to issue, view, and settle an LC document. On the blockchain side of things, we used Ethereum smart contracts to attain our objective. We built a contract for issuing and managing new Letter of Credit contracts and we built a contract interface that would serve as a template for issuing new LCs. Users could interact with the smart contracts using the various options in the frontend.

This chapter is meant to give you a comprehensive look at the power of smart contracts, specifically Ethereum contracts. They can be leveraged to quickly and effectively build cross-department or cross-organizational workflows. This can help organizations immensely when trying to build a solution with business logic that spans across multiple organizations. Additionally, it saves costs on reconciling data across organizations.

Chapter 7, *Building a Tamper-Proof Record Keeping and Document Management System,* uses Hyperledger Fabric to build a tamper-proof document and file storage system. We built a React application that asks the user to choose a directory path to be secured. It then calculates and stores the hash value of each file in the directory path, the hash value of the file tree structure of the directory path, and the hash value of the last modified time of all of the files in the directory path to the blockchain. The application then periodically checks to see whether there is a mismatch in the hash values of the file tree hash and the modified time of the files in the secured directory path. A mismatch indicates that one or more files have been tampered with. Next, it compares each individual file with their corresponding hash values in the blockchain and lets the user know which files have been tampered with. It also informs the user whether any new files have been added or old files have been removed.

Banks manage huge volumes of customer documents and other confidential private files. It is imperative to have a system that will let us know in case any tampering happens so it can instantly be rectified by replacing the information from a backup. This application allows us to do so. It can be used effectively to prevent modifications by unauthorized individuals.

In Chapter 8, *Building a Decentralized Trading Exchange on blockchain,* we built a decentralized exchange using Ethereum smart contracts to trade gold for USD. The engine for matching trades was implemented outside of the blockchain, but the executed trades and pending trades were captured to the blockchain using a smart contract. Traders can log in to their system, point their application to the trading smart contract, and view available trades in the market. They can then submit requests to the platform to buy or sell gold.

In light of several trading exchanges defaulting globally, it probably makes sense to set up a trading exchange that is not solely under the control of a centralized authority. This is where decentralized exchanges come in. In our project, whilst the trading engine is still built and maintained by a centralized authority, the actual trade offers are submitted and recorded on the blockchain. Once offers are submitted, they cannot be modified. They can only be traded against. Hence, our order book cannot be tampered with by the exchange operator.

Users can also view matching trades and detect any cases of fraudulent transactions or offers being submitted. These features make decentralized exchanges probably one of the most important blockchain use cases. They have been explored heavily by the open source permissionless community and now the permissioned enterprise blockchain community is also showing interest.

In Chapter 9, *Developing a Currency Trading Exchange for Market Making*, we use the stellar platform's order book module to build a currency trading exchange. The trading exchange allows you to exchange USD, EUR, and GBP. This chapter is meant to demonstrate the stellar platform's ability to facilitate cross-asset trades. It also shows how you can very quickly build a decentralized exchange using this powerful network. Several exchanges such as StellarTerm are actually using the order book module of the public stellar network to build exchange applications.

That covers all of the projects in our book. Let's now take a look at how you can leverage and extend the knowledge you gained in this book for building applications not covered as part of this book and what other areas you probably want to look at.

Extending concepts to other applications

You can easily extend the concepts covered in the projects in this book to other applications. Following are a few examples of modules that can be modified and extended to other applications:

- **Wallets**: As we discussed earlier, wallets are the most common module across blockchain applications. It's almost impossible to build a blockchain application without it. Wallets that hold fungible and non-fungible tokens can be used as payment wallets, digital identity cards, smart cards, ownership documents, and custodians of other transferable and non-transferable assets.
- **Tokens**: Tokens form the building blocks of many blockchain applications. Tokens can be used to represent a myriad of fungible and non-fungible assets for accounting purposes in blockchains. In cases where you need to track provenance and auditability of a real-world asset, it is typically issued or represented as a token on a blockchain system for accounting purposes. At the same time, you can use tokens to represent virtual assets as well.
- **Hierarchical Deterministic (HD) Wallets**: HD wallets are fairly common across most Ethereum and Bitcoin wallets as they are easy to maintain, operate, and transfer. This includes MetaMask. You can extend this concept to run a Custodian Wallet system for customers, where you receive payments or other assets on a public blockchain network on their behalf. The private keys in such a scenario should ideally be stored in an HSM infrastructure and the service provider should be accountable for the safety of the assets.

- **Payment gateways**: In permissionless systems, you can use the payment gateway module for receiving and tracking any kind of assets, not necessarily financial ones. Since most permissioned systems follow a deterministic consensus protocol, the block confirmation feature of our payment gateway would probably not be very useful. However, if your permissioned network uses a probabilistic block-based consensus protocol, you could easily configure the payment gateway module to receive and confirm receipt of any transferable asset.

- **Document share using IPFS**: The document share feature used in the Corporate Remittance project can be implemented across different financial services. By establishing an IPFS network between the nodes, you can easily share documents securely between network participants. By default, IPFS does not replicate documents between network participants. It only establishes a protocol by means of which you can fetch the file from other IPFS nodes on the network that have a copy of the file. You could also set up an IPFS cluster network that automatically replicates IPFS published files across all of the IPFS cluster nodes.

- **Building a Hyperledger Fabric network from scratch**: The corporate remittance chapter also walks you through setting up a custom Hyperledger Fabric network. You can modify the scripts and the `Docker Compose yaml` files for custom applications and use cases.

- **Chaincodes**: Chaincodes are Hyperledger Fabric's version of a smart contract. You can use them for different use cases owing to their flexibility.

- **Building a local Stellar network**: You can follow the steps used for setting up the Stellar network between the banks with minor modifications for setting up a development environment for various blockchain use cases implemented using Stellar.

- **Issuing and transferring assets on Stellar**: You can issue and transfer different types of assets on the Stellar network. These could be financial or non-financial.

- **Automatic blockchain workflows**: The chapter on Letters of Credit only gives a small taste of the power of Ethereum smart contracts. You can use smart contracts to re-engineer existing legacy workflows to be faster, more efficient, and transparent.

- **Tamperproof files, directories, and documents**: The tamperproof application has multiple applications as is. Additionally, you can probably connect the application to a virtual or physical backup to allow any resources that have been tampered with to be restored.

- **Decentralized trading exchanges**: Decentralized trading exchanges can be used for trading a wide variety of assets. They can include any kind of securities, financial or non-financial assets, tokens, bills, and so on.

- **Cross-asset payments**: For carrying out cross-asset remittances, you can integrate an external API to fetch conversion rates for various base and counter currencies. Optionally, you can use Stellar's order book, provided there are offers posted to it. You can look at the concept of **Path Payments** in Stellar, which carry out transactions in hops, each hop indicating the conversion of one asset into another.

Next, let's look at some additional blockchain concepts that you might want to find out more about.

The road ahead – some additional blockchain concepts

This section includes some additional concepts that the reader might want to look at to supplement their knowledge:

- **Zero-knowledge proof (ZKP)**: ZKP is a mechanism that gives the user the ability to prove that they possess some specific knowledge or information without sharing the knowledge or information with the verifier or validator. ZKP workflows have been in the spotlight after a string of cybersecurity hacks in which large volumes of customer data were lost. Cybersecurity experts have been looking at ZKP workflows to counter such attacks. The solution that this technology offers is to avoid storing any data with service providers, where it can be leaked. Instead, customers can enable a ZKP workflow to verify details about themselves. Hence, if a customer is required to prove that they are above the age of 18 at a restaurant that serves alcohol, a ZKP workflow would allow them to do so without revealing their date of birth and sharing a copy of the document for proof. From a financial services point of view, it makes sense because banks and financial institutions have, at times, a lot of customer data, which might get leaked. A ZKP workflow would permit these institutions to meet compliance norms without actually storing the data. Additionally, customers would be in control of their data. Blockchains are perfect for implementing such workflows owing to their decentralized nature.

- **Sharding**: Sharding is a database architecture that focuses on horizontal partitioning. A single table's rows are separated into multiple rows. Each partition has the same table schema but entirely different rows. This enables the developers to write to the database at high speeds. Several blockchain platforms have been playing with the idea of enabling sharding for their platform to achieve higher transaction sizing suitable for use cases such as trading or cross-border payments. The Elastico platform has successfully managed to make sharding work for blockchains. Other popular platforms, such as R3's Corda, are exploring integrating sharding with their core set of features. Given the high frequency of transactions required by many financial products, we might be seeing sharding in blockchain become more common soon.

- **Blockchain oracles**: A blockchain oracle is a third party that provides off-chain information to a smart contract to enable it to process workflows. For example, if a smart contract is supposed to transfer electricity tokens to a customer when the temperature reaches below 40 °F, you can create an application that uses a sensor to detect the temperature and then calls the smart contract to transfer the tokens. In this case, the application and the sensor is an oracle. Oracles are not a new concept in blockchain. However, with organizations integrating more and more IoT devices with blockchains, it will be especially interesting to see their role in the next age of blockchain applications.

- **Multisignature wallets:** Multisignature (Multisig) wallets are the blockchain equivalent of a secure deposit box with two locks and two keys. Transactions from the wallet need to be signed by two or more stakeholders. To enable this feature, we use the Multsig concept, which is a digital signature mechanism that makes it possible for two or more users to sign a transaction. Each user has access to a private key that they need to sign with when a transaction is to be submitted from the multisig wallet. Wallets can be 2 out of 2, 2 out of 3, 3 out of 5, and so on. The first number in this representation indicates the minimum number of key holders who need to sign to initiate successful transactions. The second number indicates the total number of keys issued for the address. These have been popular with cryptocurrency exchanges for quite some time now. With blockchains now issuing digital assets mapped to real-world assets, organizations might want to remove a single point of failure while storing assets by using Multisig wallets.

- **Stablecoins**: Stablecoins are crypto assets issued on blockchains that are pegged to a single currency or a basket of currency. This reduces volatility in their prices and makes them suitable for financial applications such as cross-border remittances. Several reputed organizations such as JP Morgan have been experimenting with building their own stablecoins for settlement instead of fiat.
- **Sidechains**: Sidechain is an approach by means of which tokens and assets in one blockchain can be moved across multiple blockchains or ledgers. Probably the best way to think about sidechains is like a ledger on top of our blockchain ledger. They have multiple uses in the real world. Consider the bitcoin network. Currently, transactions are processed at a very slow rate. We could run a ledger parallel to the bitcoin network that works on a different consensus mechanism and processes transactions much faster than Bitcoin. To do so, we can invite individuals interested in faster payments to sign up for our application and ask them to load bitcoins in their wallets on the alternate ledger. To load bitcoins into their wallet, they would transfer bitcoins to a designated address on the bitcoin network. After receiving the bitcoins in the designated address, the customer is credited with the balance on the parallel ledger. On the parallel ledger, they can transfer funds much faster than the bitcoin network. If they want to withdraw, we'll simply debit the designated address and credit the customer's address on the bitcoin network. This concept is called a sidechain, and the parallel ledger is referred to as a sidechain ledger. It is used for increasing transaction speeds, hopping between different DLT networks, lowering transaction costs, interoperability between networks, and so on.

Conclusion

That brings us to the end. In this chapter, we briefly summarized the various projects we worked on and our takeaways from each project. We also looked at how we can extend the concepts we learned to other financial projects. We closed this chapter with a description of a few additional blockchain concepts that you might want to look at to further supplement your knowledge.

So, here we are at the end of this book. I hope this book helped you with your blockchain journey and sets you on a path to create new financial services and products using blockchain or to re-engineer existing processes using this revolutionary technology.

11
Appendix: Application Checklist

Application checklist

The following checklist will aid you in building your blockchain applications.

Design checklist

The following list indicates design considerations that you should take into account:

- What is the As-Is business workflow?
- What is the To-Be workflow?
- Who are the stakeholders?
- Do identities/public-private key pairs need to be created for all the stakeholders?
- What will the high-level architecture be?
- What technical components will our architecture be comprised of?
- What is the blockchain platform to be used?
- What legacy applications need to be integrated into the blockchain application?
- How many nodes need to be set up in the blockchain network?
- What is the transaction throughput?
- What data is private and public to the blockchain network participants?
- What data can be published to the network?
- How can we keep data private from other network participants?
- What security controls need to be implemented (client ports to be opened, key management, and so on)?

Development checklist

The following is an indicative list of development activities that you will carry out during the development cycle. This checklist has been divided into four categories for ease of understanding:

1. Environment setup:
    - Setting up and installing dependencies – Node.js, React, Go, PostgreSQL, Docker, Docker Compose, and so on
    - Core Blockchain Software Installation – Ganache, Hyperledger Fabric binaries and images, Stellar images and binaries, and so on
    - Installing software modules and utilities, opening ports and setting up domains, node creation, and setup
    - Creating blockchain identities/users
    - Creating and issuing fungible/non-fungible assets

2. Blockchain app development:
    - Secure Smart Contract design and development
    - Deploying Smart Contracts and recording smart contract accounts
    - Creating contract interfaces that might be required to invoke the smart contract and interact with it
    - Creating asset interfaces for transferring assets

3. Backend development:
    - Installing and setting up a backend server for handling requests
    - Integrating with the blockchain platform and smart contracts
    - Integrating with databases
    - Exposing services that can be integrated with the frontend for transaction submission, fetching data from databases, fetching ledger data, and so on
    - Building event listeners that listen to transactions and contract events

4. Frontend development:
    - Building interfaces for all the roles
    - Integrating with backend services
    - Secure authentication

Testing checklist

The following is an indicative list of test cases and user stories that you can test your application with. You can use Chai for writing and creating test cases:

- Asset creation
- Asset transfer
- Contract methods execution
- Security protocols – access controls, fallback functions, self-destructing smart contracts, and so on

Deployment checklist

The following is an indicative list of tasks that you will have to carry out when deploying the application:

- Deploying all smart contracts to the blockchain and mapping account addresses in the contract interfaces.
- Deploying all assets to the blockchain and mapping account addresses in the asset interfaces.
- Maintain contract versions and account addresses. Ensure updated account addresses are mapped to the interfaces.
- For Ethereum smart contracts, ensure fallback methods are implemented and contracts are self-destructing for maintenance purposes.
- For Fabric, create Docker images and issue certificates to bring the network components online.
- For Fabric, create organizations and affiliations and issue identities for all the requisite network participants.
- For Fabric, install the chaincode (smart contract) on all the relevant peers and instantiate the chaincode on the required channels.
- For Stellar, ensure all the assets are issued and that trustlines have been extended with the required values to accounts that need to hold the assets.
- For Stellar, ensure the TOML files and configuration files have been updated with the local environment variables.

Other Books You May Enjoy

If you enjoyed this book, you may be interested in these other books by Packt:

Mastering Ethereum
Merunas Grincalaitis

ISBN: 978-1-78953-137-4 9

- Apply scalability solutions on dApps with Plasma and state channels
- Understand the important metrics of blockchain for analyzing and determining its state
- Develop a decentralized web application using React.js and Node.js
- Create oracles with Node.js to provide external data to smart contracts
- Get to grips with using Etherscan and block explorers for various transactions
- Explore web3.js, Solidity, and Vyper for dApps communication
- Deploy apps with multiple Ethereum instances including TestRPC, private chain, test chain, and mainnet

Hyperledger Cookbook
Xun (Brian) Wu, ChuanFeng Zhang, Et al

ISBN: 978-1-78953-488-7

- Create the most popular permissioned blockchain network with Fabric and Composer
- Build permissioned and permission-less blockchains using Sawtooth
- Utilize built-in Iroha asset/account management with role-based permissions
- Implement and run Ethereum smart contracts with Burrow
- Get to grips with security and scalability in Hyperledger
- Explore and view blockchain data using Hyperledger Explorer
- Produce reports containing performance indicators and benchmarks using Caliper

Leave a review - let other readers know what you think

Please share your thoughts on this book with others by leaving a review on the site that you bought it from. If you purchased the book from Amazon, please leave us an honest review on this book's Amazon page. This is vital so that other potential readers can see and use your unbiased opinion to make purchasing decisions, we can understand what our customers think about our products, and our authors can see your feedback on the title that they have worked with Packt to create. It will only take a few minutes of your time, but is valuable to other potential customers, our authors, and Packt. Thank you!

Index

Made in the USA
Coppell, TX
06 January 2021

47700395R00293